Women's Madness: Misogyny or Mental Illness?

Women's Madness: Misogyny or Mental Illness?

Jane M. Ussher

AMHERST
The University of Massachusetts Press

First published in the United States of America in
1992 by the University of Massachusetts Press
Box 429
Amherst, Ma 01004

Printed in Great Britain

Library of Congress Cataloging-in-Publication Data

Are available.

ISBN (cloth) 0-87023-786-1

ISBN (paper) 0-87023-787-X

To my mother,
Elizabeth Anne, with love.

Contents

Acknowledgements

Writing about women's madness is an occupation fraught with risks. The risk of offending all parties concerned: the professional experts who presently hold court, the feminist critics who vilify those same experts and the women positioned at the centre of the debate, those deemed mad. There is also the risk of falling into depression, or outraged anger, at the unfolding reality of the misery of many women's lives. The fact that I have thus far survived unscathed is thanks to the support and encouragement of a number of different people. First, Helen Malson has been a paragon of efficiency, advice and support, reading and helping with the evolving manuscript (and convincing a self-confessed sceptic of the value of feminist psychoanalytic theories!). Mairead Ussher, Julia Evans, Ros Lewis and Jackie McNeill helped at various stages and Alison Madgwick has continued to be a good and supportive friend. Karen Wraith has provided good-humoured help throughout and advice on images of mad women in art; Marcia Poynton provided the eventual choice for the jacket design. My thanks too to the editors at Harvester Wheatsheaf.

On a different level, Jan Burns and Paula Nicolson have given me continuous inspiration and encouragement through their belief in the future of a psychology which works *for* women, as well as convincing me that it is possible for women to work together – and enjoy it! I must also thank Michael, Ruth and Mairead for allowing me to tell what is also their story, and my mother for allowing her secret to be finally broken. Finally, I must thank Chris Dewberry, for all the things that one cannot discuss in print, as well as for careful comments on the text.

The author is grateful for permission from Faber and Faber, London to reproduce part of the Sylvia Plath poem 'Paralytic'.

PART One

Why women's madness?

1

Madness and misogyny: My mother and myself

When I was an adolescent my mother was mad. Because it was the 1970s, she was deemed to be afflicted by her 'nerves'. Had it been 100 years ago, she would probably have been called 'hysterical' or 'neurasthenic'. Today, it might be 'post-natal depression'. Her particular madness manifested itself in what was termed depression. Her unhappiness, pain and fear resulted in withdrawal, apathy, tiredness and a sense of worthlessness. Sometimes she cried. Sometimes she was angry. Being a 'good mother', a well-trained woman, as most of us are, she turned her anger in on herself, rather than outwards on her four children, all under twelve years old. She didn't eat a lot. She 'let herself go' by eschewing nice frocks and neatly curled hair. Her outward anger was less evident: no doubt we missed a lot, intent on pretending that everything was normal at home and that we were a happy family. As the unhappiness had no outlet in this world determined to deny women the right to their tears, to their torment, the anger was tightly controlled – stored up until it reached a breaking point, when cracked cups and saucers set aside specifically for this purpose would be taken out into the back yard and flung at the wall. We children loved it. Our mother was really potty. So we laughed, and felt relieved, because the broken cups were easier to deal with than the tears. The careful storing of any dropped and cracked cup for our mother's occasional smashing we could treat as a shared joke, shared secret; some acknowledgement of her frustration and despair, but harmless. Sometimes at night she walked for hours, wearing out her frustration and her anger pounding the darkened pavements. Her absence from the house was never commented on, even when we feared she would not return.

Looking back now, I see it all as a blatant cry for help. A plea to be noticed, for someone to listen. But we four children, preoccupied with our own games and rivalries, were the only ones who heard. And we didn't really hear at all. We didn't want to.

When my mother tried to kill herself, I was told she was really mad. They put her in the local mental hospital, the one we joked about at school, taunting each other with cries that 'the white van has arrived to take you away'. Suddenly it wasn't very funny any more. They gave her ECT[1] which left her shaking and crying, and gave her a cocktail of drugs so that she forgot everything. She forgot her pain, her misery, her loneliness, the fears which kept her awake at night and which I can even now only imagine. But she forgot everything else. Sometimes she forgot our names, confusing us, calling each name in turn before reaching the right one. So she must have been mad. My father told me she was. Her nerves had given in. She was ill. And it was a secret. We weren't allowed to tell our friends, or our relatives and we didn't talk about it ourselves. I learnt the lesson of the stigma of madness early in life: shame, fear, guilt, perhaps for many people more debilitating than the symptoms called madness. So we feigned normality, and coped.

Nearly twenty years later all this seems a distant memory. My mother weaned herself off her debilitating drug dose and carried on living. She is no longer mad. She is happy, healthy and independent, having escaped from many of the bonds that tied her. But we never talk of this time. Perhaps the fear of the madness is still with us, the shame which we did not know until the secret was made, so that the word 'madness' was never spoken. Perhaps we fear it will happen to us. That it is 'in our genes'. That one day too our nerves will snap. That we will crack. That we will split in two, fall in a heap, face the terror head on. That this madness, now called depression, or schizophrenia, or neurosis, will afflict us, and we will lose control. Or perhaps it is a wider issue: that madness, although we joke about it and fear *real* contact with it, leaves us all with a sense of loss and a sense of foreboding. For we recognize something of ourselves in the mad. And we don't know the answer to the question of madness, but turn away from it lest we find that the path which takes us there is one we are on ourselves.

For years I wanted to know: to know what was wrong, what to do, how to help. My inability to cure my mother in her earlier misery, to make her happy again, spurred me to seek solutions in an abstract, contained and academic way. Had the drugs and ECT been efficacious I might have turned to medicine, but the memories of those fearful days waiting for the slow recovery from the mind-numbing, body-breaking shocks created nothing but anger: an anger I learnt to direct outwards, not inwards, an anger which encouraged me to escape from the route so clearly laid out for me; to escape from hairdressing, shop work or an early marriage, and attempt to achieve the education which would be a passport to the world of the experts who I sometimes feared had made my mother *more* mad.

I studied psychology; this would be where I would find the answers. Nine years of undergraduate, postgraduate research and clinical psychology training equipped me with the academic armour with which to enter professional debates on the subject. But do I now have the answers? Unfortunately, I do not. My psychology gives me (or is designed to give me) a legitimate voice in the market place of the mad. It equips me with logical, well-researched explanations for madness. It gives me a myriad of labels with which to classify the different manifestations of madness, ranging from depression, anxiety, phobia, schizophrenia, to the more specific 'illnesses' such as post-traumatic stress disorder, premenstrual syndrome or post-natal depression. Symptoms – whether physical or psychological – can be grouped in neat clusters, and seen as different forms of madness, or 'mental illness' as the experts prefer, or *mental health problems* in our New Age of enlightenment. The mad can be scientifically classified – and then, supposedly, cured.

This allows me to argue that my knowledge and expertise are far greater than those who have only a loose (because untrained) understanding of the 'complex phenomenon' of madness in its many forms. I *know*; I can identify; and supposedly, I can cure. I am well trained, well rehearsed; I can give you the answers, quoting empirical research to substantiate my case. I am equipped with a whole barrage of theoretical explanations for madness, ranging from the behavioural, where absence of rewards in the environment or learned association makes us mad, to the cognitive, where it is our negative thoughts or irrational beliefs that create the problems. I can cite the psychoanalytic, where unconscious desires and childhood experiences create distress, or the social theories, where environmental deprivation and hardship are seen to cause ills. Or I can turn to the 'alternative' perspectives; to the cornucopia of newer theories advocated by experts desperate for recognition.

This knowledge gives me power. I can now use my hard-earned skills to treat other women (and men) deemed mad. Whether they are called anxious, depressed, phobic or stressed, I, as a professional clinical psychologist, can offer them an explanation for their misery, their despair. I can intervene in their pain, as the psychiatrist treating my mad, sad mother did all those years ago. As she is now happy, no longer throwing cups or hating herself, perhaps they were successful. Who knows whether *I* have been with the people I have tried to help? For I still don't know the answer. What I *do* know is that my mother was not mad, and that her anger, pain and despair were not unique to her. I know that women trapped in unhappy marriages, isolated, lonely, with young, demanding children, no money and no friends are often deemed mad. That to be a woman is often to be mad. If we stay inside our prescribed roles and routes as my mother did, or if we speak out, or move outside our designated paths we become mad. My mother may have been mad because she was adhering to the dictates of her feminine role, staying as wife and mother when she desperately wanted to flee. I can be called mad because I reject that same role. I am publicly called 'neurotic' or 'hysterical' by senior men at work if I speak out or criticize. It's a common pattern. Women members of the British Parliament are continuously hectored and pathologized when they speak. Intelligent educated men still use the threat of the label of madness very cleverly, with no shame. It silences many of us. We are all in danger of being positioned as mad. Forming part of what it is to be a woman, it beckons us as a spectre in the shadows.

Madness is no more a simple set of symptoms or problems – an individual difficulty or illness experienced by each 'interesting case' – than any individual woman's history can be seen entirely independently of the history of *all* women. As we cannot hope to understand an individual woman without looking at the meaning of what it is to be 'woman' in a patriarchal society, so we cannot understand the pain and agony which makes up 'madness' without looking at the meaning of this very concept.

Psychology, or any expert profession, any academic discipline, does not have the answer, even if those who have invested years of their lives in learning and training would have it otherwise. I wish psychology *did* have the answer. I could then turn with confidence to those whom I was trained to help, and pronounce upon their problems, confidently offering the answer. But it is a utopian dream. Women are not mad merely because of our hormones, our genes, our faulty learning, our cognition or our unconscious desires. Our madness is not an illness; it is disguised as such by the legalistically worded classifications meted out to women. And why is it *women* who are mad? Why is it that it has *always* been women?[2] Is this madness actually the result of misogyny, as many feminists would claim, and are the symptoms not madness at all, but anger or outrage?

The vague unhappiness which I felt towards the apparent simplicity of the 'official' and legitimate theories for madness, the feelings of scepticism towards their certainty, was formalized and legitimated by my reading of the critical antipsychiatry and feminist literature which I devoured voraciously, and which opened my eyes. In this, the very concept of illness was questioned. Madness itself was deconstructed. Its social, political and historical roots were exposed. In the antipsychiatry literature which blazed the trail for the madman [*sic*] as political dissident or as tortured artist in the late sixties and the early seventies, alternative explanations for the whole concept of madness were offered. The sickness was deemed to be within the system, either the family or society, not within the person. The mad were in reality protesting for the powerless. They were the ultimate scapegoats, burdened with the ills of society; categorized, castigated and separated from the rest of us, lest we see ourselves mirrored in their eyes.

The feminist critics, however, looked to misogyny. They looked to the oppression of women by men which has been taking place throughout the centuries, with the oppression of 'mad' women seen as just another form of misogynistic torture. In this view, misogyny makes women mad either through naming us as the 'Other',[3] through reinforcing the phallocentric discourse, or through depriving women of power, privilege and independence. Or misogyny causes us to be named as mad. It dismisses witches, wise women, suffragettes and battered women as mad. Labelling us mad silences our voices. We can be ignored. The rantings of a mad woman are irrelevant. Her anger is impotent.

So the psychological rhetoric filled me with knowledge, equipping me to work as a professional expert and to write as an authority on the subject of madness. The radically critical literature inspired me to question and criticize, to march and protest. The two perspectives seemed opposite and irreconcilable; contradictory. How could I practise as a clinical psychologist – as an 'expert' in madness – yet also be aware that the very concept of madness itself can be questioned; and that 'madness' serves to glorify and mystify the expert whilst dismissing the person deemed 'mad'? How could I live with the knowledge that women have been labelled and dismissed for centuries and that psychological theories and therapies, and the more invasive drug and ECT treatments still meted out to thousands, can all be seen as a means of control, comparable to other misogynistic means of controlling women such as Indian suttee, Chinese footbinding and clitoridectomy? How could I continue to practise when my head was filled with such knowledge, and especially with a realization of my own role as one of the oppressors, as the critics would describe all experts in the field of madness?

Yet I was also faced with the day-to-day reality of the misery of those deemed mad, and with the memories of my mother's madness, my childhood fear and my need to know. I knew that the despair, the anxiety, the desperate misery is far more than a label, more than a construction without firm basis in reality, far more than the voice of a tortured artist. For whilst the critiques are impassioned, thought-provoking, and inspirational, there seemed to be much left unexplained and unsaid. And what can we say, what can we do, if renouncing our professional mantles of power, we adopt the critical perspective? A theoretical deconstruction does not offer much, not even hope. A rousing rhetorical treatise may inspire, but what answer does it have? At least my training allowed me to give hope, to offer *some* answer. The fact that it might be the wrong one, or only a partial answer, I tried to ignore. The memory of the fearful child and the probably more fearful mother motivated me to seek the solution, to feel the need to offer *something*.

When I attempted to bring feminist theory into my clinical practice, it did not seem to fit. I worked with a woman who was referred by her GP for anxiety attacks and agoraphobia. As a well-trained clinical psychologist I initially worked with her to alleviate her symptoms, achieving a good measure of success. Yet in the therapy her marriage, and the lack of love, freedom or autonomy she was experiencing were what she really wanted to resolve. We spent hours discussing the implications of her relationship with a husband who would not allow her to have friends, to have work, to have a life; and who insisted on raising their son in a way which she could see was causing him to despise women. For at five years old he was ordering her around. Her husband would not engage in therapy, deriding her for making the suggestion. It was *she* who was ill. Over the course of our meetings, which were certainly as egalitarian and open as such things can possibly be, this woman became aware that her marriage was 'disastrous', that she was leading a half life, and that it was not she who was mad. But she would or could not change it. She would not leave. He would not change. Was her realization of the misery of her situation and the fact that there were alternatives merely adding to her pain? Was I holding up to her an image of a different life which she felt she could not take? I wonder if I would have served her better by helping her with her anxiety symptoms and pronouncing her 'cured'.

It is much easier to split the two worlds, keeping feminism for the conference platform, orthodox psychology for the clinic. Many of those working with the mad carry on their professional lives, aware of the critiques, often rehearsing them on the conference platform, yet clinically practising within the traditional health professions at the same time: splitting the theory from the practice, reconciling the contradictions with the need to earn a living, and remembering the investment of time and energy in the long years of training. It is not easy to give it up.[4] But I did: I had to. I no longer practise as a clinical psychologist. The contradiction between the rhetoric of my chosen profession and the rhetoric of the critics, and particularly the feminists, could be split into different (and contradictory) parts of my life no longer. I could no longer bear the dual secrecy of hiding my criticisms from my psychology colleagues and my orthodox practice of clinical psychology from myself, or from feminists. This book is an attempt to unravel the contradictions in the conundrum which asks whether feminism or psychology (feminism or therapy, whether medical or psychological) has the answer for women. It explores the conflicts between the radical critiques of the so-called antipsychiatrists and the feminists, and those who, faced with the needs of women to receive some help, affirm the desperate pleas of women to be heard. To put the question simply: is women's madness the result of misogyny, as the feminists would say, or is it an illness, which can be cured?

Whilst my exploration in this book of the many accounts of women and of men, of academic, professional and lay persons, will open up the Pandora's box of academic and popular discourse that is madness as we know it, I have started with the personal. For all of us who write about madness bring our own baggage, our own perspectives, our own politics, our own pain. Many may pretend otherwise, but we cannot leave it behind us. The least we can do is make it evident. One of the tenets of a feminist perspective is the acknowledgement of the influence of our own subjectivity on our work, on our theories, research and accounts of the world.[5] We are not blank screens, rational and objective experts with no interests and no past. It is my past which prompted the question 'What is women's madness?' which prompted the search, and which provokes me to look beyond the explanations so readily and easily offered by the experts who say they *know*.

Women's madness – misogyny or mental illness?

Why women?

One of the most common questions put to any feminist attempting to discuss women's experiences in a public forum is 'What about men?'. Any talk I have ever given about the psychology of women, or about women's madness, has invariably provoked such a response. One retort is that men have long been the (often sole) focus of interest for psychologists, and that researchers or theoreticians who exclude *women* from their analysis are never taken to task on the matter; they never have to justify *their* exclusion of women. In fact, one could posit that psychology has developed as a singularly male enterprise, with men studying men and applying the findings to all of humanity, and thus it is time to redress the balance. But I usually manage to confine myself to a less confrontational analysis – actually answering the question – even though I find it lamentable that it is the one most frequently asked. The answer is that men are 'mad' too; that men need help too; but that often men's madness takes a different form in our society. It may have different roots. It certainly exists within a different framework from that of women's madness, within a different discourse: it has a different meaning. One of the easiest ways of illustrating this is the argument that if you compare the statistics on psychiatric admissions, and those on female depression, with the statistics on prison populations, and on male violence and criminality, the scales are evenly balanced. So men may be mad – but are likely to be positioned as bad. They are likely to manifest their discontent or deviancy as criminals. Whilst women are positioned within the psychiatric discourse, men are positioned within the criminal discourse. We are regulated differently.

I will explore these arguments further in the analysis of why women are mad but I will leave the case of men here. Feminists should not have to justify their concentration on women. This does not necessarily mean a lack of interest in, or neglect of, men. But this is an analysis of *women's* madness, not of men's. And it is thus the experience of women that I shall focus on; in particular on the discourse associated with that women's madness which positions us and regulates our experiences. The research which merely describes or illustrates gender differences in madness, however it is manifested, is thus not the core of this debate. It merely provides an interesting set of validating evidence. We should not become enmeshed in the rigmarole of the sex differences research – research often carried out with little theoretical justification and no analysis of *why* it is being done,[6] or by those desperate to prove 'the existence of the Other' through the establishment of difference (Walkerdine, 1990: 62). I wish to avoid the trap of the liberal feminists' examination of difference (or absence of difference) to prove equality[7] by concentrating in this present analysis on the particular manifestation of madness in women, the reasons posited for its occurrence, and the way in which it is placed within the discourse which controls and confines our experience. Let the men dissect their own madness. I shall focus on women, with no apology!

Why madness?

Madness is an emotive term. It serves to categorize, to separate, to designate as different. Madness has a long history. It is not a concept unique to the late twentieth century, whose experts prefer the more scientifically loaded terms reified within the systems of psychiatric classification (see Chapter 9). In order to come to some understanding of what causes women to be mad, or to be labelled as mad, we need to deconstruct the very concept of madness itself. To look to the individual diagnostic categories of depression, anxiety, schizophrenia or the like, would be to lose sense of the common history, the common function, the common consequences of these different groupings of symptoms.

To use the term 'madness' is to recognize the meaning attached to the perception of illness or dysfunction in the psychological domain – the stigma attached – and to avoid entering into the discourse of the experts wherein these different classificatory systems are deemed to exist as entities in themselves, as illnesses which *cause* the disturbance in function in the first place. I would not deny the reality of the experience of the person labelled as schizophrenic, depressed or anxious, or of the person caught within any other of the nosological categories now currently adhered to (for the discussion of the idea that the diagnostic categories are not immutable see Chapter 5). But I want to look beyond any individual diagnostic category: to look to the function and experience of madness itself, especially what function it serves in society, and what it means for the individual woman. For madness acts as a signifier, clearly positioning women as the Other.

Deconstructing madness

In recent work within the field of critical psychology, as well as within other disciplines such as linguistics, film and literary theory, attention has been given to histories of the production of knowledge, to a deconstruction of discursive practices in order to challenge the given assumptions which underlie them. Much of this work is based on a post-structuralist analysis of language, in which 'those practices which constitute our everyday lives are produced and reproduced as an integral part of the production of signs and signifying systems' (Henriques *et al.*, 1984: 99). In this view, madness is much *more* than a set of symptoms, a diagnostic category. For as Taussig (1980: 3) has claimed, 'signs and symptoms of disease are not "things-in-themselves"; are *not only* biological and physical, but *are also* signs of social relations disguised as natural things, concealing their roots in human reciprocity'. Madness acts to position 'woman' within society, within discourse. For, as Valerie Walkerdine has argued:

> The 'truths' which create the modern form of sociality are fictions and therefore themselves invented in fantasy. The 'real' therefore becomes a problematic category . . . That is, both scientific and cultural practices produce regimes of meaning, truth, representation in which there are particular relations of signification. What is important about these is the production of a *sign* – is how we enter as a 'relation' and how in actual social and cultural forms we become 'positioned'.
>
> (Walkerdine, 1990: 202)

'Madness' acts as a signifier which positions women as ill, as outside, as pathological, as somehow second-rate – the second sex. The scientific and cultural practices which produce the meanings and 'truths' about madness adopt the signifier 'madness' as the means of regulating and positioning women within the social order. Thus to understand women's madness, we need to deconstruct the concept of madness itself, and look to these discursive practices which are associated with madness, recognizing the connections between discourses of madness and other discourses such as that of misogyny, power, sexuality or badness.

In this context, I use the term 'discourse' in the Foucauldian sense of a regulated system of statements, which has a particular history (which Foucault termed a 'genealogy'); a set of rules which distinguishes it from other discourses, establishing both links and differences.[8] The discourse is what organizes our knowledge about a subject – in this case about madness – and about the relation of both the individual and society to that subject. Thus, the discursive practices which create the concept of madness mark it as fearful, as individual, as invariably feminine, as sickness; and they function as a form of social regulation. The individual in distress, a distress that is undoubtedly 'real' in the sense that she is really suffering, experiences that distress in a way which is defined by the particular discourse associated with madness. She is positioned within the discourse in a way which determines her experience. Thus if madness is shameful and fearful, as it is within our current discourse, the woman is stigmatized and made an outsider. If the symptoms of madness were considered a normal part of our experience, as it is in Shamanic cultures, the woman could be celebrated as a guru, not condemned as sick. The experts and the critics adopt different discourses about madness, using these to formulate or reformulate their own practices, and as a means of positioning the 'mad' person as either sick or tortured, irrational or understandable. It is clear that different discourses are being used when Laing argues that madness is 'a perfectly rational adjustment to an insane world', and when some medical professionals maintain that madness results from 'a chemical imbalance in the brain, usually genetically transmitted'.

A deconstruction of madness does not take these discourses as isolated and independent statements, but as evidence of highly organized and regulated practices. Thus the system of dependencies of a discourse can be retraced, and a history reconstructed which demonstrates how our present practices emerged and how they came to be constituted as they are at present.[9] The deconstruction of madness allows us to see the way in which discursive regimes – called 'epistemes' in Foucault's early work (Foucault, 1970) – determine what we 'know', what we think and what we do. We can perceive how the 'truth' about madness will depend on whichever discourse is presently dominant: that is, whichever discourse is adhered to by those in power. Thus our knowledge and belief in the 'facts' about madness, the way in which we label and treat it, and the experience of the 'mad' person, the woman herself, are governed by these evolving discourses. And what Valerie Walkerdine says of masculinity and femininity is apposite here, for if, as she says, 'femininity and masculinity are fictions linked to fantasies deeply embedded in the social world which can take on the status of fact when inscribed with the powerful practices . . . through which we are regulated' (Walkerdine, 1990: xiii) then what is madness? The discourses which regulate femininity, 'woman'[10] and 'the mad' are irrevocably linked. Following Walkerdine, madness can thus be viewed as a fiction linked to fantasy, seen as fact, and experienced as 'real' by individual women; and located within a material world in which both 'madness' and 'woman' act as important signifiers. My mother's madness was real to her – her misery and pain, her hospitalization, her shame, her guilt, her anger were certainly all real. They were real to all of us. But that reality was experienced as such because of the positioning of madness as a deadly secret, a fear, a means of dismissing and controlling women, and a means of pathologizing distress. Its history is long and tragic; its relations with other regulatory practices will presently be clear.

The answers to the questions 'What is women's madness?' and 'Why are women mad?' are not easy to arrive at. There are many who would claim that *they* have the answer, that *their* knowledge is the 'truth', be they mental health experts or critics. The usefulness of the different theories for the woman who *is* mad, or whose distress or anger is understood within the discourse of madness, is certainly doubtful. A deconstruction of the different theoretical positions and their rhetorical devices and discourses, through an unravelling of the genealogy of women's madness, as well as the genealogy of misogyny and psychology/psychiatry, will allow us to examine the validity of their various claims, and attempt to address the question which forms the title of this book: is women's madness misogyny or mental illness?

But for the reader looking for the *one* answer – the magic wand which will banish madness and misery, or the endorsement of *one* theory which will explain away the pain – I would sound a note of caution: you will not find it here. For in many ways both the experts – be they psychiatrists, psychologists or therapists – and the critics, both feminists and antipsychiatrists, ultimately fail. They provide only a partial explanation for madness, spinning their webs of theories to persuade, to convince, and to regulate both knowledge itself and the individuals governed by it. So I will also deconstruct their theorizing, avoiding the trap of the simplistic and one-dimensional analysis which they all adopt: less seductive or convincing in a rhetoric debate, but perhaps more meaningful for the woman positioned as mad.

Ultimately this is far more than an analysis of madness. It is partly an analysis of what it is to be woman, of what it is to exist as the Other. Simone de Beauvoir, in arguing that 'otherness is a fundamental category of human thought', asked the question:

> Why is it that women do not dispute male sovereignty? No subject will readily volunteer to become the object, the inessential; it is not the Other in defining himself as the Other establishes the One. The Other is posed as such by the One in defining himself as the One. But if the Other is not to regain the status of being the One, he must be submissive enough to accept this alien point of view. Whence comes this submission in the case of women?
>
> (de Beauvoir, 1953, Introduction)

The influence of the discourse of madness and the pervasiveness of misogyny within the patriarchal societies may explain some of the submission of women – for it is not a submission borne easily. Yet wherever we turn women are controlled very effectively, so that they never gain the status of being the One. And madness, as a description of our fears, a category for our pain, or label for our anger, both marks us as the Other, and prevents us from challenging the One.

Notes

1. Electro convulsive therapy. See pp. 106–8, 151–3, for a discussion of this.
2. Men are diagnosed as mad, and receive psychiatric treatment, but it is women who have dominated in the psychiatric statistics for centuries, and women who are regulated through the discourse of madness. See Chapter 9, for a more complete discussion of this.
3. The concept of the 'Other' originates from Lacanian theory, where the woman is seen as always secondary in relation to the man within the symbolic order. He is the I and she is the not-I, the second sex.
4. Masson, J. M., 1989: *Against therapy*, Collins, London. This is one of the few psychoanalysts who has recognized the contradictions and publicly given up his practice, even if it has been suggested he was forced to do so by the psychoanalytic world which would not abide dissent (Malcolm, 1984). Many of the 'antipsychiatrists' continued to practise in traditional settings long after they had publicly castigated the very system which they were acting to support (Pilgrim 1990).
5. For example, see Blier, R., (ed.) 1988: *Feminist approaches to science*, Pergamon Press, New York, for accounts of feminist approaches to science, where the values of the researcher are made evident at the outset. See also Harding 1986.
6. This is a problem with a majority of simplistic sex differences research, where little or no theoretical analysis takes place, and gender is merely added as a problematic (independent) variable. See Richardson 1991; Ussher 1992d for a discussion of this.

7. See Ussher, J. M. 1991a: 'The demise of dissent and the rise of cognition in menstrual cycle research', in Richardson, J. (ed.): *Cognition and the menstrual cycle*, Lawrence Erlbaum, London, for a discussion of different feminist strategies in sex differences research in relation to menstruation.
8. See Henriques, J., Holloway, W., Urwin, C., Venn, and Walkerdine, V. 1984: *Changing the subject: Psychology, social regulation and subjectivity*, Methuen, London, p. 99, for a more complete explanation of this use of 'discourse' and 'deconstruction'. I am following these authors in 'extending signification to produce the notion of the discursive'.
9. *Ibid.*, 104.
10. In this context, to speak of 'woman', following on from Kristeva and Lacan, is not to speak of the individual woman, but to speak of the signifier. As a signifier, 'woman' is not equivalent to actual women, yet the meaning ascribed to it acts to position individual women within patriarchal discourse. For further discussion of this see Walkerdine 1990: 62 and Cowie 1978.

PART Two

The genealogy of women's madness: Deconstructing discursive practices

2

Misogyny

misogyny . . .
Misogynist: anti-feminist; male chauvinist; male supremacist; misogamist; sexist; woman hater. Antonym: feminist

(Chambers Thesaurus)

horror . . .
I would say that repulsion, horror are the very pinnacle of my desire . . . I often tend to think of the female organ as a dirty thing or as a wound, though no less attractive because of that, yet dangerous in itself like all bloody, mucous, contaminated things . . . Woman, that obscene and infected horror.

(Baudelaire)[1]

dirt . . .
Woman is a temple built over a sewer.

(Havelock Ellis, 1897)

weakness . . .
In her particular nature, woman is defective and misbegotten, for the active force in the male seed tends to the production of a perfect likeness in the masculine sex; while the production of woman is due to a weakness in the generative force or imperfection in the pre-existing matter or even from some external influences, for example the humid winds from the south.

(St Thomas Aquinas)[2]

Woman, that obscene and infected horror

A deconstruction of women's madness cannot be carried out independently of analysis of the other discursive regimes which position women as the Other; and those associated with misogyny are the most obvious starting point. For, in the eyes of the cynical feminist, women's madness is invariably linked to misogyny. Whether sexist patriarchal structures or individual oppression are the focus of attention, the implications are the same. Women are not mad. Misogynistic discourse merely deems us so. And if distress and suffering are acknowledged to be real, this is seen as a result of women's position within the misogynistic discourse, a result of institutional and individual oppression, not some individual pathology within the woman. In this view, it is society which is sick, not the women who wear the mask of madness.

In the eyes of many feminists the discourses associated with madness are only one of the manifestations of misogyny. If the ascription of the mantle of madness has overtaken other forms of misogyny as the most widespread means of controlling and confining women today, it is not because the other regulating practices were ineffective. They thus deserve attention in their own right. Many feminists would argue that in order to throw some light on the general process of female denigration and subjugation endemic in every society we might care to examine, we need to look at misogyny itself: stare the demon straight in the eye, and do not flinch. For misogynistic practices are construed as analogous to the discourse of madness, in that they act to contain us, and as a part of the constrictions which lead to madness itself because they create a culture of incarceration and oppression within which madness is the inevitable outcome for women. This misogynistic discourse has many substantive consequences, represented differently across cultures and across history. It is not a difficult search. One has only to examine the influential tomes of any established profession or academic discipline to be bombarded with treatises on women, treatises which place women firmly in their place – at the bottom of the pile.

Yet to expose one's self to an analysis of misogyny, to uncovering the poisonous barbs directed at and against women, is to risk apoplexy or anger. It belies the notion that we are in a 'post-feminist' era where women have achieved any notable measure of equality or respect. It is a depressing picture.

Confinement and constriction

> Primitive society practices its misogyny in terms of taboo and manna which evolve into explanatory myth. In historical cultures, this is transformed into ethical, then literary, and in the modern period, scientific rationalizations for the sexual politic.
>
> (Millett, 1971: 51)

As Kate Millett, in her now classic *Sexual Politics* notes, misogyny can take many forms, taboos, myths, literary representations or scientific theories, each forming the basis for organized discursive practices which work to the same end. The mysogynistic discourse prevalent in different contexts and cultures contains a number of common elements, which seem to transcend the normal divisions of nations, of history or of academic discipline. It is simultaneously pervasive and perverting. Women are objectified, associated with danger and temptation, with impurity, with an uncontrolled sexuality. They are at the same time to be worshipped and defiled, evoking horror and desire, temptation and repugnance, fear and fascination: the madonna/whore dichotomy is evident throughout all misogynistic discourse. Women are both power*ful* through their perceived affinity to nature, their ability to reproduce and their role as the mother, and power*less* through their supposed frailty, their very fecundity, their purported weakness and lability: a powerlessness maintained by the positioning of women as 'Other' within the misogynistic discourse. Women are presented as feeble, as weak vessels imbued with a dreadful temptation, unequal to men and bereft of intellectual capacity. They are labile, fickle, defective. They must be kept down, and kept outside the corridors of power. It is through the misogynistic practices that women are re-formed, re-invented, in a different guise: our bodies distorted, reshaped in a form pleasing to men; our minds controlled, ordered, altered; any threat or independent thought neutralized. Is it surprising that we are made mad?

From the taboos confining women's movement by verbal stricture, to the literal confinements of the physical constraints placed upon the woman's body throughout history, women have been maintained as the second sex. The taboos are interesting, for their richness of imagination, as well as for their pervasiveness across cultures, and they are often associated with the body – with sexuality and with reproduction.[3] One of the most pervasive is the menstrual taboo, the effects of which I have explored elsewhere.[4] Wherever women menstruate, taboos are there to contain us, as these dictates witness:

> Reading and carrying the Koran and touching any part of the body to the edges or the spaces between the writings of the Koran as well as tinging with henna and the like are acts which are an abomination for a menstruating woman.
>
> (Ayatollah Khomeini, 1980)[5]

> The very approach of menstruous women to new wine or ripe fruit caused these products to ferment and become uneatable, the seeds in the garden to become withered and, if they stood in the shade of a fruit tree, the fruit to fall to the ground. Their reflection tarnished or dimmed mirrors and rusted

> and blunted blades of steel. Metal objects became covered with rust and malodorous, and if dogs licked such objects they became rabid and their bite fatal.
>
> (Natural History VII, 64ff.; xxviii, 77ff.)[6]

The menstrual taboo[7] epitomizes the fear of women and the fantasies of men. It can be traced back as far as records are available, across cultures and social groups, and is still prevalent today, although presented in a more sophisticated guise as the 'scientific' syndrome of PMS (Ussher, 1989). The menstruating woman has been forbidden to cross a man's path, touch his food, touch children or sleep in the same house as the family. She may wither grass underfoot, cause crops to fail, butter to curdle, and milk to sour (Frazer, 1938). A man who risks sexual intercourse with a woman during this period has been warned that he will risk the destruction of his 'brain, energy, eyesight and manhood' (Weidegar, 1985: 125).

In the name of menstruation, women have been confined to menstrual huts, literally or metaphorically.[8] Seen as polluted, contaminated, dangerous, menstruating women have been barred from worship,[9] banned from work,[10] but not from worry. While our bodies bar us from the worship of the God of religion or the god of capitalism, we are marked as different and deficient, contaminated in body, castrated in mind. Whether menstruation is deemed to be woman's relic of Eve – the punishment for the Fall[11] – or merely a biological phenomenon which is inherently debilitating, the taboo ensures that, within patriarchal culture, menstruation is conceived of as a curse, not a celebration of fecundity, or a natural part of a woman's experience.

The menstrual taboos, which may seem fantastic and absurd in this age of science and reason, some would claim to be located historically in the combined fear and awe associated with women's power to bear children and her mysterious monthly bleeding. Yet these taboos are not merely isolated idiosyncrasies, dispelled by the advent of knowledge and understanding. They are part of a misogynistic jigsaw, which, when finally completed, is horrific in its magnitude and extent. Noddings has argued that menstruation is merely 'the first taboo', as 'the menstruating woman was thought to be infected with an evil spirit or to be paying the price for an essential evil spirit that is part of her nature' (Noddings, 1989: 37). The taboos effectively protect against the contaminating evil, and separate women from men. Our blood marks us as Other – as we bleed we fail, we fall. Yet these taboos are only a part of the misogynistic discourse, and, in comparison to other reified[12] rituals, may appear a relatively innocuous part, for they are often covert in their intent. Other more overt controlling practices, which Mary Daly terms the 'sado-rituals' (Daly, 1979) deserve more serious scrutiny.

The rusting chastity belt, incarcerating the wife of the absent soldier in the time of the crusades, has been seen as a literal representation of the same discourse which incarcerates women today with tranquillizers, definitions of a pathological femininity and diagnoses of madness. One could argue that our modern nosological chains[13] are merely more subtle than the misogynistic practices of the past. Confining a woman through saying she is 'mad' is more simple, and perhaps less guilt-ridden for the perpetrator, than trussing her up in the steel of the chastity belt. Feminists have argued that the organized and institutionalized misogyny throughout history has been evident in practices such as the witch trials, Chinese footbinding, female circumcision, or Indian suttee (Dworkin, 1974; Daly, 1979), practices which are seen as analogous to modern gynaecological surgery or psychological treatment in their objectification and incarceration of women. To serve – to be subject, to be subservient to a man – has traditionally been the rule for every woman. These practices ensure that women do not stray.

Sacrificial suttee

> She pleaded to be spared but her own son insisted that she throw herself on the pile as he would lose caste and suffer everlasting humiliation. When she still refused, the son with the help of some others present bound her hands and feet and hurled her into the blaze.
>
> (Walker, 1968: 464)[14]

The epitaph, 'She served in life and in death' might have graced the tomb of this Indian widow, if she had been granted a final resting place. The dictate that woman is beholden to her husband is exemplified in its most extreme form by Indian suttee, in which the widow was required to throw herself on the funeral pyre of her deceased husband, burning herself alive. She was not allowed to live after the death of her husband – her master. Suttee was commonplace in India prior to the early nineteenth century, when it was officially banned. It was almost mandatory for the women of the upper castes, and as Walker describes above, had spread to the wives of tradesmen in the lower castes before it was outlawed. Mary Daly has argued that whilst suttee might have suffered an official demise, oppression of widows is still common in India, and these derided and poverty-stricken women often commit suicide as a way out of an intolerable situation (Daly, 1979: 114). Comparisons can also be drawn with today's so-called dowry murders, portrayed by families as suicides, which occur amongst younger Indian women who are shamed by not being able to extract sufficient money from their parental family to pass to their husband's family upon marriage. Recent reports in British and North American newspapers question the innocence of 'suicides' carried out by the woman's apparently dousing herself with petrol and burning to death:[15] a nasty way to choose to die. It is difficult to prove such cases are 'dowry murders', and even suggesting in the British press that women from the Indian community might have been murdered risks accusations of racism; but the very suspicion that women are being murdered, or 'encouraged' to commit suicide because of the inadequacy of their dowry suggests a deep-seated misogyny. It indicates a belief that women are valuable only in the context of their financial worth, and useless without a dowry.

The traditional practice of suttee is the most extreme version of the dictate that a wife lives through her husband, and is redundant without him. The woman was forced to sacrifice herself on the flames of her dead marriage to be able to join her husband in the after life. She had no right to her own life, her own existence: he could claim ownership even after death. And, as it was customary practice for women to marry men much older than themselves, with girls as young as ten married to sixty-year-old men, this resulted in many young brides cutting short their lives on the searing pyres. Perhaps the woman was also being punished for being a woman, and for daring to outlive her husband, as Katherine Mayo argues in her book *Mother India*:

> That so hideous a fate as widowhood should befall a woman can be for one cause – the enormity of her sins in a former incarnation. From the moment of her husband's decease till the last hour of her own life, she must expiate those sins in shame and suffering and self-immolation, chained in every thought to the service of his soul. . . . By his death she is revealed as a creature of innate guilt and evil portent, herself convinced when she is old enough to think about it of the justice of her fate.
>
> (Mayo, 1927: 81)

Suttee legitimized the ownership of a woman by a man, through ensuring that her life will not continue after her husband's. He owns her in marriage and in death. Yet there are other means by which men have contained women, which, although they do not entail the loss of life, ensure that the life that is lived is only half an existence. One example of this, in which women are crippled in the name of beauty, is Chinese footbinding.

Chinese footbinding: the gilded stump

> When the toes have been permanently bent over the sole, a metal cylinder is placed under the sole and bandaged firmly in place. The instep, ankle and lower leg are tightly constricted with firm bandage supports, and the mother or attendants force the toes and heel together under the cylinder so that the bones of the foot are displaced. Finally the maltreated extremity is forced into a shoe with a thick convex sole. And the bandages remain in place for days, in spite of inflammation, tears, cries and feverish symptoms . . . the mother and nurses are said to console the tortured child with promises of beauty in the future and of a husband's approval.
>
> (Weidegar, 1986: 96)

The description above is clinical, factual, yet all the more horrific for its simplicity of instruction. The five-year-old Chinese girl whose feet were bound into the shape of the 'golden lotus' for the sexual gratification of men was judged as acceptable for marriage, and thus security, only on condition of her feet being distorted hooks. As Dworkin says: 'In arranging a marriage, a male's parents inquired first about the prospective bride's feet, and then about her face' (Dworkin, 1974: 104). The Chinese woman with correctly bound and disfigured feet could not walk on her gilded stumps. Her fidelity was thus unquestioned and her status as a dependant clear to the world. Her mind was as restricted as her feet, resulting in little challenge to her male protector and keeper. The woman could walk only with the aid of sticks, or on the arm of an attendant, permanently disabled in the name of man's pleasure. Chinese noble women were carried on the backs of their servants, or forced to crawl if no one was present. The degradation which footbinding entailed was justified in the interests of feminine beauty rather than being carried out openly under the name of its true function: male sexual gratification. For the lotus flower hooks were perceived to be the height of male erotic stimuli, as this Chinese commentator indicates:

> The lotus has special seductive characteristics and is an instrument for arousing desire. Who can resist the fascination and bewilderment of playing with and holding in his palms a soft and jade-like hook?
>
> (Quoted by Levy 1966: 169)

The pleasure was undoubtedly enhanced by its covert nature and its association with women's helplessness and powerlessness. The deformed and grotesque feet provided lascivious stimulation to the woman's husband, or lover if the woman was a courtesan, heightened by the symbolic constriction of the woman's power, her mobility and her independence. Yet men seemed to believe that this was something which women themselves desired, something to which they aspired. Levy notes that 'women of antiquity regarded the tiny foot as a crystallization of physical beauty' (Levy, 1966: 169). The justification that women desired this confinement, and carried it out on each other through the mother constricting the daughter, has parallels in other areas where women carry out misogynistic practices such as circumcision or the wearing of restrictive clothing, as we shall see below. A more covert justification, again part of the pretext for the confinements and treatments meted out to women at other points in history, and part of the justification for suttee, was that women's impurity needed to be controlled:

> Intellectual and physical restriction had the usual male justification. Women were perverse and sinful, lewd and lascivious, if left to develop naturally. The Chinese believed that being born a woman was payment for evils committed in a previous life. Footbinding was designed to spare a woman the disaster of another such incarnation.
>
> (Dworkin, 1974: 104)

Chinese footbinding is not the only restrictive practice carried out in the name of beauty, which provides erotic stimulation for men whilst it simultaneously objectifies and confines women. Are there not parallels to be drawn between the Chinese woman who sways from side to side 'as though on stilts' (Weidegar, 1986: 96) and the nineteenth-century woman trussed up in her corsets and stays, her waist squeezed to an unnaturally small size in the name of beauty and fashion, often until she fainted? Or the twentieth-century woman who totters on her stiletto heels, who struts in her tight short skirt, who cannot run, or even walk freely because of the restrictions of the latest fashion dictates? These women may claim to be merely exercising their right to wear the latest fashions: but are they not indoctrinated by the misogynistic discourse which decrees that women be both passive and vulnerable, not able to move freely, which may mean not able to *think* freely? The corsets and stays which restricted women in the Victorian era served a more insidious function than that of beauty or fashion. The anxiety over weight and appearance which besets the twentieth-century woman, to the extent that she will starve herself or undergo plastic surgery to change her 'imperfect' appearance, serves the same purpose. It maintains women's subordination, distracts concern and attention from our position in the world of men, for if we worry only about our own imperfections, we have no time to think or question. It maintains women as powerless. Beauty is a cruel mistress.

The connection between misogyny and the confinements imposed upon women may be shrouded under the thin guise of beauty in the case of the footbinding or twentieth-century fashion. Other practices are more difficult to present in this way – they are more obviously connected to a barbaric entrapment of women.

Enforced chastity and the cruellest cut – circumcision

> From an iron belt in four parts and about 1cm. wide, two narrow pieces of iron plate, bent to fit the curving of the body, went from back to front downwards. These were joined to the girdle by a hinge and had a broad base, then tapered to a point, like a lancet. These lancet points met in the perineal region of the woman and here also were joined together by a hinge . . . the anterior portion was provided with an opening corresponding to the vulva . . . [a] slit set with fine teeth.
>
> (Weidegar, 1986: 152)

The clinical description of the medieval chastity belt above belies the reality of the woman incarcerated in a prison of steel; her chastity ensured, her pain and humiliation denied. Inside patriarchy, where a woman has traditionally belonged to a man, passed ceremoniously on to her husband almost as a piece of property on her marriage, taking on her husband's name, as she leaves her father's behind, her purity is the prize; and the lengths to which men will go to maintain this prize are shocking in their barbarity. The chastity belt, the most literal example of this 'protection', was traditionally worn by the wife of the lord, or the errant soldier, whilst the man was fighting in the crusades or travelling the world in search of riches. It is the stuff of jokes, as when the errant lover discovers the key and cuckolds the absent husband. But in reality, the chastity belt was certainly no joke. Even the label of 'belt' given to that heavy, rusting, unhygienic cage of metal is a misnomer, belying its reality, as is clear from the description above. Women were locked in these monstrosities for years, undoubtedly suffering great agonies, as well as insult and degradation. This particular barbaric means of maintaining women's chastity was not just an archaic part of medieval history, as Paula Weidegar shows:

> In March 1931 a further case was revealed . . . John B. had forced his wife to wear a girdle of chastity . . . the belt was made of leather and steel and secured by padlocks. It is said that Mr B. had insisted on its use for twenty years. In December 1933, the League of Awakened Magyars put forward as Point 19 of their National Programme that all Hungarian girls of twelve upwards and unmarried should wear girdles of chastity, the keys being kept by the fathers or other competent authorities.
>
> (Weidegar, 1986: 153)

It is difficult to imagine that these 'competent authorities' would be other than men – legitimately controlling women through literal ownership of the key to their sexuality. A more widespread representation of the same restrictive practice, wherein a woman's honour is ensured, is provided by female circumcision, still widely carried out in many countries of the world today.

Circumcision is too innocuous a term to describe the reality of what is really a castrating practice, a process which ensures castration of both body and mind. It bears no relation to the hygienic operation of circumcision carried out on the male penis, to which it might be thought to be analogous, and has thus been renamed 'female genital mutilation' (Armstrong, 1991). In the male, circumcision involves the removal of a small piece of the foreskin; in the female, the operation is more extensive, involving removal of the whole clitoris and labia in many cases, resulting in lasting damage to the woman's sexual responsivity and pleasure. Can this compare to the minor excision carried out in male circumcision, which many would argue actually increases man's pleasure, and reduces the risk of future infection? What man would undergo the following:

> Female circumcision consists *merely* in the removal of the clitoris . . . The operator, who is generally a barber by profession, rubs ash on his fingers, grips the clitoris, draws it to its full length and shears it with a single razor stroke. Ashes are then sprinkled on the wound to staunch bleeding. [*my emphasis*].[16]
>
> [*female circumcision involves*] excision of the entire clitoris, labia minora and parts of the labia majora. The two sides of the vulva are then fastened together in some way either by thorns . . . or sewing by catgut. Alternatively the vulva are scraped raw and the child's limbs are tied together for several weeks until the wound heals (or until she dies). The purpose is to close the vaginal orifice. Only a small opening is left (usually by inserting a slither of wood) so the urine or later the menstrual blood can be passed.
>
> (Hoskin, 1979)[17]

These may seem to be extreme examples, but they are far from unrepresentative. It is estimated that over twenty million women in over thirty different countries are subjected to circumcision (Barry, 1979: 189; Armstrong, 1991: 42), yet we cannot know the reality of this custom as it is shrouded in secrecy under the legitimizing guise of 'cultural practices'. If we challenge or question it, we may be accused of racism, of not understanding. Many stay silent whilst young girls, from infancy to puberty, experience both female circumcision and artificial maintenance of the impenetrable vagina, through sewing the labial skin together, to be opened on the wedding night, either surgically, with a knife, or through forced penetration. Can this practice be right, even if it is enshrined in ritual and religion? It is not unknown for men to insist on their wives' maintaining the stitches in their labia, in order to maintain a 'tight' vaginal opening, better for tight penetration and assurance of chastity. That the woman might suffer extreme pain during intercourse, that she may have no genital sensations at all, that pain from continuous infections or from scar tissue may cripple her, is of secondary importance, if deemed of interest at all.

The confinement serves the dual purpose of maintaining chastity, and increasing the man's pleasure. As intercourse is agony for the woman, the likelihood of her taking a lover is minimalized. Women are thus remade, and controlled. As Mary Daly declares: 'Their masters have them genitally "sown up" in order to preserve and redesign them strictly for their own pleasure and reproductive purposes. These women are 100 percent pure because they are 100 percent enslaved' (Daly, 1979: 159).

The value placed on a tight vagina, on a guarantee of virginity, is again symbolic of a woman's worth as untouched goods, unsoiled sexuality, and of man's preoccupation with woman as an object for his gratification: her purity is of more import than her pain. If her sexuality is dangerous, it can be controlled by cutting out her clitoris and stitching her up. For between sixty and ninety million women today it is not a horror story; it is a reality.[18]

The ritualistic prenuptial pairing of the bride's artificially tight vagina with a wooden effigy of her betrothed's penis, in order to assure a perfect fit, may seem extreme to us:[19] but is it not a different representation of the same discourse that exhorts women to carry out vaginal exercises to ensure their man's pleasure or encourages women to take hormone replacement therapy in middle age, in order to maintain a 'serviceable' vagina? (Ussher, 1989). In a patriarchal culture women's sexuality acts only to serve men, to ensure men's pleasure. Circumcision is merely the most extreme example of the discourse of the woman as object, displaying the utter disregard for her by removing one of the centres of a woman's sexual pleasure, her clitoris. The suggestion that this may serve to increase the sensitivity of other erogenous zones only adds insult to injury. Yet women can be mentally castrated by the restrictions on sexuality in Western society, and we can directly link these physical restrictions on women's sexuality with the misogynistic discourse associated with sexuality in twentieth-century Western society.

Genital surgery, removal of the labia, the clitoris or sewing of the labia, is not practised by the average Western family, but purity and virginity are still held in high esteem, and still act to determine a woman's worth. A psycho-biologist might claim to understand this high value placed on purity. Is man [*sic*] not merely protecting ownership of his future offspring by ensuring that no other man can penetrate his bride? And is not a father protecting his property, his daughter's purity? The selfish gene[20] is at its worst in such circumstances.

Adolescent girls can engage in all manner of foreplay, but as long as they don't 'go all the way', in terms of vaginal penetration with the all-important male phallus, their virtue remains intact.[21] The bride must be prevented from penetration by anyone other than her husband. This deflowering by the male has a symbolic significance, as central to the identity of the twentieth-century adolescent as it was for the 'witch' in the dark ages, supposedly penetrated by the devil's scaly two-feet-long phallus. It is ironic that women regularly report that their most pleasurable sexual activity was experienced during adolescence, before penetration took place, and that the 'foreplay', said to be a poor substitute for 'real sex' (i.e. intercourse), was for women their most satisfying experience (Hite 1977; Dworkin 1987). Although the dissemination of the ideology of safe sex in the 1980s, because of the AIDS epidemic, has had some impact on sexual attitudes, it is still the case that sex = vaginal penetration (Jeffreys, 1990; Ussher, 1992a). But for a woman, to be sexual, to be penetrated, is to risk slipping from virgin to whore, unless she is protected by the safety net of marriage. Many would argue that this is part of the controlling belief system in which heterosexuality is 'the institution through which male supremacist society is organised' (Jeffreys, 1990: 316). Through circumcision, women are literally prepared for the penis: reshaped for man's pleasure. In twentieth-century Western society we may be equally shaped by the misogynist discourse which defines our sexuality in male, heterosexual terms. In fact, Sheila Jeffreys sees heterosexuality itself as the institution which controls women, claiming that 'heterosexual desire is eroticised power difference . . . Under male supremacy, sex consists of the eroticising of women's subordination' (Jeffreys, 1990: 229, 301). Whilst there are problems with this analysis,[22] the representation of the extreme of this subordination, in the form of sexual violence, lends credibility to her case.

Sexual violence

in life:

> We found one [young girl] hiding in a bomb shelter in sort of the basement of her house. She was taken out, raped by six or seven people in front of her family, in front of us, and the villagers. This wasn't one incident; this was just the first I can remember. I know of 10 or 15 incidents at least.
>
> (Brownmiller, 1975: III)

in fiction:

> With that, he up and ties her to the bedstead, gags her, and then goes for the razor strop. On the way to the bathroom, he grabs a bottle of mustard from the kitchen. He comes back with the razor strop and belts the piss out of her. And after he rubs the mustard into the raw welts. 'That ought to keep you warm for tonight' he says. And so saying he makes her bend over and spread her legs apart. 'Now' he says, 'I'm going to pay you as usual' and taking a bill out of his pocket he crumples it and then shoves it up her quim.
>
> (Miller, H., 1938: 128)

Perhaps one of the most pervasive forms of misogyny which reifies women's subordination is sexual violence, exemplified by rape, sexual murder, prostitution and the glorification of sadomasochism. A discussion of these issues could form a complete text in itself, and has been undertaken by many feminist writers. Sexual violence has been a part of so-called 'civilized' (i.e. patriarchal) society for as long as the latter has existed. It is not a modern-day phenomenon, a result of the supposedly permissive society of the post-sixties. Where men have power (and in what society do they not?) certain of them have exercised it over women through the use of sexual violence. Rape has been part of the spoils of war since time immemorial, a means of exacting the final pound of flesh from the defeated population, the ultimate humiliation and a degradation. As Brownmiller has outlined in her history of rape, in conditions of war it is sanctioned, almost expected, as a way of celebrating masculinity and power. And rape is not about sexual pleasure. It is about power and violence. The use of rape in prisons to establish hierarchies of power in men who would adamantly deny any homosexual tendencies, is testimony to this, if any is needed (Brownmiller, 1975: 265). Rape is not the romantic overpowering of a (willing) fainting maiden by a gallant, if overly ardent, admirer, as portrayed in romantic fiction. It is invariably brutal, often mutilating, and frequently results in long-term psychological and physical damage for the survivor. That women are penetrated with bottles, with broomsticks, with fists and with knives during rape suggests that it is carried out for reasons other than the release of sexual tension in the male, the uncontrollable passion aroused by an attractive woman, as some high court judges would have us believe. Rape is pure misogyny. Take this example of a fictional gang rape, as portrayed in the film *Last Exit to Brooklyn.* Could it exact pleasure for a perpetrator who was not misogynistic?

> They slapped her a few times and she mumbled and turned her head but they couldn't revive her so they continued to fuck her as she lay

> unconscious on the seat in the lot and soon they tired of the dead piece and the daisychain brokeup and they went back to Willies the Greeks and the base and the kids who were watching and waiting to take a turn took out their disappointment on Tralala and tore her clothes to small scraps put out a few cigarettes on her nipples pissed on her jerked off on her jammed a broomstick up her snatch then bored they left her lying among the broken bottles . . . lying naked covered with blood urine and semen and a small blot forming on the seat between her legs as blood seeped from her crotch.
>
> (Quoted by Brownmiller, 1975: 195)

This is far from the romantic version of rape. Rape represents man's ownership of woman, his power over her, and his contempt for her very self, as well as for her sexuality. The fear of rape acts to control all women. It keeps us as the Other. A society in which women can move freely without fear of sexual violence is still a feminist Utopia. Women guard themselves and their female children from the ever-present threat, confining their activities to those that reduce vulnerability. The woman who locks her door at night, who is fearful of the dark, who cannot go into the street, may be deemed neurotic, or 'agoraphobic'. But in a society where a woman who walks abroad is deemed to be fair game because she is providing sexual stimulus for a man, can we blame her? Perhaps it is misogyny she is a victim of, not agoraphobia.

It has been claimed by the authors of a recent book on sexual murders that, 'The myriad manifestations of male violence collectively function as a threat to women's autonomy. They undermine our self esteem and limit our freedom of action' (Cameron and Frazer, 1990: 164). Their analysis of sexual murder, in which the representation of male hatred towards women, manifested in sexual violence, is at its most extreme, makes for disturbing reading. Ample evidence is provided for their assertion that 'sexual murder is a distinctively male crime' where men 'murder the objects of their desire' (1990: 25, 163). The cases discussed range from the 'Yorkshire Ripper' to 'Dr Crippen' – men who have taken on the status of myth through their media representation as cases of extreme deviancy. Yet these men don't sprout horns. Rapists, paedophiles and sexual murderers do not look like monsters. They cannot be identified by their glaring, bulging eyes or their marked difference from other men, as the stereotype would suggest. The actions of the sexual murderers may be extreme, but sexual violence against women is endemic in all societies, practised by many men – men who cannot be categorized and scapegoated as monsters. As Frazer and Cameron claim:

> The common denominator is . . . a shared construction of masculine sexuality, or even more broadly, masculinity in general. It is under the banner of masculinity that all the themes of sexual killing come together:

> misogyny, transcendence, sadistic sexuality, the basic ingredients of the lust to kill.
>
> (Cameron and Frazer, 1990: 167)

The construction of masculinity in our society allows for, even encourages, the subjugation of women and the perversion of desire into oppression and pain, all in the name of male pleasure. But it is not only adult women who are victims (or, more correctly, survivors) of sexual violence. Sexual abuse of children, which has received increasing attention by professionals in recent years, has undoubtedly been present for centuries. It is on a par with sexual abuse or violence towards adult women: a manifestation of men's power over the powerless. This power is celebrated in pornography and the approbation of sadomasochism, and whilst pornography may not make us mad, it contributes to the discourse which positions woman as dirty and disgusting – an object to be used and abused.

Pornography – objectification and humiliation

> Pornography defends the coercive master–slave relationship that controls the sexual act. The supreme act, and the only acknowledged one, is coitus by brutal penetration, which coitus is performed either in the missionary position or via rear entry, but in all cases in a situation that reduces women to mere inflatable dolls. The 'success' of the 'love-making' is measured according to the amount of tears shed by the woman.
>
> (Poggie, 1986: 77)

That images of women are dehumanizing, misogynistic, and position us as objects of men's desire, as commodities infused with sexuality, is never more clear than in the case of pornography. And, as the debates about pornography rage on,[23] with politicians and campaigners on both the right and the left arguing about the supposed incitement to sexual violence which pornography provides for men, the million-dollar 'porn merchants' continue to spew out the spoils of their sexual exploitation. To them, the debate over the effects of pornography is academic: they know there will always be a market. For it seems as if men cannot be satiated by pictures of women exposed. Pornography takes many forms. The definition of what it actually is is part of the problem in its censorship. For this analysis I will take pornography to mean the depiction of women in sexual poses presented for man's pleasure, a depiction which is degrading to women because of its context; the representation of women as powerless and sexually exposed. The difference between erotica and pornography has fuelled much academic and popular debate. One major distinction is the depiction in pornography of women as objects to be used. As Dworkin argues:

> The word pornography does not mean 'writing about sex' or 'depiction of the erotic' or 'depictions of sexual acts' or 'depictions of male bodies' or 'sexual representations' or any other euphemism. It means the graphic description of women as vile whores . . . or, in our language, sluts, cows (as in sexual cattle, sexual chattel).
>
> (Dworkin, 1981: 200)

Andrea Dworkin, as one of the most vehement anti-pornography campaigners, sees it as the epitome of misogynistic control, functioning 'to perpetuate male supremacy and crimes of violence against women because it conditions, trains, educates, and inspires men to despise women, to use women, to hurt women' (Dworkin, 1981: 289). It is said to encourage men to hate women because, as exposed flesh, as powerless objects or commodities, we can be nothing but reviled. If 'pornography presents women as willing victims, as objects to be used, bodies created for the sole purpose of pleasing men' (Wallsgrove, 1987: 171) and men internalize this message, is it then surprising that women are treated as objects, used and discarded as men see fit? If pornography is 'designed to dehumanise women, to reduce the female to an object of sexual access' (Brownmiller, 1975: 32) is it surprising that men feel free to take their liberties with women's bodies, and consequently, our minds?

Pornography serves the same purpose as the other images which initially may appear more innocuous. It reinforces the archetypal view of women. As Rosalind Coward has argued:

> . . . pornography reinforces a split in the way women's sexuality is represented – between the wife and the goer. Pornography frequently promotes an ideology showing women enjoying what men want . . . pornography promotes the image of women as the place where men's depersonalised needs can be met.
>
> (Coward, 1984: 177)

The concept of woman as an independent subject is absent in pornography, which is 'an ideology and an ideology which, like racism, *requires* the creation of another, a not-I, an enemy' (Griffin, 1982: 643). In pornography, a woman's sexuality exists only to serve male pleasure, to fuel his desire; and even if she may appear to be oblivious to the male gaze, the woman frozen in the pornographic image is only simulating disdain or personal pleasure to provide further excitement for the man. As Wallsgrove contends:

> Even when the women in the stories are acting out lesbian or masturbation

> fantasies there is never any doubt that they are really performing for the reader – a man. And when they do 'speak' they perpetuate the old myths of female sexuality. The rough fuck is what they want, none of this boring foreplay or – worse – affection and communication. They are just holes asking to be humiliated and hurt.
>
> (Wallsgrove, 1987: 171)

We may not be able to *prove* that men believe that this is really what women want. But it would be surprising if it had no effect at all. And is this not what many men *wish* women were like, believing that this is what women want (the 'rough fuck', not the gentle caress), which legitimates men's treating women badly by allowing them to think that this is the way things should be. It is similar to the beliefs associated with rape, beliefs which allow men to objectify women and feel no guilt or remorse. Yet remorse should be felt. For the images of female sexuality portrayed in pornography do more than titillate or provoke men. They insult women. Our sexuality is presented in a way which is divorced from reality, from humanity, from any essence of female pleasure or pride. It is a degrading image, reinforcing the omnipotence of the penis whilst it positions the woman as shameful. As Susan Brownmiller argues:

> The staple of porn will always be the naked female body, breasts and genitals exposed, because as man devised it, her naked body is the female's 'shame', her private parts the property of man, while his are the ancient, holy, universal, patriarchal instrument of his power, his rule by force over *her*.
>
> (Brownmiller, 1975: 32)

We cannot dismiss pornography as being the stuff of bar-room jokes or bedroom fantasies. It has a much wider influence than that over man's immediate desires and pleasures. It is more than a masturbatory prop, or a voyeuristic escape to a world of power over women. For it affects the very discourse associated with women and sexuality. Rosalind Coward is right in arguing that:

> Porn puts into circulation images of sexuality that have definite meanings connected with them; sexual pleasure for men is initiation and dominance, and for women submission to men's depersonalised needs. The problem is that these meanings feed general definitions of sexual identity and sexual activity.
>
> (Coward, 1984: 176)

Pornography has a direct influence on the discourse which positions women as sexual objects; and, in a culture where sexuality is both repressed and yet represented in every visual medium, it creates a grim climate for women: a climate that is ripe for the fermentation of madness.

The defenders of pornography would vehemently disagree with this thesis. They claim that pornography is a celebration of sexuality, marking the end of repression, allowing the woman in all her glory to be worshipped and enjoyed. Women as subjects of porn have been represented as emancipated, as witness Hugh Hefner, commenting on the 'soft porn' magazine, *Playboy*:

> Women have traditionally either been put on pedestals or damned as the source of all sexual temptation and sin. These are two sides of the same coin, since both place women in a non-human role. *Playboy* has opposed these warped sexual values and, in so doing, helped women step down from their pedestals and enjoy their natural sexuality as much as men.
> (*Playboy*, January 1974)

Others have argued that many women enjoy pornography, and that a woman who does so 'is in fact a rebel, insisting on an aspect of her sexuality that has been defined as a male preserve' (Willis, 1981: 223). But the fact that women *do* read pornography and are excited by it, does not make it right. It does not mean that it is emancipatory. If the only images available to us are degrading, can we help but turn to them in our quest for sexual knowledge and excitement? It is not inherently 'bad' to be excited by visual erotica and to wish to read sexual literature. It is the perpetuation of the subjugation of women in the staple pornography which fills newsagents' shelves and pervades the works of such writers as Mailer and Miller that is offensive and reprehensible. It is women's denigration in pornography, not the depiction of sexuality or erotica, which is damaging to women. Women who pose for pornography may be willing objects of desire; they may personally profit from it. But a society where some women can receive rewards only if they bare their bodies and objectify their sex is not progressive or enlightened. It is retrogressive and misogynistic.

One of the major thrusts of the feminist debate has been the representation of pornography as epitomizing men's power over women. Pornography is seen as a celebration of that power. This would link it most clearly to the other misogynistic practices which disempower women, possibly contributing to our madness. But a contrary argument also needs to be aired – that which suggests that pornography represents men's *lack* of power over women: it proliferates as women gain strength, gain prestige, gain autonomy. Lynne Segal claims that:

> Pornography is a compensatory expression of men's *declining* power. It serves to expose not imperial strength but pathetic weakness – a gargantuan need for reassurance that, at least in fantasy, women can remain eternally objects for men to use and abuse at will. It is the last bark of the stag at bay.
> (Segal, 1987: 108)

If this is the case, the continuing growth of women's strength may signal a concomitant increase in pornography. But if we believe it may incite men to misogynistic practices – to rape, to sexual oppression, to further exploitation of women – or if we believe that the proliferation of such images is damaging to female identity, can we condone it? Can we not have erotica without denigration and oppression? Does the representation of sexuality *have* to involve oppression and degradation of women? It is a sad world if it does.

Woman – virgin or whore?

What is common throughout these forms of female sexual oppression is the representation of virgin as good woman, whore as bad, the discourse used to control women as surely as the vaginal stitches or gilded stumps. This dichotomy is exemplified, whilst most parodied and perverted, in *Justine* by the Marquis de Sade, where the image of woman as passive victim is most celebrated. Justine is abducted and subjected to a myriad sexual abuses, which subjugate both her body and her mind. She is captured, beaten, raped, sodomized and tortured. It has been claimed that 'few are the men who have not dreamed of possessing a Justine' (Paulham, 1970: 164), whom Angela Carter describes as 'a "good woman" according to the rules for women laid down by men and her reward is rape, humiliation and incessant beatings' (Carter, 1979: 38). The story of Justine and, more recently, *The story of O* (Reage, 1970) are representative of the most extreme form of rhetoric which paints women as all good or all bad, and which paradoxically espouses a high moral message in which a woman's virtue is (or should be) her most prized possession. It is also a celebration of misogyny in literature. A woman must defend her prize: or be cast out, regardless of the lengths to which she must go to protect it. A good woman is pure, a bad woman is sexual, for sexuality itself is seen as bad, as Carter argues:

> A 'bad girl' always contains the meaning of a sexually active girl and Justine knows she is good because she does not fuck. When, against her will, she is fucked, she knows she remains good because she does not feel pleasure . . . they strip her, sexually abuse her, and ejaculate upon her body. 'They respected my honour if not my modesty' she congratulates herself . . . her unruptured hymen is a visible sign of her purity, even if her breasts and belly have been deluged in spunk.
>
> (Carter, 1979: 47–8)

The story of O, written by the fictitious Pauline Reage, is a variation on this theme. O is taken by her lover to a mysterious house where she is stripped, blindfolded and manacled. She is subjected to beatings with numerous whips and riding crops, she is sexually violated, branded with hot irons on her buttocks, and taught that 'your belly and your behind are constantly at our disposal' (Reage, 1970: 15) as a succession of men take their pleasure from her. This is her first experience:

> Her hands were still fixed behind her back, her haunches were higher than her torso. One of the men gripped her buttocks and sank himself into her womb. When he was done he ceded his place to a second. The third wanted to drive his way into a narrower passage and, pushing hard, violently, wrung a scream from her lips. When at last he let go of her, moaning and tears streaming down under her blindfold, she slipped sideways to the floor only to discover by the pressure of two knees against her face that her mouth was not to be spared either.
>
> (Reage, 1970: 10–11)

O may be forced on this occasion – but she is portrayed as a willing victim, allowing the ritual degradation to occur. She permits her 'captors' to sink a ring, through her vulva, and chain her to her master. After her beatings she only cries:

> She did not want to die, but if torture were the price she was to have to pay for her lover's continuing love, then she only hoped he would be happy because of what she had undergone, and she waited, very mild, very mute, for them to take her back to him.
>
> (Reage, 1970: 24)

This is the 'good' woman who allows her lover to subject her to the worst degradations of the body and mind in the name of love – a woman who gives herself not only to her own man, but to any other man to whom he cares to offer her. It may be an erotic fantasy in the eyes of many. But it is a fantasy which exemplifies misogyny at its most obvious.

The defenders of practices such as circumcision would say that, as women are active participants (carrying out circumcision on their daughters, arguing that it is in their daughters' interests as they will not be marriageable without it), it cannot be a tool of patriarchy or be repressive. Women themselves want it, as O 'wanted' to be beaten. Women have often been the strongest advocates of these misogynistic practices, ensuring their daughters' acceptability within the particular ideology prevalent in the culture by carrying out footbinding, circumcision, enforcing suttee, or lacing ever tighter the rigid corset, in order that the daughter would not shame the family, and would be accepted as a marriageable woman. Mothers still entreat their daughters to maintain their purity, not to 'ruin their reputation', thus preventing their daughters from exploring their own sexuality in an open honest manner. Such women Daly terms the 'token torturers' (Daly, 1979: 137). This does not, however, devalue the criticism of these practices as examples of misogyny and control: mothers are as indoctrinated by patriarchal ideology as their daughters will come to be. Women who are mentally castrated themselves cannot be solely to blame for wishing the same on their daughters. If oppression does stem from the mother, is it not, as Irigaray has suggested, that she merely 'reproduces the oppression to which she is subjected'? (Irigaray, 1980: 156)

Misogyny in action: madwomen and witches

The different manifestations of misogyny discussed above have served to maintain our position as the Other within the phallocentric discourse, which both regulates and reifies 'woman' whilst maintaining women's subjugation. These discursive practices invariably locate the danger of woman in the body, and invariably focus on the body as a means of access to the woman herself, literally confining or chaining us through the reified rituals of footbinding, genital mutilation, suttee, sexual violence or pornography. Under the guise of religion, culture, or sometimes merely male entertainment, women are confined and condemned. But these are not the only manifestations of misogyny. Other misogynistic practices are more overt, one of the most widely discussed being the control of large sections of the female population by accusations of 'witchcraft'. The witch has come to symbolize female oppression and female powerlessness, and her treatment to exemplify men's cruelty. In many feminist analyses both the witch and the mad woman have been portrayed as women who dared to question, who attempted to rebel, and who thus speak for us all. Witchcraft and madness are seen as analogous means of controlling women. But in the Law of the Father[24] witches are seen as sick, or as evil. Who is right? And is either explanation sufficient? There is no one thesis unanimously shared by the numerous experts on the subject, each authority advocating a different explanation for the systematic torture and immolation of women as witches. Were they evil women or innocent scapegoats? Young or old? Engaged in devil worship or unwitting victims of a misogynistic fantasy fuelled by the theological rhetoric of the era? What is clear is that each self-proclaimed authority on the subject of witchcraft is adamant that his (for they are invariably male) theory provides *the* key explanation. To peruse the literature on witchcraft, a fascinating exercise in itself, makes it easy to imagine that the 'experts' are referring to quite different phenomena. But they are not.

Each is presenting evidence which supports his own thesis, looking at the 'problem' of witches through his own distorting prism.

This certainty in those who pronounce upon their pet theories, together with the narrowness of their vision, is analogous to the deconstruction of women's madness. Just as a cornucopia of explanations is offered either to justify the witch trials or to exonerate the victims, with no one theorist accepting the reality of the complexity of the issue, so it is with madness. By demonstrating that no *one* explanation is sufficient to understand the witch trials, and then drawing the analogy with women's madness, I hope to demonstrate that, as we need to widen our field of vision and turn our critical gaze on the authorities on witches, so must we do with madness.

Notes

1. Quoted by Groult 1986: 64.
2. Quoted by Morgan 1989: 43.
3. See Martin 1989 for a fascinating study of reproduction from both the medical and the woman's own perspective.
4. In *The psychology of the female body*, Ussher 1989.
5. Quoted by Morgan 1989: 223.
6. Quoted by Weidegar 1985: 123.
7. Laws 1990 prefers the term 'etiquette' to 'taboo', as she believes this term 'derives far more strongly from the intricate social rules that people in society attach to . . . menstruation' (43). I will stick to 'taboo', following Millett's (1971) analogy of taboo as misogyny.
8. The literal menstrual huts are described by Frazer 1938 in *The Golden Bough*, who provides a cross-cultural account of the taboos associated with menstruation. The metaphorical huts could be said to be the general effect of the taboos on women's identity.
9. Banned from churches and other places of worship during the menstrual period – to be readmitted only after a ritual, cleansing bath. See McLaughlin 1984.
10. Menstruation has been used as a justification for not employing women for many centuries, on the erroneous assumption that menstruation makes women labile and their work inefficient; see Ussher 1992d.
11. Noddings 1989 traces the role of menstruation in the positioning of women as evil.
12. Reified in patriarchal culture through their elevation to the status of legal, religious or scientific practice.
13. Nosology is the term used to describe the classification of madness under diagnostic categories, such as depression, schizophrenia, etc. Szasz (1961) coined the term 'nosological chains' in his claim that the modern categories serve the same functions as the literal chains which bound the mad in the early asylums.
14. Quoted by Daly 1979: 117.

15. As an example of this, Daly 1979: 115 refers to the 1977 *New York Times* report of a woman strangled and burned in kerosene by her husband and in-laws.
16. See Weideger 1986: 70, who discusses this circumcision in more detail.
17. Quoted by Daly 1979: 154.
18. See Armstrong 1991 for a recent discussion of this.
19. The bride would be 'fitted' for her wedding night by having the wooden effigy of her husband-to-be's penis inserted into her tightly sewn vagina, in order that intercourse could take place on the wedding night. The 'little knife' would be used to ease the passage of this effigy and often of the penis.
20. Dawkins 1976 presents a case where psycho-biological factors determine behaviour, the desire to reproduce one's own genes being of primary concern. Wilson 1988 discusses this in relation to sexuality.
21. Cowie and Lees 1987, in a study of adolescent sexuality, found that girls were still greatly influenced by the madonna/whore dichotomy, and that they were classified as either 'slags' or 'drags', depending on their willingness to engage in sex with boys.
22. One of the major difficulties being the emphasis on heterosexuality as the root of women's difficulties. See Chapter 9.
23. The debate about what can actually be defined as pornography has heightened recently amid attempts to make it illegal on the grounds that it incites men to sexual violence; but the results of research are actually equivocal, with many studies suggesting those who commit sexual crimes use *less* pornography. See Segal 1990, versus Dworkin 1981.
24. Lacan first discussed the Law of the Father, a formulation for language as the medium through which we are placed in culture, enforced by the figure of the father in the family. See Lemaire 1977.

3

Witchcraft – wickedness or woman hatred?

> *wildwomen . . .*
> Why witches? Because *witches dance*. They dance in the moonlight. Lunar lunatic women, stricken, they say, with periodic madness. Swollen with lightninglike revolt, bursting with anger, with desire, they dance wild dances on the wild moors. Wildwomen, uncivilised, as the white man says of other races; wildcats as the government and the unions say of some strikes; as they say of some of our schemes. The witches dance, wild and unjustifiable, like desire.
>
> (Gauthier, 1986: 199)

> *evil women . . .*
> 'The witch . . . really was – an evil liver; a social pest and parasite; the devotee of a loathly and obscene creed; an adept at poisoning, blackmail, and other creeping crimes; a member of a powerful secret organisation inimical to Church and state; a blasphemer in word and deed; swaying the villagers by terror and superstition; a charlatan and a quack sometimes; a bawd; an abortionist; the dark counsellor of lewd court ladies and adulterous gallants; a minister to vice and inconceivable corruption; battening upon the filth and foulest passions of her age.
>
> (Summers, 1929: xiv)

> *destitute women . . .*
> Witches did dance in the moors and they hid there too. The wilderness was for the most destitute women the only place of survival that society allowed them. The witch, the queen of the forest, is like the domesticated wife who is queen of the home. Queen of one domain because excluded from all others. Mystery, night, forest, it all resembles the clandestineness of pariahs and

heretics. The underground where one may indeed fight is nonetheless not equivalent to freedom.

(Marks and de Courtivron, 1986: 220)

madwomen . . .

Almost all mentally sick were considered witches or sorcerers, or bewitched.

(Zilboorg, 1941: 253)

Witches – women reviled, feared, condemned

Witches have been known to man [*sic*] for centuries. Witchcraft in different manifestations has been documented since records have been kept, since the written word became a means of transmitting and perpetuating belief and ideology. And witches have always been women, in reality and in imagination: as have the 'mad'. Just as there are a myriad explanations for madness, a plethora of experts holding court, so there are with witchcraft.

Whilst persecution of individual 'witches' is part of women's history within patriarchy, the organized witch trials which are commonplace, if not endemic, in Europe and North America from the late fourteenth century until the seventeenth century were notably different from individual persecutions which may have gone before. The trials have been seen as the embodiment of a hatred of women, organized and ritualized through patriarchal dictate, resulting in the torture and death of millions of women under the catch-all term 'witch': the ultimate in misogynistic annihilation. Or they are seen as the persecution of the insane, or of those who were evil.

It is difficult to specify how many 'witches' were actually condemned and killed: estimates vary between hundreds of thousands, to many millions. This disparity is probably because 'few subjects have gathered about themselves so large concentrations of misinformation as English witchcraft' (Notestein, 1911: v) and records were not always kept, or noted by modern historians. However, we do know that more women than men were burned as witches. Again, estimates of ratios vary: Dworkin (1974) suggests a ratio of twenty to one, Notestein (1911) six to one. It is interesting that the latter, an acclaimed historian, presents little analysis of this gender difference in his history of witchcraft, treating it as if it were almost coincidental, or accidental.

Every society has its scapegoats, every society has the Other, the outsiders, the aliens. Women as the Other are already represented in all patriarchal discourse but as witches women are doubly guilty, for being both woman, and wicked. The tacit assumption that women witches were quite *incidentally* victims or scapegoats – perhaps because of their position in society, or their age, attempts to excuse the witch trials instead of seeing them as an example of the underlying misogyny found in other cultures and other times in history, even though expressed in different ways. The women burned as witches were *not* co-incidental victims; and the discourses associated with witchcraft have much in common with discourses which condemn and confine women under various other guises.

Evil women: a threat to god and church

> The witch has abandoned Christianity, has renounced her baptism, has worshipped Satan as her God, has surrendered herself to him, body and soul, and exists only to be his instrument in working the evil to her fellow creatures which he cannot accomplish without a human agent.
>
> (Lea, 1906: 206)

The witch has become a personification of the discourse which positions woman as evil. Supposedly the devil incarnate, a witch was said to be able to kill with a look, tear an unborn baby from the womb of its mother, ruin crops, destroy livestock and 'alter men's minds to inordinate love or hate' (Scot, 1584: 31). The *Malleus maleficarum* (the *Witches' hammer*) published in 1487 by the notorious clerics turned witch-hunters, Sprenger and Kraemer, outlined in inordinate and lurid detail the evil crimes of witches. It became the bible of the inquisition, acting to legitimate licentious speculation about the behaviour of *all* women. At a time when books were a rarity, available only to a select few, the *Malleus maleficarum* was produced in vast quantities, to be read and its message internalized by judges, clerics and scholars (all male of course); and given virtually the same degree of status and importance as the Bible, the other 'holy book'. The unholy *Malleus maleficarum* cannot be accused of manufacturing the condemnatory discourse of woman as evil harlot, as the Bible itself conveys a similar message. The myth of Adam and Eve emphasized woman's role in man's fall from grace, providing a justification for women's oppression and punishment for her 'sin'. For, as St Ambrose decreed in the third century AD, 'Adam was led to sin by Eve and not Eve by Adam. It is just and right that woman accept as lord and master him whom she led to sin.'[1] It was only a short step to the belief that this lack of morality would be manifested in active evil – in witchcraft.

The society of the sixteenth and seventeenth centuries was ripe for the promulgation of the discourse of the evil woman. For prior to the regulation of society through scientific discourse, all disease, madness and unexplained misfortune was assumed to be the result of evil spirits, inhabiting the body of the victim, who may or may not be deemed to have deserved the invasion. If the cause of a disease was uncertain, it was perceived to be the result of something 'shot' into the body by an unknown, and probably malevolent force, often a witch (Alexander and Selesnick, 1966).[2]

In the thirteenth and fourteenth centuries the mind and body were regarded as the province of the clerics; and madness and illness were, therefore inevitably conceptualized in terms of good and evil. The treatment for the unfortunates said to have been invaded by evil spirits ranged from appeals, bribery and supplication to exorcism, magical rituals and punishments. Any failure on the part of the exorcist or spiritual healer could be attributed to the recalcitrant evil spirit rather than to the failings in either the theory or practice of the expert. These ideas concerning disease and madness were perhaps an inevitable product of the then current state of the evolution of scientific knowledge, for as Alexander and Selesnick remind us:

> Primitive man . . . could not know that bacterium caused wounds to become infected . . . wind was destructive, hence he assumed an angry being who blew it to attack him. Rain was sent by spirits to reward or punish him. Disease was an infliction sent by invisible superhuman beings or was the result of magic manipulations by his enemies.
>
> (Alexander and Selesnick, 1966: 9)

The witch as scapegoat

But how exactly did the witches come to be blamed for all manner of ills? It has been argued that the evolution of witch hunts was a response to the crumbling of feudalism and threats to the church in the medieval period. Agricultural misery, plague, civil war and religious changes and reversals, enforced by death penalties (Rosen, 1969: 35), resulted in a disruption of society and the system of beliefs that had maintained the social order. As explanation for misery or infection could not be found in traditional religious discourse, which was changing and uncertain, another source was sought. And women became the scapegoats. As witches, women were a convenient source of evil, for their absence of morality was 'known'. So continued the centuries-old practice wherein women have 'served as scapegoats for the evil men fear in themselves' (Noddings, 1989: 37). The witch trials have been seen as analogous to the Spanish Inquisition, or to anti-semitism (Szasz, 1971), recently expressed in the Nazi persecution and mass destruction of Jews, an ideology infectious in its transmission, often created and maintained by the elaborate pronouncements of the inquisitors themselves, who stir the fires of prejudice, fear and hatred through their florid rhetoric and webs of fantasized horror. As Trevor-Roper writes:

> Just as anti-semites built up, out of disconnected titbits of scandal, their systematic mythology of ritual murder, poisoned wells . . . so the Hammers of Witches built up their systematic mythology of Satan's kingdom and Satan's accomplices out of the mental rubbish of peasant credulity . . . and the one mythology, like the other . . . generates its own evidence.
>
> (Trevor-Roper, 1967: 15)

If the authorities could attribute misfortune to the evil in witches, they could ensure some semblance of control, because the witches could be eradicated. Thus the witches were blamed for causing illness in both adults and children, for crops failing, for causing 'possession' (often of children), for cattle dying, for the spoiling of brewing or baking, for impotence and for death. And in the 'dark ages' infectious diseases in animals or humans were rife, as were both illness and premature death in newborn infants and adults, probably resulting from the general living conditions. As Rosen argues:

> The countryside at this date was exceedingly damp . . . Huts of the poor were often earth-floored, and infested with vermin of all kinds (this explains the visits from toad familiars; toads and frogs were just naturally around) . . . Childbirth was the occasion for family . . . visits, with everyone congregating around the mother and handling the new baby with most unsterile hands: 'rheums' must have been like tuberculosis, too common to mention.
>
> (Rosen, 1969: 47–8)

Phenomena attributed to witches would be explained today by our knowledge of disease, of diet, or of environmental hardship. Childcare and dietary practices may have produced the violent convulsions or 'wasting away' of children which were attributed to the witches. Babies were frequently put out to nurse or weaned from an early age, on 'pap', a flour and water paste, while their mothers continued to work, or were absorbed in the care of subsequent children. The combination of a calcium-, protein-, and vitamin-deficient diet and the insanitary habits of the poor, would have predisposed children to 'wasting away', if not to rickets and convulsions (Rosen, 1969: 44). Some of the descriptions of violent illness suffered by children indicate the likelihood of meningitis, pneumonia or epilepsy, illnesses which would certainly not be attributed to witches today.

The spiritual possession of older children and adolescents by the witches may also be explained either through illness, undiagnosed and misunderstood, or through trickery: possession feigned out of malice for the supposed witch, or for the gaining of power and attention by the one possessed. The possession of a number of adolescents in the Salem witch trials as late as the seventeenth century has been interpreted in this way (Stone, 1980). It is commonly acknowledged that belief in witchcraft can result in psychosomatic illness (Mappen, 1980): if you believe that the burning of a wax effigy of yourself will cause illness, it almost certainly will. So the witch provided a powerful depository for the unknown or feared phenomena besetting the closed village community. Confidence in the evil of witchcraft was more acceptable than uncertainty or self-blame.

The lonely old hag

The witch hunts functioned partly to allow scapegoating and persecution of individuals as solutions to problems which were deeply embedded in the system. The most vulnerable groups in society – women, the poor, the socially isolated, those who needed charity – could be blamed for all manner of social ills which could not otherwise be explained (Stone, 1980). Thus a poor woman within a closed village community, or one who had elicited resentment from others, became a convenient and powerless scapegoat. One authority, Midelfort, describes the witches as 'evil' and 'melancholic' women, who were in a 'depressed state characterised occasionally by obscure or threatening behaviour' (Midelfort, 1972: 185) and delineates the 'witch' as an old woman living alone, with her pet animal, her 'familiar', acting as her only companion throughout a lonely winter. Yet any peculiar behaviour exhibited by these women was more likely to be a result of their isolated position in the rural village community, than a result of their 'monthly humours', or their relationship with Satan (Rosen, 1969). The old women living alone would have made a pet of any animal willing to be their companion, to stave off loneliness, thus opening themselves to taunts of unnatural relationships with the animal; taunts of being a witch with her familiar. However, the prototypical witch, immortalized in both fairy tales and more learned documents, was not the single woman, the 'spinster': twice as many *married* women were branded witches (Notestein, 1911). As with many other of our stereotypes of witches (that of the old woman, the hag) the image is erroneous.

The juxtaposition of the witch and the spinster is in reality a continuation of the discourse wherein the woman outside of the controls of a relationship with a man is deemed a threat. The lonely old woman has traditionally been portrayed as an aberration, almost an insult to womanhood, and juxtaposed with images of beautiful (and usually acquiescent) maidens, who fall in love with their prince and achieve true happiness. Thus it is her very 'failure as a woman' which leads her to witchcraft: not being attractive to men, what other option than witchcraft does she have? As a result authorities can declare that:

> A woman usually becomes a witch after the initial failure of her life as a woman; after frustrated or illegitimate love affairs have left her with a sense of impotence or disgrace.
>
> (Baroja, 1973: 256)

If only she had been lucky, a man would have saved her from disgrace. This discourse, however, of the ugly, wicked witch conceals the reality of many women's experiences of the tortures inflicted under the label of witchcraft, allowing us to dismiss their persecution, rather than enabling us to ignore the rhetoric, and examine the real.

It is the description of the witches as sexually crazed and instigators of unnatural passions that most clearly links the inquisition to other persecutions of women.

Lewd and Filthy Women

> Centuries of imposed celibacy had not inhibited the erotic drives of monks and nuns, and underground passageways were known to connect some monasteries and nunneries. Townspeople often had to send prostitutes to the monasteries in order to protect the maidens of the village. It became increasingly imperative to the Church to start an anti-erotic movement, which meant that women, the stimulants of men's licentiousness, were made suspect . . . they (were seen as) carriers of the devil.
>
> (Alexander and Selesnick, 1966: 67)

The scapegoating of women during the collapse of feudalism was intrinsically linked to sexuality, unsurprisingly as madness and badness have been associated with women's sexuality from the mythical representations of Eve's tempting Adam in the Bible to the twentieth-century discourse of the psychotic woman as sexually disinhibited. The association of badness and sexuality during the Middle Ages provided a convenient and seductive explanation for the crumbling edifice of celibacy which was a mainstay of the medieval church, as well as locating the temptation and sexuality within the women. As Adam would not have fallen without the temptation offered by Eve, the errant clerics of the Middle Ages were able to attribute their fall from celibacy to the lewdness of women, and the latter's provocation of uncontrollable desire. The sexuality of women, most noticeable in the witches, was perceived to be both terrible and terrifying, for as the *Malleus maleficarum* dictated, 'all witch craft comes from carnal lust which in women is insatiable' (Sprenger and Kraemer, 1487).[3] Thus the learned cleric, Reginald Scot, declared that it was thought that:

> . . . the cause why women are oftener found to be witches than men: they have such an unbridled force of fury and concupiscence naturally that by no means is it possible for them to temper or moderate the same.
>
> (Scot, 1584: 236)

A woman who was openly or actively sexual was in danger of being considered a witch. Sexuality, womanhood and witchcraft became synonymous. The combined fear, disgust, and suppressed sexual attraction felt for all women is clearly reflected in the fantasies and accusations surrounding the witches. The representation of a woman's sexuality was linked to her alleged weakness, her closeness to animals and to creatures of the lower order. As Bodin declared, women were 'reduced to this extremity [witchcraft], by bestial cupidity . . . For one sees that women's visceral parts are bigger than those of men whose cupidity is less violent' (Bodin, 1530: 96).[4] As women were seen to be more vulnerable and closer to nature, closer to bestiality, it was an easy step to declare that 'since they are feebler in body and mind, it is not surprising they should come under the spell of witchcraft' (Sprenger and Kraemer, 1487). Thus to talk of witches, is to talk of woman. As Shuttle and Redgrove argue, 'whenever we use the word "witch" we mean a certain aspect of "woman" ' (Shuttle and Redgrove, 1986: 202). All women could be witches – their sexuality and fecundity made this so.

Menstruation and the witches' curse: impotence and castration

One of the foundations of the discourse of woman as Other, as dangerous, and as liable to witchcraft was this fecundity, and particularly menstruation, as Reginald Scot illustrates:

> Women are also monthly filled full of superfluous humours, and with them the melancholic blood boils; whereof spring vapours, and are carried up, and conveyed through the nostrils and mouth, etc., to the bewitching of whatsoever it meet. For they belch up a certain breath, wherewith they bewitch whosoever they list. And of all other women, lean, hollow-eyed, old beetle-browed women are the most infectious.
>
> (Scot, 1584: 236)

When women menstruate, they become witches, and the fears and fantasies associated with witchcraft can be seen as analogous to the fears associated with menstruation itself. In fact, it has been claimed that 'witchcraft is the natural craft of the woman. It . . . is the subjective experience of the menstrual cycle' (Shuttle and Redgrove, 1986: 198). In a thesis which presents menstruation as power incarnate, Shuttle and Redgrove have claimed that the wholesale condemnation and burning of women in the Middle Ages could be seen as 'nine million menstrual murders': the fears associated with the witch (that she would render men impotent, spoil crops or bring illness and famine) were identical with the fears of the menstruating woman.[5] So, was the fear of the witch in reality a fear of woman, a fear of sexuality, of fecundity and of blood? Was the positioning of women as evil, and to be tried and burnt, a way of containing that fear?

There are many explanations for man's fear of women's sexuality and fecundity and in particular man's fear of menstrual blood. One of the most easily identifiable in the context of the witch trials is the fear of impotence and castration. The association of sex and menstruation has traditionally evoked terror and dread, the sight of blood on the penis a foretaste of the horrors imagined, making sex during menstruation taboo in many cultures, an activity abhorrent to the male imagination, for:

> whosoever shall lie in sexual intercourse with a woman who has an issue of blood . . . does no better deed than if he should burn the corpse of his own son, born of his own body, and killed by a spear, and drop its fat into the fire.
>
> (Fagarel–Zoroastrian text).[6]

Intercourse during menstruation may symbolize castration, the apparently bleeding penis awakening the dread of men, fear of 'the bleeding vagina which might swallow a penis' (Shuttle and Redgrove, 1986: 211), and thus it is not surprising that when women bleed they are seen as dangerous and to be avoided. The witch personified this horror – for not only did she bleed, but she was seen to be blessed with power literally to strip men of their sexual potency, having stirred man's ardour with her 'unnatural passions' in the first place. As the *Witches' hammer* declared:

> When the member is in no way stirred and can never perform the act of coition, this is a sign of frigidity of nature; but when it is stirred and becomes erect, yet cannot perform, it is a sign of witchcraft.
>
> (Sprenger and Kraemer, 1487)[7]

The more serious accusation, and for men the more terrifying, was that witches could and would remove the penis by casting a spell, a fantasy which may reflect the repression of sexuality and fear of women in the celibate male clergy. Although some of the supposed castration acts of the witches were so far-fetched as to be almost laughable, they would have incited hatred and fear in a society which was both closed (Rosen, 1969) and superstitious. Take this example from the *Witches' hammer*:

> And what then is to be thought of those witches who in this way sometimes collect male organs, as many as twenty or thirty members together, and put them in a birds nest, or shut them up in a box, where they move themselves like living members and eat oats and corn, as has been seen by many as is a matter of common report? . . . a certain man tells that when he had lost his member, he approached a known witch to ask her to restore it to him. She told the afflicted man to climb a certain tree, and that he might take which he liked out of a nest in which there were several members. And when he tried to take a big one, the witch said: you must not take that one, adding, because it belongs to a parish priest.
>
> (Sprenger and Kraemer, 1487)[8]

This may seem fantastic and somewhat risible – but is it? Are not traces of this belief alive today? That men fear the loss of the phallus whilst simultaneously imputing inordinate powers to that same member, is a part of phallocentric discourse from prehistory to the twentieth century, and is invariably accompanied by hatred and fear of women. The phallus is positioned as all-powerful, woman as liable to mock or destroy its power. It is interesting that whilst the witches were said to cause impotence in mere mortal men, they were also said to be able to excite and accommodate the devil himself, with his mythically powerful sexual drive.

Sex with Satan

The *Malleus maleficarum*, which can almost be described as a hand-book of pornography, attributed all manner of salacious practices to the witches, fornicating with the devil, or with his familiar, probably being the most commonly cited. The fantasies of the inquisitors are at their most graphic in this context. For example, the phallus of the devil, with whom the witches supposedly fornicated, was believed to be both long (twenty-three inches), twisted, rough and sometimes sharp, compelling women to scream out with pain when 'enjoying' the Satanic rituals. Other sources believed the Satanic phallus to be horned, with scales emitting ice-cold semen: it was as 'cold as ice and burned like fire when it was withdrawn' (Hughes, 1965: 146). That these fantasies were both fantastic, phallocentric and sadistic goes without saying (what woman would want to be penetrated by a two-feet-long scaled penis?). Yet the witches were reputed to take part in such sexual rituals not just frequently, but with relish: what further proof was needed to condemn them as lewd and wicked harlots? Reinforcing the message centuries later, Montague Summers, in his *History of witchcraft* (Summers, 1929: 32) asserted that: 'Witchcraft was in truth a foul and noisome heresy', peopled by 'lewd and filthy' women. Summers describes in lurid detail the practice of devil worship which he argues most commonly took the form of 'kissing the fundament' (the buttocks) of the Lord of the Sabbat. His disgust and distaste betrays his misogyny, as in this extract:

> . . . those wretches [the witches] met at night in a secret chapel, and after the most hideous orgies, which included the paying of divine honours to Satan and other foul blasphemies of the Sabbat, they donned masks fashioned to imitate goats' heads, cloaked themselves with long disguise mantles, and sallied forth in bands to plunder and destroy.
>
> (Summers, 1929: 136)

This whole discourse exemplifies the combination of fear of women's supposedly uncontrolled sexuality, and the salacious pleasure men obtained from fantasizing about the degradation of woman through that same sexuality, a degradation at its most obvious in the actual witch trials, where the cruelty of the inquisitors is transparent.

Torture and confession: male fantasies fulfilled

> . . . at the time and place of torture . . . the length of Christ in wax be knit about her bare naked body . . . they are racked and tortured, so they can hardly stand or hold themselves from confession. In which case I doubt but that the Pope would blaspheme Christ, and curse his mother for a peacock, curse God (as) a piece of pork, with less compulsion would have renounced his Trinity, and have worshipped the devil on his knees.
>
> (Scot, 1584: 47)

Women branded as witches were subjected to trial, to torture, often to rape and public humiliation, and then to death by burning or hanging for their supposed sins. Many women were condemned on the basis of their own confessions, wrung out of them in public in a way that must have satisfied the sexual fantasies of the persecutors, assuring them of the righteousness of their persecution. Once in the possession of the authorities, who considered themselves bound by their duty to cast out the devil, the 'witch' was stripped and shaved of all body hair. Her body was searched for proof of her relations with the devil and frequently subjected to sexual abuse by her voyeuristic captors, abuse which ranged from the humiliating public stripping and sexual interrogation to gang rape.[9] Tortures might include beating, severe blood-letting, thumb screws, or the notorious water ordeal in which the victim was thrown trussed into a pond to sink and drown if innocent and float if guilty. If she floated, she was burned. Whilst the ducking of witches has taken on legendary proportions, it is interesting that many of the historians who document the tortures do not include the rape and stripping. Perhaps they choose to ignore the less palatable persecutions – or overlook the perverse power of the torturers.

These ritualistic trials and tortures were not isolated or random practices. It became a profitable occupation to scour the countryside, acting as an expert who could search out witches. One of the most common practices in the mid-1600s was for a 'pricker' to examine the naked bodies of suspected 'witches' (invariably women), looking for the 'devil mark', an infallible proof of guilt. Marks which today we would probably describe innocuously as moles, blemishes or birthmarks, sealed the fate of many innocent victims. And was this procedure of investigation not guaranteed to extract every ounce of salacious gratification for the investigator, the 'pricker'?

> The Pricker . . . *stripping them naked*, he alleged that the spell spot was seen and discovered. After *rubbing over the whole body with his palms*, he slips in the pin, and, it seemes, with shame and fear being dasht, they felt it not.
>
> (Summers, 1929: 74; my emphasis)

The pricker had the power to stride into any village, claiming his right to strip and prick any woman he chose to suspect – then condemn her to trial should she fail his test. And for this he was royally paid, making a healthy living out of the torture and destruction of women, for after the pricking the woman was invariably deemed a witch.

The confessions exacted from the witches were remarkable for their similarity, including perversions at the sabbat, sex with the devil, the murder and boiling of children, followed by the eating of their bodies. The similarities do not necessarily attest to the truth in the tales, but perhaps suggest that the inquisitors' demands for a particular set of evidence were being fulfilled. Is this not comparable to more recent examples of confession under pressure, such as those of the 'Birmingham Six' or the 'Guildford Four' convicted wrongly of IRA terrorist bombing in Britain?[10] The televised admissions and 'confessions' of captured allied pilots in the 1991 Gulf War provide more recent evidence of this. Many 'experts', however, have argued that the similarity of the witches' confessions was testimony to the accuracy and truth of the accusations levied against them. Thus Hughes claims that:

> Witches themselves, all over Europe, confessed, often freely, to practices which were substantially the same . . . presupposing that these practices . . . were, with minor differences, evidence of a general system which did actually exist. One feels this in spite of admitting that there were set

> patterns of question and answer, which might well elicit the general picture required by the examiners.
>
> (Hughes, 1952: 91)

This reputable author, oft-quoted as a good source for an 'honest' text on witchcraft, claims also that the inquisitors were 'sober and sincere men, with the highest regard for truth' (Hughes, 1952, 91), and that only 'third-hand journalists' would claim that they were cruel. Such bigotry is horrifying in its blatancy. Hughes claims that physical torture was outlawed in England, a claim refuted by other sources (i.e. Scot, 1584); and one which appears to ignore the psychological torture and pressure suffered by the accused women, which may have been more crucial to their confessing. It is difficult to imagine anyone maintaining their silence in the face of both physical and psychological punishment. We have too much evidence of the fact that persecutors' desires for confession or for specific statements are almost invariably fulfilled.

Sexuality was not the only 'crime' of the witches and the only reason for their persecution. Many authorities have claimed that the witches were actually mad, and that it was merely the ignorance of the marvels of modern medicine on the part of the inquisitors which resulted in the failure to acknowledge their illness.

Madwomen, neurasthenics, simpletons: persecution of the innocent

> Many of the witches were neurotic subjects . . . today they would be writing obscene letters to curates, or practising the emotional masturbation of the Groupists.
>
> (Hughes, 1965: 88)
>
> Demonics of all description are to be classed either with maniacs or with melancholics.
>
> (Pinel, 1806: 238)

It was as early as 1563, at the height of the witch trials, that a physician, Johann Weyer, attempted to demystify witchcraft, arguing that witches were not evil or possessed, but merely deluded individuals – the undiagnosed mad. This was the beginning of the conceptualization of the witch as a person suffering from mental illness, an analysis which has now become an 'accepted' part of psychiatric history, used by medical personnel to exempt from criticism their own 'caring' treatment of disturbed women, which seems benign when juxtaposed with the barbarism of the witch trials.

The sixteenth-century pioneers, Johannes Weyer and Reginald Scot, argued that witches should be subjected to 'compassionate treatment under the auspices of doctors, or the physicians of the mind, rather than subjected to persecution as devil worshippers' (Bynum *et al.*, 1988). Centuries later, Charcot argued that the modern manifestations of neurosis and hysteria were present in women charged with witchcraft, and were the cause of their deviant behaviour and subsequent accusation. Thus the hallucinatory experiences of the witches, in which they described in great detail their dealings with the devil, have been interpreted as the rambling of psychotic women, the confessions as the product of a fertile imagination, or a result of the hallucinatory qualities of the ointments which the witch rubbed on the 'broomsticks' which were actually used as masturbatory tools.[11]

This has become the most widely accepted interpretation of the witch trials: that the undiagnosed and oppressed, those who were poor and unable to cope with society, or were exhibiting psychotic symptoms, were wrongly labelled witches. It seems a plausible explanation. Yet it allows the focus of guilt to shift from the inquisitors, the oppressors, who could be seen to be acting in innocence of the 'real' cause of suffering, and it passes the focus of attention and the blame, however unintentionally, onto the women themselves. It was their behaviour which brought about their 'diagnosis', and hence their death.

In recent years it has been argued that the witches were labelled as mentally ill by modern psychiatrists eager to reinforce their own propaganda, as they attempted to produce an argument in support of their analysis of all deviance as madness. They have been pronounced guilty of 'shallow and idealized self-historiography' (Micale, 1990a), for their blinkered view of medical and psychiatric history as seen through their own rose-coloured glasses; for their use of 'the past to comfort the present' (Pilgrim, 1990: 212). Thus, Thomas Szasz has compared the witches' inquisition with modern psychiatric treatment, claiming that the tortures are analogous, at the same time as he challenges the very existence of mental illness itself:

> The concept of mental illness has the same logical and empirical status as the concept of witchcraft; in short, witchcraft and mental illness are imprecise and all-encompassing concepts, freely acceptable to whatever uses the priest or physician (or lay 'diagnostician') wishes to put them.
>
> (Szasz, 1971: xix)

In this view the witches were not mad, but labelled as such by the patriarchs in their attempt to gain control, in the same way as the 'mad' woman is today. One of the alternative explanations for witchcraft proposed by some feminists is not that witches were 'mad', but that they were actually powerful women who represented a threat to male privilege and power. Her condemnation as 'witch' stripped woman of her power.

Powerful women healers

> Witch–healers are persecuted for being practitioners of 'magic'. It was witches who developed an extensive understanding of bones and muscles, herbs and drugs, while physicians were still deriving their prognoses from astrology and alchemists were trying to turn lead into gold. So great was the witch's knowledge that in 1527, Paracelcus, considered the 'father of modern medicine', burned his text on pharmaceuticals, confessing that he 'had learned from the Sorceress all he knew'.
>
> (Ehrenreich and English, 1974: 15)

The feminist view of the witch as healer presents one of the more convincing alternatives to the thesis of the witch as madwoman. The pathologization of women as 'mentally ill' can thus be viewed as a process of ignoring powerful women, of pathologizing those who challenged the social order. In this view, rather than dismissing the witches as mad, feminists have argued that they should be celebrated as a part of our 'herstory', celebrated as strong and independent women who were threatening to patriarchy, and thus condemned. The psychiatric explanation for witchcraft is seen as adding insult to injury, and is thus akin to other patriarchal tactics for neutralizing women's power, such as suttee or footbinding: mass misogyny in action.

One of the major contributions of the feminist critique of the witch trials is the recognition that many of the women condemned were practising as healers or midwives, a source of succour and wisdom, rather than of evil or death. In a culture where illness and afflictions were conceptualized within a theological doctrine, women healers were often the only ones in the community able to offer reliable treatments and remedies, using their knowledge of natural herbal cures, tested and perfected through trial and error. Gage has argued that 'the witch was in reality the profoundest thinker, the most advanced scientist of these ages' (Gage, 1972), as she used her knowledge to cure both physical and psychological ailments. It has been argued (Szasz, 1971) that the women healers were in actual fact the mothers of modern medicine, using empirical experimental methods long before their male counterparts. The latter, steeped in theological methodologies, were blinkered by their belief in evil as the cause of sickness. In this analysis, the witch is not a mentally ill but undiagnosed patient. She is actually the person successfully treating those in distress. A very different interpretation of the 'facts'.

As an expert midwife, the 'witch' was able to provide both physical and psychological support to women during labour, and to relieve the pain of childbirth using herbal remedies such as those derived from ergot, still used today to hasten labour (Ehrenreich and English, 1974: 16). The woman healer was also skilled in obstetric practices which would have been life-saving for women. But perhaps even more undermining to patriarchal society: she was an expert in abortion. Peregrine Hughes comments thus on this particular skill of the witches: 'they could cause lameness, abortion and many evils by physical means' (Hughes, 1965: 147). Hughes betrays his own moralistic stance through his association of evil and abortion, an association still made today by the pro-life movement and exemplified in a recent paper which sees abortion as a form of 'deathmaking' (Abrahams, 1990).[12] In a society where effective contraception was virtually nonexistent, women who wanted any control over their fertility would have depended on the skills of the women healers. No wonder they had power.

The women healers, however, were not rewarded or praised for their skills, or elevated to a position of high status in the society: they were condemned as evil because their skills challenged the privileged patriarchs, the male experts who believed that a monopoly on healing was their God-given right. In fact, the church declared 'that if a woman dare to cure without having studied, she is a witch and must die' (Michelet, 1862: xix). Since women were barred from any form of medical training, this condemned any woman healer outright. Even those few women who *were* educated were at risk of being deemed guilty of witchcraft. For example, in 1322 Jacoba Felicie was brought to trial by the Faculty of Medicine at the University of Paris, for healing patients whom orthodox physicians were unable to cure. Her crime was that she was able to:

> . . . cure her patient of internal illness and wounds or of external abscesses. She would visit the sick assiduously and continue to examine the urine in the manner of physicians, feel the pulse, and touch the body and limbs.
>
> (Ehrenreich and English, 1974: 16)

This was her crime; the effectiveness of her interventions was merely further proof of guilt, for, as a woman, her place was not to cure at all. The church, the patriarchal state, comprising both clerical and secular powers, invoked moral theological arguments to defend their own monopolistic control of medicine and its secrets. The success of the 'witch' healer was seen as corroboration of her guilt, for if she could effect a cure after orthodox male physicians had failed, she must be employing magic. Does this treatment not have a parallel today in the treatment of modern midwives by the British medical establishment, exemplified by the castigation and systematic expulsion of the feminist obstetrician, Wendy Savage?[13] Women who challenge orthodox practice in the twentieth century may be seen to be as dangerous as the witches were in the thirteenth.

This analysis of the witch as healer is notable for its absence from many orthodox psychiatric or psychological analyses of witchcraft. Perhaps it is because any acknowledgement of the existence of these wise women would be to admit the historical precedent of the threat to the supremacy of the orthodox medical model, and to challenge the belief that medicine and psychiatry developed in a direct male line from Hippocrates, as argued by psychiatric historians such as Alexander and Selesnick (1966). Any woman-centred perspective is devalued. Ignoring the women healers denies their importance, and is a profound derogation of women's power. Thus, as Szasz declares, 'man (the masculine Physician) robs Woman (the White Witch) of her discovery: he declares her mad, and himself the enlightened healer' (Szasz, 1971: 92).

Diana worshippers: remnants of a matriarchal religion

> The records of the middle ages show that the ancient god was known in many parts of the country, but to the Christian recorder he was the enemy of the New religion and was therefore equated with the Principle of Evil, in other words, the Devil.
>
> (Murray, 1921: 9)

The 'witch as healer' is not the only woman-centred explanation that has been ignored or neglected. A thesis presented by the anthropologist Margaret Murray was that the witches were part of an old religion, involving cult worship, effigies of horned gods, ritual practices, and the burning of the 'divine victim' as a sacrifice. In this conceptualization of witchcraft, the shocking behaviour of the witches as described at the witch trials and the gatherings of the sabbat, are seen to be firmly based in reality. These practices were not interpreted as being akin to devil worship, but recognized as part of an ancient religion in which women played a powerful role, and where their sexuality was celebrated rather than denigrated. It was because this ancient, matriarchal religion challenged the patriarchal dictates of Christianity that it was equated with evil.

The palaeolithic cult worship which has been documented by many historians (for example, Frazer, 1938) was undoubtedly a threat to the patriarchal church, as its adherents attracted allegiance from a people beset with war, famine and disease. Such communities were ripe for conversion to belief systems which promised some relief, if only temporarily, from the harsh realities of daily life. A religion in which matriarchy was a dominant practice, and the woman seen as a 'guardian of the sacred fire and giver of life' (Hughes, 1965: 84) would have offered great solace to women who were oppressed and denied autonomy. The 'old' religion would have provided a forum for women to meet with each other, to escape from their subjugation, to practise pagan ritual, to trade folklore, to organize rebellion and to celebrate their sexuality (Ehrenreich and English, 1974). But women's meeting and organizing has always presented a threat to patriarchal society, so it is not surprising that it was suppressed in a way that ensured that women attracted to the 'cult' or the organization of women could be controlled or dismissed. Peregrine Hughes dismisses them as somehow feeble for needing each other's support:

> The cult would serve, too, as a psychological Cave of Adullam for emotional women, repressed women, masculine women, and those suffering from personal disappointment or from any nervous maladjustment which had for some reason not been resolved by the local resources of the church.
>
> (Hughes, 1956: 85)

This patronizing catch-all categorization of women is similar to many male descriptions of women organizing today, and particularly those women organizing to oppose patriarchal control. Hughes reinforces the frequent accusation that we are neurotic, anxious and *really* want to be men. Substitute 'feminism' for 'the cult' in the above quotation, and you could be describing the comments of any number of twentieth-century men such as the recent literary critic who berates feminists for attempting 'to become a rather nasty type of man' because they 'dress like men or bathe naked from the waist down' (Holbrook, 1989: 54).

The witches, as healers or worshippers of ancient goddesses, were as threatening to the patriarchal society of the Middle Ages as any acknowledgement of their skills would appear to be to the psychiatric historian of today. The witch hunt was effectively used to curb, or extinguish these women, and was seen by some to be a useful means of social control:

> Women were a socially disruptive element, at least when they lived outside the family and without patriarchal control. In this restricted sense the small witch trial may have been *therapeutic*, or functional.[73]
>
> (Midelport, 1972: 195–6; my emphasis)

A strange 'therapy', burning women at the stake, after systematic torture and public trial. This raises the question: therapeutic for whom? Certainly not for the women themselves. Is this an analogy we can make with therapy today: is it to serve the needs of the women, or the needs of society, of patriarchy?

Witchcraft and madness

The inquisition and the witch trials did not continue after the eighteenth century, with the exception of sporadic and localized persecutions such as the infamous Salem witch trials. There are many different interpretations for the decline in the persecution of witches (Hughes, 1965; Veith, 1965). One argument is that the witches had been neutralized through the ritualistic torture and murder, and thus women refrained from practising their 'arts', be they sorcery, healing or goddess worship. A more convincing case is that science was overtaking theology as the philosophy underpinning the state, and thus 'illness' rather than 'evil' was the concept invoked to control women. Towards the beginning of the nineteenth century the medical profession was emerging as an organized and cohesive (patriarchal) body, ritualizing diagnosis, treatment and cure. Science was being rediscovered and theology passed over for empiricism. Many psychiatric historians would argue that this directly resulted in the 'dark ages' coming to an end. But not for women. The scientific discourse which replaced theology was, for them, as restrictive and damaging. As Thomas Szasz noted, there was a

> replacement of the theological concept of heresy with the medical concept of mental illness, and of the religious sanctions of confinement in a dungeon or burning at the stake with the psychiatric sanctions of confinement in a hospital or tortures called treatments.
>
> (Szasz, 1971: 138)

Madness, hysteria or insanity came to replace the catch-all description of 'witch' as a label applied to women who were in some way deviant, in some way different: women who did not fit. The seeds of this movement were sown by many critics of the witch trials, such as Weyer, or Scot, who advocated a psychiatric or pathological diagnosis of the women labelled witches. Yet as I argued above, a simple analysis which interprets witchcraft as undiagnosed madness is too simplistic and does not account for the many different women who were persecuted and condemned. Many women were called witches, but one explanation cannot completely explain the myriad reasons for their persecution, or their supposed deviancy. The 'witch' may have been a healer, a devout worshipper of Diana, a lonely spinster, a hated rival, a random woman picked by the pricker for his own gratification. She *may* have been evil, or have practised strange sexual rituals. She may have been 'mad' or 'melancholic', was possibly depressed, anxious and unhappy. 'Witch' described all of these women, dismissing them all. Yet any exploration of witchcraft which looks at only one explanation is equally inadequate. It will be simplistic and ultimately useless in its narrow limitations. Each of the self-proclaimed authorities on witchcraft is guilty of this, as are the experts on madness.

The feminist may see the concept of witchcraft as evidence of misogyny, as an attempt to strip women of autonomy or power; and the witch trials as analogous with other tortures. The psychiatrists may see it as madness, as illness, a dysfunction within the woman herself. The view of the woman herself, the witch, is absent – her voice is not heard. She is used as a pawn in the debates and disagreements of the self-proclaimed authorities on her condition.

The witch and the madwoman share analogous positions within misogynistic discourse, and must be seen in the context of other misogynistic practices used to control women. As witchcraft died out, and the clerics of the inquisition lost their power, the psychiatrists moved in. The nineteenth century saw the roots of our present logical positivist position on madness, where science replaced theology, and the female malady replaced the curse of the witch.

This madness, rife during the nineteenth century, which some have termed the 'cult of female invalidism', apparently spread through the population of women in the same way that witchcraft had previously spread through Europe and America – in almost epidemic proportions (Veith, 1965). It is no coincidence. The label may have changed, the treatment may appear more humane, but the process is the same. Women who are rebelling; women who are depressed, are being categorized, chastized and imprisoned in their bodies, which are intrinsically linked with illness or badness. Numerous different reasons can be produced to explain this madness, many different roots to it can be found – but the 'treatment', the label, is the same for all. The madwoman, like the witch, no longer has an identity as an individual, as autonomous subject, she has disappeared under the enveloping label attached to her. The critics who fail to see this actually contribute to her subjugation, maintaining her position as the Other, and preventing her from challenging the One – men.

Notes

1. St Ambrose quoted by Morgan 1989: 10. Woman was clearly to blame for the fall of man from the Garden of Eden, for it was asserted that 'woman, through a grievous lack of moral sense or will, caused the fall of man by accepting the serpent's enticement and tempting Adam to eat the forbidden fruit' (Noddings, N. 1989: 51).
2. The devil, or evil, was blamed for a cornucopia of illnesses – from colds, to fever, to plague – as there was no knowledge of 'germs'.
3. The *Malleus maleficarum*, quoted by Hays 1965: 143.

4 Quoted by Morgan 1989: 229.

5. In this view, all women can be seen as witches. 'The image of the witch is consistent because it is an image of the transforming and changing menstrual cycle; it occurs all over the world because women occur all over the world . . . it is very, very old in human history because menstruation is as old as Eve; it is thought to be evil because men fear the power and abilities of women' (Shuttle and Redgrove 1986: 210).
6. Quoted by Morgan 1989: 227.
7. Quoted by Hays 1972: 143.
8. *Ibid.*: 144.
9. The details of the witch trials are outlined by Hays 1972. Also see Easlea 1980. Rape was one of the most common 'treatments' meted out to those supposed to be witches, who ranged in age from adolescents to elderly women.
10. The Guildford Four were convicted of an IRA bombing campaign and sentenced to life imprisonment on the strength of their own confessions which they claimed were beaten out of them. They were vindicated and released in 1989. The Birmingham Six were convicted in 1975 on their confessions and, subsequently invalidated, forensic evidence. They were released in 1991, the judiciary finally admitting that their 'confessions' were exacted by beatings.
11. Hughes 1952 discusses this argument in more detail, claiming that the ointments were rubbed on the body to enhance sexual arousal and on the broomstick, which was then rubbed between the woman's legs.
12. Pope John Paul II reinforced this view in June 1991 when he compared abortion to genocide.
13. Wendy Savage was relieved of her position as a consultant in the British National Health Service for attempting to introduce women-centred practices and natural childbirth. Her colleagues challenged her competence, an action which resulted in her dismissal. (Although after her appeal and an outcry from her women patients she has been vindicated and reinstated.) See Savage 1988.

4

The female malady and the medicalization of sex: The Victorian madwoman

hysteria. . .

The frequency of hysteria is no less remarkable than the multiformity of shapes which it puts on. Few of the maladies of miserable mortality are not imitated by it. Whatever part of the body it attacks, it will create the proper symptom of that part. Hence, without skill and sagacity, the physician will be deceived; so as to refer the symptom to some essential disease of the part in question, and not to the effects of hysteria.

(Sydenom, 1848: 85)

feminine. . .

Hysteria is assimilated to a body as site of the feminine, outside discourse, silent finally, or at best, 'dancing'.

(Rose, 1986: 129)

woman. . .

Women and madness share the same territory . . . they may be said to enter a concentric relationship around a central point occupied by a fundamentally male normality. Like some insidious virus, insanity therefore invades the mythology of woman, finding therein a semiotic fluid that it may use for the purposes of self-definition.

(Martin, 1987: 42)

hysterical woman. . .

John laughs at me, of course, but one expects that in marraige . . . You see he does not believe I am sick! And what can one do? If a physician of high standing, and one's own husband, assures friends and relatives that there is really nothing the matter with one but temporary nervous depression – a slight hysterical tendency – what is one to do? . . . So I take phosphates or phosphites – whichever it is, and tonics, and journeys, and air, and exercise, and am

> absolutely forbidden to 'work' until I am well again. Personally, I disagree with their ideas. Personally I believe that congenial work, with excitement and change, would do me good. But what is one to do? . . . But these nervous troubles are dreadfully depressing. John does not know how much I really suffer . . . Of course it is only nervousness. It does weigh on me so not to do my duty in any way!
>
> (Charlotte Perkins Gilman, 1892: 10, 14)

The rise of the Victorian madwoman marked a turning point in both the history of women's madness and in institutionalized misogyny. Madness was certainly not a new concept in itself. Eminent scholars had speculated on the origins of insanity or melancholia from the time of the ancient Greeks. The institutionalization of the application of science and rationality to the problem of the insane, a particular hallmark of the Victorian epoch, was not new either. Hippocrates had advocated a scientific analysis for both physical and psychological problems in 430 BC, anticipating the present scientific discourse by over two millennia. Yet the Victorian era marked an important change in the discursive regimes which confined and controlled women, because it was in this period that the close association between femininity and pathology became firmly established within the scientific, literary and popular discourse: madness became synonymous with womanhood. It was also the era when madness became firmly conceptualized as mental illness, under the scrutiny and control of the rising medical establishment, where it remains today. Hence, I would like to take a more careful look at the Victorian madwoman, who some would say was the immediate fore-mother of the modern-day woman diagnosed as neurotic, phobic, anxious, depressed, anorexic or schizophrenic . . . the list is endless. Both feminist revisionists and professional experts turn to the Victorian 'mad' woman to support their own case, for either a continuous history of misogynistic medicine or for the logical progression of scientifically based interventions. From whichever perspective, the Victorian view of women's madness provides an insight into madness today.

The age of enlightenment: the age of repression

> we let them in chains rot in their own excrement. Their fetters have eaten off the flesh of their bones, and their emaciated pale faces look expectantly towards their shallow graves which will end their misery and cover up our shamefulness.
>
> (Reil, 1803)

> Bedlam . . . was a favourite Sunday excursion spot for Londoners,

> who came to stare at the madmen through the iron gates. Should they survive the filthy conditions, the abominable food, the isolation and darkness, and the brutality of their keepers, the patients of bedlam were entitled to treatment – emetics, purgatives, bloodletting, and various so-called harmless tortures provided by various paraphernalia.
>
> (Alexander and Selesnick, 1967: 114)

The history of the Victorian madwoman has to be seen in the context of the dramatic changes in discursive regimes and practices taking place during the nineteenth century. That the Victorians removed the chains from the insane, following the revolutionary practices of Pinel who released the chains of the mad men and women housed in the Parisian asylums, tends to be cited as an exemplary case of the Victorian Enlightenment. The horrific treatment and conditions of the pre-nineteenth-century madhouses have been well documented and discussed elsewhere (Scull, 1979, 1981; Porter, 1987; Foucault, 1967). They make fascinating, if uncomfortably voyeuristic reading. Prior to the 'enlightenment', the mad were seen to be closer to animals, their loss of reason resulting in the loss of their very essence of humanity. Consequently, the mad deserved no better treatment than that meted out to a bad or difficult dog. As Scull argues 'The resort to fear, force and coercion is a tactic entirely appropriate to the management of brutes!' (Scull, 1979: 64).

The fact that 'madness borrowed its face from the mask of the beast' (Foucault, 1967: 72) is demonstrated by the quotation from La Salpetriere at the end of the eighteenth century:

> Madwomen seized with fits of violence are chained like dogs at their cell doors, and separated from keepers and visitors alike by a long corridor protected by an iron grille; through this grille is passed their food and the straw on which they sleep; by means of rakes, part of the filth that surrounds them is cleaned out.
>
> (Foucault, 1967: 62)

The very fact that the mad managed to survive such maltreatment and neglect, that they managed to survive sleeping on dirt in the freezing temperatures without clothing, that they could survive the degradation and filth, was more confirmatory proof to the asylum keepers and expert observers that they were closer to animals, and should thus be treated as such. For as Foucault has argued, if madness was animality it 'could be mastered only by discipline and brutalizing' (Foucault, 1967: 75).

The nineteenth century heralded a change in this particular view of madness, as the discourse of madness as illness began to gain pre-eminence, during what Foucault (1967) has termed the advent of the 'age of reason'. Care, exercise and cleanliness replaced brutal incarceration as appropriate treatments for the afflicted. Whilst some critics have argued that the Victorians were not the first to apply a humanitarian approach to the insane – the Spanish were the first to remove the chains and have humane asylums which promoted exercise, occupation and diet in 1409 (Alexander and Selesnick, 1967: 116) – it is clear that the Victorian period did mark an increase in humanitarian treatment, accompanied by the establishment of the scientific experts, who promoted the rise in the formal state institutionalization and 'expert' care of the mad.

Science came to be espoused by these experts as a means of rising out of the mire of quacks and mavericks; as a means of achieving both status and monopoly. From a cynical viewpoint, it was a calculated move based on fiscal reasons, rather than any adherence to the greater good of science itself. But science clearly worked as their ticket to success. For as Littlewood and Lipsedge (1982:43) have noted: 'By 1800 . . . science, not religion, determined what were acceptable thoughts within the heads of the average citizen. Reason instead of faith became the new measuring stick'. This is echoed in the declaration of Thaddeus Wakeman in 1890:

> The answer [to the question of what is the new creed] . . . in one word is Science. The majority of the American people are already practically secularists – people of this world . . . Our people are unconsciously welcoming the incoming sway of Science and man; and this is proved by their absence from the Churches.
>
> (Quoted by Ehrenreich and English, 1978: 71)

There are a number of important implications of the scientific philosophy becoming dominant in the nineteenth century. First, it legitimated the male scientific experts who held pre-eminent positions in the community, for scientific expertise brought with it the power to define reality.[1] Second, women were excluded from power through the dominance of the myth of the masculine scientist, as science itself emerged as a singularly male enterprise, which it remains to this day (Keller, 1985; Ussher, 1992c). And third, 'science' was effectively used to provide a smoke-screen for the more insidious role of the professional experts; to neutralize criticism and dissent through the belief that 'science' was rational and objective.[2]

Those who had speculated in the market of madness in the eighteenth century, whom Porter has termed the 'medical entrepreneurs' (Porter, 1987: 166), had stimulated the demand for asylum space through casting a wide net for potential customers, and had demonstrated that there was a living to be made in caring for the newly emerging class of outcasts. Yet as science became the guiding philosophy, as illness rather than demonic possession became accepted as the explanation for deviancy or madness, the newly established professions of psychiatry and medicine, which had come to espouse positivistic principles,[3] could claim monopoly in treatment. As Henry Maudsley, the English psychiatrist, argued in 1873:

> The observation and classification of mental disorders have been so exclusively psychological that we have not sincerely realized the fact that they illustrate the same pathological principles *as other diseases*, are produced in the same way, and must be investigated in the same spirit of *positive research*.
>
> (Baruch and Treacher, 1978: 35; my emphasis)

The Victorians had thus invented what Scull has termed 'an ingenious metaphysical argument dressed in the trappings of science (Scull, 1979: 159) in order to support their case that madness had a somatic basis. It was no longer the *mind* which was at fault, but the *brain*. Thus the only profession with any right to provide diagnosis and cure was that of medicine. Thus in the 'great confinement', the madhouse became a hospital, even though 'treatment' continued to be offered within secure and often brutal regimes.

The first victory of the medical profession in Britain over the lay asylum keepers came in 1828, when it was decreed by law that asylums must have medical supervision.[4] The 1845 Lunatics Act reinforced their power, cementing the medical claim to have sole authority over the mad. After this period, medicine had established its right to control the insane, and had only to concentrate on retaining it by perpetuating the belief that continued medical treatment for diseases of the mind was needed. Both the cult of science, and public indifference about the plight of the mad, whom they wished to be separated and controlled, reinforced this process (Scull, 1979; Treacher and Baruch, 1982).

Whether the rise of the experts in madness was a result of the rise of capitalism and the concomitant power of the bourgeoisie, as some have claimed (Foucault, 1967), or the availability of wealth in the newly emerging middle classes, which provided employment for opportunistically minded men (Ehrenreich and English, 1978), or purely the result of the scientific developments of the nineteenth century (Alexander and Selesnick, 1967) which allowed an 'unveiling' of both nature and madness for what they really were, the implications were the same. Madness was placed firmly within the scientific discourse, the professionals (mainly medical) took control of the treatment, excluding those they deemed mavericks, the lay healers and women. The medical practitioners and the developing psychiatric profession had their state mandate for control, a mandate they have to this day.

The gentleman doctor – the masculine scientist

> In the eighteenth century . . . the successful British physician . . . was, beyond question, a gentleman. As with the medieval physicians before him, his classical education had not been sullied by too much practical training (though he spent some years 'reading' medicine, usually in Latin): he mingled with the best people and would perform no task unworthy of his rank, such as surgery or concoction of drugs.
>
> (Ehrenreich and English, 1978: 142)

> Writings by male practitioners commonly implied that midwives were dangerous and ignorant by comparison with surgeons and physicians. The claim was made by potentially rival practitioners in the context of widespread concern about the control of medical practice. Midwives appeared especially suspicious to enlightened savants because their territory was the intimate and tightly knit circle of women, at least in the imagination of their detractors.
>
> (Jordanova, 1989: 32)

As we saw in Chapter three, women healers had been a common feature of society for centuries. Whilst the witch trials may have served to deplete their number, they were still very much in evidence in the nineteenth century. Yet whilst the so-called age of enlightenment validated the role of the professional, it virtually extinguished the female healers. It is interesting that the same discourse was used both to position women as liable to suffer from melancholy or madness, and to claim their unsuitability for any form of intellectual employment, particularly that in the emerging 'expert' professions. A woman doctor or psychiatrist was unthinkable. Women were seen to be pallid, pathetic creatures, in need of care themselves and incapable of extending treatment or advice to others. Any woman who aspired to such a role was seen as a freak, for 'femininity' would be appalled by the reality of madness or illness, as this nineteenth-century physician believed:

> More especially is medicine disgusting to women, accustomed to softness and the downy side of life. They are sedulously screened from the observations of the horrors and disgusts of life. Fightings, and tumults, the blood and the mire, bad smells and bad words, and foul men and more intolerable women, she but rarely encounters, and then, as part of the privilege of womanhood, is permitted, and till now, compelled, to avoid them by a not, to her, disgraceful flight.
>
> (Dr Augustus Gardener, 1872)[5]

The Victorian woman who was held (as declared in a medical text of 1848) to have 'a head almost too small for intellect but just big enough for love' (Shfrock, 1966: 184) was risking not only offence to her femininity, but all manner of disability to both herself and her future offspring if she attempted to transcend the gender role laid down for her by the male élite. As Herbert Spencer declared in 1896, whilst bemoaning the lack of 'reproductive power' in many women:

> [it] may be reasonably attributed to the overtaxing of their brains – an overtaxing which produces a serious reaction on the physique. This diminution of reproductive power is not only shown by the greater frequency of absolute sterility; nor is it shown only in the earlier cessation of childbearing; but it is shown in the very frequent inability of such women to suckle their infants.[6]

Just as the edicts on witchcraft served to strip the sixteenth-century woman of power and autonomy, so the scientific dogmas of the nineteenth century ensured that women were confined to the home and to their reproductive role, to avoid damage to their health, and their future offspring. Women were thus firmly excluded from the professions, particularly those requiring the skills of a 'rational scientist'. For, as one nineteenth-century educationalist claimed, if a woman were to 'violate the natural laws of organisation' by studying or working on intellectual tasks, she would be prone to a 'mental persecution . . . which has fated the cerebral structure of woman, less qualified for these severe ordeals, than those of her brother, man' (Maddock, 1854: 17).

It was not only medicine from which women were to be excluded, but education, politics, law, economics, writing – in fact any occupation which might challenge the authority of men. If science was becoming the guiding philosophy of society in the Victorian age, the key to a future of enlightenment and knowledge, those who investigated and disseminated it were determined that it would be not placed in the hands of women. 'Women' and 'science' were contradictions in terms.[7] Nineteenth-century discourse placed women firmly on the side of nature, infirmity and superstition, and men on the side of learning, direction, management and science. Science was personified as male. Nature was female – to be 'unveiled, unclothed and penetrated by masculine science' (Fee, 1988: 44). Through their use of the tool of science men could uncover and control nature, and, by extension, uncover and control women.

Buttressed by the scientific rhetoric, the medical profession was consolidating its monopoly over healing, and now the woman who was pregnant, who felt sick, or depressed or simply tired, would no longer seek help from a friend or a female healer, but from a male physician. And so throughout the nineteenth century, and into the twentieth century, the psychiatrists looked to extend their power through widening their definitions of madness (Scull, 1979). The general belief underlying the doctors' practice as well as their public pronouncements was that women were, by nature, weak, dependent and diseased. Thus the doctors attempted to secure their victory over the female healer: 'with the "scientific" evidence that woman's essential nature was not to be a strong, competent help-giver but to be a patient' (Ehrenreich and English, 1978: 91). So to talk of 'mad' came to mean to talk of 'woman'.

Madness as synonymous with femininity

> Whilst the name of the symbolic female disorder may change from one historical period to the next, the gender asymmetry of the representational tradition remains constant. Thus madness, even when experienced by men, is metaphorically and symbolically represented as feminine: a female malady.
>
> (Showalter, 1987: 4)

There is some controversy about the gender balance, or rather imbalance, in the population deemed mad prior to the mid-nineteenth century. This lack of agreement is interesting, for it is a further reflection of the different interpretations of the history of madness, heavily coloured by the authors' own interests. For example, Foucault (1967), in his much-lauded history of madness, has claimed that during the great confinement which took place after the mid-fifteenth century, men and women were incarcerated in fairly equal numbers – if for different reasons. More recently, Porter (1987) has criticized Foucault's concept of a great confinement, claiming that prior to the mid-nineteenth century more men were treated as mad and admitted to asylums, arguing that:

> Georgian asylum admissions lend no support to the view that male chauvinist values were disproportionately penalizing women with mental disorders, or indeed that the asylum was significantly patriarchy's device to punish difficult women.
>
> (Porter, 1987: 163)

Others, such as Elaine Showalter, have claimed that women formed the majority of psychiatric cases as early as the seventeenth century, citing as evidence the files of a doctor, Richard Napier, who reported 'nearly twice as many cases of mental disorder among his women patients as among men' (Showalter, 1987: 3). Unfortunately, Scull (1979), in his excellent history of Victorian mad doctors and their patients, omits any mention of the notion of gender, a blindspot in an otherwise exemplary thesis. Do these differing positions echo the controversy over witchcraft, where evidence is selected to fit the argument of the critic concerned?

There does seem to be some evidence that prior to the Lunatics Act of 1845, which compelled all local authorities to provide asylum care for the mad, men outnumbered women in terms of actual bodies in the madhouse

– even if many women were confined as mad in other spaces, such as the attic.[8] Whatever the case prior to the mid-nineteenth century, all commentators seem to agree that subsequent to this period, women began to predominate in the statistics of the insane. The 1850s saw an unprecedented increase in the number of women admitted to asylums. As early as the 1830s it was being recommended that 'in the case of a public asylum, a larger proportion of the building should be allotted to females, as their numbers always predominate' (Browne, 1837: 184). In the 1871 census, for every 1,000 male lunatics, there were 1,182 females, and 1,242 female pauper lunatics for 1,000 males (Showalter, 1987: 52). The mad woman was moved out of the home and into the public asylum, taking up a more prominent place in the overall conceptualization of madness, for, as Elaine Showalter argues, in the nineteenth century madness itself became synonymous with femininity, and was firmly institutionalized as such.

A central component associating madness with femininity and with the female body was the continued association between female sexuality and deviancy, construed as madness. It was present in the fear and fantasy surrounding the persecution of witches, and it is not surprising that it was also endemic in the pontifications of the Victorians.

The dangerous sex

> Females are naturally libidinous, incite the males to copulation, and cry out during the act of coition.
>
> (Aristotle)[9]

> In females who become insane the disease is often connected with the peculiarities of their sex.
>
> (Haslam, 1817: 4)

> [in the eighteenth century] the female body was analyzed – qualified and disqualified – as being thoroughly saturated with sexuality; whereby it was integrated into the sphere of medical practices, by reason of a pathology intrinsic to it.
>
> (Foucault, 1967: 104)

The connection between women's unfettered sexuality and danger, evil or insanity was not an invention of the Victorians, despite the traditional association of the Victorian era and sexual repression. Women's unbridled lust has concerned men for centuries, as I have argued, being blamed for the fall of man from grace, and his continued passage into promiscuity. As Foucault has eloquently argued, sexuality emerged as a central component in the apparatus of power in the seventeenth century, when sex first became 'a means of access both to the life of the body and the life of the species' (Foucault, 1979: 146). Just as science, in the guise of psychiatry or medicine, was brought in to legitimate the connection between the womb and the brain, so it was used to reify the connection between sexuality and madness, particularly in the female. As the *Malleus maleficarum* (discussed in Chapter 3) decreed that woman's sexuality was at the root of her propensity to witchcraft, so the nineteenth-century physician looked with horror upon women's supposedly unbridled carnality. A woman's body was disgusting; her 'unholy desire', or her 'animality and sexuality' seen as inevitable antecedents of madness. As Henry Maudsley declared:

> We have to note, indeed, to note and bear in mind how often sexual feelings arise and display themselves in all sorts of insanity.
>
> (Maudsley, 1873: 83)

Sex itself – or sex outside of the hallowed confines of marriage – first became pathologized and 'psychiatrized' in the nineteenth century (Foucault, 1979). Although the discourse within which sexuality was associated with insanity and pathology can be traced through history, its legitimization as a form of illness, and the inclusion of masturbation, illegitimate pregnancy, homosexuality, frigidity, promiscuity and nymphomania under the umbrella of psychological nosology, was a Victorian achievement. These 'disorders' in women, closely associated with reproduction, were believed to be capable of turning the metaphorical angel into a voracious, sexualized monster. As Henry Maudsley reminded his fellow psychiatrists: 'the irritation of the ovaries or uterus is sometimes the direct occasion of nymphomania – a disease in which the most chaste and modest woman is transformed into a raging fury of lust' (Maudsley, 1873: 82).

This seems to be the rationalization and scientific validation of the discourse which declared witchcraft to be the result of women's uncontrolled passions. Now madness was seen as 'inseparable from notions of vice' (Porter, 1987: 201) and the 'solitary vice' of masturbation in particular was 'recognized in all countries as a common cause of insanity' (Esquirol, 1845: 41). Both women and men were envisaged as victims of insufferable ailments resulting from masturbation, a belief first heralded centuries before, as we see in Tissot's 1766 diagnosis:

> Digestion, concoction, perspiration, and other evacuations, are no longer performed as they ought to be: hence arises a sensible diminution of the powers of the memory and even of the understanding: the sight is hereby clouded: all kinds of gout and rheumatism; weakness in the back, and all consumptions, arise from the same cause [masturbation].
>
> (Tissot, 1767: 62)

Although both men and women were liable to incarceration in an asylum for symptoms seen to arise from masturbation, it was women who experienced one of the most severe and disabling 'treatments' – clitoridectomy – as a cure for their unnatural sexuality. Whilst I have already explored clitoridectomy in the discussion of misogyny, it is important to note that it was specifically tied to insanity during the Victorian era. Whilst it was a controversial practice in its day, and not widespread, it *was* inflicted upon many women. There was no logical reason for it, other than the belief that female madness, melancholia or discontent were somehow associated with 'unnatural desires', that madness was located in the female body. This extract from Issac Baker Brown's case notes of his first clitoridectomy performed on an hysteric testifies to the absence of any medical justification for the treatment. Could he not just as easily have chosen to cut off her toes, or her nose?

> She was very melancholy, and expressed a most earnest desire to be cured. I advised her admission to the 'Home' . . . and divided the clitoris subcutaneously. This being my first operation, I did not know the consequences of performing the operation in this manner. For two whole days the haemorrhage was profuse and uncontrollable. Sleep was procured by opiates.
>
> (Baker Brown, 1866)[10]

Can you imagine a man allowing his penis to be 'divided subcutaneously' in the name of an exploratory treatment, with no proven efficacy? Although this removal of what was perceived to be the offending organ was the most extreme representation of the discourse of sexuality = mad/bad, the routine treatment of women in Victorian asylums fulfilled the same controlling function. Both treatments, as Elaine Showalter has noted,

> expressed the power of male psychiatrists over definitions of femininity and insanity. Instead of the surgical knife, moral management looked to the physical design and domestic routine of the asylums to regulate even the most deviant female behaviours.
>
> (Showalter, 1987: 78)

Women who were promiscuous, who bore an illegitimate child, or even women who were sexually assaulted or raped, and understandably traumatized by the event, were sent to the asylum.[11] The 'whore', the woman who was pregnant out of wedlock, the masturbator, the sexually proactive woman – in one case a woman merely guilty of sending visiting cards to men she was sexually attracted to (Showalter, 1987: 77) – all provided a threat to the discourse of woman as passive, virginal and sexually innocent. Such women were a bad influence, and needed to be hidden away, either literally or by process of definition. If these sexually nonconformist women could be treated as madwomen their threat to the discourse of femininity was neutralized. Women were again in a double bind, for the association of femininity with sexual innocence and purity or conversely, with insatiable lust, could be used to categorize women as mad. Thus the rigid image of 'woman' or 'femininity' could be used to punish, to convict, to control – women out of control were clearly sexual and dangerous, and mad.

The woman paid the price for the sin of sex outside of marriage. As the prostitute, the 'mistress', the rape survivor are today perceived to be the source of temptation and thus to blame for inciting men's uncontrollable desire, the madwoman in the nineteenth and twentieth centuries may have been guilty of nothing more than this: guilty of a crime which, in the appropriate context, is seen as woman's main function within the discourse of woman as sex object. For as Hallisey, perhaps cynically, notes: 'the woman's proper role is to render service to others, to be nurturant and sexual in the house' (Hallisey, 1987: 4), yet if caught (i.e. out of the hallowed confines of marriage) it is she who has traditionally paid the price. But it was not only for sexual activity outside the accepted bounds of patriarchy that women were condemned. Women's bodies, their reproductive systems, were deemed to be seething with sexuality, leading in many instances to the infamous daughter's disease: hysteria.

Hysteria: the daughter's disease

> Nervous, susceptible women between puberty and thirty years of age, and clearly the single more so than the married, are most frequently visited by hysteria; and such constitutions have always a greater aptitude to strong mental emotions, which on repetition, will superinduce mental derangement.
>
> (Burrows, 1828: 191)

The supposed role of the 'wandering womb' in the etiology of madness has been well documented by feminists from different disciplines (Ussher, 1989; Showalter, 1987; Sayers, 1982). Madness was seen to be closely associated with menarche, menstruation, pregnancy and the menopause. The womb itself was deemed to wander throughout the body, acting as an enormous sponge which sucked the life-energy or intellect from vulnerable women (King, 1990). Madness was almost inevitable, given the female constitution; and the maintenance of sanity was seen as 'the preservation of brain stability in the face of overwhelming physical odds' (Showalter, 1987: 74). Energy could be spared for the intellect only at the expense of the womb, as Fitch claimed in 1890:

> In regard to the possible effect on health and physical vigour of women students, it was feared that the opening of new facilities for study and

> intellectual improvement would result in the creation of a new race of puny, sedentary and unfeminine students, and would destroy the grace and charm of social life, and would disqualify women for their true vocation, the nurturance of the coming race and the governance of well-ordered, healthy and happy homes.
>
> (Fitch, 1890)

The womb acted to preclude women from work, and position them as 'mad'. Hysteria, termed by one recent critic 'the joker in the nosological pack' (Porter, 1990) became the accepted diagnosis of all aspects of female madness, as well as a whole cornucopia of other female maladies. Whilst hysteria has a long and chequered history, initially discussed by Hippocrates,[12] it is only in the late eighteenth and nineteenth centuries that 'the hysteric' became an object of professional gaze (Porter, 1990). Hysteria became a 'metaphor for everything unmanageable in the female sex' (Micale, 1990a), the categorization of the powerless, as Showalter (1990) puts it. As Foucault has pointed out, 'the hysterization of women, which involved a thorough medicalization of their bodies and their sex, was carried out in the name of the responsibility they owed to the health of their children, the solidity of the family institution, and the safeguarding of society' (Foucault, 1979: 146–7). Nineteenth-century psychiatrists saw themselves as playing for the highest stakes: the future of both society and civilization – a society they wanted to continue as it was, with their own power intact.

There has been an enormous resurgence in the interest in the discourse associated with hysteria in recent years, possibly because of the fact that 'feminists see hysteria as a semiotic language which speaks to patriarchy in ways which can't be expressed' (Showalter, 1990). A new journal, the *History of Psychiatry*, launched in 1990, focused almost the entire contents of its first issue on hysteria. Books and conferences on hysteria are being prompted in many different countries.[13] Hysteria is being reinterpreted by feminists as an expression of women's anger, women's oppression, and of the power of a misogynistic discourse to define what 'woman' means, and to exert control over women's lives – as 'witchcraft' may have been in the Middle Ages.

But it is the treatments for hysteria which have been most carefully analysed by those rewriting the history of women's madness. One most frequently discussed, the rest cure of Silas Weir Mitchell,[14] merits mention, if only because it is used as part of the argument that current psychological treatment is equally prone to use torture and confinement, if in a different guise.

At the peak of his career in 1874, Silas Weir Mitchell advocated as a treatment for hysteria: seclusion, enforced bed rest, and the absence of mental activities such as reading, as well as plenty of regular bland food and daily massage. At first glance this may appear innocuous, but more than one author has compared this treatment to the solitary confinement and sensory deprivation used on today's political prisoners (Ehrenreich and English, 1978: 31; Ussher, 1989). Mitchell's guiding philosophy was that the hysteric should be broken, almost like a wild horse, which will eventually be cowed and tamed. In his own words:

> There is often no success possible until we have broken up the whole daily drama of the sick-room, with its selfishness and its craving for sympathy and indulgence. . . . A hysterical girl is . . . a vampire who sucks the blood of the healthy people about her.
>
> (Mitchell, 1877: 36–7)

The rest cure was used on a number of prominent American women, including Edith Wharton, Jane Addams, Winifred Howells and, most notable, Charlotte Perkins Gilman, who immortalized the cure in *The yellow wallpaper*, a personal account of depression, 'treatment' and eventual escape, as cited at the beginning of this chapter. (Mitchell apparently abandoned his rest cure when he read of the reality of its effects, in Gilman's book – Gilbert and Gubar, 1979: 136). Recent feminist work on hysteria, observing that strong and outspoken women were the ones diagnosed and treated within this oppressive regime, (Showalter, 1987; Ehrenreich and English, 1978), lends support to the case that diagnosis and treatment were used as methods of social control, and that symptoms were in reality a form of protest.

However, many other women, less famous, less outspoken, were also treated for hysteria and associated disorders. In particular Mitchell's rest cure was also deemed appropriate for those suffering from the newly emerging disorder of anorexia, young women whom Brumberg termed the 'fasting girls' (Brumberg, 1988), a further group of women whose madness was firmly located in the body and sexuality.

The fasting girls

> That mental states may destroy appetite is notorious, and it will be admitted that young women at the ages named are specially obnoxious to mental perversity.
>
> (Gull, 1874: 28)

It was natural for Mitchell's rest cure to be embraced by physicians treating women diagnosed as anorexic in the late nineteenth century: rest and excessive feeding appeared to be the most appropriate remedy for the potentially life-threatening disorder. But the earlier history of anorexia is interesting,[15] having many parallels with the history of women's madness: indeed, it is often treated in the same vein by feminists who interpret anorexia as protest 'against the way women are regarded in our society as objects of adornment and pleasure' (Brumberg, 1988: 34). There are claims that anorexia was evident in the Middle Ages: saintly women were renowned for their prolonged periods of fasting, living only on communion wafers and the fragrance of flowers (Schwartz, 1986: 116). Anorexia as protest is not the 'modern disease' nosologists might have us believe.

Scholars rewriting the history of the women saints have suggested that anorexia was evident as early as 1694; and it has been claimed (Bell, 1985) that many women saints of the medieval period, such as Catherine of Siena, were suffering from anorexia nervosa rather than wasting away out of piety. Whilst Bell, in his *Holy anorexia*, appears to adopt a feminist perspective, in that he interprets both the anorexia mirabilis of the medieval saints and the anorexia nervosa of the twentieth-century adolescent as a reaction to patriarchal oppression, he is in practice committing the same mistake as those who labelled the witches as mentally ill. He is pathologizing women who were independent, who were significant in their time. He is also simplifying a complicated and many-faceted phenomenon, in a way which is both naïve and dismissive of the women concerned. No single explanation for madness, anorexia or witchcraft is sufficient, be it the protest against patriarchy, or the explanation of distempered organs advocated by many nineteenth-century medical men.

Whilst there were many infamous cases of starving women over the centuries (some perhaps fraudulent),[16] it was not until 1873 that anorexia nervosa became a recognized clinical syndrome. That the 'fasting girl' had become a serious problem for Victorian medicine is apparent from the image of the wasting invalid in Victorian art and literature. One explanation for the emergence of anorexia is that its symptoms were an expression of the cultural context of Victorian society, and in particular, a reflection of the attitude of the Victorians towards both femininity and food. It was in the Victorian era that food became a focal point for female distress, a symbolic communication, as well as one of the visible aspects of life over which women had some control. Food took on a significance far greater than that represented by its nutritional function. Denying food became a means of exemplifying femininity, of reaching a physical and spiritual ideal. As Brumberg argues:

> Young women searching for an idiom in which to say things about themselves focused on food and the body. Some middle class girls, then as

> now, became preoccupied with expressing an ideal of female perfection and moral superiority through denial of appetite.
>
> (Brumberg, 1988: 188)

To be frail, pallid and wasted was fashionable for the middle-class Victorian woman. Her working-class counterpart had little time for wasting of any kind; she needed to eat to work. Starvation became associated with femininity, and food became synonymous with everything which was distasteful to the upper-class woman: appetite, defecation, animality, working-class drudgery, obese ugliness, indulgence, and worst of all, uncontrolled sexuality. Thus, within the same discourse in which madness and hysteria were seen as a result of unnatural sexuality, disorders of appetite were associated with masturbation or with sexuality. Control of food intake was seen as a reflection of the body, and thus of sexuality, that fiend which bespoiled the purity of the 'angel in the house'. Mothers trained their daughters to control themselves, 'to train the appetite . . . so that it represented only the highest moral and aesthetic sensibilities' (Brumberg, 1988: 175).

Freud declared, 'The famous anorexia nervosa of young girls seems to me . . . to be a melancholia where sexuality is undeveloped' (Freud, 1895: 200). Again we come full circle: woman's madness or pathology, be it anorexia or hysteria, is seen to result from the animality and sexuality of the female body. Hysteria and anorexia are similar in that they locate the dysfunction in the body, requiring treatment invariably involving some drastic measure of control of the afflicted woman. They are also similar in that both are deemed by feminists to be symptoms of protest – as is modern-day madness.

It would be useful at this juncture to explore two other beliefs associating sexuality with madness which have made their mark on present-day discourse of women's madness: the belief that sex itself is therapeutic and a cure for madness; and the related belief that a celibate woman, a spinster, or a lesbian (for lesbians were deemed not to be sexual in the Victorian mind – Jeffreys, 1985), is somehow deviant and dangerous, and will be 'cured' through a good dose of sex – with a man, naturally. For female sexuality outside of the bounds of patriarchal discourse has always been deemed deviant; in the Victorian woman a deviance seen as madness, to be cured by the penis.

Sex as therapy

> When these places [the heart and lungs] are filled with blood, shivering sets in with fevers. They call these erratic fevers . . . The

fact is that the disorder is cured when nothing impedes the downward flow of blood. My prescription is that when virgins experience this trouble, they should co-habit with a man as quickly as possible. If they become pregnant they will be cured. If they don't do this, either they will succumb at the outset of puberty or a little later, unless they catch another disease. Among married women, those who are sterile are more likely to suffer what I have described.

(Hippocrates)[17]

The womb is an animal which longs to generate children. When it remains barren too long after puberty it is distressed and sorely disturbed and straying about in the body and cutting off the passages of the breath, it impedes respiration and brings the sufferer into extreme anguish and provokes all manner of diseases besides.

(Plato)

The belief that 'woman's madness, hysteria and abnormality are a result of the deprivation of male company' and that 'regular sexual intercourse' (Martin, 1987: 16) is the appropriate cure, is an interesting reversal of the dictum that rampant sexuality causes madness. Perhaps we should not be surprised at the contradiction; many others are evident within the dicta of the patriarchal experts. And whilst there is evidence that sexual deprivation was deemed dangerous for both men and women, it is the focus on the apparent curative powers of the male penis which is of interest to feminist analysis. From the time of Hippocrates, who recommended regular sexual intercourse for the preservation of mental health to the infamous antipsychiatrist David Cooper who more recently advocated 'bed therapy' for his female patients (Cooper, 1974: 41), the power of the phallus in restoring sanity has been a common theme. As Martin notes, 'the presence of the man, and more specifically the phallus, is a constantly suggested remedy for derangement' (Martin, 1987: 44). How simple life would be if madness could be cured by a 'good fuck' as authors such as Norman Mailer might put it. Fortunately, for woman at least, it is not. The image of the mad woman's being subjected to regular unwanted intercourse as a 'cure' does not bear thinking about.[18]

I cannot help but relate this viewpoint to the discourse surrounding rape: the belief that women fantasize about rape, and, once forced to undergo the penetration by the all-powerful male, actually enjoy it. It is as if the phallus is both all-powerful, and impossible to resist, whatever the context. Literature was redolent with images of this all-conquering male, as exemplified in this extract from Ayn Rand's novel, *The fountainhead*:

> It was an act that could be performed in tenderness, as a seal of love, or in contempt, as a symbol of humiliation and conquest. It could be the act of a lover or the act of a soldier violating an enemy woman. He did it as an act of scorn. Not as love, but as defilement. And this made her lie still and submit. One gesture of tenderness from him – and she would have remained cold, untouched by the thing done to her body. But the act of a master taking shameful, contemptuous possession of her was the kind of rapture she had wanted.
>
> (Rand, 1943: 220)

The belief that all women want to be raped, and enjoy the domination of men, is akin to that which prescribes sexual intercourse as a cure for madness, even if the woman herself is not willing. This is all evidence of the underlying faith in the power of the penis – both the symbolic and actual power of the phallus. For whilst men's sexual contact with women has traditionally been deemed fraught with dangers, necessitating humiliation and control of woman's lethal sexuality, it is also a necessary part of men's maintenance of power over women. Rape and the attendant mutilations of the female body[19] mark the most extreme representation of this discourse, as we saw in Chapter 1. But the Victorian belief in intercourse as therapy is not far behind, and is still found in present-day writings on sex.[20] Freud's comment, that 'I do not think I am exaggerating when I assert that the great majority of severe neuroses in women have their origins in the marriage bed' (Breuer and Freud, 1957: 246), may be interpreted as part of the same discourse, even if the penis was not so crudely offered as the cure. What is clear is sex = power: as Foucault argued, 'sex was a means of access both to the life of the body and the life of the species' (Foucault, 1979: 146).

Given the preoccupation with the power of the phallus, it is not surprising that men flattered or deluded themselves into believing that women's madness was merely the result of an absence of male sexual contact. That women were, and still are today, subjected to unwanted intercourse as a result of this belief is less amusing (see Jeffreys, 1990).

Yet whilst men could advocate their sexual attentions as the ideal therapy for Victorian madness, the women who provoked the most disdain and mistrust, risking the zealous attentions of expert healers, who pronounced them misguided and deranged, were the celibate spinsters and lesbians, women who had completely rejected the sexual attentions of men.

The spinster: our social Nemesis

> The Spinster . . . unobtrusive, meek, soft-footed, silent, shamefaced, bloodless and boneless, thinned to spirit, enters the secret recesses of the mind, sits at the secret springs of action, and moulds and

> fashions our emasculate society. She is our social Nemesis. For the insult of her creation, without knowing it, she takes her revenge.[19]
>
> The subnormal is a type chiefly prevalent among celibate women. They tend, for instance, to enjoy a less rich and varied diet than married women.
>
> (Haldane 1927: 137)

Whilst women were, and still are, exhorted to maintain their purity and virginity, they are also expected to enjoy and relish a 'normal' sexual life – i.e. sexual intercourse with a man. The misogyny directed towards women who were outside the confines of men – those who were celibate, or living as a spinster – reached a zenith in the first half of the twentieth century, as the 'frigid' woman (by definition, any who did not want to have sex with a man) was seen as a threat to civilization: both a threat to patriarchy and to themselves. As one commentator, Weith Knudsen, declared in 1928:

> It is not possible to dismiss the lurking social-biological danger that this sexual anaesthesia, so prevalent among civilised women, will intensify the misunderstanding between the sexes and contribute to make them greater strangers to each other than nature has already made them. Thus (relative or absolute) feminine erotic sensibility actually reinforces the threats to our civilisation.
>
> (Weith Knudsen, 1928: 119)

But as the late nineteenth and early twentieth centuries marked a demographic phase of a preponderance of women, partly due to the death of men in war, it was inevitable that many women would be enforced to 'endure' a life without the sexual attentions of a man. Such women were pitied or reviled, if they appeared to be happy in their spinsterly state, or to have actively chosen it. The horror of celibacy might seem a contradiction within the discourse which defines women's sexuality in itself as dangerous and reviles the female body, yet there is no contradiction: it is women's sexuality *outside the controls of men* that is the threat. The creation of the term 'frigid' to describe 'the deviant women who failed to respond with enthusiasm . . . to sexual intercourse' (Jeffreys, 1985: 169) allowed the threat to be dismissed by pathologizing it. The label 'frigid' could be used to control women. As Jeffreys argues:

> The fear of being labelled frigid was to be used as a weapon, by the sexologists and their populisers, to force women to adapt themselves to the demands made by the new role for sexual intercourse.
>
> (Jeffreys, 1985: 169)

This pathological frigidity was deemed to be a symptom of illness or madness, and consequently descriptions of it were couched in medicalized language. 'Sexual impotence' or 'deficient' sensibility'

(Stekel, 1930: 251) was considered to be the result of repression, and described in psychoanalytic terms, such as 'arrested development', which led to 'psychosexual infantilism' or 'genital infantilism' (Van de Velde, 1931: 227). Other factors, such as 'cerebral defects, defective secretion of the sexual glands . . . nervous disorders . . . ovarian insufficiency, amenorrhea, prolapse of the womb, vaginitis and constipation' (Maudsley, 1874) were also seen to be at the root of woman's reluctance to engage in sex. And women who expended energy on mental activities were believed to be in danger of suffering from 'sexless sterility' as 'what nature spends in one direction she must economise in another' (Maudsley, 1874: 15).

At the same time, this very refusal to have sex, this 'sterility', was thought to cause grave problems, as a Dr Browne declared:

> The woman who has neither husband or lover and is not under vitalised and sexually deficient, is suffering mentally and bodily – often without knowing why she suffers; nervous, irritated, anaemic, always tired, or ruthlessly fussing over trifles.
>
> (Browne, 1923: 101)

The diagnosis of both psychological and physical consequences of sexual abstinence parallels the attribution of witchcraft or hysteria to such gynaecologicalized aetiological factors. It is a double bind: women's biological or cerebral 'defects' can be seen to *cause* deviance in almost any form; but they also can be seen to be the *symptoms* of deviance. Thus 'nervous disorders' could result from frigidity, or be the cause of it.

During the late nineteenth century a growing number of women publicly advocated celibacy (interpreted by men as frigidity), as a reaction to what was perceived to be the sexualization of women, and the widespread exploitation inherent in prostitution, sexual abuse of children and sexual violence. These women presented a particular threat to the patriarchal order, and it is not surprising that they were pathologized.

The history of the feminist revolt against the worst excesses of the Victorian institutionalization of what some have termed sexual slavery (Barry, 1979), which was epitomized by the Contagious Diseases Acts of the 1860s, has been documented elsewhere.[22] As a direct result of the horror felt towards the sexual abuse of women and girls by Victorian men, nineteenth-century feminists such as Swiney and Sibthorpe advocated a denial of the flesh, an abstinence from sexuality for woman, in order that they could rise to a higher level and achieve spiritual purity.[23] This obviously posed a serious threat to the dominant order in which women were expected to submit to the pleasures of men. Not only were the feminists challenging the misogynistic discourse, they were attempting to incite other women to deny what men perceived to be their natural rights – the woman's body. Yet it was also acknowledged by some women that celibacy, whether enforced or not, could have its negative effects on women. For it was claimed in an anonymous article by 'The Spinster' in 1911 that,

> The Spinster must either keep her womanhood at the cost of suffering inordinate for the thing it is . . . or she must destroy the faculty itself, and know herself atrophied . . . This social slaughter can no longer pass without challenge, and . . . if prurience has slain its thousands, chastity has slain its tens of thousands.
>
> (Jeffreys, 1987: 605)

This is a different argument from that advocated by the reactionary patriarchs, who promoted intercourse as a 'cure' for difficult or rebellious women. It is a plea for the acknowledgement of the damaging effects on women of denying their sexuality or confining it to an institutionalized relationship, which in reality was out of many women's grasp. As women's sexuality was confined to marriage and men, the 'atrophy' discussed above must have been the fate of many women. For the patriarchs could conceive of sexuality as being expressed only in a relationship with a man, who would simultaneously control and contain the danger in women. As Jeffreys notes:

> Wilhelm Stekel and other experts on women's frigidity, argued that feminism, manhating and the threats to male dominance and 'civilisation' that spinsters, lesbians and resisting women provided, would be abolished if most or all women could be subjected to sexual 'pleasure' with men.
>
> (Jeffreys, 1990: 29)

Sex is the saviour of society again! But the woman who provided the most serious threat in the nineteenth century, the woman who was deemed the most deviant, was the woman who preferred the sexual company of women – the lesbian. Like the celibate woman she rejected men, but rather than denying her sexuality she was enjoying it!

The lesbian

> When they still retain female garments, these usually show some traits of masculine simplicity, and there is nearly always a disdain for the petty feminine artifices of the toilet. Even when this is not obvious, there are all sorts of instinctive gestures and habits which may suggest to female acquaintances that such a person 'ought to have been a man'. The brusque energetic movements, the attitude of the arms, the direct speech, the inflexions of the voice, the masculine straightforwardness and sense of honour, and especially the attitude towards men, free from any suggestion either of

> shyness or audacity, will often suggest the underlying psychic abnormality to a keen observer.
>
> (Havelock Ellis, 1897: 250)

The woman who chose to be sexually active – but not with a man – was, and still is, beyond the pale in the eyes of patriarchal society. She was certainly at high risk of being diagnosed as mad, as Jeffreys argues in her discussion of a spinster female novelist, Rhoda Broughton, who, looking back on her youth in 1850, noted that women who wished to love and live with each other would have been 'consigned to Bedlam' or to 'utter ostracism' (Jeffreys, 1985: 111). Whilst the supposed danger and deviancy of lesbians has been part of the misogynistic discourse surrounding women for centuries, it was in the nineteenth and twentieth centuries that the lesbian became officially pathologized, her sexuality being part of her supposed 'condition'.

The fear of the lesbian, and the fear that the very knowledge of such 'perverse acts' would have an unhealthy influence on other more innocent women was reflected in the reluctance of the Victorian law makers to publicize the 'deviancy' by making it illegal. So whilst homosexual acts between men were made illegal in England in the Victorian era, homosexual acts between women were legally deemed not to exist and could therefore not be officially regulated. It was feared that otherwise safely heterosexual women might be led astray by the very knowledge of the possibility of sexual relations between women (Weeks, 1989). How insecure these men must have been. Their belief in the powerful phallus was obviously incomplete.

It is significant that it is within the world of the lesbian spinster that the description of woman as witch or woman as mad creature again comes full circle. For the lesbian was portrayed as both a witch, and a sick, misguided soul. This is illustrated in a short fictional tale of two 'spinster ladies' inadvertently caught by their friend engaging in sexual acts, who, shocked, observes:

> The two ladies, Miss Jones and Miss Evans, were performing some unspeakable ritual, which would bring ruin on some unfortunate soul, maybe even herself! . . . They say that the innocent always suffer the most in these things, that was why 'they' captured virgins . . . (For these) old maids . . . who were easy prey to the devil himself, in their childless and disappointed lives, the dark arts must be a way of getting back.
>
> (Hall, 1985: 22–3)

This nicely encapsulates the view in which lesbians, spinsters or barren women can all be seen as witches. They are deviant. They challenge our concept of femininity, of fulfilment through children and marriage: and if they appear happy in their 'deprived' state, as Miss Evans and Jones undoubtedly were, they must be engaging in evil acts, for how could any normal woman be happy with that particular lot? Perhaps the sweeping away of the theological explanations in the wake of the Victorian scientific revolution was not as complete as we might care to believe.

The image of the lesbian woman as witch is only one example. Victorian literature is awash with images and representations of the witch, the madwoman, the angel or the monster, and can provide as clear a representation of the general societal consensus about women as the scientific pontifications of the experts. One could fill a whole book with examples of such material, as others have,[24] but it is worth taking at least a fleeting glance over some of the images of women, and particularly mad women, presented in nineteenth-century literature, as they mirror the views fully sanctioned by science. This view, particularly that offered by female novelists, is often a very accurate one, for, as Zeman claims, 'as woman's predicament has shifted and changed, as she has gained advantages and lost them, the serious woman novelist has made it her business to depict the state of play in her time, noting, guiding, warning, exhorting' (Zeman, 1977: 2). Thus literature is important, for it reflects the beliefs and myths associated with women and madness, and, in the form of the female author, it represents one of the few outlets for the woman's voice.

The evil behind the veil: women in nineteenth-century literature

> Some upheld that the veil covered the most beautiful countenance in the world; other – and certainly with more reason, considering the sex of the veiled lady, – that the face was most hideous and horrible, and that this was her sole motive for hiding it. It was the face of a corpse; it was the head of a skeleton; it was a monstrous visage, with snakey locks, like Medusa's, and one great red eye in the centre of the forehead.
>
> (Hawthorne, 1958: 127–8)

The belief that any and every woman potentially housed evil, a 'raging' passion, an insanity, is represented in literature by the discourse of woman as evil, the woman behind the veil. The prevalence of the veiled wicked woman in literature in the nineteenth century is striking. For example, Shelley's Witch of Atlas, was a 'creative lady [who] weaves "a subtle veil" to hide her beauty, which is dangerous for mortal eyes since it "makes the bright world dim" ' (Gilbert and Gubar, 1979: 471). The associations between beauty and temptation, evil and witchcraft are transferred from the pornographic *Witches' hammer* to romantic nineteenth-century literature. The message is the same: woman as powerful temptress and as evil, with the potential to be either, or both. Man's most fearful fantasy, the witch with her power to castrate, was transformed in Victorian literature into the fear of woman. As Holbrook argues:

> The witch aspect of woman could always display the capacity to reduce us to nothing . . . what we mean by castration is really annchilala. The witchwoman can remove from us all the capacity to deal effectively, which she gave us in the first place.
>
> (Holbrook, 1989: 225, 229)

The juxtaposed images of woman as angel and as the castrating sexual monster were prevalent in nineteenth-century literature, medicine, psychiatry and popular discourse. It is no wonder that women themselves internalized this imagery – madonna or whore, angel or monster – which split them from their true sense of self. Images of the angel and the witch are reminders to women of the consequences of rebellion: Snow White and her wicked stepmother; Cinderella and her stepsisters; Hansel and Gretel and the witch; Jane Eyre and Bertha Mason. Medusa, Lady Macbeth, Delila, Salome, Eve, all portray woman as evil or a temptress. As Gilbert and Gubar argue, 'For every glowing portrait of submissive women enshrined in domesticity, there exists an equally important negative image that embodies the sacrilegious fiendishness of what William Blake called "The Female Will" ' (Gilbert and Gubar, 1979: 28). Whilst we are asked to applaud the purity and innocence of the heroine, who represents all that is good and ideal about woman, we are invited to vilify and revile the depraved sexual witch/madwoman. Yet even the image of the angel in the house which the Victorian woman was entreated to emulate was a double-edged sword. As Noddings argues:

> As an 'angel in the house', woman has been credited with natural goodness, an innate allegiance to 'a law of kindness'. But this same description extols her as 'an infantile, weak, mindless creature' in constant need of male supervision and protection . . . the alleged angel was an image that all Victorian women were supposed to internalize.
>
> (Noddings, 1989: 59)

But, whilst the angel may not have been a positive image, its counterpart was worse. As Philip Martin notes in his analysis of Bertha Mason and Jane Eyre, perhaps the archetypal pair, 'Bertha Mason . . . combines the myth of women's madness with the myth of her ungovernable libido . . . [her] "depravity" remains as a means of defining Jane's sanity and chastity' (Martin, 1987: 124, 128). Bertha Mason, confined to the attic of her husband, is a raving, aggressive sexual woman, out of control, out of her mind. It is because of her sexuality, her transgression of femininity, that Bertha Mason is mad. Let that be a lesson to us all. Bertha also mirrors the psychiatric discourse which associated madness with reproduction, as Elaine Showalter demonstrates:

> Bertha's madness is also linked to female sexuality and the periodicity of the menstrual cycle. Her worst attacks come when the moon is 'blood red' (chap. 25), or 'broad and red' (chap. 27); at these moments she is vicious and destructive, although at other times she is lucid and calm. Still a prisoner of her reproductive cycle . . . Bertha suffers from the 'moral insanity' associated with women's sexual desires.
>
> (Showalter, 1987: 67)

These representations of women may reflect man's ambivalence about his own power, as suggested by Simone de Beauvoir (1953), or his dread of maternal power and control (Dinnerstein, 1973) emanating from his early infantile experiences. Yet it is clear that, as Holbrook argues, 'beneath all these figures there is the underlying fantasy of the dangerous fertility of woman' (Holbrook, 1989: 225). What is certain is that these representations exclude women, mark us as the Other, dividing us and categorizing us through labels of 'witch', 'madwoman', 'whore'. Only as 'wife' is one safe. The image of the evil woman in nineteenth-century literature positions women as the second sex and acts as a mirror for all women; a mirror showing the danger and weakness inherent in the female condition. As Hallisey claims:

> The image of the venomous woman depends on a combination of misogynistic notions and traditional role expectations; in other words, evil women stand as representatives for all women. In the literature of misogyny, women are seen as weak reeds, lacking physical strength and dependent upon men in all things.
>
> (Hallisey, 1987: 10)

Evil and madness were almost synonymous in nineteenth-century literature, at least where women were concerned. Madness has been represented by male authors and through male characters: but madness in literature takes on a different form when it is portrayed in women. Madness in male characters often represents access to truth, a mirror of the horrors we cannot bear for ourselves. As has been said of Shakespeare's King Lear, 'the frantic king tears off the mask and speaks the sane madness of vital truth' (Melville, 1962: 894). But, as Martin argues:

> the female lunatic is assigned a very different role. Here eccentricity is less easily tolerated and finds no place in the history of comedy. Far from being accused of an idiocy that lies somewhere beyond ignorance, seldom created with the fool's perceptions, she is more usually condemned by being in possession of a dangerous knowledge or desire.
>
> (Martin, 1987: 14)

The bifurcated images of women in the Victorian novel were a reflection, or interpretation, of the reality of women's lives in that era. Yet the image of woman as angel, the worshipped madonna, was perhaps the further from the truth. As Monter notes: 'The sad truth is that, in women's "real" social history, the pedestal is almost impossible to find, but the stake is everywhere' (French, 1985: 170). Women were categorized, confined and sexualized; and, as sexuality became increasingly confined during the eighteenth and nineteenth centuries, so were women. As Foucault has argued, during 'the monotonous nights of the Victorian bourgeois sexuality was confined; it moved into the home. Women, by the very nature of their personification of fecundity and sexuality, were literally confined to the home' (Foucault, 1979: 3). It was a home which offered the protection of a gilded cage.

The gilded cage: symptom as protest?

> Three general vices appear to have special domain over wicked women, namely, infidelity, ambition, and lust . . . Women being insatiable it follows that those among ambitious women are more deeply infected who are more hot to satisfy their filthy lusts.
>
> (Summers, 1928: 47)

> Nature has not simply distinguished the sexes by a single set of organs, the direct instrument of reproduction: between men and women there exist other differences of structure which relate more to the role which has been assigned to them.
>
> (Cabinis, 1958: 275)

I have examined the witches, whom feminists have claimed were powerful women oppressed and tortured for daring to challenge their repressive role, for challenging the authority of men. In the Victorian era, there was no longer any need to burn women at the stake. They could be incarcerated in the asylum, or inside their own 'weak and afflicted bodies', which were treated with leeching, solitary confinement, clitoridectomy, frequent intercourse, or a good beating from a 'concerned' husband. Silence, spirituality, decorum, self-government and control were the heights to which these women were encouraged to aspire. The experts deemed it appropriate to protect woman from the pressures of the world, postulating the belief that women would be happy and satisfied if only allowed to recline in the gilded cage. Woman should follow the dictates of her 'natural' destiny, as the sociologist, Durkheim, argued:

> Women's sexual needs have less of a mental character because, generally speaking, her mental life is less developed. These needs are more closely related to the needs of the organism, following rather than leading them. Being more of an instinctual creature than man, woman has only to follow her instincts to find calmness and peace.
>
> (Durkheim, 1897: 272)

The message was clear: follow the path nature has provided and you will be happy. Attempt to follow the masculine path and all manner of illness could befall. Thus, women in the nineteenth century who attempted to create a life of their own, striving for independence, could be thwarted and dismissed through being diagnosed as mad. As female psychology was linked with reproduction, any woman deviating from the prescribed role of good wife and mother was liable to be treated by one of the available 'cures'. The latter were, quite simply, an extension of the general ethos which prevented women from achieving autonomy; from finding an outlet for artistic or literary talent; or discovering an opportunity to develop skills or follow a profession. To attempt to throw off these chains of patriarchy was to risk a diagnosis of madness, just as in earlier centuries one risked being called a witch.

As Gilbert and Gubar state, women 'who did not apologize for their ambition, their literary efforts, were defined as mad and monstrous: freakish and unsexed or freakish because sexually "fallen" ' (Gilbert and Gubar, 1979: 63). Such suggestions about women who strove to obtain outlets for their talent can be heard in the dictum of the influential nineteenth-century thinker, Nietzsche: 'When a woman inclines to learning there is usually something wrong with her sexual apparatus' (quoted in Morgan, 1989: 161). Virginia Woolf recognized that, though there have been difficult ways of labelling women – witch, whore or madwoman – the process is the same:

> When one reads of a witch being ducked, of a woman possessed by devils, of a wise woman selling herbs, or even of a very remarkable man who had a mother, then I think we are on the track of a lost novelist, a suppressed poet, of some mute and inglorious Jane Austen, some Emily Brontë who dashed her brains out on the moor or mopped and mowed about the highways crazed with the torture that her gift had put her to.
>
> (Woolf, 1928: 48)

The process throughout is that of misogynistic control and oppression. Madness has become the heir to witchcraft.

It is, however, important to note that, in the nineteenth century, it was the affluent women of the upper middle-classes who were mad or hysterical. Working-class women were too busy working a fourteen-hour day in the pits or the factory, or caring for numerous children, to have time to be 'mad'. These women did not need to be controlled by the same patriarchal discourse which confined the upper-middle-class woman in the gilded cage of hysteria or anorexia. Their lives were controlled through the dual oppression of class and gender. Their reproductive role served to restrict them, binding them to husband and children (or in the case of childless women, binding them to a life of ostracization from society) whilst their poverty and oppression as working women neutralized any threat of autonomy or power. If it did exist, their 'madness' was unnoticed: exhaustion and extreme poverty provided an effective control for their 'unnatural passions'.

By contrast, as we have seen above, in the middle and upper classes sickness and invalidism for women were almost in vogue: 'it was acceptable, even fashionable, to retire to bed with "sick headaches", "nerves" and a host of other mysterious ailments' (see Ehrenreich and English, 1978: 125). The importance of such female frailty to the medical profession and to the emerging industrial society cannot be overestimated. As patients women could have no autonomy, no power; and if frailty was essentially intertwined with femininity, women could certainly not act independently. That women were seen as essentially 'sick' is clear from the words of the eminent surgeon, Silas Weir Mitchell: 'The man who does not know sick women, does not know women' (Ehrenreich and English, 1978: 129).

This line of argument has led to the feminist retort that symptoms are protest; that madness is the result of oppression; and that, as women are powerless, they cannot express their discontent in any way other than madness, hysteria or anorexia.

Feminist literary critics and historians have been most vociferous in associating Victorian madness with protest against women's oppressive role, among them Gilbert and Gubar, who have shown that 'dramatizations of imprisonment and escape are so all-pervasive in nineteenth century literature' and 'the "mad" woman . . . [is] sentenced to imprisonment in the "infected" house of her own body' (Gilbert and Gubar, 1979: 85, 92). To illustrate this collective voice of feminist critics, I would like to offer a number of extracts from different texts where the same message, that symptoms are protest, is being given.

On hysteria

> With hysteria, the cult of female invalidism was carried to its logical conclusion. Society had assigned women to a life of confinement and inactivity, and medicine had justified this assignment by describing women as innately sick. In the epidemic of hysteria, women were both accepting

their inherent 'sickness' and finding a way to rebel against an intolerable social role.

(Ehrenreich and English, 1978: 139)

On anorexia

> Anorexic girls paraded physical starvation as a way of drawing attention to the starvation of their mental and moral faculties.
>
> (Showalter, 1987: 128)

> Anorexia nervosa is a freely chosen method of communicating and asserting power – in essence, an exercise in free will.
>
> (Brumberg, 1988: 37)

On domesticated death

> The Victorian domestication of death represents not just an acquiescence in death by the selfless, but also a secret striving for power by the powerless.
>
> (Gilbert and Gubar, 1979: 25)

Elaine Showalter has posed the relevant question: 'Was the hysterical woman a feminist heroine, fighting back against confinement in the bourgeois home? Was hysteria – the "daughter's disease" – a mode of protest for women deprived of other social or intellectual outlets or expressive options?' (Showalter, 1987: 147). Many would answer, Yes. As we can see from the small sample above, there has been a good deal of discussion of the feminist heroine in the incarnation of the hysteric, the neurasthenic, the anorexic, the madwoman, as well as the witch. And whilst it is the literary theorists who at present hold highest the banner of feminism and madness, in their re-analysis of the madwoman in literature, others are also foraging for heroism in the annals of history. As Zeman, in her analysis of recent 'champions of women' has noted, 'sociologists are busy with the rites of their favourite tribes, Victorian Women, and their skinny descendants, Captive Wives' (Zeman, 1977: 1). Medical professionals, sociologists, literary theorists, psychologists and historians are all attempting to reclaim Victorian woman as their own.

Whilst the Victorian madwoman is seen as a heroine, the male doctors have been rewritten as the oppressive persecutors, as we can see from Showalter's statement:

> Whether the disorder was anorexia, hysteria, or neurasthenia, English psychiatric treatment of nervous women was ruthless, a microcosm of the sex war intended to establish the male doctor's total authority.
>
> (Showalter, 1987: 137)

Ehrenreich and English agree, declaring that 'medical treatment, which had always had strong overtones of coercion, revealed itself as frankly and brutally repressive' (Ehrenreich and English, 1978: 139). Thus the Victorian mad women have been seen as victims of a misogynistic and oppressive society. Such a society, it is agreed, either created their illness through a process of confinement, or produced conditions necessitating starvation and invalidism as the only available protests against repression. This is a seductive argument, but it is very simplistic and incomplete. In some senses, this is the issue at the crux of this book. For, whilst feminist arguments are both persuasive and appealing in their rhetoric and in their veneration of the Victorian madwoman, they are simplistic in their analysis of the phenomena of madness; and, as Brumberg argues, 'the madhouse is a somewhat troubling site for establishing a female pantheon' (Brumberg, 1988: 35). I tend to agree.

Whatever interpretations we make, it is interesting (and faintly voyeuristic) to peruse the fantastic assumptions and beliefs held by the Victorian forefathers of the present-day expert keepers of women's minds. Many of their concepts would now be lodged in the realms of the ridiculous: the idea of the wandering womb which sucked energy from the woman; the association between masturbation and insanity; the belief that women were at the mercy of raging and uncontrolled passions which would ensnare any available man; the fear of woman's unbridled sexuality. But are they merely an historical tale, of interest only in the context of our modern-day enlightenment, useful in that they throw a positive light on present-day experts? Perhaps not. Much of the discourse associated with women's madness, like that associated with women and witchcraft, is still present today, disguised in a more palatable form.

The legacy of victorian madness and witchcraft

> Those mythic masks male artists have fastened over her human face [serve] both to lessen their dread of her 'inconsistency' and – by identifying her with those 'eternal types' they themselves have invented – to possess her more thoroughly.
>
> (Gilbert and Gubar, 1979: 17)

The witch trials are now in the distant past, of interest to anthropologists, historians or students of the occult, commented upon for their mysterious associations rather than as a means of confining many thousands of women to death by burning. Witchcraft has almost a glamour today: the image of the sweeping black cloak, the power, the mystique. The twentieth-century witch in Western countries is not associated with the same dread as her fifteenth-century counterpart. She is more likely to be portrayed as a powerful, sexually attractive woman, her danger anaesthetized, as illustrated by the recent film *The witches of Eastwick* where the witches, stripped of their horror, conform to some vision of female beauty. The sexual element in the cornucopia of symbols and images of witchcraft has remained; but the evil element has been reduced to provide a more anodyne image.

The nineteenth-century practice of labelling women as hysteric, of fearing the spectre of the madwoman in the attic has also disappeared. The image of the hysterical woman has become a cliché: the fainting maiden in the Victorian pastiche, the reality of whose illness or oppression is diluted and eclipsed in the parody of her weakness. Our representations of these women, and of the 'female malady', acts to disguise the real nature of their 'treatment' which, in its ritualized objectivity, assumes a distorted semblance of rationality and reality. Does the labelling, categorization and stereotyping of these women as witches, whores or madwomen conceal the misogyny underlying confinement, as well as concealing the nature of the individual's experience? Or is it a 'rational' diagnosis of their problem, an underlying illness? The process of stereotyping women's behaviour, of categorizing women as mad or bad, of diagnosing and applying a label which marks women as the Other, whilst maintaining our powerlessness, is still with us. The discursive practices have merely become more entrenched.

Notes

1. See Keller 1985 and Bleir 1988 for an interesting analysis of these arguments.
2. See Ussher 1992c for an analysis of this.
3. The physicians and psychiatrists have not always commanded the respect and automatic authority they do today, for the medical profession in the nineteenth century were still firmly wedded to the classics, and a degree in medicine was more likely to suggest a knowledge of classical literature, of Greek and Latin, rather than any practical medical skills. At the lower end of the medical hierarchy, the surgeons had not yet dissociated themselves from the barber shop image of their immediate predecessors. Positivism was adopted to give legitimacy and stronger control of the sick.
4. See Scull 1979 for a discussion of this history.
5. Quoted by Barker-Benfield 1976: 87.
6. Quoted by Sayers 1982: 8.
7. Jordanova, L. 1989: 31 demonstrates the way in which women were firmly positioned on the side of nature and irrationality, men on the side of science and reason, in the eighteenth and nineteenth centuries.
8. The madwoman in the attic was the subject of much nineteenth-century literature, epitomized by the characterization in Charlotte Brontë's *Jane Eyre*.

9. Aristotle, *Historia animalium.*
10. Quoted by Jeffreys 1987: 11.
11. One of the first women I worked with as a trainee clinical psychologist had been institutionalized for forty years, under a diagnosis of 'psychosis' after she had been sexually assaulted in World War Two, and reacted with 'nervous symptoms'. Her family could not deal with her anxiety, and did not want to be associated with the 'shame' of her assault. She was instead labelled and treated as mad.
12. King 1990 argues against this view, saying that it was not hysteria that Hippocrates referred to, and that there has been a mistake in the translation. However, she concedes that hysteria has a long history in the annals of medicine.
13. See Micale 1990b: 39 for a review of recent work on hysteria, and a summary of forthcoming literature.
14. See Showalter 1987; Ehrenreich and English 1978; Ussher 1989; Gilbert and Gubar 1979.
15. See Schwartz 1986 for an excellent historical account of 'Diets, Fantasies and Fat' and Brumberg 1988 for a specific account of anorexia. Both examine the cultural antecedents of women's eating disorders.
16. Brumberg has argued that many of the early infamous cases could not possibly have survived such a long period without any food, as they had claimed. Anne Moore was a famous 'fasting woman' who later confessed to being 'fed through wet towels and her daughter's kisses' (Schwartz 1986: 116).
17. *About virgins*, quoted by Leflowitz 1981: 13.
18. Jeffreys 1990 makes a strong case against heterosexual sex as a means of regulating women and maintaining society.
19. Brownmiller 1975 describes in horrific detail atrocities committed by men during rape.
20. Szasz 1981 makes a damning critique of modern sex therapy and in particular the notion of sexual surrogacy, in the context of the belief that sex *is* therapy.
21. Quoted by Jeffreys 1987: 602.
22. The Contagious Diseases Acts legalized and encouraged the physical (vaginal) examination of women suspected of prostitution in garrison towns and ports. Women's campaigns against the acts resulted in their being repealed in 1886. See Jeffreys 1985 for a discussion of this history.
23. Jeffreys 1985: 40.
24. See Gilbert and Gubar 1979; Martin 1989; Hallisey 1987; Showalter 1987.

PART Three

The experts and the critics

5

Twentieth-century madness: the heir to witchcraft and hysteria?

biological. . .
Mental illness is . . . caused by both psychological events that disrupt certain neurotransmitter systems and by a constitutional tendency for these systems to malfunction.

(Sutherland, 1987: 269)

psychoanalytic. . .
Psychoanalysis continues the rationalist spirit of Greek philosophy, to 'know thyself'. . . . As far as the individual is concerned, the sources of his neurotic suffering are by their very nature 'unknowable'. They reside outside the realm of consciousness, barred from awareness by virtue of their painful, unacceptable quality. By enabling the patient to understand how his neurotic symptoms and behaviour represent derivations of unconscious conflicts, psychoanalysis permits the patient to make rational choices instead of responding automatically.

(Arlow, 1989: 19)

cognitive. . .
The goals of cognitive therapy are to correct faulty information processing and to help patients modify assumptions that maintain maladaptive behaviours and emotions. Cognitive and behavioural methods are used to challenge dysfunctional beliefs and to promote more realistic adaptive thinking. Cognitive therapy initially addresses symptom relief, including problem behaviours and distortions in logic, but its ultimate goal is to remove systematic biases in thinking.

(Beck and Weishaar, 1989: 299)

Community care

If the Victorian era marked the beginning of the monopoly of medicine over madness, the twentieth century has marked the establishment of a myriad different theories and therapies, each firmly supported by the scientific discourse which buttresses the rhetoric of therapeutic efficacy. Madness has become firmly positioned as pathology, as *mental illness*; and, whilst the medically trained psychiatrists are still very much in control of its regulation, the new professions of therapy, clinical psychology, social work and counselling are vying for recognition as the rightful carers (or keepers).

From the end of the nineteenth century, the institutionalization of the insane had become an accepted part of society – the segregation of the mad within the psychiatric discourse the norm. The custodial sentences meted out to these unfortunates in the eighteenth and early nineteenth centuries may have reduced them to a life of passivity and psychological deprivation, or in extreme cases to the status of animals, but the institution was deemed to be the most appropriate place of cure. From the middle of the nineteenth century, until the beginning of the twentieth, the expansion in the number of hospital beds continued, and, for many years, admissions appeared to be increasing on an almost exponential curve.[1]

The mid-twentieth century marked a change in this policy of institutionalization when the policy of 'community care' became the guiding light of mental health policy, as attention moved away from the hospital into the (some would say mythical) community.[2] At the same time, the establishment of syndromes and the classification of madness within discrete categories marked the reification of the medical approach by the god of taxonomy,[3] simultaneously widening the net of psychiatric jurisdiction. For, whilst the early psychiatrists concentrated on the classic syndromes of schizophrenia, hysteria and melancholia, their twentieth-century counterparts widened their definitions of madness to include the neurotic disorders, including depression, anxiety and phobias within their remit. The Victorian psychiatrist may have concerned himself with selective groups of mad, such as the hysterical middle-class women and the paupers. The new diagnostic categories could include almost anyone.

Elaborate and highly complex theories, which explained the aetiology of the symptoms of those positioned as mad, evolved, each suggesting different forms of intervention or cure. And whilst many of these early theories were both crude in their theoretical analysis and in their establishment of appropriate 'cure',[4] their legacy is still with us today. The scientific discourse associated with madness in the official annals of psychiatry and psychology may not be gender-specific. It may be used to regulate both men and women. But it is this discourse which forms the basis for the positioning of women as mad today, and so is worthy of analysis here.

The widening of the psychiatric net did not diminish the focus on femininity and insanity: the cultural conflation of 'woman' and 'madness' still prevails. The scientific theories of the twentieth century merely entrench it more firmly in legitimated discourse; and the move away from the asylum allows a wider spectrum of experts to pronounce on causes and cures, fortified by the new taxonomies adopted as official classifications of 'madness'. It is important to examine these new categories within which madness is positioned, as this will illustrate how knowledge of, and thus power over, madness has moved away from the lay person, through taking on a complex and mystifying status which is both difficult to understand and to challenge.

Classification and categorization

Physical medicine has increased by leaps and bounds over the last two hundred years, as the blood-letting and leeching of the eighteenth-century physician was replaced with more complex theories, aided by advances in organic chemistry and the development of germ theory (Busfield, 1986: 37). Whilst the rhetoric celebrating the scientific validity of medicine has permeated popular discourse to the extent that doctors are still rarely questioned and invariably revered as all-knowing and -seeing,[5] psychiatry, with its jurisdiction over the mad, has not fared so well. Within the profession of medicine, to specialize in psychiatry is seen as slightly suspect, as Littlewood and Lipsedge argue:

> Psychiatrists are seen by medical students as unstable and confused, and as working in the least desirable speciality after dermatology. Medicine has been described as a scientific parvenu, anxious to discard those mystical elements which remind it of its own disreputable past, and to be interested in the insane is still regarded as slightly suspect.
>
> (Littlewood and Lipsedge, 1982: 21)

It is not, therefore, surprising that in order to maintain respectability, psychiatrists adhered to those concepts and constructs deemed closest to the positivistic scientific method – to taxonomy, and to classification – in order to accrue the status automatically given to their colleagues specializing in physical medicine, and to maintain control over the other professions which were vying for a foothold in the market place of madness.[6] Establishing the existence of a plethora of distinctly different mental illnesses, each encapsulated within the disease model which focuses attention on aetiology, symptoms and treatment, allowed analogies to be made between physical and mental illness, reinforcing the belief that similar models could be used for diagnosis and cure.

The classification system of the German psychiatrist, Kraeplin, first published in 1883, formed the basis for the descriptions of syndromes and diagnostic categories still used by mental health professionals today. Madness is no longer the vaguely ethereal notion of the past, but a systematically organized collection of distinct syndromes which the authorities claim can be isolated and considered as independent entities. The resultant categories are now established within the bibles of psychiatry devised by the American Psychiatric Association or the World Health Organization: the DSM III R (*Diagnostic and statistical manual of mental disorders*) and the ICD-9 (*International classification of diseases*). Theoretically, those making diagnoses and extending treatment can operate on uniform principles, thus sharing the fruits of their research and clinical practice by means of this agreement on diagnostic categories.[7]

Now reified within the classificatory system, and described as 'mental disorder', madness is to be distinguished as

> a clinically significant behavioural or psychological syndrome or pattern that occurs in an individual and that is typically either associated with either a painful symptom (distress) or impairment in one or more important areas of functioning (disability). In addition, there is an inference that there is a behavioural, psychological or biological dysfunction, and that the disturbance is not only in the relationship between the individual and society.
>
> (ICD-9)

The DSM IIIR, which is the more comprehensive, divides madness into a number of different 'axes', the first two being the means of classifying 'abnormal behaviour', to be used in the diagnosis of madness.[8]

Axis I

Disorders usually first evident in infancy, childhood or adolescence (mental retardation, attention deficit disorder, conduct disorder, anxiety disorders of childhood or adolescence, other disorders of infancy, childhood or adolescence, eating disorders, stereotyped movement disorders, other disorders with physical manifestations, pervasive developmental disorders).

Organic mental disorders (dementia, delirium, amnesic syndrome, organic delusional syndrome, organic hallucinations, organic mood syndrome, organic anxiety syndrome, organic personality syndrome).

Psychoactive substance use disorders (including: alcohol, barbiturate, amphetamine, tobacco and cannabis abuse).

Schizophrenic disorders (disorganized, catatonic, paranoid, undifferentiated, residual).

Delusional (paranoid) disorders

Neurotic disorders

Affective (mood) disorders (bi-polar disorder, major depression, other specific affective disorder, atypical affective disorder).

Anxiety disorders (phobias, obsessive compulsive disorder, panic disorder, generalized anxiety, post-traumatic stress disorder).

Somatoform disorders (conversion disorder, psychogenic pain disorder, hypochondrias, atypical somatoform disorder).

Dissociative disorders (psychogenic amnesia, psychogenic fugue, multiple personality, depersonalization disorder).

Sexual disorders (gender identity disorders, paraphilias – i.e. fetishism, transvestism, paedophilia, sexual masochism/sadism – psychosexual dysfunctions – i.e. inhibited sexual desire/excitement, inhibited orgasm, premature ejaculation, vaginismus).

Sleep disorders

Psychological factors affecting physical condition

Axis II

Personality disorders (paranoid, schizotypal, histrionic, narcissistic, antisocial, borderline, avoidant, dependent, obsessive–compulsive, passive–aggressive).

Developmental disorders (academic skills disorders, language and speech disorders, mental retardation, pervasive developmental disorder).

To illustrate the way in which these classifications might be applied, I shall provide descriptions of a few 'cases'.[9]

Case example, Deborah (diagnosed as suffering from unipolar depression)[10]

Deborah was listless, constantly tired, and felt continuously unhappy.

She had a poor appetite, and had lost a considerable amount of weight over the last few months. She had very little energy, and found it an effort even to get dressed in the morning. She said that she could no longer concentrate even to read the newspaper. She no longer went out of the house, and experienced no pleasure in activities which were previously enjoyable. During the day she sat at home, often in her night clothes, and gazed out of the window. At night she could not sleep, and would wake many times during the night if she did achieve sleep. She felt bad about herself, thinking that no one would want to be with her, and that she was boring. Sometimes she thought about killing herself, as it seemed the only way out of her misery. She felt very afraid, and did not feel that she had any control over her life any more.

Case example, Helen (diagnosed as suffering from panic attacks and agoraphobia)

Helen experienced panic attacks whenever she went on the underground train. She had been experiencing this for a year, and had had to reorganize her working life around this as she needed to travel across the city a lot. Recently she had been avoiding going out as she had begun to fear that the panic would happen at any time when she was out of the house. Even thinking about the train, and sometimes thinking about going out, brought on symptoms of panic. When this happened her breathing would increase, she would experience chest pains, heart palpitations, dizziness, sweating, trembling, and feel terrified about what was going to happen to her. She thought that she might have a heart attack or faint, and then would be trampled on by lots of people.

Case example, Susan (diagnosed as suffering from obsessive–compulsive disorder)

Susan was obsessed by a fear of contamination, and believed that germs were potentially wrecking her and her family's life. She was particularly afraid of wooden objects, and could not bear to touch anything wooden, having removed all such objects from her home. To cope with her anxiety, Susan carried out a number of compulsive rituals which took up most of her day. In the morning she spent an hour washing the bathroom, cleaning every surface with bleach, then an hour washing herself in a ritualistic manner. She would then start at the top of the house and clean each room thoroughly. Doors had to be left in the right position, and objects always in the same place. Susan could not touch her husband or her children until they had washed their hands in the same ritualistic manner, and could not kiss them until they had washed their faces. Susan could not touch objects which had been brought in from outside until they had been placed in the refrigerator, or had been boiled, and was thus unable to cook or to go shopping.

Case example, Patricia (diagnosed as suffering from schizophrenia)

Patricia had been a qualified accountant, but had recently deteriorated in both physical and mental health so that she could no longer work. She had difficulty in communicating, both because of incoherence in her speech and because she wandered from topic to topic during any conversation. She would not sit in the same room as a television, as she believed that she was being spied upon through the screen. She often heard voices inside her head, repeating the same phrases over and over again. These voices were sometimes so loud that Patricia had to scream in order to drown them out.

Each of these women experienced numerous symptoms which were interpreted as evidence of a specific form of madness, and thus were categorized under a particular diagnostic umbrella. Whilst these classification systems are adhered to most rigorously in research trials and are central to academic debate within the arena of modern madness – having been designed for psychiatrists in research settings – their utility as systems for day-to-day treatment of the mad has not gone unquestioned. Mental health professionals outside the medical sphere are less concerned with classification and exact diagnosis[11] because the symptoms of the various syndromes are often indistinguishable[12] and the syndromes are not immutable,[13] issues which will be discussed in more detail in Chapter 6. Additionally, as the classification systems are in a state of flux, with revisions being proposed on a regular basis,[14] it seems as if our very notion of the way in which madness should be categorized is continuously changing.

Even if we suspend our disbelief and accept the contention that these classifications of madness are valid and reliable, the implications are unpredictable. For the experts who claim to offer the key to understanding our modern miseries are in constant battle for pre-eminence and power. There is little agreement over the cause, the course and the consequent treatment for *any* sort of madness. The naïve person, attempting to find the right diagnosis and the right treatment, will be given different information depending on the expert they consult. There are as many theories for the aetiology, course and, therefore, treatment for the different manifestations of madness as there are experts pronouncing. Psychiatrist or psychologist, sociologist or humanistic therapist, to whom should we listen, whom should we disregard? It is not clear.

A woman who is unhappy, angry and withdrawn may be told by a psychiatrist that her hormones are in a flux, by a psychologist that her cognitions are faulty, by a sociologist that her environment is responsible, or by a psychoanalytic therapist that she is repressing her unconscious desires. She might be categorized as anxious, as depressed, as schizophrenic, or as having a psychosexual problem, depending on the symptoms that accompany her unhappiness, and the framework that guides her clinician. Who is right? Or is it the case, as with the witches, that no single perspective, no single categorization, can fully explain our madness?

What the different theories and paradigms invariably fail to do is examine the gender differences in diagnosis and in madness. The theories are presented as gender-neutral. And thus the question of *women's* madness will not necessarily appear to be of central interest. Yet these are the paradigms which are used to explain, to diagnose and to treat twentieth-century *women* – to categorize, to compartmentalize, to control. I shall, therefore, briefly examine the major models, in order to illustrate the lack of agreement between experts – the different aetiological explanations given[15] – and to demonstrate how women are treated by present-day experts. I shall begin with the dominant model in the health care system still governed by the medical professionals: the biologically reductionist model, where madness is deemed to be in our genes, our biology, our hormones, in the brain.

Madness in our genes

> The majority of cases of depressive illness appear to be genetically transmitted and chemically produced. Stated differently, the disorder seems to be hereditary, and what is inherited is a tendency to chemical imbalance in the brain.
>
> (Klein and Wender, 1988)

The traditional 'medical model', that which reduces madness to physical aetiology and treatment, has been transformed from crude analogies between the various 'humours' and manifestations of disorder, to a sophisticated scientifically validated array of theories. The science which rescued the Victorian psychiatrist from the mire is still wielded today by his twentieth-century descendant. Many of these theories claiming biochemical abnormalities to be at the root of madness postulate that there is some genetic basis for the abnormality, as exemplified by Gold's statement that 'depression runs in families. Children who receive the depressive gene or genes become vulnerable, or predisposed, to affective disorder' (Gold, 1986).[16]

The whole gamut of psychiatric classifications, including anxiety,[17] alcoholism,[18] schizophrenia,[19] depression[20] and personality disorder,[21] has been related to organic or genetic factors. These organic theories clearly site the root of madness, and thus its treatment, in the brain. Consequently, the theories and therapies are in the domain of a reductionist technology, which looks at madness in an abstract context, as related to dysfunctioning organs.

For example, attention has been focused on 'synaptic events' such as noradrenaline, 5-HT, dopamine and actetycholine as neurotransmitters at the root of psychological illness (de Fonseca, 1989: 280). In schizophrenia, 'structural and functional abnormalities' in spinal fluid circulation, or malfunctions in dopamines, norepinephrine, serotonin, platelet monoamine oxidise, or various viruses (Meltzer, 1987) have been postulated as causal. Others advocate more structural problems in the brain such as

> patterns of hypofrontal/hyperparietal regional cerebral flow and glucose utilization, left hemispheric dysfunction, and deficits of interhemispheric information processing.
>
> (Kovelman and Scheibel, 1986: 1)

In depression, it is the hypothalmic–pituitary–adrenal cortical axis that has been deemed to be over-active (Caroll, 1982). Depression has also been related to malfunctions in neurotransmitters, with low levels of either serotonin or norepinephrine being posited as of aetiological significance because of the finding that these drugs relieve symptoms. Yet recent research has dismissed these theories as it has become clear that the tricyclic antidepressants and the monoamine oxidise inhibitors are not acting in the way previously thought (Heninger *et al.*, 1983) – they increase the levels of the neurotransmitters only when they are first taken, which then return to their existing levels after a couple of days. As the drugs take between seven and fourteen days to work, the neurotransmitter theory cannot hold at all! More recent researchers have started to look to postsynaptic receptors as the key to depression (McNeal and Cimbolic: 1986) but have concentrated on animal models, as it is difficult (if not impossible) to study receptor sensitivity in humans.

In the traditional medical view, the key to understanding madness is undoubtedly seen to be in biochemical research advances, which are said to be only impeded at present by the lack of sophisticated research tools, or the absence of a biochemical breakthrough. Or as de Fonseca puts it in a recent discussion of 'Psychiatry in the 1990s':

> An impediment to progress has been the difficulty of studying mental illness in animals. There are no good animal models of either depression or schizophrenia. A further search for such models if successful would assist progress.
>
> (de Fonseca, 1989: 281)

Is it not a sad indictment of psychiatry that the attention should be given to simulating mental illness in animals when we are surrounded by enough distress in people? Can we say that our experience of 'madness' and of the discursive practices which regulate it is analogous to the experience of an animal – a laboratory rat? This position derives from the belief that the root of madness is firmly in the brain – if only we could test out the experimental drugs on animals, or correctly identify the malfunctioning synapses, we could find the cure. Psychiatry at its most simple. From the same source springs the recent conclusion that:

> Community surveys suggest that psychiatric morbidity is common and that its management is essentially a matter for general practitioners. It, therefore, seems appropriate that *new psychotropic agents, intended for the treatment of these conditions*, should be assessed under the condition they are most likely to be used – in general practice.
>
> (Beaumont, 1989: 137; my emphasis)

No mention of the other roles the general practitioner might play – merely a focus on madness as a biochemical abnormality. The juxtaposition of these two quotations illustrates psychiatric discourse at its most crude: madness *is* biology. What else could it be?

Physical treatments

> ECT entails the deliberate induction of a seizure and momentary unconsciousness by passing a current of between 70 and 130 volts through the patient's brain. Electrodes were formerly placed on each side of the forehead, but now the standard procedure is to put one on the temple of the non-dominant cerebral hemisphere. In the past the patient was usually awake until the current triggered the seizure, and the electric shock often created frightening contortions of the body, sometimes even causing bone fractures.
>
> (Davidson and Neale, 1990: 241)

To take a biological or genetic position on madness is inevitably to lead to the position that the appropriate treatment is physical. If madness is located within the body, the logical conclusion is that treatment should concentrate on the body. Physical treatments and their descendants, the biochemical restraints, have a long history in psychiatry. From the physical incarceration of the early asylums, to the leeching, the rest cures, or the crude electrical treatment of the nineteenth century,[22] the belief in the efficacy of a corporal cure was an intrinsic part of the medical monopoly over madness. Three of the treatments most commonly used in the early part of the twentieth century were insulin shock, where the patient was loaded with insulin until a coma ensued; electro convulsive therapy (ECT), where electric shocks were sent through the brain, usually under anaesthetic; and lobotomy, less frequently used, but most clearly demonstrating the reductionist viewpoint as the offending organ – part of the diseased brain – is literally removed.

These treatments are worth a brief discussion as they represent a continuation of the practice wherein physical treatments, which appear to work without any clear reason for their effectiveness,[23] are used on passive patients, the heirs of Baker Browne's victims of clitoridectomy. Insulin was first discovered and used in the treatment of diabetes in the early 1920s, and introduced as a treatment for madness in the 1930s. It involved controlled injections of insulin which reduced blood sugar level and induced either coma or shock up to one hour after the administration of the drug. Bed rest and the reduction to a childlike state, as well as substantial weight increase, were the effects of this treatment – reminiscent of Mitchell's rest cure imposed upon the Victorian hysteric.

Psychosurgery was the other invasive treatment, introduced in the 1940s, and known as leucotomy or lobotomy. This procedure involved the surgical removal of parts of the temporal lobe, or the severing of nerves connecting the cortex and hypothalamus through entering an instrument under the eyelid. The supposed effects were the reduction of fear, anxiety, depression and obsessional behaviour, and it was used most frequently with schizophrenics. Whilst it is rarely used in either Britain or the USA today, following the development of sophisticated methods of control in psychopharmocology, and the recognition of the side effects resulting from the massive damage of brain tissue, thousands of patients deemed mad were treated with this irreversible treatment during the decade after its inception.

Whilst psychosurgery and insulin treatment died out in the 1950s (although the latter was still used in many institutions until much later, as Sylvia Plath immortalized in *The bell jar*), ECT continues to be used today. ECT was based on the same premise as insulin therapy, that shock-induced convulsions were efficacious in the treatment of madness. First introduced into Britain in 1938 by two Italian psychiatrists, Cerletti and Bini,[24] ECT rapidly became one of the major treatments for all types of depression. It involves the application of electric current to the 'alterior temporal areas of the scalp', whilst the patient is gagged (to prevent biting of the tongue) and restrained. In the early applications of ECT the patient was physically tied down in order to control the convulsions. Today an anaesthetic and muscle relaxant are administered prior to treatment. Despite widespread disquiet over its mode of operation and the ethics involved in its (often involuntary) administration, researchers continue to advocate its use in the treatment of depression[25] (and particularly puerperal depression),[26] schizophrenia[27] and mania.[28] In those diagnosed as depressed, ECT is more commonly prescribed for women than men[29] by a ratio of two or three to one (Showalter, 1987: 207).

Today, the medical treatment for madness is invariably pharmacological. Psychiatrists may use psychological therapies, but these are invariably seen as supplements to the 'real' treatment, the treatment of the diseased mind. Hospitalization for madness is certainly on the wane, as it has been for half a century, and 'care in the community' is the catch-phrase on everyone's lips.[30] An array of different drugs is available,[31] heavily buttressed by research (and advertising) financed by the pharmaceutical companies. For depression, tricyclic antidepressants (such as amitryptaline and imipramine) and monoamine-oxidase inhibitors (such as phenelezine and tranylcypromine) are most commonly prescribed; for anxiety tranquillizers (such as benzodiazepines), sedatives or lithium; and for psychosis the anti-psychotic phenothiazines. The majority of those positioned as mad will be treated with medication. And the likelihood of receiving medication, as opposed to therapy, is increased if the person is working-class (Mollica and Mills, 1986) or female (Miles, 1988: 11).[32]

Yet physical treatment for madness is not the only solution open to the experts. As a result of critiques of the physical interventions (reviewed in Chapter 6), the realization of their limitations, and the expansion of the non-medical professionals' role, alternatives such as psychological therapy have blossomed.

The birth of therapy

> Psychotherapy is . . . the systematic use of a relationship between therapist and patient – as opposed to pharmacological or social methods – to produce changes in cognition, feelings and behaviour . . . far from being a diversion or a luxury, psychotherapy, like education, may well be essential in a modern industrial society.
>
> (Holmes and Lindley, 1989: 3, 13)

Medicine is not the only voice within orthodox mental health care. Physicians are not the only group to claim expertise in the diagnosis and treatment of the mad. During the late nineteenth and twentieth centuries the evolution of psychological interventions, and particularly therapy, has had an enormous impact upon the theories and treatments for madness. The movement away from physical treatments has resulted in the development of a myriad new professions vying for the market in madness. In this way, the monopoly of the medical men has been seriously challenged; and the jurisdiction of the experts simultaneously widened – for the 'talking cure' of psychotherapy (the leader in the non-invasive field) is not advocated merely for serious disturbance, but also for 'problems with living' and a multitude of minor disorders. If the authors quoted above are to be believed, therapy should be as widespread as education, part of our experience of living in a 'modern industrial society'.

As there is a cornucopia of different therapies available in the modern market place of madness, each proffering *the* explanation of and solution to distress (usually at a price), any analysis in this context will inevitably be both cursory and selective. I cannot describe every therapy available, but I can provide a number of examples of the different modes of intervention most widely practised in the Western world today. What the description of these various forms of therapy will demonstrate is the roots of the present treatment in the historical developments of our scientific forefathers [*sic*], and the way in which modern methods arose out of work carried out far from the central arena of the mad – out of research carried out in sumptuous consulting rooms in Vienna; in clinical laboratories filled with confined animals; or in undergraduate psychology classrooms. Therapy may now be widely available and practised by a range of professionals far from the leading edge of science, but its roots are firmly in this arena. Much of the therapeutic discourse is still tied to science,[33] and thus to power, to prestige and to patriarchy.

The budding professional carer, be she clinical psychologist, social worker, counsellor, psychiatrist, psychiatric nurse or therapist, will be trained in one or more of the orthodox therapies discussed below. She will be taught the language of the profession: its rhetoric of efficacy[34] associated with each intervention, which allows her to offer her services to the mad in order to treat their distress, to remove their problems.

Psychoanalysis: the founding father of therapy

> Psychoanalysis aims at producing a certain kind of knowledge, providing explanations of human conduct and experience by revealing the mental forces that underlie them . . . In Freud's words 'We do analysis for two reasons: to understand the unconscious and to make a living.'
>
> (Frosh, 1987)

Psychoanalysis, based originally on the work of Freud (1856–1939), was the first recognized 'talking cure' offered as an intervention for madness. The knowledge that some form of discussion, some conversation or verbal support, could alleviate suffering was not new – anthropological and historical evidence will attest to such a fact. Yet Freud was the first to study systematically and formalize psychological interventions for madness – particularly neurosis – through his acknowledgement of the effects of the unconcious on the mind, and the relationship between childhood experiences and adult distress. Whilst Freudian psychoanalysis has spawned a succession of imitators or alternative therapies, it remains the centre of many debates on therapy both because of its historical significance, and because of the penetration of Freudian ideas into popular discourse. The lay person asked to discuss psychology will invariably mention Freud – despite the fact that academic psychology is at pains to distance itself from psychoanalysis, and thus the student of literary theory is more likely to study Freud than is the psychology student. Yet whatever the criticisms of the theory,[35] Freudian psychoanalysis has had a remarkable influence on modern theories of madness, and continues to be practised today.[36]

Freud theorized that unconscious mental life is the major determinant of behaviour – and hence at the root of all madness. He also stressed the importance of sexuality in the formation of the individual identity, in motivation, and in behaviour, a sexuality which is present in the infant, and influential throughout the life-span.[37]

Freud argued that a constant battle for dominance between aspects of the unconscious mind resulted in the neurotic anxiety which he deemed to be at the root of the majority of psychological disturbances, and the blockage or repression of unconscious impulses.[38] Freud theorized that the early experience of the child and the successful resolution of the stages of psychosexual development – the oral, anal, phallic and genital stages, as well as the resolution of the Oedipus complex[39] – lay the foundations for the adult personality, successful resolution leading to a healthy psyche, unsuccessful resolution, accompanied by introjection and repression, to neurosis – to madness.

Over the many years of his writing, Freud developed and modified his theories, producing a volume of work impressive in its clarity, its complexity and its impact on twentieth-century thinking. The theory which has perhaps received the most vilification from those interested in the psychology of women has been his theory of female development, and particularly the theory of penis envy. Freud argued that women are biologically disadvantaged because of their lack of a penis, a lack which they realize at the Oedipus stage of development, and thus:

> the little girl, dependent on her clitoris for sexual stimulation becomes aware of its inferiority as an organ, and feels a mixture of damaging emotions: a general sense of her own inferiority in the world, her distance from power, a hateful revenge at the mother for having created her like that, in her own image, and a passionate envy of the real thing, the penis possessed by father and brother alike.
>
> (Frosh, 1987: 56)

Women are thus biologically destined to a life of envy and inability to realize their full potential because they lack the essential key to superiority – the penis. Women are deemed to be closer to nature, more passive, and 'weaker in their social interests and as having less capacity for subliminating their instincts than men' (Freud, 1933: 169) – altogether inferior. Revisionists, such as Juliet Mitchell, have argued that Freudian theory is not necessarily sexist as it reflects in a symbolic context the *cultural* reification of the penis as all-powerful. But Freud himself conceptualized women's inferiority in terms of the literal biological penis – the envy as envy of precisely that organ. Thus underlying women's psychology – and women's madness – is what results from 'the predominance of envy in their mental life' (Freud, 1933: 168).

Psychoanalytic therapy, the intervention aimed at resolving the unconscious conflicts of the patient that lead to neurosis, aims at creating an alliance between the therapist and the healthy part of the patient's ego. The patient is allowed to resolve the earlier conflicts which are at the root of distress through facing the repressed feelings in the safety of the analytic setting, and moving towards resolution in the light of adult reality. If the repression is no longer in operation, the ego should be able to develop normally. Classic psychoanalysis employs the use of free association, dream analysis and interpretation to allow the patient to express unresolved conflict and to loosen defence mechanisms. Much of the emphasis in the treatment is on the therapeutic relationship and particularly on 'transference' – the feelings directed towards the therapist in the analytic sessions which are actually feelings for significant figures in the patient's past. The interpretation of these feelings (for example, anger at the analyst being interpreted as anger at the rejection by a parent) can allow the patient to realize her repressed feelings and, through expressing them, resolve them. The analysis can take many years, and can be a painful (as well as expensive) process for the individual.[40] The realization of the impracticability of long-term daily psychoanalysis has led to the evolution of short-term 'psychodynamic therapy' wherein the basic concept of resolution of unconscious desires is adhered to, but the intervention is more focused, and of a shorter duration.[41]

Freudian therapy is not the only model of psychoanalytic therapy practised today. The last fifty years have seen the development of clearly delineated schools of therapy, based on the work of post-Freudians such as Carl Jung, Alfred Adler, Melanie Klein, Karen Horney, Anna Freud, Donald Winnicot, and, more recently, Jacques Lacan, among others. This is not the appropriate context to examine the contradictions and inconsistencies between these different approaches. But it is important to note that psychoanalytic thinking has had enormous effect on the culture of Western society – and particularly on the current discourse of madness.[42] Whilst psychoanalysis was restricted to medical practitioners in the early part of the century, it is now practised by non-medical professionals, thus opening up the monopoly on madness to a wider group of experts (although one which is extremely élitist, given the restrictions placed on training and the arduous initiation necessary in terms of personal therapy and supervision), experts who may have seen the root of madness as within the individual, but who do not see it as a biological or physical problem.

Yet, despite its pre-eminence in the minds of the public as the epitome of psychology, it is not psychoanalytic theory which dominates therapy in many countries – and particularly Britain. Other theorists have gained a strong foothold in the market for treating madness, particularly those of the behavioural or cognitive schools. These are the direct product of 'rational, objective science' supported by the prestigious nature of their proponents – the American psychology professors of the post-war generation.

Behaviour therapy: learning and reinforcement

> Behaviour therapy is an attempt to change abnormal behaviour, thoughts, and feelings by drawing on the methods used and the discoveries made by experimental psychologists in their study of both normal and abnormal behaviour.
>
> (Davison and Neale, 1990: 538)

Behaviourism and its descendant, behaviour therapy, originated from the work of experimental psychologists in the early twentieth century – the scientist in his laboratory determining the practice of the scientist–practitioner[43] in the field. Behaviourism does not concentrate on the unconscious, but on observable behaviour and the environment, arguing that all behaviour is learnt, and that madness is a result either of faulty learning, or of problems in the environment.

Behaviour therapy has been used most extensively with the form of madness diagnosed as anxiety, phobias and depression. In the case of anxiety or phobias, the most common treatment since the 1950s has been based on the principles of 'classical conditioning'.[44] Learned associations have been seen as the cause of anxiety, and treatment involves exposure to the feared object, resulting in the experience of the anxiety as non-threatening, which thus then reduces it and the person is cured. If this is carried out gradually it is called *systematic desensitization* (Wolpe 1973) and involves a gradual introduction of the feared object (such as the spider) or situation (such as an open space in the case of an agoraphobic) for increasing lengths of time, until the person is no longer anxious. If it is carried out in one trial (probably literally a trial for the patient), it is called *flooding*. For example the patient is presented with the spider for a prolonged period until the fear finally abates. The theory is that it is avoidance of the feared object which maintains the fear, and thus exposure to it will reduce the anxiety.

Case example, Mary

Mary had been afraid of lifts since she was trapped inside one as a child and had thought that she was going to suffocate. As she now worked in a high-rise office, her fear was causing her difficulty. She was worried that she would have a heart attack or suffocate if she went in a lift, and thus she felt anxious even when she thought about lifts. Using systematic desensitization, the behaviour therapist first taught Mary to relax, so that she was able to feel in control of her body. They then worked on progressively introducing images of lifts into Mary's mind, whilst she was in a state of relaxation. When she no longer felt anxious with these images, they moved to standing outside a lift, and to Mary opening and closing the doors, whilst practising her relaxation and breathing exercises. The next stage was to open the lift and to stand inside. When this could be accomplished without anxiety, Mary went inside the lift with the therapist, and closed the door, but did not go up in it. When this was accomplished, Mary went up in the lift for one floor, with the therapist. On succeeding sessions she went up to the top of the building, and on the final session was able to accomplish this on her own. She no longer felt anxious as she had learnt that nothing catastrophic would happen in the lift, as she had feared.

Operant conditioning,[45] based on principles of learning, has been used as a basis of therapy (as well as in classrooms, in prisons and in hospitals) as means of controlling behaviour. Skinner, the most renowned advocate of operant conditioning, moulded a whole generation of adults who used 'star charts' and reward or punishment in a systematic way, in order to (attempt to) control their children. The use of a gold star on a child's essay or the 'time out' in the corner for a naughty child[46] is based on the operant theories of behavioural psychologists. The regulated version of this which has been used in institutions is called a *token economy*. In this, the 'residents' are controlled through a system of rewards in the form of 'tokens' which can be traded (one might argue that our whole culture is based on a token economy if we work for monetary reward). A further type of therapy is *aversive conditioning*, although for ethical reasons this is less common. Noxious stimuli are paired with the undesired behaviour in order to reduce the occurrence of the behaviour. Thus, smoking can be paired with an emetic, so the person learns that smoking makes them feel sick; or sexual behaviour deemed deviant is paired with electric shocks, in order to reduce desire (Bancroft, 1974). Aversive conditioning has not been found to be particularly effective, and is rarely used, although it is a common occurrence in the research literature on behaviour therapy.[47] One of its most controversial applications has been in the treatment of homosexuality, which until 1968 was deemed a psychiatric syndrome. It is still used with some paedophile sex offenders who are rewarded for sexual responsiveness to adult female pornography, and punished for arousal directed at children.

A further form of behavioural theory which has been influential is that of *modelling*, in which it is argued that we learn to behave in a particular way by observing the behaviour in others – learning to be afraid of dogs because we witness others' fear; learning to be mad because our mother was mad. Thus in treatment, *modelling* can be used where the person is able to view desired behaviour and model it; or the therapist may use *role playing* – the most well-known form of which is *assertiveness training*. These therapies assume that any deviant or maladaptive behaviour is the result of faulty role models and thus by relearning the person can be helped. Assertiveness training, widely used with women, is based on the assumption that unassertive behaviour is a cause of women's unhappiness, and that 'assertiveness training can play a key role in enabling women to break out of stifling and passive roles resulting in boundless improvements in health' (Pattenson and Burns, 1990).

There have been many controversies surrounding the subject of behaviour therapy over the last few decades, as the original theories have not been able to provide complete explanations for distress nor for madness in its many forms, and the treatments have not always been as effective as the experimental psychologists who support them predict (see Shapiro and Firth, 1987). Various extensions and sophisticated developments within the area of behaviour therapy have been proposed in order to answer criticisms, leaving a complex web of theory almost impenetrable to the uninitiated (those who are not experimental psychologists), and resulting in a situation where only the most simple forms of behaviour therapy are generally practised in the clinical field. The gap between research and practice is perhaps at its most acute in this area, the sophisticated experimental psychology experiments having little impact on the clinician who is often unfamiliar with the terminology or the subtle complexities in the arguments. Anyone who has witnessed the (mal)practice of 'time out' (which has turned into seclusion: used, for example, in the 'pin-down' British children's homes as recently as 1991), the rigid adoption of token economies, and the misuses of punishment, all in the name of 'behaviour therapy', would have to acknowledge that this makes a mockery of the original theorizing, and lends little credence to its efficacy in the real world of health care – which in this context often seems to be health coercion.

Despite these difficulties, behaviour therapy continues to exert its influence in the management of the mad. There are a number of different academic journals devoted to the publication of behavioural research; and experimental or academic psychology, which forms the basis of the profession of clinical psychology, continues to hold behavioural theories in high esteem (although there is also much dissent). Yet one of the major criticisms of behavioural models, leading to its slipping from a position of pre-eminence in therapeutic contexts over the last decade, has been the simplicity and reductionist nature of the theories, and the lack of attention given to thought processes, as the attention is given over solely to the environment. In order to overcome this, there has been a great deal of research in the area of cognitive psychology, which looks at the mental processes, at cognitions.

Cognitive theories

> The main distinguishing feature of a cognitive approach to psychological investigation lies in the emphasis given to mental processes that intervene between an environmental event and the reaction of a person . . . explaining how people perceive, attend to, classify, store and remember information, and how they use this information to make decisions.
>
> (Brewin, 1990: 466)

During the 1970s and 1980s there has been what has been termed a 'cognitive revolution' in psychology. The backlash against behaviourism, as a result of what was seen as its inability to view man [*sic*] as an active agent, led to the development of theories which looked to the realm of the cognitive. That is, they looked to the role of thoughts, beliefs, attitudes and memories as the factors which determined behaviour, and thus, in the area of mental health, are at the root of madness. Depression,[48] anxiety[49] and schizophrenia[50] have all been put under the cognitive microscope, the assumption being that maladaptive thinking patterns (alternatively termed negative schemata irrational thoughts, faulty cognitions, or styles of attribution) are the cause of psychopathology. These cognitions are deemed to have a direct effect on the person's mood, on their view of the world, and on the way they act within it. Madness is, in this model, in the mind.

The cognitive approach looks to a number of key concepts in order to describe behaviour, including: information processing; beliefs and belief systems; memory attitudes and expectations; self-statements; attributions;[51] perception of helplessness and control;[52] expectancy; mental representations; self efficacy;[53] problem solving; and coping.[54] These concepts are then used directly in therapy in order to ameliorate madness, resulting in a myriad different cognitive therapies.

The cognitive approach differs from the behavioural in that the person is seen as an active processor in his or her environment, and the processing of information is central to its theories of madness.[55] One of the ways in which these theories are used in therapy can be demonstrated by a brief discussion of Beck's cognitive therapy (Beck, 1976) which is based on the premise that faulty cognitions lead directly to biases in perception, and thus to depression. Beck argued that negative thoughts based on previous experiences exist in the form of schemata, which are activated when similar events are experienced, and thus influence the interpretation of these events. These errors and negative automatic thoughts lead to negative evaluations of self, world and others: to depression. Cognitive errors include arbitrary influences, selective abstraction, overgeneralization, magnification and minimalization, personalization, and dichotomous thinking. Beck's therapy relies on uncovering these faulty cognitions and correcting them. This is not dissimilar to the therapy devised by Albert Ellis, 'rational emotive therapy' (Ellis and Bernard, 1985) which assumes that depression is the result of negative irrational thoughts, which the therapy concentrates on challenging.

Case example, Alison

Alison was feeling depressed. She was unhappy in her marriage, she felt a failure at work, and thought she was unattractive, unpopular, incompetent and boring. She avoided social situations because she believed that people would not talk to her. At work she always had lunch on her own, as she thought that others would not want her to join them. She did not put in for promotion, as she 'knew' that she would not get it. She was over-concerned with losing weight in an attempt to make herself more attractive, which she thought would make her more popular. In the cognitive therapy, her beliefs about herself, the future and the world were examined. She was encouraged to name all the negative things she felt about herself, and spent time talking about the way these beliefs stopped her doing things which she might enjoy; how they precipitated her feeling bad about herself. Evidence for the validity of these negative thoughts was sought, and Alison realized that many of her beliefs were unfounded. She carried out behavioural experiments at the behest of her therapist, to see if people did like her, and found that her fear that she would be rejected was unfounded. She also examined the relationship between her desire to be liked and her desire to be thin, realizing that losing weight would not make her any more popular or happy. She would have to change how she felt about herself. She applied for promotion and was given positive feedback, again disproving her belief in her incompetence.

Within psychology, the field of cognition is one of the areas which is experiencing the greatest growth and productivity and it is a relatively high-status area in which to research (Ussher, 1991a; Bowers, 1990). The profession of clinical psychology, following the scientist–practitioner model, is very much based on the utilization of therapy deriving from empirical research findings, and is wedded in the main to cognitive–behavioural methods.[56] The theories may be impressive, they may seem to offer some explanation for misery, for anxiety, for unhappiness. But there are many problems inherent in these approaches. First, are negative cognitions an antecedent or consequence of depression (Lewinsohn *et al.*, 1981)? Second, although much of the cognitive research is impressive as laboratory demonstrations, how relevant is it to the subjective experiences of the individual? How much does it really explain a woman's position as mad? Is Smail's criticism, that 'the sedulous accumulation of the research findings' in textbooks on cognitive approaches to madness 'reveals little more than how people react to sometimes bizarre experimental conditions', valid (Smail, 1991: 62)?

It was partly disenchantment with the positivistic bias and rhetoric of objectivity in these approaches that led to the development of therapies which did not ignore the subjective, and which eschewed the models of rational man [*sic*] inherent in the cognitive–behavioural models; that is, the development of humanistic psychology and psychotherapy.

Humanistic psychology – caring and sharing

Humanistic therapies blossomed in the 1960s. Based on the premise that 'self-actualization' (Rogers, 1961) was the road to happiness, that the acceptance and understanding of a person's madness in a therapeutic setting will result in change, humanistic therapy valued the person and preached a philosophy of caring; and the 'principle of equal respect' (Holmes and Lindley, 1989: 46) was a prominent part of these therapies.

In the literature on humanistic therapy there is a great deal of emphasis on the necessary conditions for successful therapy, focusing on a caring relationship in which the client (never the 'patient'!) receives 'unconditional positive regard', empathy genuineness and warmth. Feeling heard, their pain and difficulties acknowledged, the person would be healed. Thus, the characteristics of therapists are emphasized more than the actual therapeutic techniques (see Parloff *et al.*, 1978). Humanistic therapy has blossomed in both Britain and the USA, forming the basis for many interventions aimed at 'problems in living', and being at the foundation of the growing profession of counselling. It is not really aimed at treating severe deviations in behaviour, or serious disturbance. Rather it attempts to 'enable its beneficiaries to become more autonomous, to assume more control over their lives' (Holmes and Lindley, 1989: 98).[57] Yet it still focuses on the individual as the source of the problem. In an attempt to move away from the individual as the focus of attention many humanistic therapists have adopted group therapy, where the philosophy is the same, but the experience of therapeutic cure is in the group context, the group being central to the experience of shared pain, and shared support.

Family therapy

In recent years there has been considerable development in the area of family therapy, based on the premise that it is not *individuals* who are mad – but the systems within which we live. Thus, systems theory (Selvini-Palazzoli *et al.*, 1980) in which dysfunctions within a system are seen as being manifested by one person, who is often scapegoated, has become influential in the treatment of madness. It is argued that the individual who is designated as mad is merely manifesting the problems present within the family, and treating her in isolation will not be of any help. It is the family which needs to be treated, with the therapist working at changing the troubled relationships so that the symptoms disappear. So, for example, within structural family therapy attention is given to alignments and splits, and to the family processes which are seen as enmeshed or disengaged (Minuchin, 1974).

These long-established therapies, presently the core of mainstream professional training for many different practitioners, are not unchallenged in the market-place of the mad. For example, a recent textbook on 'innovative therapies' considers primal integration therapy, feminist therapy, encounter, co-counselling, psychodrama, bio-energetics, biosynthesis, psychosynthesis, transpersonal therapy and neuro-linguistic programming (Rowen and Dryden, 1988). Therapy is becoming more widely accepted by the populace and is expanding accordingly, with an ever-increasing professional grouping becoming involved. One of the consequences of this growth in the number of experts competing for care of the mad is that more and more 'patients' are needed to satisfy the demand. Thus the definition of what is madness, of what can be 'treated', is widening all the time. We are all potential prey for the experts – we can all have a problem which can be theorized, treated and tacitly controlled. Are we all at risk of being deemed mad?

Competition for care

As we approach the twenty-first century, the explanations offered for madness by the numerous experts are multitudinous. The medical profession may have wrested control from the layman by the end of the nineteenth century, but the end of the twentieth marks a time when its monopoly is being seriously challenged if not overturned. Psychologists, psychoanalysts, counsellors, therapists, social workers and nurse therapists are among the professional groups asserting their own expertise and proficiency in the diagnosis and care of the mad. And this is not an easy situation, a situation without fray, without open hostility and competition. As the nineteenth-century physicians successfully usurped the lay asylum keepers, today's rising stars in the market place of madness are attempting to topple the medical profession from its position of power. This has led to a number of important outcomes. First, an increasing move towards professionalization in the non-medical professions,[58] evidenced by the move towards registration and professionalization in the field of therapy in Britain,[59] country in which therapy is at present unregulated. This is justified as a means of protecting the public from charlatans, as was the recent registration of British clinical psychologists. The reaction of many practitioners to critiques of therapy seems to be not to examine the utility of therapy, but to tighten up practices, and further to legitimate the practitioners, as these recent authors make clear:

> The need for some regulation of psychotherapy training has . . . become apparent . . . the solution for it being used for doubtful purposes is to insist on proper controls rather than to oppose its expansion.
>
> (Holmes and Lindley, 1989: 11, 13)

But who is actually being protected? Is it not the professionals who can limit practice to those who have entered their portals, as did the physicians who successfully marginalized the midwives and the asylum keepers in the eighteenth and nineteenth centuries?

The person at the centre of debate, the person said to be in need of help, the woman who is deemed mad, may feel confused: which profession has the answer? What is the explanation for the madness? How can it be effectively treated? To return to my own experience, if I had been looking for a useful alternative for the medical care which seemed to offer little to my mother, where should I have turned? Having examined the alternatives I feel no more certain about which is the better. Maybe the psychological therapies are not as physically invasive as some of the biologically based interventions, but which one should a woman in distress choose? And how do we know which one works?

Effectiveness of therapy

Researchers, determined to 'prove' that their own brand of therapy is efficacious, or 'rational scientists', intent on unveiling the 'truth' about effectiveness of theories and therapies, have embarked upon a succession of controlled research studies which compare treatments and therapies, look at outcome, and examine the object of the researcher's gaze with a cool and objective eye.[60] The results are nothing but equivocal. It does seem clear that therapy in itself *is* effective for the majority of people[61] in alleviating symptoms of distress, but that some benefit more than others.[62] In addition, whilst psychotherapy (and particularly cognitive therapy) has been reported by some researchers to be more effective that psycho-pharmacology[63] in treating depression, and both cognitive and behavioural therapy more effective than psychoanalytic therapy,[64] it has been suggested that there are actually very few differences between therapies. The verdict would seem to be similar to that of the Dodo in *Alice in Wonderland, 'Everyone* has won and all must have prizes' (Lewis Carroll).[65] One of the difficulties in assessing the effectiveness of therapy is how successful outcome is measured. A positive result for behavioural or cognitive therapy is easier to obtain because more reactive or behavioural measures are looked to for indications of success. A change in unconscious processes is both more difficult to achieve, and more difficult to measure. So the very concept of a meaningful comparison of different therapies can be put into question.

The research also suggests that therapies are actually more similar than they are different, and that the 'common factors' in therapy may account for successful outcome.[66] Thus, the presence of a warm understanding relationship with the therapist, the feeling of being understood, encouragement, support, reassurance, credibility, attention and expectancy for improvement are all positive indicators. Obviously they can be present in any therapeutic framework, so some of the theoretical underpinnings of the various therapies may be questioned. It may be that the characteristics of the therapist are more important than the framework she is adopting.

However, the outcome of this complicated theorizing and heated debate,[67] where academic and professional reputations are the stakes being played for, is that we still have little knowledge of what madness is, what causes it, and what really is an effective intervention for those in distress. We have many theories and therapies, offered in good faith by their protagonists, each effective to some degree in helping alleviate pain, but if any one person attempts to consider the breadth of answers offered by the conflicting theories and therapies, one can only conclude that any therapy is as good as another – if therapy is any use at all. For the psychological approach to madness, still focusing on internal pathology, on psychological causation, and thus on therapy as intervention, has not gone unchallenged. One criticism of the very notion of therapy is that we look merely for the alleviation of symptoms, and that these are not the *real* problem: the person is manifesting distress only as a result of deeper or wider injustices.

Hence, one of the major developments in the explanation of madness in the last twenty years has been the sociological approach, seeing the cause of unhappiness within the social environment, rather than within the person.[68] This perspective views poverty, isolation, oppression – the material reality of life – as the problem, and unhappiness as the inevitable consequence. It is the community which is sick, not the person. In this view, therapy acts merely as 'a palliative, diverting attention and energy away from the true causes of human misery' (Holmes and Lindley, 1989: 97). Yet, apart from advocating social change on a mass level, or the deconstruction of madness (discussed in the next chapter), the sociologists have offered little directly to alleviate the misery of those individuals positioned as mad.

The suspended revolution

At the end of the twentieth century, despite the movement away from reductionist models, and the development of alternative therapies, as well as the sociological critiques of the psychological approach to distress, the medical profession is still very much in control. Despite the growth of professions such as clinical psychology, social work and non-medical therapy, the psychiatrist still holds the purse strings and thus the power. Reductionist models of research and practice are consequently maintained (Pilgrim, 1990: 223). If we adopt David Healy's somewhat optimistic stance that there is a 'suspended revolution' in the treatment of the mad, we might expect change, for he argues, following Kuhn (1962), that it is as a result of the investments in traditional theorizing and practices endorsed by the old order, that change is slow to take place. Change only occurs when the old are replaced with the new, who can envisage a different future. Yet the very entrenchment of views makes the future unclear. As Healy argues:

> Within psychiatry there is a suspended revolution with a very uneven battleline drawn between the combatants, many of whom have a foot in both camps. Between the smoke of battle and the political manoeuvring behind the scenes, newcomers to the field, and indeed most of the combatants, cannot be expected to see what is happening, or what the likely outcome will be.
>
> (Healy, 1990: 41)

This is a battlefield where the players are fighting for control, fighting for the right to pronounce on madness – each individualizing the distress presented to them, reducing it to part of an academic equation, a dogmatic debate. And as each profession asserts its professional identity, its right to pre-eminence and the accuracy of its theories, it marginalizes and ignores the other approaches, attempting to render them impotent by leaving them out of the debate. But this battle, this debate between the theories or paradigms, is not where we should be looking for the answers to the question of women's madness – or at least not without taking a position of serious scepticism. How many of them consider the issue of gender? How many of them consider women? The object of these theorists' and therapists' gaze appears to be gender – neutral; they are blind to her sex and her oppression. The only approach which places women's concerns firmly on the central agenda – the psychoanalytic approach – appears to reduce us to envious and inferior neurotics.

Yet it may not be a case of deciding which theory is more appropriate – choosing between psychoanalytic, behavioural, cognitive or humanistic approaches, deciding whether to work with the individual, the group or the family – for *all* of these theories and therapies have been vilified and vociferously condemned by critics who have challenged the very foundations of the therapeutic approach. Such critics have looked beyond the individual to the political role of the 'mental sciences', which 'play a key role in providing the vocabulary, the information and the regulatory techniques for the government of individuals' (Rose, 1990: 121). Thus, the foundations of the expert professions are under threat, and the 'suspended revolution' may result in their being overthrown altogether. The battle of the dissenters versus the experts is on, for the antipsychiatrists and feminists *will* have their say.

Notes

1. The history of madness from the nineteenth to the twentieth century has been documented elsewhere (see Scull 1979; Busfield 1986), and the interested reader should consult these texts for a detailed coverage of the transition from the asylum to the modern policy of community care.

2. The movement away from the institution took place for a number of different reasons. The standard psychiatric explanation is that it was because of the evolution of psychotropic drugs, which allowed the control of madness to take place outside the hospital. Physical strait-jackets were replaced by chemical constraints, not so visible but certainly as powerful. Yet this view of a natural evolution of psychiatric practice is not without its detractors. Scull 1979 argues that the development of psychotropic drugs did not take place until the 1950s, when the move to community care was well under way. Scull's own explanation for the move is that of finance: segregation was becoming increasingly expensive, and thus impossible to justify. For him, the move was from 'segregation in the asylum to neglect and misery within the community' (Busfield 1986: 328). The long-term chronic patient was ejected into the community with little thought or care, to sink or swim as circumstances decreed. The very notions of community or care were a nonsense in this context.
3. A taxonomy is a system of classification: in this sense, the classification of certain behaviours as being part of a syndrome such as depression, schizophrenia etc.
4. For example, Hippocrates, the founding father of medicine, distinguished only two states of mental illness, mania and melancholia.
5. But there has been a resurgence in 'alternative medicine' in recent years, and patients' lobbying groups are increasingly questioning the medical dictates. Legal action against the medical profession has also increased in recent years.
6. Professions like clinical psychology, therapy, social work and counselling.
7. But it is not so clear-cut. What is interesting is that the two most widely used systems of classification are not entirely in agreement – they provide a slightly different method of dividing up the symptoms of mental illness. See Skodal and Spitzer 1983 for a discussion of this.
8. Any grouping of symptoms can be categorized under one of the cited groupings; and, using the axes system, a person may be categorized under both axis. For example, a person categorized under 'mental retardation' on axis I may also be categorized as having a 'language and speech disorder' under axis II.
9. These are descriptions of cases from my own clinical work. Details have been changed to protect anonymity.
10. Unipolar depression is where the symptoms are low affect (mood), sadness, loss of appetite and sleep problems. Bipolar depression includes irritability, talkativeness and mania as well as depression.
11. One might argue that exact classifications are taken more seriously by some authorities. For example, those making diagnosis in the USA, where health insurance determines the measure of treatment given, and where diagnosis is of vital importance in determining the ability of the psychologist or psychiatrist to receive remuneration, classification is a central part of health care. In Britain, where treatment is (at present) free under the National Health Service, classification and exact diagnosis are of less importance, and mainly of interest to the physician who is determining the particular treatment to be given, or to the researcher examining the effects of a given intervention on a designated group of clients. The mental health expert is more likely to attend to symptoms than to diagnostic categories in this context.

12. For example, a major distinction made by psychiatric authorities, learnt and regurgitated by generations of psychology and psychiatry students, is that between the categories of psychosis and neurosis.
13. For example, Bentall, 1990 has questioned the validity of schizophrenia as a syndrome and Ussher 1989 has questioned the validity of the reproductive syndromes of PMS and PND.
14. For example, the DSM was revised in 1989.
15. This can only be a relatively cursory analysis, covering the major arguments and approaches inherent within the different paradigms.
16. One of the ways in which the biological theories are substantiated is through the demonstration of common patterns of disorder in family members, and particularly those who share identical genetic make up – monozygotic twins.
17. See Pauls *et al.* 1980.
18. See Goodwin *et al.* 1973.
19. Gottesman, McGuffin and Farmer 1987 review the genetic studies of schizophrenia.
20. See Gold 1986, also Biron *et al.* (1987) proposed a genetic link for depression.
21. Cadoret 1978 argued that adopted children of parents with antisocial personalities were likely to receive the same diagnosis.
22. See Scull 1979; Showalter 1987.
23. There is no clear agreed medical justification for the efficacy of insulin therapy or ECT.
24. See Busfield 1986: 334; Clare 1979, Chapter 6, for a discussion of this history.
25. Avery and Winokur 1976; Carney and Sheffield 1974.
26. Sneddon and Kerry 1984.
27. May *et al.* 1976.
28. Berkwitz 1974; Aden 1976.
29. Malla 1988 in a study which examined 5,729 psychiatric admissions over three years reported that the 1,236 patients who received ECT were more likely to be female and older than the patients who received other treatments. Breggin 1979 reported that 80 per cent of patients who receive ECT in one USA hospital are women, because its disabling effects are deemed less problematic in women.
30. This is not to suggest that hospitalization is a thing of the past. Many mad people *are* hospitalized (in the main women, ethnic minorities and working-class people) in Britain under the regulations of the 1983 Mental Health Act (see *A practical guide to the Mental Health Act* [1983]) Mind publications, London. Also see Nairne and Smith 1984: 193–6 for a simple description of the Act. This defines who can be 'sectioned' (taken into hospital against their will) under the authorization of a psychiatrist and a relative or approved social worker. Most treatment, however, takes place outside of hospital, with psychotropic drugs administered by a general medical practitioner or a psychiatrist.
31. For a review of the different psychotropic drugs and their brand names see: British National Formula, no. 5 (1983); Nairne and Smith 1984: 199–208; Duquesne and Reeves (1982).
32. See Chapter 9 for a discussion of this.
33. The more humanistically orientated therapies may be the exception to this rule, but they are still evaluated within scientific frameworks.

34. Frank 1985 has argued that belief in the effectiveness of the therapist, largely determined by therapist confidence, is an essential component of therapeutic efficacy.
35. Psychologists have invariably argued that psychoanalysis is unscientific, that it cannot be proven or disproven, and that it is specific to the middle-class Viennese patients whom Freud analysed and then interpreted to fit in with his own theories. See Kline 1977.
36. For a detailed analysis of Freudian therapy the reader is referred to the Penguin editions of Freud in the original, which are both readable and clearly expressed – more so than some of the interpretations or analyses of Freud's work.
37. Freud conceived of the psyche as being divided into three components, the id, ego and super-ego, which competed for energy within a closed system. The id is the basic foundation of the personality, present at birth, and consisting of the basic urges for food, elimination, warmth and sex – the primary processes. The ego develops during the first six months of life and deals with reality through negotiating between the needs for 'pleasure demanded by the id and the constraints of the reality of life. The third component, the super-ego, develops through the Oedipus complex, and serves the role of moral regulator, or conscience, through internalizing the moral standards of the parents, and thus society.
38. The ego acts as a regulator of the desires of the id, pushing acceptable desires or impulses into the unconscious through repression, which is then manifested as anxiety. Other mechanisms at the root of madness are projection, wherein desires experienced by an individual are attributed or projected on to external forces or people, because they are unacceptable to conscious awareness; displacement where emotions are directed away from their real target for fear of the consequences; reaction formation, converting a feeling to its opposite – such as love to hate; and introjection, turning feelings of anger or anxiety inwards, thus experiencing mourning or depression – outside causes for madness turned upon the individual. Failure to realize physical needs, sexual needs or to express anger can thus be manifested as depression.
39. The Oedipus complex is the stage where the child sexually desires the parent of the opposite sex, and through fear of punishment from the parent of the same sex, transfers desire, and identifies with the parent of the same sex. It is at this stage (age four) that the super-ego is developed and the child learns the moral values of society.
40. For more detailed descriptions of psychoanalysis see Mitchell 1986; Kline 1977; Frosh 1987.
41. See Malen 1979 for a typical description of short-term therapy. See also Casement 1987 for a readable description of the issues pertinent in such therapy for client and therapist.
42. See Sayers 1986; Frosh 1987 for a discussion. The implications of certain psychoanalytic theories for women's madness are discussed later in the book, in the context of the feminist reinterpretations.
43. See Ussher 1991 for a review of the scientist–practitioner in relation to clinical psychology.
44. Classical conditioning, originating in the work of the Russian physiologist Pavlov, is based on the premise that learned associations between different stimuli motivate behaviour. Pavlov carried out experiments on dogs, where

it was discovered that dogs given food (the unconditioned stimulus) accompanied by the sound of a bell (the conditioned stimulus), eventually salivated solely to the sound of the bell (the conditioned response). Thus the dog had learnt to associate the bell with the food, and whilst initially the dog would salivate at the sight of the food (the unconditioned response), after a period of time the bell took on the same properties as the food, because of the association, and produced the salivatory response. In the shorthand used by learning theorists:

ucs (food) = ucr (salivation)

ucs (food) + cs (bell) = ucr (salivation)

cs (bell) = cr (salivation)

It is claimed that the association of fear with an innocent stimulus (such as a spider) produces a phobic reaction, which is reinforced by avoidance of the object in question. To use the same diagrammatic approach:

spider (cs) + fear (ucs) = ucr (anxiety)

spider (cs) = cr (anxiety) → maintained by avoidance

45. Operant conditioning is based on the work of Thorndike and Skinner, who carried out experiments with cats, rats and pigeons using the classic 'Skinner box' in which the rat is observed pressing a lever with increasing frequency because the lever press produces food. Within this particular paradigm, the influences of reward and punishment on behaviour were observed, renamed by the theorists the 'principles of reinforcement'. Put simply, behaviour which is rewarded will increase, behaviour which is not rewarded will be reduced. Behaviour is thus 'shaped' in a desired way through the manipulation of reinforcement. Negative reinforcement (such as the withdrawing of attention) is generally found to be more effective than punishment in moulding behaviour, and reward is the most effective motivator. Thus, logically, imprisonment is less effective as a means of changing deviant behaviour than is providing incentives or rewards for desired behaviour. Behaviour theorists have also proposed that behaviour can be mediated by avoidance learning, as classical conditioning between a noxious stimulus and a neutral stimulus (such as pain and the dentist's chair) can result in a fear-response on presentation of the neutral stimulus (the dentist's chair), which is thus avoided. This has been termed 'motivated-fear response' (Miller and Mowrer 1948).
46. 'Time out' from reinforcement, meaning: absence of rewards.
47. For example, see Bachman 1972 on the discussion of electric shock as a negative reinforcer for self-injurious behaviour.
48. Beck 1979.
49. Salkovskis and Clark 1986.
50. Frith 1979.
51. This interest in attribution evolved from the work of social psychologists (see Weiner 1985b for the original theorizing), and assumes that individuals make causal explanations about things which happen to them, or about moods and symptoms which are experienced, in order to attempt to exert control over the environment or to understand what is happening. Attribution theorists look at the way in which labelling of 'symptoms' occurs, and predict that this is dependent upon available knowledge. Thus the

person's memory, beliefs and attitudes are closely involved. The label provides information about the possible cause. Generally, causal attributions distinguish between internal and external sources, distinguishing whether a problem is caused by the environment, or by another person, or is caused by the individual themselves. Thus it is claimed that attributing successful outcomes to stable, unchanging factors leads to raised expectations of future success. Peterson and Seligman 1984 suggest some individuals have a 'vulnerable attributional style'; i.e. a tendency to attribute positive experiences to external, unstable and specific factors, and negative experiences to internal, stable and global factors. Similar theories have been proposed to explain anxiety, which is deemed to be the result of misattribution or inaccurate labelling of bodily symptoms. For example, panic caused by overbreathing may be interpreted as a heart attack, and because of catastrophic thoughts a spiral of anxiety is entered which causes more overbreathing, further anxiety and fear, and so on (Salkovskis and Clark 1986).

52. One of the earliest research areas in the area of cognition, arising out of developments in experimental psychology, is that associated with learned helplessness – a theory engrained on the minds of succeeding generations of psychology undergraduates, who perhaps identify with its message! The original work on learned helplessness was very behavioural (Seligman 1975) based on the finding that when dogs were confined to an experimental setting where they received electric shocks which they were unable to avoid or escape, they developed an expectation of lack of control in other situations. They had thus learned to be helpless, learning that they could not expect there to be a relationship between their own actions and the environment. Subsequently, this theory has been used to explain depression, and lack of coping, which is deemed to result from an absence of perceived control, learnt from previous experience.

    However, human responses to situations where they are made helpless are more complicated than those of the laboratory-confined dogs, perhaps unsurprisingly! Thus it was proposed (Abramson, Seligman and Teasdale 1978) that the person's perception of the cause of an event affected their response, and determined whether they became depressed or not. Thus, depression was said to result from the tendency to attribute events to internal, stable and global causes, resulting in a 'depressogenic attributional style'. The person's attributions of control were also found to be important, based on the idea that each person has a 'locus of control', a belief that events are caused by either internal or external factors (Rotter 1966). This concept is still central to psychological theories such as the health belief model (Becker and Maimen 1975). The health belief model (proposing that internal perceptions of causation of ill health are more likely to result in preventative behaviour) is used to explain people's preventative health behaviour. Leading on from this concentration on control, coping and feelings of helplessness, therapy which changes the source of a person's attributions and improves their coping has been claimed to relieve depression. See Antaki and Brewin 1985.

53. Bandura 1977. Examining the different outcome expectancies associated with actions and behaviour, and how these relate to the decision to perform one action rather than another, Bandura argued that people vary greatly in the confidence they have in coping with situations. The more confident people feel about coping with a situation, the higher their self-efficacy, the

harder they will try to overcome the situation.

Self-efficacy depends on:
- information the person has about past performance
- vicarious learning
- verbal persuasion
- emotional arousal (high arousal = lower self-efficacy).

54. See Brewin 1990 for an excellent review of the application of cognitive psychology to clinical practice. For a general introduction to cognitive psychology see Eysenck 1984.
55. Information processing theories of depression (Teasdale 1983) suggest that cognitions affect mood, and mood affects cognitions.
56. There is a movement away from these models in clinical psychology but the profession is still wedded to a model of science, behaviourism and cognition (see Ussher 1992c).
57. This is a description of psychotherapy in general, but applies most appropriately to the humanistically orientated therapies.
58. For example, the registration and chartering of clinical psychologists in Britain in 1988 established boundaries around the profession, restricting clinical practice to those who, having undergone an appropriate academic and professional training, have satisfied the criteria of the professional body, the British Psychological Society. In the USA clinical psychologists have been licensed for decades, as they have in the majority of European countries.
59. See Holmes and Lindley 1989 for an argument supporting the professionalization of therapy.
60. See Lambert, Shapiro and Bergin 1986 for a useful review of this literature.
61. A meta-analysis (an evaluation of a number of outcome studies), carried out by Smith *et al.* 1980, reported that out of 475 studies there was an effect size of ·85: 80 per cent of treated patients were better than control subjects who received no treatment.
62. Some people do not benefit from therapy, or are made worse.
63. Rush *et al.* 1977 found that in a study of depressed patients, 79 per cent benefited from cognitive therapy, whereas only 20 per cent of those taking imipramine were improved.
64. Eysenck (1952) started an ongoing controversy by suggesting that in 80 per cent of cases patients spontaneously improved, and that behaviour therapy is more effective than psychoanalysis. Eysenck is the editor of a behavioural psychology journal.
65. Quoted by Luborsky, Singer and Luborsky 1975.
66. See Strupp and Hadley 1979; Lambert, Shapiro and Bergin 1986.
67. Debate about the effectiveness of therapy has been going on for over forty years now.
68. These theories are discussed in Chapter 9.

6

Dissension and revolt: Antipsychiatry and psychopolitics

alienation . . .
One must conclude that the ultimate impact of the mental health industry is to increase alienation and false consciousness . . . by the content of what it conveys, namely the myth of individual psychology and cure in the midst of a diseased society; and . . . by the . . . form . . . i.e. that of expertise itself: technocracy descending from above, like white gods coming from the skies to colonise the natives.

(Kovel, 1982: 100)

oppression . . .
The role that psychology plays in legitimizing the oppression of this society is by no means minor.

(Brooks, 1973: 317)

sickness . . .
While psychoanalytic theory recognises that the sickness of the individual is ultimately sustained by the sickness of his civilisation, psychoanalytic therapy aims at curing the individual so that he can continue to function as part of a sick civilisation without surrendering to it altogether.

(Marcuse, 1966)[1]

ignorance . . .
Modern man has discovered the atom, but not himself. He remains as ignorant of intra- and interpersonal relationships as the medieval alchemist who tried to make gold by mixing bird shit and bees' wax. Most of what goes down as psychiatric treatment is simply an attempt to perpetuate this ignorance. If the patient is docile, a few sweet words will keep both the psychiatrist and his client from uncovering what each might find disturbing in himself and in the

> other. If the patient is recalcitrant, then progressive violence in the form of tranquillising drugs, forced hospitalisation, electric shock, or lobotomy . . . will . . . shut him up.
>
> (Barnes and Berke, 1971: 349)

> *torture . . .*
>
> A prison warden, a slaveholder, and a psychotherapist have in common the desire to control another person . . . many slaveholders thought of themselves as kindly and argued that slaves were lucky to have them as masters, for others would be worse. Medical doctors at Auschwitz argued that if they didn't do what they did, others would do it more brutally. People who participate in causing suffering to others often employ this argument.
>
> (Masson, 1989: 189)

The politics of sickness

> Nature . . . weeds out those who have not got the innate power of recovery from disease and by means of the tubercle bacillus and other pathogenic organisms she frequently does this before the reproductive age, so that a check is put on the *multiplication of idiots and the feeble minded.* Nature's methods are thus of advantage to the race rather than to the individual.
>
> (Sir James Barr, President of the British Medical Association 1912; my emphasis).[2]

Dissension and revolt, resulting in attempts to overthrow the dominant discourse of madness, have been endemic in every society where the concept of madness has existed.[3] Latterly it was the archetypal sixties radicals, the 'antipsychiatrists',[4] who popularized the critiques of madness, placing them firmly in the public arena and declaring openly that 'the emperor has no clothes'. The rejection of the medical model by critics such as Laing, Szasz and Cooper, combined with their arguments that diagnosis of madness was a moral judgement based on value-laden conceptualizations of health and illness, proved both seductive and convincing. As a result, their arguments were embraced by radical mental health professionals, the media and – most importantly – those at the forefront of battle, the men and women positioned as mad.[5] These critiques, further discussed in Chapter 8, whilst they have many flaws, form an essential part of any deconstruction of women's madness, for they outlined the political implications of adherence to the official discourse of madness as illness, and provided the theoretical background for the feminist rejections of orthodox theories and therapies.

One of the common elements among the dissenters is that they take a relatively sociological or social constructionist perspective on madness.

The genetic or biological view of madness as mental illness, dominant within the psychiatric discourse, is seen as reactionary and dangerous – a danger illustrated by the extreme view above, where Barr argues that madness could be dealt with by letting nature take her course, as those most vulnerable would die through natural selection. The implications of this belief that nature in her wisdom would identify the idiot gene – the blueprint for madness – and eradicate it, are indeed horrifying. 'Care' of those deemed mad would certainly not be advocated, lest nature be impeded in her task. The Nazi persecution of the mad in the 1930s was based on this philosophy, and used genetic theories to justify mass murder (Pilgrim, 1990: 226). They argued in favour of the purity of the race and protection of the sane from the invading gene of madness to justify the slaughter and incarceration of millions of 'feeble-minded' – those deemed mad and therefore dispensable. This fear that madness could be 'bred' into the normal population was present within psychiatric discourse as recently as 1947, as this textbook citation testifies:

> Unfortunately, psychopaths (i.e. those 'stocks' which breed the 'bulk of the inefficient members of the community') also inter-marry with the sound and normal members of the community. In so doing they drag fresh blood into the vortex of the disease and it is this which keeps the process alive, and which reduces the aggregate mental vigour, stamina and effficiency of the nation.[6]

The fear of infiltration of madness into the community was both reactionary and misguided, but it was on the basis of this fear that thousands of supposedly mad people were forcibly sterilized during the nineteenth and twentieth centuries. It is also the justification used to permit those deemed 'mentally handicapped' to be sterilized today (Roberts and Burns, 1989). Such fears and discrimination against those deemed mad, coinciding with fears about their uncontrolled sexuality, prompted psychiatrists in the past to claim that the 'unruly element' were increasing at a greater rate than the 'better classes', and thus birth control was not to be recommended for the 'better classes' (Littlewood and Lipsedge, 1982).

It was as a reaction to those reductionist philosophies that critics such as Thomas Szasz, the libertarian psychiatrist, distinguished very clearly between organic (or physical) illness and madness, and proposed that all mental illness is a myth. Szasz argued that madness was erroneously termed 'mental illness'. In reality it was 'problems in living', a 'fictitious entity similar to witchcraft' (Szasz, 1961) and labelled as an illness by the medical profession in order to legitimate their own authority. Rather than being a biological or genetic phenomenon, behaviour is deemed mad because it breaks social rules; and the classification and diagnosis of the behaviour results in the individual's being scapegoated by an oppressive society. In this view, to discuss madness in terms of illness is to mystify and falsely legitimate a moral judgement. In this vision (elucidated by others such as Erving Goffman, the American sociologist) physical and mental illness can be clearly separated: diagnosis of the latter is to be based on a social construction of health or normality whilst the former is said to be objective and value-free. It was therefore argued by many of the dissenters that, whilst physical illness, which is deemed to be based on underlying physical pathology, can be studied within the (supposedly) apolitical natural scientific framework as a reality, madness can not. Goffman argued:

> Signs and symptoms in a medical disorder presumably refer to underlying pathologies in the individual organism, and these constitute deviations from biological norms maintained by the homoeostatic function of the human machine. The system of reference here is plainly the individual organism, and the term 'norm', ideally at least, has no moral or social connotation.
>
> (Goffman, 1968: 345)

By contrast, it is argued that madness must be seen in its cultural context, and thus cannot be studied scientifically, as those adhering to the rhetoric of science would claim. Many of the dissenters based their critiques on the distinction between psychological and physical problems, conceding that medical experts could have legitimate authority over the physically ill, but not the mad. As Szasz explains:

> Disease means bodily disease. Gould's *Medical Dictionary* defines disease as a disturbance of the function or structure of an organ or part of the body. The mind (whatever that is) is not an organ or part of the body. Hence it cannot be diseased in the same sense as the body can.
>
> (Szasz, 1971: 94)

This distinction, widely embraced by the radical health movement, has been used as ammunition for throwing out the medical experts, together with their nosology, and for questioning the very existence of institutionalized treatment of madness. For the implications of *illness* are that the person is not in control of their own condition, and must be treated by those with the appropriate knowledge and power to heal. Yet as Conrad notes: 'illness, like beauty, is in the eye of the beholder' (Conrad, 1982: 106) and thus the healers can delineate their own areas of expertise, their own areas of control, creating the 'illness' by process of definition. The implications of the ascription of the label of illness, the adoption of the 'sick role', are significant. For the sick role acts both to legitimate the doctor–patient relationship, and to prescribe behaviour for the individual designated as 'ill'. The consequence of this is that the 'sick' individual is exempted from normal responsibility for their own condition, and thus cannot recover by an 'act of will'. They must recognize that being ill is in itself an undesirable state, but must want to recover, and seek appropriate help or treatment (Conrad, 1982: 107). Further, the treatment for 'illness' is bound up with the reductionist model, as Baruch and Treacher show:

> . . . the sick role absolves the patient from responsibility for his condition – the use of drugs strangely confirms this passivity. The patient not only becomes dependent upon the doctor for his 'cure' (because the doctor alone can be responsible for prescribing drugs), but he also runs the risk of becoming physically dependent on the drugs.
>
> (Baruch and Treacher, 1978: 85)

The concept of madness as illness is, however, seductive and appealing, for if our misery is an organic dysfunction we have only to wait for the cure dispensed by the physician and we will be relieved. As Dorothy Rowe has noted, 'the belief that our suffering has a physical cause is always persuasive, because it relieves us of all responsibility' (Rowe, 1990: 15). Hence, every new 'breakthrough' in the physical sphere is greeted with excitement, as Gilman illustrates:

> When in the 1960's there seemed to be evidence that sociopaths all showed similar genetic errors, a great sigh of relief was heard in society. There was a clear, unrefutable marker that provided a specific sign and a direct etiology for sociopathic and psychopathic acts.
>
> (Gilman, 1988: 14).

Despite the critiques, the temptation remains to seek a physical cure for today, just as in the nineteenth century, 'asylums . . . get rid of troublesome people for the rest of us' (Scull, 1979: 260). The twentieth century has seen a movement away from the monolithic asylum, but the control of the mad is still in the hands of the medical profession, either through outpatient clinics in hospitals, or through the medical dominance of therapy and clinical psychology. This dominance, based on the belief in a physical aetiology for madness, serves political ends: it allows psychiatrists to maintain the continuity between physical and mental illness, and to deny the role of social, economic or political factors in madness. It has therefore been argued by many of the dissenters that it is important to recognize that madness is *not* illness; that it is a distinctly different phenomenon from physical pathology. If we acknowledge this, the focus of attention could be shifted to what many see as the *real* problem, that of society. And then the medical experts would no longer be in control and their edicts would be seen as the labelling of discontent within a medical model, which acts to persecute the individual in distress.

Power and persecution in practice: diagnosis and labelling

> Diagnosis is the Holy Grail of Official Psychiatry.
>
> (Kovel, 1982: 86)

> Clinical judgement [is a] blank cheque which can be filled in with any amount of tacit biases and unwritten rules, and completely undermines psychiatry's claim to be based on observations more solid than lay judgement.
>
> (Ingleby, 1982: 30).

One of the other major tenets of the antipsychiatry argument was that the supposedly objective diagnosis of madness, based on 'clinical judgement', is subjective, arbitrary, and founded on values, morals and political allegiances – a medicalization of deviance in order to maintain social control. The aura of legitimacy given to the diagnosis of madness by the professionalization of treatment is seen to obscure the reality of the oppression. For the diagnosis of madness, the decision to ascribe the label to any particular person, is ultimately dependent on the views of the individual expert. As Scull has argued, 'Psychiatrists possess the power to assign one person to the status of being mentally ill, and to refuse the designation to another' (Scull, 1975: 221). Many, such as Szasz and Laing, have compared the subjective diagnosis of madness to what they see as a more objective process, that of the medical expert diagnosing physical illness, an argument which can also be seen as flawed, as I shall outline below.

With madness, the professionals are assigning a label which fits their own philosophical framework of 'illness' as did the medieval clerics who defined any deviant outsider as 'evil'. Thus Szasz has claimed, 'To the zealous psychiatrist all men are mad, just as to the zealous theologian, all men are evil.' (Szasz, 1971: 39). Diagnosis, whether of witchcraft or madness, is seen as applying a label to deviancy – of categorizing aliens or outsiders.

Under the umbrella of 'labelling theory' these arguments have been absorbed and reiterated to generations of undergraduates as well as to readers of popularized texts on psychiatry. Even those who dispute much of the work of the dissenters have tended to assimilate the basics of labelling theory into their analyses, even if they do not act on it.[7] Even the conservative medical student, normally fed on a strict diet of biological reductionism, will now be aware of the power of labels, of the sociological analysis of labelling.

Labelling theorists, such as Scheff or Goffman, see madness as the 'labelled violations of social norms' (Scheff, 1966: 25), arguing that all madness is dependent on social and cultural values, not scientific objectivity. Psychiatry is thus seen as an agent of social control. Within this conceptualization, madness or mental illness does not exist as objective reality; it exists only in the mind or eyes of the beholder. Society creates madness through a process of definition. A person may commit a particular act, or exhibit a particular type of behaviour, yet not receive the label of deviant, of mad person, either because the behaviour makes sense in the context within which it is performed, or because the person exhibiting it is within a social category less vulnerable to labelling. As Peter Sedgewick illustrated:

> It is all right to be 'out of contact' if you are a young woman who ignores suggestive remarks from men as you walk along the street; it is all right (or at least it is no concern of a psychiatrist) if you hear supernatural voices in the course of a Pentecostal meeting; you may take off your clothes and dance at a hippie festival of joy and music, you may hector and dominate in the classroom or parade ground, you may refuse attention to onlookers if you are fishing, writing a PhD or meditating on St John of the Cross: but if you try these things at home, in the wrong kind of public place or on the observation ward of a mental institution, heaven help you because you are then 'mad', 'mental' or eligible for some more technical diagnosis.
>
> (Sedgewick, 1981: 45)

Thus, a diagnosis of madness depends on some subjective evaluation that the behaviour is inappropriate in the viewer's judgement to place it within the realms of illness, and thus the jurisdiction of the experts. Behaviour itself is not necessarily mad; it depends who is doing it and in what circumstances. Goffman argued that the inability or reluctance of the mad person to play their designated social role, and thus fulfil the expectations of others, was the primary cause of their being labelled mad. So a woman who neglects her children, has sexual relationships with men other than her husband, becomes angry and violent, or consumes large amounts of alcohol is at risk of being labelled mad. She is categorized for not playing her designated social role. A man is not in danger of diagnosis of madness for these very same behaviours, which are seen as part of the accepted male role.

Others have noted that 'ceremonies of transition' play an important role in the transformation of the sane rational person into the mad person (Becker, 1963; Ericson, 1962). This might involve a psychiatric case conference, a meeting to 'confirm' the diagnosis, or incarceration into a psychiatric hospital. Once a person is labelled, he or she becomes part of a deviant group, which, as a consequence, develops a deviant subculture (Becker, 1963) resulting in common patterns of behaviour and ways of seeing the world. The labelled individual will internalize their description, resulting in low self-esteem and a self-fulfilling prophecy. It is thus a downward spiral. If you are told that you are mad, you take on the mantle of madness.

It has been argued that everyone performs actions that correspond with our definition of mad behaviour, and, in certain circumstances, we may be referred to those in authority, or receive the stigmatizing label; and thus everyone has the potential of being labelled mad – or mentally ill (Scheff, 1966). And once the person is labelled as mad, everything they say or do will be interpreted within this context, as their behaviour is selectively interpreted by the outsider to provide confirmation of the diagnosis. R. D. Laing illustrated this process in his thesis which fundamentally challenged the medical reality of schizophrenia as a syndrome, reinterpreting the discourse of those labelled schizophrenics within a framework which gave their language and thought a new meaning. For example, in his early book, *The divided self* (1960), Laing reanalysed the description of the 'bizarre behaviour' of the schizophrenic patient outlined by the influential nineteenth-century psychiatrist, Emil Kraeplin, arguing that the patient was ridiculing the nonsensical questions of the great doctor, rather than exhibiting mad behaviour. He thus described a scenario in which the patient was cleverly, and understandably, reacting to the situation he was in. This contrasts sharply with the interpretation of both Kraeplin, and legions of subsequent observers, that the case example was that of prototypical madness.

Equally it has been argued that behaviour meaningless to one person may be meaningful to another, and that we should not use our own perspectives to judge. As Berke claims:

> (We should) always try to observe another person from his or her social experiential reference points. This means that one cannot assume a knowledge of another's interpersonal field, nor prejudice peculiar behaviour as 'sick'. What is peculiar in one situation may well be 'normal' in another.
>
> (Barnes and Berke, 1971: 80)

Thus, it may be only because behaviour deviates from social norms that it is deemed mad, or because the observer who makes the judgement holds a different view of the world. As Smith has argued:

> I suggest that the behaviour of persons who came to be labelled as mentally ill fails to confirm that they share the same version of reality as does the observer. What they do and say indicates that they do not construct reality in a way that the observer can understand . . . Behaviour is recognised as odd, funny, bizarre, etc., because it does not make sense in terms of the rules for producing intelligent behaviour in a given cultural community.
> (Smith, 1967: 11)[8]

The ability to interpret behaviour as madness in those officially diagnosed was most clearly illustrated in the now infamous research carried out by Rosenhan (1973). Psychiatric and nursing staff in twelve institutions diagnosed 'pseudopatients' – colleagues of the experimenter who had been instructed to report auditory hallucinations – as schizophrenics. The twelve 'patients' behaved in a perfectly sane way following their admission to the hospital, but their insistence on their sanity, their habit of writing down observations, and their very demeanour was interpreted as symptomatic of their illness. The patients themselves described the experience as alienating, and it was argued that this whole process of diagnosis and 'treatment' produces an irreversible mental patient identity. As well as casting doubts on the validity of diagnosis, this research illustrates how the ascription of a label affects our interpretation of behaviour and our willingness to see it as deviant.[9]

Rather than use the concept of illness, Laing argued for a re-conceptualization of madness (and specifically schizophrenia) as a 'special strategy that a person invents in order to live in an unlivable situation' (Laing, 1967: 79) positing that if we see schizophrenia as comprehensible, even adaptable, we *cannot* see it as illness. Within this framework, traditional psychiatric treatment is seen as the quest to enforce the patient to abandon his or her subjective perspective for the psychiatrist's supposedly 'objective' one – a process which Laing sees as inevitably dismissing and opposing the patient. Thus traditional mental health services, and the labelling process, seen as central, are implicitly rejected:

> Psychiatry is not a specialism of medicine, but of mythology.
> (Szasz, 1979: 49)

> The committed person labelled as patient, and specifically as 'schizophrenic' is degraded from full existential and legal status as human agent and responsible person to someone no longer in possession of his own definition of himself . . . More completely, more radically than anywhere else in our society, he is invalidated as a human being. In the mental

> hospital he must remain, until the label is rescinded or qualified by such terms as 'remitted' or 'readjusted'.
>
> (Laing, 1967: 84)

Labelling theorists would thus argue that madness is not an objective reality, but a socially constructed concept, changing and developing. Behaviour 'normal' at one point in time, or in one society, is mad in another. Some have used statistical models of deviance to account for this. For example, Durkheim declared: 'we shall call "normal" these social conditions that are the most generally distributed, and the others "morbid" or "pathological". So if a majority of a population are engaged in a particular behaviour, by definition, it cannot be mad' (Durkheim, 1938: 56).

A further explanation is that behaviour which is at odds with that of the ruling élite will be deemed 'mad'. This can act to stigmatize particular social groups, such as women, blacks or the poor – or those deemed outside, the 'alienists'. Yet what each society deems to be alienists differs, as is illustrated by cross-cultural analysis, an analysis which the dissenters use as further evidence of the social construction of madness.

Madness and culture

> Why bother with political trials when we have psychiatric clinics?
>
> (G. Morozov)[10]

The native Indian of the north west coast of America who gives away all his possessions after being beaten in a competition (Schwab and Schwab, 1978: 132) is not deemed mad. The Yanomamo woman who leaves her newborn female infant outside the encampment to die, because she does not want another child (Chagnon, 1977), is not deemed mad. The women of Islam who claim to be possessed by the 'Sar' spirits, which have to be placated by riches and presents from their husbands (Littlewood and Lipsedge, 1982: 197) are not deemed mad. Yet in twentieth-century Western culture, these individuals would be at risk of receiving a psychiatric diagnosis, their 'symptoms' seen as clear evidence of insanity.

It is important to note that definitions of madness are consistent within, though not necessarily between, cultures, as Wallace noted, for whilst, 'what we recognise as pathological behaviour is usually a matter of common consensus in a society, the standards of consensus vary from one society to another' (Wallace, 1967: 195). The fact that anthropological literature is rich with examples of behaviours deemed mad because they deviate from strong cultural or religious norms leads to suggestions that madness is actually the distance from the ideal or basic character type in a given society (Schwab and Schwab, 1978). But it is not just the distance from the *ideal* character type; it is the distance from the strict roles we are expected to play as 'good' citizens. Thus the Islamic woman who refuses to conceal herself under the veil runs the risk of being called mad, because she is transgressing the strict moral code of behaviour which confines and controls women. The Russian, Zhores Medvedev, was diagnosed as suffering from 'hypochondriac delusional condition, causing an irregular, aggressive attitude in the patient towards individuals, organisations or institutions' (Medvedev and Medvedev, 1973: 73) and hospitalized by psychiatrists because of his scientific writings which directly contradicted the then party line in the Soviet Union. In this way, diagnosis of madness can be used to dismiss political opponents, or those whom one would care to see deposed. This is a dangerous process, as Littlewood and Lipsedge argue:

> Ex-President Amin of Uganda was described by a Professor of Medicine as suffering from 'grandiose paranoia, hypomania, probably schizophrenia, hypomanic paranoia, possibly GPI and the Jekyll and Hyde syndrome'. To characterise political opponents as insane is unhelpful to those with psychological difficulties. It is also a facile abnegation of political responsibility . . . Insanity is a seductive explanation both of antagonistic societies and of political opponents.
>
> (Littlewood and Lipsedge, 1982: 201)

The satirical ascription of madness to the then British Prime Minister, Margaret Thatcher, during the political crises at the beginning of the 1990s is also representative of this discourse:

> What happens is that the old cow, or Mrs Thatcher (to give her full medical name), starts foaming at the mouth and mooing in a strident, harsh, aggressive voice that can be heard for miles. Sadly there is no cure for Mad Cow Disease, which is so virulent that unless the cow is forced to resign the whole nation becomes infected and dies.
>
> (*Private Eye*, 10 November 1989)[11]

Similar too was the description during the 1990–1 Gulf Crisis of the Iraqi President, Saddam Hussein, who was seen as the 'Mad despot who wants to rule the Arab world' (*Daily Express*, 3 August 1990).

Some of the ascriptions of labels of madness to those in other cultures are clearly reflections of xenophobia or racism, and a diagnosis of madness acts as a means of both dismissing behaviour, and controlling what is 'normal' in a given society. Thus women can be labelled mad for not conforming to stereotypes of femininity, and immigrants labelled mad for not becoming part of their host culture. Research has shown that immigrants are at greater risk of being diagnosed as mad (mainly as schizophrenic) (Littlewood and Lipsedge, 1989; Rack, 1982; Fernando, 1988) as are more working-class people (Hollingshead and Redlich, 1958) and women (see Chapter 9), which suggests that to be part of an 'alien' group is to be at risk of falling into madness, or at least to be at risk of being ascribed the label. It is clear that this risk of descent into madness, and the consequences of diagnosis, serve two important functions. First, the function of social control, and second, the function of scapegoating individuals – scapegoating the outsider, maintaining the existence of the 'Other'.

Scapegoats and social control

> Aliens have a role in our society. They demonstrate to the average individual what he or she should avoid being or even avoid being mistaken for – they define for him the limits of his normality by producing a boundary only inside which can he be secure.
>
> (Littlewood and Lipsedge, 1982: 39)

Outsiders and aliens maintain the cohesion of social groups and play an important part in defining the identity of the in-group, defining what is normal behaviour. The 'Other' is needed to define the 'One'. Through defining what is mad, we denote what is sane, what is 'normal', a process carried out by psychiatrists, and other social control experts, who negotiate reality on behalf of the rest of society. In fact, it is the fear of the fall into madness which determines our need to position the mad person as being fundamentally different from ourselves, as Gilman argues:

> The construction of the image of the patient is, then, always playing out of this desire for a demarcation between ourselves and the chaos represented in culture by disease . . . it is in this world of representation that we banish our fear of disease, isolating it as surely as if we had placed it on a desert island.
>
> (Gilman, 1988: 4, 2)

By marking groups out as different, as deviant, as mad, we can affirm our own normality, or even ascertain what it is. Thus the boundaries between 'normal' and 'abnormal' are an important part of the maintenance of society itself, of sanity and order. For 'the mentally ill and witches (like foreigners and the dead) may show us normal behaviour by doing the opposite' (Littlewood and Lipsedge, 1982: 195).

But the mad have not always been the outsiders. Foucault has argued that lepers were the archetypal outsiders in the fifteenth century (Foucault, 1967). We have also seen how witches served this role prior to the advent of science and reason. Foucault argued that one group of outsiders was literally replaced with another when many of the institutions built as leper colonies were reinstituted as asylums to house the newly defined aliens, the mad.[12]

Other 'outsider' groups such as prostitutes, criminals, child abusers, rapists, and more recently, people with AIDS, serve the same purpose, people positioned always as the Other because they are both different and deviant. The Victorian iconographic representations of melancholia, the depictions of the sexually-diseased nineteenth-century 'harlot' are analogous to the representations of outsiders today, as exemplified by the person with AIDS: as Gilman argues, 'the AIDS patient remains the suffering, hopeless male, both the victim and the source of his own pollution' (Gilman, 1988: 262).[13]

The outsiders are not merely functional in defining ourselves and our social groups. They have an intrinsic fascination – possibly because they represent that part of ourselves which we most fear, as Foucault has pointed out:

> On all sides, madness fascinates man. The fantastic images it generates are not fleeting appearances that quickly disappear from the surface of things . . . When man deploys the arbitrary nature of his madness, he confronts the dark necessity of the world; the animal that haunts his nightmares and his nights of privation is his own nature, which will lay bare hell's pitiless truth.
>
> (Foucault, 1967: 23)

Whether this is a process of projection of our own fears or a vicarious enjoyment of those impulses to which we cannot allow free rein, there is ample documentation of the voyeuristic nature of society's enjoyment of the mad. The Victorians institutionalized it: visits to the asylum, to view the mad, became a routine part of social life (Showalter, 1987; Scull, 1979).

Twentieth-century representations of madness and the outsider serve the same functions, denoting the boundaries of our own sanity, our own normality. There is consistency: 'the images of disease, whether in art or literature, are not in flux, even though they represent collapse. They are solid fixed images that remain constantly external to our sense of self' (Gilman, 1988: 2). These images are to be found in medical journals, representing the 'before and after' power of the psychotropic drug (Jordanova, 1989), in newspaper stories on madness, and in the images of art and literature. The dissenters would argue that, whilst these images allow us to distance ourselves from the mad, we can also attribute negative features that belong to ourselves, or to our social group, to them. They thus act as scapegoats. As Berke argued:

> 'Mental illness' reflects what is appearing in a disturbed and disturbing group of people, especially when internalized in and by a single person. More often than not, a person diagnosed as 'mentally ill' is the emotional scapegoat for the turmoil in his or her family or associates, and may in fact be the 'sanest' member of this group.
>
> (Barnes and Berke, 1971: 77)

The mad are not the only scapegoats for society's ills. Jews, women, blacks, teenage drug-abusers, homosexuals can all serve this function. It is not, however, only the labelling and scapegoating inherent within the medical monopoly which is disputed by the dissenters, but the very validity of the scientific philosophy underlying the expert care of the mad – the validity of positivism itself.

The politics of positivism

> Positivistic models not only generate techniques through which the psychiatrist can carry out his socially ordained function, but provide an essential smoke-screen behind which the real nature of that function is concealed.
>
> (Ingleby, 1982: 43)

Positivistic science rescued the nineteenth-century physicians from the mire, and has continued to be 'the lynchpin of psychiatric practice' (Busfield, 1986: 17), as we have seen. The positivistic view of madness assumes that objective diagnosis can identify a set of known syndromes, classified by the modern medical profession as depression, schizophrenia, anxiety etc., which are entities underlying the pathology in the individual patient. Thus, research in psychiatry and, to a certain extent, psychology, is founded on the positivistic premise that 'good' science, with reliable and rigorous methodology, will systematically identify the factors associated with madness, allowing a numerical taxonomic approach to be applied to human suffering.

The applicability of positivism, of the scientific methodology, to the study of human behaviour has, in fact, been repeatedly challenged – within the disciplines of sociology (Durkheim, 1938) and psychology (Harre and Secord, 1972; Gould and Shotter, 1977; Ussher, 1992c) and by the antipsychiatrists or dissenters (Laing, 1960; Szasz, 1961; Sedgewick, 1987; Ingleby, 1982). For example, Szasz argued that whilst physical illness can be viewed within a positivistic framework, madness must be understood in terms of role play, rule breaking and an analysis of meaning and communicative language (Szasz, 1961). Laing also emphasized subjectivity, a factor anathema to the positivist, whilst rejecting any mechanistic causal explanations of human behaviour (Laing, 1960). More recently, Ingleby has attacked the very basis of the 'objective science' upon which psychiatry and psychology are based as 'science whose conceptual foundations have not been properly thought out' (Ingleby, 1982: 24), dismissing the view that psychiatry is value-free as 'pure whitewash [with] pretensions to objectivity' (Ingleby, 1982: 28).

Why is positivism deemed so inappropriate? To begin with, it assumes that observations can be made rationally and objectively, without any contamination from values, beliefs or politics. In fact, the absence of such concepts is a central goal of the scientific exercise. A 'true' scientist is a blank screen who manipulates variables and factors in a neutral apolitical way. It is assumed that concepts and questions can be defined operationally, and investigated in an *exact and replicable* fashion. Theories are then constructed in a causal, deterministic fashion; hypotheses are presented which can be tested using experimental methods, ideally using a laboratory situation, and, at the very least, rigorous experimental methodologies. Positivists delineate a clear distinction between 'facts', which are the objects of the scientists' attentions, and 'values', which are not. 'True science' is declared to be value-free: the scientist is rational, objective and, seemingly, has no values which affect his (for the scientist is prototypically male) research. The positivistic approach implicitly assumes (Ingleby, 1982: 28) that human action is no different from the rest of nature and can be thus be studied objectively. But this has been strongly refuted with the claim that human behaviour, and particularly madness, can be judged only subjectively, as Ingelby argues:

> Descriptions of . . . human activities and states of mind . . . are always subjective interpretations – subjective not in the sense that there are no criteria, but that the criteria are unstated ones, lying in the culture itself . . . judgements of insanity are even more dependent on cultural competence, since they assert that no conventional interpretation can be successfully applied. The first point undermines the possibility of objective description in the human sciences generally, the second applies to psychiatry in particular.
>
> (Ingleby, 1982: 32)

Ingleby precludes the role of positivism not only in the treatment of madness, but also in the whole of the human sciences – an argument which would raise the hackles of many academics and researchers in the Western world today. Yes this criticism is a central component in the deconstruction of the discourse of madness as it is officially represented, and in the attack on the expert professions and their monopoly on madness.

It is the positivistic paradigm that perpetuates the assumption that behaviour can be categorized and classified in the same way that the scientist might categorize atoms or particles. This has led to a concentration on classification of psychological disorders, and the dominance of the taxonomic approach to madness. But there has been a great deal of criticism of the very basis of diagnosis, and of its fundamental validity and reliability, for reliability across diagnostic agencies is poor (Busfield, 1986: 66–73). Symptoms are rated differentially by different psychiatrists (Kreitman, 1962), and any given set of symptoms may be rated as depression, schizophrenia, or some other syndrome, depending on the person carrying out the diagnosis.[14] Thus, the validity of the supposedly objective diagnostic categories is thrown into doubt. For as Mechanic states:

> The usefulness of a diagnostic disease model depends on its level of confirmation, which in turn depends upon the reliability of the diagnosis (the amount of agreement among practitioners in assigning the diagnostic label) and its utility in predicting the course of the condition, its etiology and how it can be treated successfully.
>
> (Mechanic, 1969)[15]

Equally, the validity of the syndromes as discrete entities has been questioned, as similar symptoms can be found across a range of disorders, and the ascription of a label such as schizophrenia or depression does not act as a predictor of an individual's symptoms, behaviour or aetiology.[16]

One of the other central tenets of positivism is the maintenance of the division between subject and object: the assertion that the observer, the expert, is neutral. Thus psychology and psychiatry assert that politically neutral value-free judgements are made in the process of research, diagnosis and treatment of madness. Yet this is a false assumption, as Ingleby has argued above, acting as a smokescreen for the reality of the psychiatric battlefield. The very notion of objectivity is seen as a 'whitewash'. The very assertion that 'objective' psychology and psychiatry exist is challenged, and the very notion of positivism is seen as political, as Kovel has outlined:

> The notion of (positivism) also has a political power, since what is repressed out of the medical model of mental illness is that which considers the person as an active social agent, defined by what class, community and history have for him.
>
> (Kovel, 1982: 86)

The very principle of scientific neutrality is deemed to be a fallacy. Yet confidence in the existence of the unemotional and neutral observer, the researcher or practitioner who believes he or she is 'unbiased and distanced from the emotional bullets of politics' (Tizard, 1990: 436) is used as a justification for the ascendancy of the experts and their continued control of the reins of power. The object of the scientist–practitioner's attention, whether it be an individual, group or community, is not a value-free 'variable' able to be fitted into some neat experimental design, or examined and explained within a set of testable hypotheses. Each individual, each group, is shaped by many forces, historical, social and political – factors absent from the positivistic agenda, and therefore deemed to be immaterial. The positivistic assessment can, therefore, be only partial, and invariably biased by the foundations of the science itself, a reflection of the interests of the ruling élite in the profession. As one commentator notes:

> Contemporary analysts recognise that, whatever their intentions, scientists are the products of their society and time, and their construction of social reality is shaped by the world view and values of the culture in which they are reared. These belief systems can influence all phases of the research in which scientists engage, from choice of problem to interpretation of results.
> (Spence, 1985: 1285)

In fact, according to some observers, there are 'certain biases built into experimental design and data interpretation which lead the scientist to retain theories despite disconfirming evidence' (Grover, 1981: 17). Thus, rather than being objective and apolitical, positivism acts to mystify the conditions of those deemed in need of treatment, at the same time as it reifies the power of the expert.

The glorification of the expert

One of the more insidious implications of the positivistic paradigm is to glorify the role of the 'expert' – researcher, psychiatrist, psychologist or therapist – as they are the only ones deemed capable of diagnosing and treating this thing called madness, a process analogous to the reification of those with religious authority in the past. The mystification of professional training, with its long and poorly paid initiation and strict entry criteria, separates the expert from the patient, attributing seemingly omnipotent powers to the former, so that the professional becomes power incarnate. What Foucault says of doctors we could say of all mental health experts:

> As positivism imposes itself upon medicine and psychiatry . . . the psychiatrist's power [becomes] more and more miraculous . . . the authority he has borrowed from order, morality, and the family now seems

> to derive from himself; it is because he is a doctor that he is believed to possess these powers . . . and it was thought, and by the patient first of all, that it was in the esotericism of his knowledge that the doctor had found the power to unravel insanity; and increasingly the patient would accept this self-surrender to a doctor both divine and satanic.
>
> (Foucault, 1967: 275)

Once the experts – whether theorist or therapist – attain power, they are loath to give it up. Thus professional hierarchies, institutions and practices are erected to protect it. The prolonged sacrifices and hurdles of the professional training also ensure little dissension from within the ranks of the professions – how many would expose to the world the inadequacies of their own training, the fact that *they* are the emperor without clothes? It is much easier to join the charade and maintain the traditional practices and customs. The élitism and mystification is thus maintained. The attribution of these 'divine and satanic' powers to the expert, a process which Foucault sees as a 'reification of a magical nature' (Foucault, 1967: 276) in the form of objectivity, clearly separates the expert from the lay person – the One from the Other. It thus acts to disqualify the views of interventions of people outside the hallowed confines of the 'caring professions'; and most clearly those of individuals positioned as mad. But as the mad are clearly without reason, is their exclusion from power not natural?

Madness as unreason

> If we go back to first principles, what the 'mentally ill' have lost is not their bodily health, nor their virtue, but their reason: their conduct simply does not 'make sense'.
>
> (Ingleby, 1982: 128)

That madness is the absence of reason or rationality is seen as an explicit assumption of the positivistic argument, for the model which sees madness in terms of 'cause' and 'effect' implies the person is not a rational agent, he or she having been *made* to behave in a particular way. It is implicit within the positivistic discourse that the mad person has no control. The absence of reason is what distinguishes her madness from badness. As Conrad argues: 'Deviance that is seen as *willful* tends to be seen as crime; when it is seen as *unwillful* it tends to be defined as illness' (Conrad, 1982: 107). This has often been the central debate in cases of what are seen as horrendous crimes, such as mass murder, as exemplified in the case of Peter Sutcliffe, the 'Yorkshire Ripper', the British man who murdered and brutalized women between 1976 and 1982. His murdering of prostitutes could be conceptualized as *bad*, but when he began to murder 'innocent women' it veered towards the *mad*, as it was then seen as completely irrational. This is well illustrated by the comment from Jim Hobson, a detective involved in the case:

> He has made it clear that he hates prostitutes. We, as a police force, will continue to arrest prostitutes. But the Ripper is now killing innocent girls. That indicates your mental state and that you are in urgent need of medical attention. You have made your point. Give yourself up before another innocent woman dies.
>
> (*Evening Post*, 26 October 1989)

Within a misogynistic culture, to murder prostitutes is understandable, to murder 'innocent' women represents a lack of reason – we cannot believe that a sane person would commit such outrages. As Joan Smith, in her analysis of the Ripper case, comments:

> Madness is a closed category, over which we have no control and for which we bear no responsibility. The deranged stand apart from us; they cannot be *blamed* for their insanity. Thus the urge to characterise Sutcliffe as mad has powerful emotional origins; it is as much to do with how we see ourselves and the society in which we live as it has to do with the perception of him and his crimes. It is a distancing mechanism, a way of establishing a comforting gulf between ourselves and a particularly unacceptable criminal.
>
> (Smith, 1989: 137)

The values ascribed to madness, badness and illness were parodied in Samuel Butler's novel *Erewhon* (1872) in which a traveller visits a country where men are imprisoned for illness and sent to hospital for crime. Illness is shameful, and seen as being within the control of the individual, who must be punished; crime, out of the individual's control, deserves sympathy and treatment. This nice twist on our own social mores illustrates that the ascription of intention can determine our reactions to behaviour.

The critique of the concept of unreason to distinguish madness was central to Laing's critique of schizophrenia. He objected to the notion that behaviour seen as irrational, meaningless or unintelligible is labelled as schizophrenic, and argued that 'mad' behaviour was understandable in the context of the person's life: 'a perfectly rational adjustment to an insane world' (Laing, 1967). If we can explain behaviour, or see it as logical in the situation, it cannot be madness. In Laing's description of schizophrenic families it was the influence of the 'monstrous Mrs Doublebind' that resulted in the behaviour deemed mad in the unfortunate offspring – behaviour that was a rational reaction to the mother's contradictory communications, rather than evidence of unreason.

This fear of unreason is a powerful controlling force, as Foucault has argued:

> The scandal of unreason produced only the contagious example of transgression and immorality; the scandal of madness showed men how close to animality their fall could bring them; and at the same time how far divine mercy could extend when it consented to save man.
>
> (Foucault, 1967: 81)[17]

Thus, from their different stables, the dissenters provided an analysis of madness which depicted it as a label ascribed to unreason, to deviancy; a label which acted to instil fear and functioned to control those outside the boundaries of insanity. This is not, however, the only function of madness, for it has been argued that the discourse of madness serves to mystify reality, to mystify and conceal oppression – and that this process was a part of the basic features of therapy.

Mystification of reality

> Mystification serves to buttress the prevailing mode of social organisation when that mode includes domination, as capitalism most certainly does. Viewed in this light, then, the use of a purely psychological view of human difficulties is a handy way of mystifying social reality.
>
> (Kovel, 1982: 73)

The concept of madness implicitly locates the problem within the individual who is sick, a contention strongly contested by the critics who would locate the sickness within the system, the society. The discourse of madness serves to divert attention away from the problems within society, focusing attention on to the individual, who is suffering only as a direct result of societal pressures. The symptoms labelled as part of the illness called madness are thus seen as a reflection of the inequalities and conflicts within society. The mental health professionals disguise the reality of the misery experienced by individuals, and add to their oppression by providing individualized technological solutions for social problems. As Brooks has argued:

> the role that psychology plays in legitimating the oppression of this society is by no means minor . . . the entire concept of oppression as an illness fundamentally obscures an understanding of the impossible lives people are forced into in this society.
>
> (Brooks, 1973: 317, 325)

As for the psychiatrists and psychologists themselves, 'theirs is a moral enterprise' (Scull, 1979: 265) not the rationally based healing exercises they would claim. The dissenters, in this context, consider their own role to be that of putting 'back into the world what has been placed in the psychic structure of the individual' (Brooks, 1973: 333).

This analysis recognizes that there is some reality in the experience labelled madness, that individuals are distressed – but that this phenomenon is caused by society. Laing viewed this as problems caused by the family; Marxist theorists, such as Brooks, as problems in the wider social system. This was most clearly elucidated by Herbert Marcuse when he argued that capitalism is inevitably accompanied by 'surplus repression', as the system can only satisfy the needs of the few, and thus the power imbalances and inequalities will generate oppression and repression for the majority. Thus 'the sickness of the individual is ultimately caused and sustained by the sickness of his civilisation' (Marcuse, 1966). Szasz saw madness as a direct result of the conflicts inherent in the tensions between individual needs and the needs of society. Whatever the exact location of the 'problem' in the views of the different theorists, it is most certainly not within the individual who is labelled mad. It is within the wider system. The concept of madness together with its subsequent treatment is seen as a reflection of power structures in society; the symptoms are a reaction to oppression, or a protest at inequality.

Symptom as protest

> The madman, like the poet, would refuse Wittgenstein's proposition that 'that of which one cannot speak one should be silent'. It is precisely the unsayable and the unspeakable that must be expressed in mad and poetic discourse.
>
> (Cooper, 1978: 28)

The analogy of the mad as artist or poet, or the claim that 'all madmen are political dissidents' (Cooper, 1978: 23) was one of the torches held high during the antipsychiatry heyday of the late 1960s. The glorification and romanticization of madness became the flag-bearer in the most popularized fight against psychiatry. The madman (*sic*) was seen as a misunderstood genius. A thwarted artist. A protester. By incarceration in the hospital, or confinement through the bonds of nosology, doctors and scientists were seen to be preventing the expression of creativity and talent.

It is a seductive argument – and one which might appear persuasive at a first glance. The view that psychosis is 'our culture's means of archetypal renewal of the inner self ' (Barnes and Berke, 1971: 87) provides a more attractive view of madness than the traditional medical view. Joseph Berke's views on 'renewal', juxtaposed with the image of the tortured artist, Mary Barnes, whose career, before release from her 'nosological chains' by Laingian therapy, was that of schizophrenic, were presented as proof of the reality that schizophrenia was not madness, but creativity and protest. Barnes herself eloquently describes the trap of her madness from which she was freed by her art:

> My whole being was raring to get free. I was like a butterfly fluttering in a net. Not until I was released did I really know how caught I'd been. The net was so big. The flutter so violent, a panic of movement, like a moth on the window pane, unable to make my own way.
>
> (Barnes and Berke, 1971: 56–7)

This description is reminiscent of the 'bell-jar' described by Sylvia Plath (Plath, 1963) – the invisible film within which madness confines. Thus the expression of symptoms could be seen either as a protest against society, or as an attempt to escape from the trap within which the person is confined. Others, such as Goffman, saw *all* expression of deviancy as protest, declaring:

> If you rob people of all customary means of expressing anger and alienation and put them in a situation where they have never had better reason for having these emotions, the natural recourse will be to seize on what remains – situational improprieties.
>
> (Goffman, 1968)

This argument was not confined to antipsychiatry – it was current in 'alternative' literature and political theorizing in the late 1960s. Sartre and Marcuse conceptualized 'the "dregs" of the capitalist system – the deviants and drop outs as . . . in Hegelian terms, the "determinate negation" of that system' (Ingleby, 1981: 56). So deviants, drop-outs, the mad, all become 'culture heroes'. Foucault went further – seeing art itself, or at least modern art, as simultaneously protest and expression of madness, as well as seeing madness as a means of understanding art:

> Through madness, a work that seems to drown in the world, to reveal there its nonsense, and to transfigure itself with the features of pathology alone, actually engages within itself the world's time, masters it, and leads it, by the madness which interprets it, a work of art opens a void, a moment of silence, a question without reconciliation where the world is forced to question itself.
>
> (Foucault, 1967: 288)

Attention has been paid to artists who have been mad – Nietzsche, Van Gogh, Goya, Artaud, de Sade (in addition to women artists discussed below by the feminists) – implying that madness both inspired art and was at the very basis of its creation. The madman locked in the asylum, or bound by the chains of nosology, could be resurrected, elevated to the pedestal and revered as a tortured artist.

Whether in literature or in art, expression of madness is seen to serve a function: the ability of the madman to speak his mind, to speak the unspeakable, awakens both a horror and a longing in ourselves. Thus:

> Through the mouths of the dark characters of Hamlet, Timon, Lear and Iago he [Shakespeare] craftily says, or sometimes insinuates, the things which we feel so terrifically true that it were all but madness for any good man, in his proper character to utter, or even hint of them.
>
> (Melville, 1962: 894)

This juxtaposition of madness and art or protest may shed some light on the experience of a number of people who are deemed mad or in distress. Art or protest may protect a person from madness. It may provide a release for the individual person who can express fears and desires through art or literature – fears which may otherwise be expressed through various symptoms. But neither view, tempting and attractive though it might be, can be applied to many of those who are called mad: both are far too simplistic and romantic (a view discussed in detail in Chapter 8).

The most vociferous criticism, however, and one levelled from all avenues of dissension, has been that directly criticizing the role of professional intervention, of therapy, of psychiatry and psychology.

Physical treatment: physical torture

> Psychiatry based on force and fraud, and justified by medical necessity, the prime purpose of psychiatric treatments – whether utilizing drugs, electricity, surgery or confinement – . . . is there to authenticate the subject as a 'patient', the psychiatrist as a 'doctor' and the intervention as a form of 'treatment'.
>
> (Szasz, 1967)

> Once somebody is declared 'mentally ill' you can do anything you want to them, including torture, as long as you claim that you are doing it for their own good.
>
> (Masson, 1989: 204)

The physical treatments have perhaps received the most consistent condemnation from the dissenters. The physical treatments arising directly from the supposition that madness has a biological basis and thus by altering the physical functioning of the maladaptive brain, the person will be cured, have received the most widespread criticism. Lobotomy, insulin therapy and ECT, treatments which burgeoned in the 1950s, as we have seen, provided the focus for a series of academic and popular critiques in the 1960s. Represented in literature such as Kesey's *One flew over the cuckoo's nest* and Pinter's *The caretaker*, ECT in particular was seen as the epitome of treatment as torture. The treatment itself was seen as synonymous with the oppressive, barbaric nature of psychiatry – tying the patient to a bed and sending electric shocks through their skulls in order to induce obedience; to remove rebellion. As the novelist Janet Frame noted, in *Faces in the water*:

> [ECT was] the new and fashionable means of quieting people and making them realise that orders are to be obeyed and floors are to be polished without anyone protesting and faces are made to be fixed into smiles and weeping is a crime.
>
> (Frame, 1961: 24)[18]

The exposure of maltreatment in famous cases, such as that of the 1930s film actress Frances Farmer who was forcibly incarcerated by her mother and subjected to ECT, drug treatment and psycho-surgery, have provided fuel to dissenters' fire. ECT has thus passed into the popular consciousness as part of the mythology of psychiatry, seen as ineffective, oppressive, and of no validity in anything other than quieting the patient and reinforcing the power of the physician. The end did not justify the means, in the view of the critics and many of the general public. Yet ECT is still used by many psychiatrists, who reject the criticisms, and attest to the benefits of the therapy.[19] In fact, recently there has been a plethora of research attesting to the benefits of what one author terms 'this relatively sage and effective form of treatment' (Taub, 1987) and case after case is presented to 'prove' that ECT works. One interesting factor is that recent research papers invariably advise 'further research' to examine the efficacy of the treatment, as instanced by de Fonseca's comment: 'Although available for many years the actions of ECT are not yet fully understood. Further research is needed' (de Fonseca, 1989: 281). This can be seen as analogous with other, now rejected, treatments of the past, such as the treatment of women's madness with clitoridectomy, another untested practice.

As Browne was unclear why clitoridectomy 'cured' his nineteenth-century female patients, today's practitioners are uncertain as to why ECT would 'work' – if one accepts that it actually does. If, however, one looks at what one advocate, who has catalogued and evaluated thirty years of ECT in his patients, claims, one can easily produce an explanation as to why it is still used. It has been shown (see Ganesan, 1986) that ECT produces memory loss, interruption of 'abnormal mental processes' and a generalized sense of well being – as well as disorientation and confusion in some patients. For many medical experts, the memory loss is compensated by a change in state, a dissipation in the madness. It is of little consequence that the 'patient' may be incapable of *any* thought – good or bad.

Drug treatment, which has also borne the brunt of dissension, also continues growing from strength to strength, based on the psychiatrists' belief that madness is inherited, and due to a chemical imbalance in the brain.[20] As this very concept is rejected by the dissenters, drug treatment itself is seen as a nonsense, its iatrogenic effects often adding to a person's misery.[21] Drugs are seen to function through quieting and placating those protesting against the wrongs of society, whilst at the same time maintaining the power of the medical experts, who are the only ones with the authority to dispense drugs – as well as lining the coffers of the drug companies. In answer to the question 'Why do psychiatrists insist that depression is a physical illness?' Rowe answers simply 'Money, prestige, power' (Rowe, 1990: 24).

One might have expected the dissenters, having dismissed physical treatments, to embrace therapy with open arms. It did not have to be carried out by medical practitioners; it did not have to diagnose the patient. But no. Therapy is vilified as vociferously as medical intervention – if not more so.

The trouble with therapy

> Psychiatry [is a] . . . discipline where it was still fashionable to talk to the patient . . . the reverse was true. Both the interview and treatment situations were carefully structured to prevent any genuine exchange between patient and therapists. The hospital ward was a factory farm designed to label, process and dispose of the human fodder fed into it.
>
> (Barnes and Berke, 1971: 78)

Since the advent of the Freudian revolution in the early twentieth century, psychotherapy, in one form or another, has been a common treatment for madness. Yet the apparent humanity of the treatment, which involves talking rather than physical interventions, has not been accepted by the dissenters as a great advance. They would argue that the philosophy underlying therapeutic treatment was the same as that underlying the physical intervention: treatment for illness, imposed by the expert. And whilst Ingleby has argued that psychiatry 'attempts to provide short-term solutions for what are at root political problems'

(Ingleby, 1982: 44), others have criticized and condemned professional intervention more completely. The institution of health care has been seen as self-serving:

> . . . a fairly seamless empire, almost exclusively responsive to its own needs as an institutional network, no matter how much individuals working within it may separate themselves from its imperatives.
>
> (Kovel, 1982: 84)

Therapy is seen as oppression incarnate, 'offering adjustment rather than liberation' (Brown, 1973: 482) from the problems inherent within society. Through the imposition of the therapist's beliefs on to the patient, social control is ensured as 'therapy demands the filial subordination of the patient, as well as acceptance of their therapist's values, which are usually similar to accepted social values' (Brown, 1973: 482). Szasz objected to the paternalistic nature of therapy, which he saw as a process restricting the autonomy and liberty of the individual. He argued that because of the covert nature of the social control, psychiatry results in 'dehumanisation, oppression and persecution of the citizen branded "mentally ill" ' (Szasz, 1971: xvii). He saw as a central problem in therapy the unequal power relationship which acts to reinforce or create many of the symptoms exhibited by patients.

Therapy's concentration on the individual was seen to reinforce the belief that the problem was inherent within that invidual, whereas critics such as Laing believed that intervention was necessary at the level of the system rather than the individual. Whilst this spawned the development of family therapy, focusing no longer on the individual, this is a form of intervention which has been criticized in its turn.

It is not just the psychiatrists who have borne the brunt of the condemnation: the attendant professions have also been berated. For whilst the twentieth century saw the birth of the non-medical professions of clinical psychology, social work, counselling and therapy, critics have pointed out that these professions are still dominated and influenced by the medical model, and are mostly under the wing of the psychiatrists. Thus Smail, discussing the evolution of clinical psychology in Britain, has argued:

> Clinical psychologists were dwarfed by a medical guild whose powers, self-determination and freedom of action . . . did not permit psychologists to adopt anything but a secondary role. The physical methods of treatments appropriate to the so-called mental illness obviously necessitated possession of a medical degree, and non-physical methods stemming, in this country, largely from the psychoanalytic school, could only be practiced by people (usually doctors) who had undergone an expensive and lengthy initiation ceremony . . . the licence to practice treatment was based on a

> system where authority was accorded to would-be healers on the basis of membership of the appropriate (medical) club.
>
> (Smail, 1973: 212)

More recently, Rowe has argued: 'In the USA many clinical psychologists are dependent on psychiatrists for their work, either directly in the management structure or indirectly through referrals. So they must preach the psychiatric gospel' (Rowe, 1990: 25). And whilst many individual practitioners in these non-medical professions do undoubtedly reject the reductionist paradigms, and would reject the premise that they are beholden to psychiatrists, it cannot be denied that their work is still based on professional intervention and on supposedly scientific, objective methodology – all within the traditional structures of organized health care. It is to this that the dissenters object; it is not care but coercion.

One of the most unreserved in his condemnation has been Jeffrey Masson, who declared that 'psychiatry . . . has always been intrusive, destructive, and vicious' (Masson, 1989: 39) – leaving no doubt as to his own position. Masson outlined a both seductive (in its persuasiveness) and shocking (in its content) case against therapy in support of his basic thesis, which is:

> [that] abuse of one form or another is built into the very fabric of psychotherapy, that power corrupts, that psychiatric power corrupts just as political power does, and that the greater the power (and a psychiatrist's power is great indeed), the greater the propensity for corruption . . . The ways that a therapist can harm a patient are as varied as they are in any intimate relationship. A person can be harmed financially . . . emotionally, physically . . . or sexually.
>
> (Masson, 1989: 211)

Masson leaves us in no doubt as to the reality of this exploitation and harm in his catalogue of therapeutic abuse, ranging from the therapists who sexually assault, torture and murder their patients, to those who worked with the Nazis during the Second World War in both 'medical' experiments and psychological torture. Strong stuff indeed. And the academic reputation of the therapists offers no protection from Masson's acerbic tongue: Freud, Jung, Rogers – all come in for scrutiny and annihilation. Yet perhaps the most complete denigration is reserved for John Rosen, the American psychiatrist who pioneered 'direct psychoanalysis'. Rosen's work is held up as the epitome of therapeutic exploitation. It is useful to look at Masson's case because it exemplifies a particular facet of much of the dissension – that which represents extreme cases as the norm.

According to Masson, Rosen was certainly extreme in his methods, believing in confrontation, in using 'cunning, guile, shrewdness and seductiveness' to stalk the secrets of the patient; to shock the patient into sanity. This included physically striking patients, starvation, involuntary incarceration in a cellar, and sexual degradation. One example which Masson gives was of evidence cited in a court case against Rosen:

> He explained to her that her mother had had a breast like a rock, with no milk to give her, and consequently she had never 'negotiated her oral phase' of development, and had never properly satisfied her instinct for sucking. He then proceeded to lie down and take off his pants and boxer shorts down over his penis and he commanded the Plaintiff to suck his penis . . . and continued to philosophize 'this is what it's all about, this is when a baby is at peace, when it is sucking'.

The same patient was induced to 'lick his anus and orally take in as much faeces as she could, which she did' (Masson, 1989: 185) as well as being forced to engage in three-way sex, and cunnilingus with a woman. All part of the 'therapy'.

Masson uses this extreme example of Rosen, and others analogous to it, to support his contention that 'even when therapy is voluntary, there is an emotional and mental coercion' (Masson, 1989: 287). Therapy is thus seen as corrupt, regardless of the benevolent veneer. It is profiting from the problems of others; depending on the continuation of misery for its very existence. Could any self-respecting therapist read these criticisms and continue to practise? I could not.

Conclusion

Yet this – perhaps the strongest – critique leads me to the point where the critics themselves need to be put under the microscope. Their accusations are serious. For the consequences are surely an abolition of psychiatry, of clinical psychology, of any therapeutic intervention. The whole process of diagnosis, classification and labelling has been exposed. The professionals themselves have been vilified; the philosophy underlying their interventions denounced. The dissenters have laid bare many of the problems in models of madness, in psychiatry and therapy – and leave us asking the question, 'What now?' Should we accept their critiques unquestioningly? Is the implication of their critiques – the removal of services – any more positive than the barbaric practices they delight in exposing? Many would say not. And most central to this thesis, what about the issue of gender – of women?

The antipsychiatrists and dissenters were not the knights in shining armour they have sometimes been depicted as, ready to transform the institution into a haven, by breaking down the nosological battlements and spiriting the misdiagnosed to freedom. There are many weaknesses and limitations within their analysis, which I will consider in detail in Chapter 8. But one major omission in their work is the analysis of the specific problems and oppression experienced by women. Gender, patriarchy and misogyny were not high on the agenda of the so-called radicals – if on their agenda at all. To read their work one would imagine that the mad person was gender-neutral, when we know that women make up a large percentage of those who are positioned within the discourse of madness. For, since the Victorian era, madness has been synonymous with femininity, and women predominate in both the 'official statistics' and popular discourse. But the dissenters seem to ignore this fact. Perhaps this should not surprise us. None of the radical movements of the sixties which provided impetus for present-day critiques is notable for its concern about women – with the obvious exception of the feminist critiques. The dissenters were happy to expound theories of oppression whilst continuing to objectify and pathologize the women they used as case examples. They implicitly dismissed misogyny by referring to women as *just another* oppressed group. Their blindspot perpetuates the oppression. It was the feminist critics who redressed the balance.

Notes

1. Quoted by Holmes and Lindley 1989: 97.
2. Baruch and Treacher 1978: 31.
3. For example, in the early nineteenth century, Andrew Halliday argued: 'Philosophers by deviating from the known path of common sense and accurate observation have occasionally been so bewildered in the mazes of metaphysics, as to doubt the existence of the matter [mental illness] altogether' (Halliday 1828: 1). In the 1930s many anthropologists, who advocated a cultural perspective on madness, cast doubt on the legitimacy of a biological approach to treatment. As Ruth Benedict, an anthropologist

   > writing in 1934, argued: 'Just as those are favoured whose congenial responses are closest to that behaviour which characterizes their society, so those are disordered whose responses fall in the arc of behaviour which is not capitalized by their culture. These abnormals are those who are not supported by the institutions of their civilisation. They are the exceptions who have not easily taken on the traditional forms of culture' (Benedict 1935: 258, quoted by Busfield 1986: 83).

4. Called such in the face of their own ardent disclaimers that they were not to be categorized together, each claiming that their work certainly could not be subsumed under such an ignominious label. For example, R. D. Laing (1972) has stated, 'I have never called myself an antipsychiatrist'; and

Thomas Szasz has claimed that antipsychiatry is an 'imprecise, misleading and cheaply self-aggrandizing' concept with all antipsychiatrists being 'self-declared socialists', or 'communists' (Szasz 1979: 49).

5. In texts on this subject, it is customary to provide an almost historical account of lives of the antipsychiatrists, outlining the theories of each of the 'great men' in turn. This only perpetuates the cult of the individual, the assumption that it was the 'single-handed author of germinal ideas' (Sedgewick 1982: 10) who originated and developed the critique, when in reality, as many have acknowledged, any development of theory in either the arts or sciences is by its very nature a collective or accumulative exercise: very little is the product of divine revelation to a single author – even if the authors themselves would have us believe otherwise. Although analyses of these great male lives may be interesting from an historical point of view, at least to some people, particularly in terms of the development of dissent from within the folds of the psychiatric profession, it serves my own purpose more adequately to consider the critiques of the dissenters across the decades *en masse*, in order to be able to use them to inform an analysis of women and madness.
6. Quoted by Baruch and Treacher 1978: 31.
7. David Ingleby 1982 discusses the adoption of some of the tenets of the antipsychiatrists by liberal psychiatrists such as Clare 1976. Lipservice can be paid to the critiques, and present practices maintained. The experts are subsequently strengthened in their own position.
8. Quoted by Busfield 1986: 100.
9. The research itself has been criticized, and its interpretations questioned, as certain of the 'stooges' were not deemed mad. The ethics of this type of research are also questionable.
10. Quoted by Medvedev and Medvedev 1971: 67.
11. This political satire refers to the scare in Britain in 1990 about BSE, commonly known as 'mad cow disease', which resulted in British beef being banned from many countries.
12. Porter 1987 has disputed this thesis, arguing that the simple replacement of leper colonies with asylums did not take place, and that it is a romanticized version of the history of psychiatric care. There is perhaps a stronger case to be made for a replacement of the poor house with the asylum.
13. Gilman 1988 provides an interesting overview of the iconography of outsiders, drawing analogies between the prostitute of the nineteenth century and the sexual outsiders of today.
14. See Spitzer *et al.* 1983 for a discussion of this.
15. Quoted by Baruch and Treacher 1978: 235.
16. See Bentall 1990 and Bentall *et al.* 1988 on schizophrenia; Ussher 1989 on the female reproductive syndromes.
17. The mad were closer to animals specifically because of their absence of reason, and represented a reminder of the fate which could befall any who strayed beyond the bounds of normality.
18. Quoted by Showalter 1987: 216.
19. See Scott 1989, for a recent example.
20. See Gold 1986; McGuffin and Katz 1989, and the discussion in Chapter 5.
21. See Pilgrim 1990, who argues that the effects of drugs are often more debilitating and long-lasting than the original symptoms they are prescribed

to treat. Jenner 1989 provides an insightful account of his own experiences as a psychiatrist in which his confidence in physical treatments waned as a result of his growing awareness of the damaging effects of both minor and major tranquillizers.

7

The feminist critiques

perpetual therapy . . .
First, there is a fallen state, formerly named sinful and symbolized by Eve, presently known as sick and typified by the powerless but sometimes difficult and problematic patient. Second, there is the restored/redeemed state of perfect femininity, formerly named saintly and symbolized by Mary, presently typified by the weak, 'normal' woman whose normality is so elusive that it must constantly be re-inforced through regular check-ups, 'preventative medicine', and perpetual therapy.

(Daly, 1979: 231)

privatized distress . . .
The monolithic grip of the old romanticist experts has been broken, and the horde of pop psychologists, sex therapists, counsellors, liberal gynaecologists etc., who take their place, offer no answer – or all answers. Their only consistent interest in the Woman Question is that it remain, insofar as possible, privatized – compressed into the psyche of each individual woman, for this is the only terrain on which they can operate.

(Ehrenreich and English, 1978: 322)

psychology . . .
Psychology has nothing to say about what women are really like, what they really need and what they want, essentially because psychology does not know.

(Weissten, 1973: 394)

men . . .
the whole psychological thing is based on the premise that there are *Individual* problems rather than a social problem which is

> political . . . My oppressors are not institutions. My oppressors are *Men* – and all the superstructures which are set up by men.
>
> (Miller, 1973: 488)

Dismantling patriarchal views of madness

The critiques put forward by the dissenters may seem on the surface to be pro-feminist, to offer solutions to the problem of women's madness. For if madness is viewed as a strategy, a communication, the result of oppression within a contradictory patriarchal society intimately related to restrictive social roles, it might appear that the dissenters have 'bequeathed to the women's movement a vocabulary of protest' as Juliet Mitchell has argued (Mitchell, 1974: xix). But, although I would not completely dismiss this claim, since many of the dissenters' arguments are an essential background for any feminist analysis, I would dispute any contention that they are deliberately or consciously *pro*-feminist, because their theories considered women only by default, almost coincidentally. Even when the case studies concentrated on women, as did those of both Laing and Cooper, the issue of gender was not a central part of their analysis. The women whose cases are described in almost voyeuristic detail are presented from a male perspective. The women, and their families, are judged within a framework where traditional gender roles are not questioned – in fact, where deviation from these traditional roles is seen as evidence of pathology, or the cause of pathology in others. As Elaine Showalter has observed:

> In *The Divided Self* . . . Laing analysed the situation of Mrs. R., a twenty-eight-year-old agoraphobic, as a 'lack of ontological autonomy', although to a feminist reader, her infantilization and dependence on male approval seem more immediately relevant. Similarly, Mrs. D., a forty-year-old woman in an acute anxiety state, was treated coldly by Laing, who argued that in withholding comfort, he gave her the existential freedom to take responsibility for her life. But Mrs. D.'s main symptom was intense anger toward her husband, an anger Laing calls 'unaccountable' and never takes seriously.
>
> (Showalter, 1987: 231)

There was also a great deal of misogyny inherent within the theorizing of the dissenters. Laing's argument that the madness was not within the person, but within the family, invariably placed the blame firmly at the door of the mother. It was her overbearing nature, her emasculation of her husband, which was said to cause the symptoms of the scapegoated individual labelled schizophrenic. The role of the father in these problematic families was ignored, and the influence of wider social processes on the women's internal conflict (for almost all of his cases were women) frequently neglected.

The very nature of the depiction of the antipsychiatry movement, with its emphasis on the individual male ego, the conquering, radical, hero–innovator, is dangerously distant from the needs of individual women. It is the dissenters themselves on whom the spotlight is turned, the attention given to their theories, their lives. The proper focus for attention, the mad woman herself, is curiously absent from their discourse. But the reality of the misery and the intensive care needed to heal woman's pain was often far from the ideals of the radical quest, and may have reinforced their pattern of giving attention to theoretical arguments at the expense of practical realities, as the decades rolled on. As Showalter says:

> The image of the schizophrenic voyage that Laing had created drew upon his own heroic fantasies; it was a male adventure of exploration and conquest . . . Faced with the obligation to play mother on the psychic journey, Laing seems to have lost enthusiasm for it.
>
> (Showalter, 1987: 236)

The recognition that the original dissent had failed to address the problems of women provided the impetus for the feminist critiques of madness. The existing order was obviously failing – yet the alternative theories and critiques were still inadequate, if not misogynistic. As Ehrenreich and English note: 'Where sociologists saw "roles" and "institutions", psychiatrists saw "feminine adjustment" and the medical authorities saw "biological destiny".' Thus the door was wide open for a feminist analysis to fill the gap.

The feminist critics took many of the basic arguments outlined by the antipsychiatrists and used them as a basis for analysing the position of *women* in relation to madness. For the statistics seem to make the position clear – it is *women* who are positioned as mad.

Gender and madness: facts and fantasies

> All the data on mental illness indicates that in modern western industrial societies more women than men are mentally ill.
>
> (Gove, 1979: 54)

This is a statement made with confidence, referring to the mass of empirical data attesting to women's dominance in psychiatric statistics. It seems as if the legacy of the Victorian era, in which women were present in far greater numbers in the asylums and in the consulting room, is still with us. But is it? Wearing his empirical hat, the sociologist, Walter

Grove, feels confident in his case. He refers to community surveys of psychological disturbance, statistics on treatment by general practitioners, and admission to psychiatric hospitals, to support his assertion that gender differences in 'mental illness' are a reality, not merely a figment of the statistician's imagination. Yet the ability of the seemingly objective statistics, the scientifically exalted empirical study, to provide a false sense of security in assertions of 'fact', presents a trap we should avoid. For the multifarious group of authors who look no further than the bald statistics in their search for an understanding of women's experience are themselves falling into the trap of naïveté, and unquestioned acceptance of positivism. But the statistics *are* convincing.

Research published in many different societies, including Britain,[1] the United States[2] and Europe,[3] seems to point to the same conclusion: women are much more likely than men to come under the scrutiny of the expert eye of the psychiatrist, and be positioned quite firmly as in need of 'care'. Whether the researchers looked at in-patient treatment, private psychiatric care, or general practitioner statistics, the results were the same. Women predominate.[4] For example, in England, the most recent statistics on psychiatric in-patient care, published in 1986, record 482 females and 364 males per hundred thousand admitted for treatment. Of first admissions the rate is 100 men to 119 women per hundred thousand, and for readmissions 264 men to 350 women. Overall, there were 83,865 men admitted for psychiatric care in 1986, and 113,386 women. The picture for the USA is similar: women predominate in the majority of diagnostic categories (Russo, 1990).

These cases are the tip of the psychiatric iceberg, for only a minority of officially diagnosed cases will show up on the statistics for hospital admissions, since a majority of 'cases' will be treated in the community. Yet the gender imbalance is also reflected in community treatments – women are more likely to be referred to a psychologist, psychiatrist or therapist than men (Briscoe, 1982), are twice as likely to be prescribed psychotropic drugs (Cooperstock, 1976, 1978; Chioton *et al.*, 1976), and more likely to be given ECT (see Chapter 9). Thus, from the 'official' perspective the position is clear: more women are diagnosed, and treated as mad.

The second area of ammunition for the theories of women as mad comes from the ubiquitous 'community survey' in which assessments are made of psychological distress in those men and women living in the community, unknown (as yet) to mental health professionals.[5] These surveys show that women are more likely to report psychological distress, and particularly depression, than men.[6]

Yet what is interesting is that the gender difference, in both officially diagnosed 'psychopathology' and rates of disorder in the community, is actually *reversed* in children: boys present with far more psychological problems, and 'disordered behaviour' than girls (Gove, 1979; Stevenson, 1985). Boys experience far more developmental delays, language and perceptual difficulties, behaviour disorders, physical difficulties such as enuresis and encopresis (bedwetting and soiling). In fact, across the board, boys are twice as likely as girls to experience some developmental difficulty, and come to the attention of the experts. It is evidently only in post-adolescence that women become notably 'mad'.

The case might seem to be clear – women *are* more mad. But, perhaps not surprisingly, there are a number of dissenters. In 1969 Dohrenwend and Dohrenwend attacked the basic premise that gender differences in psychopathology exist, particularly criticizing the community survey, so beloved of the sociologists. They argued that, as the estimates of the prevalence of mental illness vary between 1 per cent and 64 per cent in the different surveys, or between 16.7 per 1,000 and 333 per 1,000, the validity of the research must be questioned. They also argued that different community surveys use different techniques to evaluate 'madness', including clinical diagnosis, interviews and questionnaires, and that the definition of 'disorder' used varies from study to study, with a different cut-off point used by the various researchers, and little consensus concerning the interpretation of the data collected (Goldman and Ravid, 1980: 32). So we cannot say unequivocally that the research paints a clear picture.

We are faced with the limitations of positivistic frameworks again. And the significance of these findings is unclear – is it that women actually *are* mad, or that they are merely *diagnosed* as such because of the discourse associating femininity and psychological infirmity? There are suggestions that women are more likely to be given a psychological diagnosis for a non-specific problem, whilst a man will receive a physical diagnosis (Penfold and Walker). Some suggest that women are more likely to report symptomatology than men (Cooperstock, 1976; Nathenson, 1975) and, in particular, that women will report psychological distress more readily than men (Philips and Segal, 1969) – although others contest this (Weissman and Klerman, 1977, 1979: 59) claiming that, 'women are no more likely than men to articulate their symptoms' (Gove, 1979, 1959).

Women also dominate only in particular categories of madness – namely depression, eating disorders, anxiety and phobias (Gove, 1979; Briscoe, 1982). When it comes to the schizophrenias, the evidence is not so clear and it has been claimed that there is no gender difference in psychosis at all (Rosenthal, 1977). Yet Gove argues that women are more likely than men to be diagnosed as schizophrenic, because women's 'deviant' behaviour is more likely to fit within the diagnostic category of

Table 7.1 Mental illness hospitals and units – England: all admissions by diagnostic group 1976, 1982–6: number and rates per 100,000 population[7]

Diagnostic group	Rates per 100,000 population for 1986	
	Males	Females
All diagnoses	83,865	113,386
Schizophrenia, paranoia	15,271	14,148
Affective psychoses	8,107	16,526
Senile and presenile dementia	7,624	13,234
Alcoholic psychoses	509	266
Other psychoses (including drug psychoses)	7,455	10,537
Neurotic disorders	4,978	10,291
Alcohol dependence syndrome	8,301	3,508
Nondependent abuse of alcohol	2,095	1,204
Drug dependency	1,382	806
Nondependent abuse of drugs	614	278
Personality and behaviour disorders	6,531	7,667
Mental retardation	305	284
Depressive disorders not elsewhere classified	11,740	23,469
Other psychiatric conditions	287	346
Mental illness – diagnosis not stated	65	48
Other conditions and undiagnosed cases	8,601	10,774

schizophrenia, citing examples of women's 'uncontrolled sexuality' as a prime 'symptom'. The statistics above on hospitalization for psychiatric illness in England in 1986 provides a useful illustration here.

Thus, there are also particular disorders from which *men* are more likely to be diagnosed as suffering, namely 'irresponsible and antisocial conduct',[8] as well as drug- or alcohol-related problems.[9] This has led to the argument that 'women can be considered *both* overserved and underserved by mental health delivery systems' (Carmen *et al.*, 1984: 33): a woman with depression will be labelled and treated very quickly (if not *too* quickly), a woman with an alcohol-related problem may be ignored, her problem denied. The reverse may be said for men.

There is not, therefore, a clear-cut case for saying that more women are mad, or that more women are diagnosed as mad. But we can say that women are more likely to experience, or be diagnosed as experiencing, particular manifestations of madness, classified and reified as 'female disorders' within our current psychiatric discourse. It may be that categories such as depression, anorexia and neurosis have firmly taken over from hysteria and neurasthenia as the 'daughter's disease'. They have become 'female problems' and thus, in a circular way, women are more likely to be categorized as suffering from such disorders.

It is also important to note that women are not all equally at risk. The statisticians would agree that particular groups of women are more at risk of coming under the psychiatric microscope: those who are married, those with children, those who are unemployed or poor, and those who experienced death of a mother in childhood. I shall explore the implications of these findings below. But it is important to note at this point that it is a nonsense to claim (as many have done, both feminists and biological reductionists) that in our society more women are mad. Women are not a homogeneous group. *Particular* women are more at risk of diagnosis and treatment, as are particular groups of men.[10] The discourse of madness regulates all women – but some of us are more likely to be positioned within it.

Whilst this is an interesting debate, we must be wary of missing the point of the argument. If we accept labelling theory and the critiques of diagnostic classifications (discussed in Chapter 6), the altercations between the researchers may be somewhat irrelevant, for we can safely say that none of the diagnostic categories, such as 'depression' or 'schizophrenia', is immutable.[11] It cannot, therefore, be a clear-cut case wherein we can argue that schizophrenia is more or less prevalent in women than men, for we must take a step back and look at the very category of schizophrenia itself – or indeed any other diagnostic category – before making a judgement.

Labelling women's anger

> Most twentieth-century women who are psychiatrically labelled, privately treated and publicly hospitalised are not mad . . . they may be deeply unhappy, self-destructive, economically powerless, and sexually impotent – but as women they're supposed to be.
>
> (Chesler, 1972: 25)

One of the foundations of the critiques discussed in the last chapter was that madness is not an illness but a social construction. In the feminist analysis this social construction is seen to be based on misogynistic or patriarchal principles. Thus as women have been controlled through witch-hunting, suttee, Chinese footbinding or sexual slavery, they are now controlled through labels of madness and the subsequent therapy, therapy which some feminists see as 'mind rape' (Daly, 1979: 287). Hence, many feminists would accept the dissenters' arguments that definitions of madness are based on value judgements and prescriptions for normality which support existing power structures. But, since the power structures are clearly patriarchal, it is no coincidence that women predominate in the corridors of madness.

The feminist argument – that the concept of madness is used to control deviant women and to maintain the dominant order – was not new. As we saw in the last chapter, sociologists, historians and antipsychiatrists had presented much documentation to demonstrate that madness was socially constructed and 'expert care' a means of enacting the oppression of the mad within the cloak of professional legitimacy. What the feminist argument added was the dimension of misogyny. They placed gender firmly at the head of the agenda.

The basic concepts outlined by the male dissenters – of labelling, culture-bound definitions of madness, social control and scapegoating, mystification of reality, symptom as protest and therapy as oppressive – were taken on board and reinterpreted within a feminist framework. Where the male dissenters of the 1960s and 1970s clearly saw society as oppressive, the feminists saw the problem as patriarchy.

Within the feminist analysis, the labelling process is seen to serve the function of maintaining women's position as outsiders within patriarchal society; of dismissing women's anger as illness – and so exonerating the male oppressors; and of dismissing women's misery as being a result of some internal flaw – and thus protecting the misogynistic social structures from any critical gaze. The earlier dissenters may have been correct in pointing out that psychiatric labels serve society: what they omitted from their analysis was that it is a *patriarchal* society.

In the historical analysis of women's madness, we have seen how nosological categories were ascribed to women who were actually archetypally feminine. The Victorian maiden wasting away in her darkened boudoir, the hysteric, the neurasthenic, the anorexic – all were aspiring to heights of femininity within the narrow confines which patriarchy dictates. The twentieth-century mad woman is no different. As madness itself is synonymous with femininity, those women who wholeheartedly embrace the gender role assigned to them, or those who reject it, are at high risk of being diagnosed as mad. As Chesler has commented:

> Madness and asylums generally function as mirror images of the female experience, and as penalties for *being* 'female', as well as for desiring or daring *not* to be.
>
> (Chesler, 1972: 16)

The socialization of women can be seen to prepare women for the mask of madness, the 'desperate communication of the powerless' (Showalter, 1987: 5). Having no legitimate outlet for feelings of frustration, anger and misery evoked by the reality of living in a patriarchal society, women fall into the psychiatric trap. Madness in the twentieth century has become institutionalized as a discourse which legitimates the positioning of women as good/bad – attractive and seductive, dangerous and fearful. The discourse, associated with the fear of women and the confining power of madness in the nineteenth century, has merely taken on a tougher veneer of respectability, as well as extending its authority to greater numbers of women.

Thus the labels applied to women, labels which so cleverly place the problem within her as a person, distracting from the social reality of her life, serve to mystify the reality of her oppression, a process buttressed by the gender bias in psychiatric nosology, the labelling process itself.

The now classic study of Broverman and his colleagues (1970) illustrates this bias wherein femininity itself is seen as pathological. They demonstrated the paradox that women who *conform* to the female role model, as well as those who *reject* it, are likely to be labelled psychiatrically ill; that cultural stereotypes of femininity and masculinity are accepted and internalized by mental health professionals of various disciplines, and are used in the evaluation and diagnosis of madness. The description of a *healthy* adult, either male or female, conformed to the masculine stereotype, whilst the feminine stereotype, of passivity, conformity, less aggression, lower achievement motivation etc., was seen as psychologically *unhealthy*. Adult women were generally seen as

> more submissive, less independent, less adventurous, more easily influenced, less aggressive, less competitive, more excitable in minor crises, having their feelings more easily hurt, more conceited about their appearance, [and] less objective.
>
> (Broverman *et al.*, 1970)

Thus women who are archetypally feminine will be more likely to be defined as mad; as will men who exhibit feminine characteristics.[12] Conversely, women who *reject* the female role are also likely to be labelled mad. Although masculinity is associated with more positive mental health,[13] it seems that this is only for men; and women who are adventurous, competitive, sexually active, independent, women who reject the role of wife and mother, to name but a few examples, may be at risk of being designated psychiatrically ill. In fact, the woman who reports symptoms which are seen as 'male', such as alcohol abuse or aggressive antisocial behaviour, will be seen as much *more* psychologically disturbed than the man who exhibits the same symptoms. Thus, as the woman in the 1870s who attempted to take advantage of the new divorce law was subjected to the 'treatment' of clitoridectomy for her madness (Showalter, 1987), the woman in the 1990s who is *too* 'liberated' may be equally classified and controlled.[14] The reverse process can operate with men: those who are 'feminine' (i.e. dependent or passive) are liable to be labelled 'mad'. For example, Kayton and Biller demonstrated that diagnosis of schizophrenia in men was associated with so-called 'feminine' traits (Kayton and Biller, 1972), and dependent behaviour is seen as more pathological in men than in women (Costrich *et al.*, 1975), as is depression and anxiety (Waisberg and Page, 1988). Thus, as Chesler argues:

> What we consider 'madness', whether it appears in women or in men, is either the acting out of the devalued female role model or the total or partial rejection of one's sex role stereotype.
>
> (Chesler, 1973)

In my own clinical work in the field of AIDS, where gay men then formed the majority of the client population, I heard the usually very rare diagnosis of 'hysteria' applied to men – men who were crying and freely expressing their emotions, behaviour which is deemed unacceptable within our present construction of masculinity. Yet, as these men were infected with the HIV virus, and often facing the death of a partner, was crying not appropriate behaviour? Many of the men I worked with were referred for psychological treatment precisely because of this 'inappropriate affect'.

It is not only in diagnosis that there is some evidence of the sexism in clinical judgement. There is some suggestion that therapists use gender stereotypes in their treatment of women. For example, Rickles has described the *clinical* phenomenon of the 'angry woman' syndrome, where the juxtaposition of the aggressive woman who has an uncontrollable temper and drinks excessively with the husband who is passive and inactive is seen as the central reason for therapeutic intervention (Rickles, 1971). Were this anger exhibited by a man, it might not been seen as pathological, as a syndrome, but merely as a normal aspect of male behaviour. It is because it is a woman who is angry that treatment is necessitated, and intervention is aimed at changing the gender roles exhibited by the couple to ensuring that the woman conforms to the 'proper' role of passive wife. On the same lines, Houck has described his treatment of the 'intractable woman' in therapy, whom he describes as 'not easily governed, managed or directed; obstinate; not easily wrought; not easily relieved or cured; unruly' (Houck, 1972). These 'problems' were ameliorated in therapy with the resumption of appropriate feminine behaviour.

Freud's infamous case of the hysteric 'Dora' has also been seen by some feminists as women's anger being pathologized. In response to Dora's disgust at the attempted seduction by her father's friend, Freud pronounced:

> I should without question consider a person hysterical in whom an

> occasion for sexual excitement elicited feelings that were preponderantly or excessively unpleasurable.[15]

The Dora case has been seen as a typical example of the substitution of a psychological analysis for the acknowledgement of a real oppression, as Freud interpreted Dora's revulsion as a pathological reaction to men, that is, a reflection of her own neuroticism. Others could interpret her rejection of her seducer and her subsequent rejection of men as an understandable reaction – certainly not as evidence of madness.

Blaming the woman

Not only is the case of Dora exemplary of the presentation of a psychological explanation for a real oppression, it is also an example of the case where women are blamed for their own distress. The sexually abused girl is blamed for her 'seductive' nature, the depressed woman blamed for her own misery, for not making an effort, and the woman is repressed – as was Dora. As Jaqueline Rose argues:

> Dora is repressed as a woman by psychoanalysis and what is left of Dora as somehow reliable is the insistence of the body as feminine, and since it is a case of hysteria, in which the symptom speaks across the body itself, the feminine is placed not only as source (origin and exclusion) but also as manifestation (the symptom).
>
> (Rose, 1986: 28)

Blaming the woman herself effectively controls her. She is denied her anger. As women were once controlled by fear of witch hunts, by Indian suttee and by circumcision, they are now controlled by the label of madness, and the dictates of therapy. As Juliet Mitchell, herself a feminist psychoanalytic theorist, argues:

> . . . there seems overwhelming justification for the charge that the many psychotherapeutic practices, including those that by the formal definition are within psychoanalysis, have done much to re-adapt discontented women to a conservative feminine status quo, to an inferiorized psychology and to a contentment with serving and servicing men and children.
>
> (Mitchell, 1974: 299)

What is *mad* within patriarchy is that which is at odds with the dictates of the patriarchs. Women who reject their designated role can be positioned as mad, and therapy helps us to conform. What is interesting is that it is not the institution of psychiatry which is used to control *men's* deviancy or rebellion, but the penal institutions, the prisons. Thus, whilst women are mad, men are bad.

Mad women – bad men

> Whether as suspects, defendants or offenders, women are dealt with in accordance with the degree to which their criminal and social behaviour deviates from appropriate gender role expectations.
>
> (Edwards, 1986: 79)

The relationship between madness and badness is an interesting one, and an area already touched on in the examination of the historical discourse on madness and femininity. In the dark ages deviant women were clearly bad – the theological discourse placed them thus and the witches are testimony to this charade. But many today would argue that whilst women are likely to be deemed in need of psychological or psychiatric help if they commit a deviant act, men will be deemed in need of legal incarceration, or punishment. The same behaviour (e.g. violence) is treated differently, depending on whether it is committed by a man or a woman. As Jan Burns argues, '. . . if one is female and commits an offence one is much more likely to be seen as having a psychiatric problem than if one is male' (Burns, 1991: 16). This is not to suggest that men and women carry out a similar amount of violent or criminal acts – it is clear that few women murder, carry out burglaries, or commit violent crimes in general. But if they do, women will be likely to be seen as mad – a man as bad. In 1986 in England, 36,743 men (compared to 1,229 women) were given a prison sentence. Psychiatric discourse positions women as mad whilst the medico-legal discourse clearly positions men as bad.[16]

The courts are liable to sentence women to psychiatric treatment for a 'crime' for which men will receive a prison sentence, and even women given prison sentences are more likely to be deemed in need of psychiatric treatment, or to be prescribed psychotropic drugs once inside, evidenced by the fact that female prisons prescribe far more psychotropic drugs (i.e. antidepressants, sedatives and tranquillizers) than do male prisons (Edwards, 1986: 81). Conversely, when men receive a psychiatric diagnosis, they are far more likely to be sentenced to secure psychiatric treatment (in Britain, detained under sections 3 or 37 of the Mental Health Act)[17] than are women. For example, in England in 1986, 1,376 men but only 337 women were 'detained' in 'special hospitals' such as Rampton or Broadmoor (HMSO, 1986). This is an interesting anomaly in the psychiatric statistics, as it is the only area of psychiatric care within which men are in the majority. Is it that men's madness is more dangerous, that it somehow needs to be contained, as a wild lion would need to be put behind bars? Is it that because women are expected to be mad, their diagnosis is not a surprise and offers no threat whereas men's does? As Jan Burns argues:

> Within our present gendered discourses women are expected to be unstable and out of control, and as such women who offend frequently come under the psychiatric remit . . . they are also seen as less deranged than men who come under this remit, and, as such, enter the less restrictive facilities. Men, on the other hand, being sane and rational the majority of the time, are deemed as exceptionally mad if they do manage to enter into the psychiatric services, needing very secure provision, and may also be seen as too intractable and too dangerous to be treated in anything other than the prison system.
>
> (Burns, 1992)

So for behaviour which is deemed in need of control, men will be more likely to go to prison, and women to hospital, or to a regional secure unit.[18]

With good behaviour parole is automatic after two-thirds of a prison sentence, but not at any time during a compulsory psychiatric detention. The implications for this are serious as women will be invariably confined for longer; and as many would argue that the stigma of a psychiatric detention is greater than that of a prison detention, the implications for women of this differential sentencing could be more long-lasting.

Similarly, as a diagnosis of madness denotes an absence of reason, this implies that women who commit crimes, who are violent, are not in control of their senses. Is this because criminality, violence or aggression cannot be reconciled with our conceptualization of femininity, and thus the woman *must* be mad? This is an invidious process, which strips the woman of even the power to be actively 'bad'. It pathologizes rather than criminalizes, and women do not necessarily welcome this. As Camp indicates:

> For most women in prison the implication of psychiatric treatment is that she has committed an offence and is not fully responsible for her actions, and must be taught what is best for her. As they see it, most women who commit crimes, or even minor offences, would prefer to be considered bad than mad.
>
> (Camp, 1974: 154)

The ascription of the label of criminality to men is less stigmatizing, as well as somehow more 'natural'. We know that men commit crimes, that they are sometimes *bad*, and thus we merely punish them for their anti-social actions, without looking any deeper for an explanation for their behaviour. The man who stabs his lover is merely acting like a man. He must be punished, but his behaviour causes no particular surprise. Whereas the women who stabs her lover must be mad.[19]

In an analysis which posits that the female violent offender is *neither* mad nor bad, Susan Edwards has presented a depressing litany of cases where women have been provoked into murdering their husbands or lovers in circumstances which would certainly have been deemed 'mitigating' had the murderer been a man. Case after case of women abused, oppressed, degraded and finally driven to uncharacteristic violence for which they are convicted, can be juxtaposed with cases where men are freed for carrying out violent acts against women, where the woman was deemed to have provoked the attack. What is interesting is the finding that 'it is assumed that women homicide offenders are bad, if there is evidence of premeditation, or mad if there is no evidence of provocation' (Edwards, 1986: 84). In neither case is there any analysis of the reality of the woman's previous pain and degradation. Women do not kill strangers. When they kill (which is rare) it is invariably their own man. And why? Not for reasons of random aggression, but in the cases of the women Edwards cites, because of persistent cruelty, rape, humiliation, torture and subjugation. The violent or criminal woman is not the living image of the scheming monster who populates mythology. Her sad reality is very different:

> She is neither some monstrous dangerous person, nor sick, maladjusted and mentally impaired. Instead she frequently responds to a trained incapacity for spontaneous retaliation by waiting neither through scheming nor cunning, where the frustration and strain of the familial environment and her helplessness within it result in the violent response out of defensive reaction and self-preservation, or as with children, sheer desperation.
>
> (Edwards, 1986: 86)

This does not *justify*, or excuse, the woman's violent behaviour, but it provides an alternative explanation for it, outside of the woman herself. For this feminist analysis clearly demonstrates the discriminatory bias operating in both penal and psychiatric institutions.

Physical barbarism

> 'Don't worry,' the nurse grinned down at me. 'Their first time everybody's scared to death.'. . . Doctor Gordon was fitting two metal plates on either side of my head. He buckled them into place with a strap that dented my forehead, and gave me a wire to bite. I shut my eyes. There was a brief silence, like an indrawn breath. Then something bent down and took hold of me and shook me like the end of the world. Whee-ee-ee-ee-ee, it shrilled, through an air crackling with blue light, and with each flash a great jolt drubbed me till I thought my bones would break and the sap fly out of me like a split plant.
>
> I wondered what terrible thing it was that I had done.
>
> (Plath, 1963: 151–2)

The analysis of the process and power of the labelling and diagnosis of women as mad, our positioning within the psychiatric discourse, was only one aspect of the feminist critique. Expert interventions were equally vilified. And the physical treatments rejected most vociferously by the male dissenters were judged with particular disdain by feminist critics, as women form by far the majority of recipients of such invasive 'care'. Just as the physically-mediated Victorian treatments of the rest cure and sexual surgery were used predominantly on women, so have today's treatments of ECT, insulin therapy and secure hospitalization. All reduce women to a childlike dependent state, literally confining her to her bed, to her home or to the hospital, increasing her weight (with insulin therapy), reducing her to an infantile state after the administration of her treatment, and ensuring she is both helpless and hopeless. Her madness abates because she can no longer think; she cannot remember. As Sylvia Plath described ECT:

> Now they light me up like an electric bulb.
> For weeks I can remember nothing at all.[20]

This description of a case of a woman who became *sad* after forty years of organizing her husband's life is illustrative:

> After four or five alternate-day [ECT] treatments the woman no longer recognised me; she no longer recognised anything. But her behaviour changed dramatically. She started using large amounts of make-up and wearing dresses she had saved from the 1930s . . . One day . . . she wore an enormous white flower in her hair . . . she flashed [her doctor] an alluring smile, and winked. The doctor blushed . . . He considered her improved.
> (Milner, 1960: 42)

In this case the ECT has 'worked' by removing the woman's sadness – as well as having the added benefits of resulting in more stereotypically acceptable feminine behaviour. No wonder it was deemed a success. But would the woman herself have thought so?

It has been claimed that women are more likely to be given amnesia-inducing treatments such as ECT because 'they are judged to have less need of their brains' (Breggin, 1979).[21] This is described most poignantly in Marion Milner's account of psychoanalytic work with a woman who 'since the ECT [said] something was missing in her, for she had no feelings and nothing mattered anymore' (Milner, 1960: 3).

> Not only does she say there is something missing that she did have before and that she does not care anymore, nothing makes any difference, but also she had no will power and she did before. When she tries to describe further what is missing she talks of her loss of power to appreciate, particularly music which meant so much to her and is now just a 'jungle of

sound', also that her fingers are now all thumbs, whereas before skilled work with her hands was her greatest comfort.

(Milner, 1969: 17)

The justification for lobotomy being more frequently practiced on women was similar: lobotomy did not interfere with their ability 'to assume or resume the role of a housewife' (Berke, 1979: 96). In fact, psychiatric textbooks published in the 1970s recommended lobotomy to enable a woman to cope with her marriage (Showalter, 1987: 210).

The depiction of the physical treatments, epitomized by the typical photographic images of a female patient and male doctor, celebrates female dependence and male control, as Showalter has argued:

> Following the iconographic conventions of the mesmerist and his subject, the vampire and his victim, Charcot and his hysteric, and the prison doctor and his suffragette, the representation of shock treatment too makes use of archetypal patterns of masculine dominance and feminine submission.
>
> (Showalter, 1987: 207)

That institutionalization, and its attendant physical treatment (deemed torture by many of the recipients) was the epitome of misogynistic control over women, legitimated as 'psychiatric care', was the cry of women novelists, patients and critics, from the 1960s onwards.[22] In novels such as Janet Frame's *An angel at my table*, recently made into a film, Sylvia Plath's *The bell jar* and Antonia White's *Beyond the glass*, the connection between femininity and the methods and aims of the interventions are made clear. The women are incarcerated in monstrous and frightening institutions, as they are incarcerated in their rigid feminine roles. They are naughty if they disobey, they are punished for misbehaving, they are washed, watched and wronged through their treatment as objects. The codes of femininity to which they must conform in order to escape are rigid, defined and decreed from above by those in control. Artificial beauty (successful application of cosmetics was applauded), passivity and gentleness are to replace the anger, the rantings, the depression for which these women are condemned. Madness (aberrant femininity) is replaced by acquiescence (acceptable femininity). Women represented in feminist novels are not positioned as heroines. They are not celebrating their madness as a release of thwarted creativity, but are tragically repressed and misplaced, as Janet Frame clearly demonstrates in her (autobiographical) description of the hospitalized schizophrenic:

> It is seldom the easy Opheliana recited like the pages of a seed catalog, or the outpourings of Crazy Janes who provide, in fiction, an outlet for poetic abandon. Few of the people who roamed the day rooms would have qualified as acceptable heroines in popular taste.
>
> (Frame, 1961: 112)[23]

The modern psychiatric strait-jacket – psychotropic drug treatment – serves the same purpose: suppressing and silencing women, making sure that we forget. We may forget the pain – but we forget everything else as well.

Although the physical treatments were notable grist to the mill of the feminist dissenters, the talking cure of psychotherapy was given equally short shrift. Whilst it may appear less invasive and more 'caring', the basic premises behind the intervention were seen as being based on phallocentric models of normality, which therapy coerced women into following. And, whilst therapy *can* be practised by professionals who are not medically trained, and therefore might be assumed to take a less reductionist standpoint, it has in reality been hijacked by the experts; hijacked by the psychiatrists and the other patriarchal professionals such as clinical psychology, psychoanalysis, social work and counselling. Such professions may adopt the rhetoric of care and concern, but they serve their own interests as strongly as did the nineteenth-century medical men whom we can clearly see as monopolistic and machiavellian. Thus therapy is not deemed to be the panacea it is painted.

Therapy as tyranny

> Therapy acts to enforce the whole male structure, and ultimately forces women upon an area which, founded and documented by men, has been used against women.
>
> (Miller, 1973: 485)

In the feminist view, therapy is not gender-neutral. It is based on patriarchal principles and supports a patriarchal and misogynistic culture. The transformation of oppression into illness during the course of therapy is seen as rewriting women's lives, women's pain, within a framework which conceals misogynistic control of women, encouraging women to conform and be controlled. The 'helping professions' are seen as agents who coerce women into accepting situations they do not want and that they are unhappy with. The woman herself is taught to see her misery as illness, and to direct attention and cure at herself. This means that women fail to look to factors outside themselves, factors outside their own madness, for explanations for unhappiness. But this is a situation which many women are beginning to challenge, as expressed by Miller:

> I am tired of thinking of myself as crazy – a nice way to ensure that I never throw off oppression – a way to keep women dependent upon the oppressors.
>
> (Miller, 1973: 48)

To pathologize the individual woman is to neutralize her as a threat to the dominant order. There is no need to look to society – to men – to political factors to understand and ameliorate her situation. There is no need to heed her comments or her complaints, her cries for help. Everything she has previously experienced can be seen as part of her pathology, and her previous life rewritten to fit the psychiatric scenario. As Mary Daly argues:

> Perpetually pushed into this revised past, the patient patiently re-learns her history, which is reversed and rehearsed for the therapist's records. The patient learns to fixate upon herself as an object, to objectify and label happenings in her process until process is re-processed into processions of thoroughly impersonal, explainable events.
>
> (Daly, 1979: 285)

The woman is thus separated from her own feelings, which are compartmentalized and dismissed. She must integrate them into a therapeutic 'normality', which simultaneously labels and dismisses her anger, her despair. The woman must also look for help to relieve her of her 'illness' – and those who offer help are firmly entrenched in the medicalized models (or their positivist-biased equivalents) in the helping professions. Her oppressors, the therapists, are imbued with definitions of normality based on misogynistic assumptions – assumptions which the feminist critics have exposed in no uncertain terms, as we see in Daly:

> . . . women who have been seduced, brow-beaten, and mind-raped by individual therapists or by gangs of mini-therapists in marathon encounter sessions should re-consider the meaning of 'normality' in such a setting.
>
> (Daly, 1979: 287)

Mary Daly does not mince her words: therapy is mind rape. And she is not alone in condemning mental health treatments and the experts who peddle them, as the following extracts from femininist texts illustrate:

> Traditional mental health treatment has done little but provide a label for emotionally disturbed women, often adding to their hardships with no plan for empowerment.
>
> (Fulini, 1987: xiii)

> Since clinical experience and tools can be shown to be worse than useless when tested for consistency, efficacy, agreement and reliability, we can safely conclude that theories of a clinical nature advanced about women are also worse than useless.
>
> (Weissten, 1973: 402)

> The Woman question . . . has no answer in the market place or among the throngs of experts who sell their wisdom there.
>
> (Ehrenreich and English, 1978: 323)

One of the major criticisms of therapy is that it is practised by men, on women; that 'from the beginning men have been therapists . . .' (Ernst and Goodison, 1981: 307); that in North America women 'currently number less than 10% of the psychiatrists and more than 60% of the patients' (Penfold and Walker, 1984: 26). The fact that certain 'caring' professions, such as clinical psychology in Britain, have a larger proportion of women (currently 50:50 – Williams and Watson, 1992; Nicolson, 1992) can be seen as irrelevant because men are still at the top. They still maintain the positions of control, and thus deploy the departmental budgets, determine training, and decide the type of services offered, as well as the types of client groups served. In addition, women trained as therapists have had to train within an androcentric profession, which may value the male perspective over the female, as Chesler suggests:

> Most contemporary professionals (like most non-professionals) unthinkingly consider what happens to men as somehow more important than what happens to women. *Male* psychiatric illness or 'impairment' is viewed as more 'disabling' than female illness. The ghost of female expendability and 'outsideness' haunts almost every page of psychiatric and psychological journals.
>
> (Chesler, 1972: 65)

Women who want to succeed within their chosen professions invariably adopt the male mode, not wanting to be cast as outsiders. Examples of women who have rallied against the system and failed are plentiful.[24] In my own clinical experience, when I naïvely attempted to suggest alternative models for understanding women's (and men's) distress, alternatives to the cognitive–behavioural methods of intervention, mentioning the feminist perspective, I was laughed out of the room. 'Keep your politics for the conference platform,' was the message. No wonder many women choose to follow the pattern in which they have been well trained, electing to practise the patriarchal therapies so expertly taught, to achieve a happy (and blind) progress up the career ladder. Even feminist therapists can be deemed dangerous, seen to be taking on the language of the patriarchs and using it against women; thus betraying feminism itself, as Kitzinger has claimed:

> Instead of subverting or supplanting psychology, as feminists initially intended, many have accepted its language as their own, and it has often been professional feminist psychologists who first offered these personalized concepts to the feminist communities . . . In consequence, feminism has moved from a political movement into a 'lifestyle' or 'state of the mind'. Psychology is, if not an agent of, at least a willing participant in the depoliticization of feminism.
>
> (Kitzinger, 1990: 132)

Feminist critics would argue that women therapists, feminist or not, are no different from women in other male-dominated professions; and the therapists themselves are analogous to other groups in their organized control of women in general. Therapy will merely mirror the oppression and systematic treatment of women as the Other which takes place in all organizations in society. Thus it can be claimed, as Chesler says, that:

> Psychiatrists and psychologists are no more sexocidal than politicians, soldiers, poets, physicists, or bartenders are. However, they are no less so – despite their rather special concern with power over individual women. (Chesler, 1972: 60)

From this view, a critique of therapy is just one part of a general critique of misogynistic practice which oppresses women in patriarchal society. And as sexual abuse of women is seen by many feminists to be a fundamental component of misogynistic discourse, as evidenced by the earlier discussion of rape and pornography, is it surprising that such abuse is also present in therapy?

Sexual oppression in therapy

> SHEILA: . . . he never even took his clothes off. He just dropped his pants . . . He told me I was blocked, that there were things I had to work out with my father and that maybe we could solve it on a non-verbal level if I would just trust him . . . Then he got up, dropped his pants, said, 'Take your pants down,' or something really insensitive, unsensual, and he just got on top of me. He came, I didn't come. And then I said, 'I'd like to get on top of you.' And then he told me that that was my problem, that I wanted to be in control . . .
>
> (Chesler, 1972: 147–8)

The fact that women are sexually assaulted, or 'seduced' by their therapists is a matter of much controversy – a fact covered up by many professionals and seen as 'probably infrequent' (Strickler, 1977) in the official view. The issue of the seduction of patients by their physicians was of concern to the 'founding father' of medicine, Hippocrates, who declared that physicians should keep themselves 'from all intentional ill-doing and all seduction and especially from the pleasures of love with women'.[25] It was also present in both the nineteenth-century treatments of madness, as we have seen, and in some of the early psychoanalytic cases. But it was not until the 1970s that public discussion of the extent of the abuse began to take place.[26] Perhaps not surprisingly, this was met with great resistance, and publication of material documenting the extent and nature of sex between clients and therapists was dismissed or even suppressed.[27]

Studies attempting to investigate the question of therapist–client sex have suggested that up to 15 per cent of therapists *admit* to such activities, and over 50 per cent engage their patients in physical contact which they deem 'non-erotic', such as kissing, hugging and touching (Kardener *et al.*, 1973, Holroyd and Brodski, 1977). These are not isolated incidents, for of those therapists who admit to having had sexual relationships with their patients, over 80 per cent have done so with more than one woman patient; and many have done so repeatedly, the *average* being twenty-nine times (Holroyd and Brodski, 1977). The question of the boundaries between what is and is not erotic is debatable, and kissing or touching patients may be deemed abusive. But what is astounding is the high percentage of therapists who actually own up to sex with their patients. Is this merely the honest few? For as Masson rightly comments:

> The problem with all of these surveys is that they are taken of offenders. Imagine attempting to find out how many men had raped by asking nonconvicted rapists whether they were guilty of rape. Or imagine attempting to find the number of incest victims in a given community by asking all the fathers in that community how many of them had committed incest.
>
> (Masson, 1989: 224)

Surveys of women patients (for female therapist/male client sexual relations are infrequent)[28] who have been seduced by their therapists present a disturbing picture. It is difficult to know the extent of the problem, for many women are afraid to come forward, often not realizing that 'sex between therapist and patient is unethical or actionable'.[29] It is estimated that only between 1 and 4 per cent of women who have been sexually abused by their therapists come forward,[30] partly because women are ill-advised as to the appropriate channels for action. If women *do* come forward, they are likely to be treated like the rape victim: guilty until proved innocent. One authority claims that neurotic women fabricate their evidence because their 'lives of quiet desperation' lead them to 'react with allegations of sexual improprieties' (Brownfain, 1971: 26). Professional organizations invariably will act to protect the therapist – who protects the woman? She may be accused of seducing the therapist, of enjoying the 'sexual treatment', and the myth of the powerfully palliative phallus is again resurrected as women are persuaded that sex with their therapist will 'improve the transference relationship', cure frigidity, cure their madness.[31] The attraction between the therapist and client is seen as emanating from the woman herself: she is the one who has provoked these feelings, she is responsible for them. Women's sexuality is to blame, yet again.

And women do believe they are to blame. These women often feel guilty.[32] They have internalized the blame for men's desire, as these extracts from interviews with women, carried out by Phylis Chesler, demonstrate:

> MELISSA: I think that he finally just couldn't resist me any more. I think I finally just put too much pressure on him . . .
> ROSLYN: Actually, in a certain way, I was seducing him all along . . . unconsciously . . .
> CINDY: He'd interpret everything I said as 'transference love' or sexual desire for him . . .
>
> (Chesler, 1972: 145–7)

What is the response of the expert professions to allegations of misconduct, to stories of sex between client and therapist? Invariably there is an attempt to vilify the culprit, who is depicted as extraordinary, and not representative of his profession – a process similar to the positioning of the rapist or sex offender as a monster, allowing us to dimiss him as different from ourselves. Claiming that sexual abuse by therapists is rare, Stone argues from this perspective:

> The sexual abuse of patients is an egregious manifestation of deficiencies in character and competence . . . the vast majority of psychiatrists are ethical and competent. They are deeply troubled by the unethical conduct of the *very few* who sexually abuse and mistreat patients and discredit the profession. We may feel that these offending colleagues need treatment rather than punishment.
>
> (Stone, 1984: 374; my emphasis)

The *very few* unethical therapists are seen as being ill (or perhaps mad), a convenient explanation for their behaviour. Pathologized, they are dismissed. For example, in a study of 'seductive therapists', Dahlberg described them as men who were both 'grandiose . . . withdrawn and introspective, studious, passive and shy' (Dahlberg, 1970). Psychologizing the abuser allows professional distance to be maintained, permitting the therapeutic professions to maintain their veneer of integrity. They can claim that there is no problem, since only a few of their members are acting with impropriety, and there is thus no need for an examination of the institutional structures which, in practice, allow and protect such abuse: if we sweep it under the carpet, pretend it isn't there, we can carry on as normal:

> In all the cases that have been reported in the literature, not one raises the question of what to do with the psychiatrist who seduces patients in the course of therapy – whether it is called transference or countertransference, love or acting out (or up), incest or rape.
>
> (Davidson, 1984: 365)

Can it be right that we turn a professional blind eye to sex between therapist and client for fear of damaging the profession, for questions of ethics of disclosure, for fear of damaging the family and reputation of the therapist and the woman client?[33]

There are no connections made between abuse inside and abuse outside the consulting room. It is presented as an aberration rather than an experience of many women's lives in many contexts. What is ignored is the gender issue, the misogyny, the misuse of power. Therapy is presented as a cure for women's pain, an intervention for madness, for unhappiness, for misery. For the therapist to seduce his patient is an abuse of that privilege and power. To claim that she was willing, that she wanted it, that if it had been rape she would have screamed, is to ignore the unequal position of the two protagonists, and to ignore the dangers in using the consulting room as an arena for seduction, and in blaming the woman for whatever ensues.

Academics may argue about the niceties of whether a therapist can marry his patient and still practise, or how long a period should elapse after 'treatment' before such an engagement can take place.[34] They may declare that to prevent such liaisons would be an infringement of the liberty of both client and therapist. What they ignore is the desperation of many of the women involved in therapy, their need for love and affection, and the ease with which physical abuse can take place in this context. If, as women, we have been taught that power is attractive and seductive, is it surprising that the therapist, who combines this power with the appearance of understanding and caring, finds his patients an easy target for his sexual advances? Women live in a culture where men's power is eroticized – through romantic fiction, pornography and film – and we cannot deny that many women find it erotic, and, indeed, may then feel guilty for doing so. In order to understand women's reactions to therapeutic sexual abuse, and their apparent willingness to engage in these relationsips – a willingness used to exonerate the therapist – we need to acknowledge the sexual attraction of power.[35]

In therapy, the power imbalance is *not* a fantasy; it is a reality. The women involved may not scream; they may appear willing; but the effect of these sexual relationships is invariably damaging (Schoener *et al.*, 1984; Chesler, 1972). The therapist does not carry the woman off into the sunset on his proverbial white horse, as many of the women, caught up in the seduction, hopefully fantasized. *He* invariably ends the 'relationship', leaving the woman distraught.[36] In 90 per cent of reported cases the women were harmed (Bouhoutsos *et al.*, 1973) and as many of these women have previously been sexually abused,[37] we should ask, Is their 'treatment' merely adding to their pain? Or is it allowing the therapist to attribute the 'problem' to the woman, reinforcing the misogynistic myth of the seductive personality which is wheeled out with disastrous consequences in child sexual abuse cases? A minority of women may suffer no ills from sexual contact between patient and therapist. A few women may marry their therapist and speak positively about the relationship. But such women are rare.

It may provide some satisfaction to feminist critics to reveal the fact that many of the therapists who engage in sexual activity with their patients may be suffering from sexual inadequacies; that 'seductive male therapists have unenviable track records as lovers, suffering frequently from impotence and premature ejaculation' (Davidson, 1984: 364),[38] or that 'one might simply conclude from this information that "seductive" therapists are lousy lovers' (Chesler, 1972: 114). But this is similar to falling into the trap of pathologizing the therapist, painting him as abnormal. These men are not aberrations. They do not behave in a way that deviates greatly from men in other positions in society. Pathologizing or ridiculing them conveniently ignores the fact that sexual contact between powerful men and powerless women is part of the fabric of our society. Erotic stimulation is provided by the imbalance of power. Women are blamed for the resulting sex. Why should therapy be any different?

Sex therapy – objectification and forced heterosexuality?

Whilst psychiatric and psychological models of madness are unequivocally rejected by the feminist critics, specific forms of therapy have come in for scrutiny as being particularly misogynistic – forms such as that of sex therapy (Ussher, 1992a), which is said to be based on a 'phallocentric model of sexuality' (Stock, 1988: 26) which acts to confine and control women through the imposition of marriage and heterosexuality as 'normal' (Jackson, 1984). Women who deviate from this norm, through choosing either to be celibate, or to be lesbian, may be deemed in need of treatment, as happened in the nineteenth century. As sexuality itself can be seen as a social construction therapeutic interventions are not based on rational objective theories as claimed by their proponents, but on current social constructions of 'normal' sexuality, and therefore of sexual dysfunction. Just as the diagnostic categories of masturbation, nymphomania and frigidity were pathologizing inventions of the Victorians, so women today who reject sexual intercourse can be pathologized, with vaginismus elevated to the status of a phobia, a 'dread of the penis' (Jeffreys, 1990: 33). That women may have any other, perhaps logical, reasons for refusing penetration is ignored or denied. The problem is again firmly placed within the woman herself. Sexuality itself is considered in a reductionist manner, with all attention focused on those attributes deemed most important within current medical discourse, as Stock's example illustrates:

> In this culture, the inability of the male to have a cylindrical tube of flesh between the legs become sufficiently rigid to insert in a vagina or other bodily orifice is considered a major and incapacitating sexual dysfunction; the inability to be emotionally intimate or to communicate clearly with a sexual partner is not diagnosed as a sexual dysfunction, and is certainly not researched as frantically as sexual dysfunction.
>
> (Stock, 1988: 31)

The actual mechanisms of sex therapy have been denounced by many feminists as being objectifying for women (Ussher, 1990a) in their frequent use of pornography (Stock, 1988: 26), and their use of mechanistic interventions such as 'intravaginal retention of the larger dilators for a matter of several hours each night' (Masters and Johnson, 1981: 96). Others have argued that sex and marital therapy has a more invidious function, that of maintaining oppressive (and heterosexist) patriarchal power structures, as Jeffreys claims:

> The setting up of the Marriage Guidance Council, the work of sexologists and the development of sex therapy are all instances of how men's power over women was to be supported through the regulation of marital sex.
>
> (Jeffreys, 1990: 5)

Jeffreys sees marital therapy as a 'tinkering with the husband/wife relationship so as to bolster the man's power and subordinate the woman' (Jeffreys, 1990: 11). Marital and sex therapists are seen as being 'dedicated to the maintenance of marriage and heterosexuality' (Jackson, 1984), which means that lesbian women are at risk of being treated within a heterosexist framework if they come forward for therapy (Ussher, 1991b).

Family therapy: Blaming the woman, ignoring gender

Sex therapy is not the only specific intervention to be rejected. Family therapy has received equally short shrift. One of the most common findings within psychological literature is the blaming of the mother for the ills or sins of the child. The mother has been a convenient scapegoat throughout the centuries, but psychology and psychiatry have elevated mother-hating and mother-baiting to the status of scientific fact: for example see Yager (1982) in relation to blaming the mother for anorexia. The mother has been blamed for the gamut of childhood illnesses, disturbances and delinquencies; for schizophrenia, depression psychopathy and personality disorders; for homosexuality; for autism, anorexia and anxiety; for child sexual abuse (the mother's rejection of the father causing him to abuse the child). You name it, the mother has caused it. This fits in very conveniently with the misogynistic discourse where the mother is feared, envied and reviled: the psychiatric discourse keeps her in fear of being hauled before the diagnostic court, accused of a heinous crime if she fails to toe the line.

Hence, family therapy has been carefully scrutinized by feminists. For whilst it may appear to be enlightened in its focus on the system rather than the individual women, it is seen as operating from an androcentric point of view which reinforces traditional gender stereotypes.

The system which the therapists are supporting is seen to be one which may not be healthy for the woman, for families themselves may be breeding grounds for madness (see Chapter 9). Women's roles within the nuclear family being a common root of distress from the feminist perspective, a family therapy which does not even question these roles will be deeply flawed. Family therapists have been accused of reinforcing male dominance, of ignoring politics, ideology or extra-familial contexts, such as social, economic and historical determinants of distress (Taggart, 1985) and of generally being 'conformist and confused' (Kovel, 1976).[39] The idea that individual rights and needs of the woman should be subjugated to the needs of the family as a whole has been questioned and the specific interventions based on systems theory (Selvini Palazolli *et al.*, 1978) have been criticized for adopting an inappropriate stance of neutrality in the face of 'the most harsh realities of family violence and other forms of intra-familial exploitation and abuse' (Grunebaum, 1987: 647). As the very notion of the therapist's neutrality has been questioned again and again (Ussher, 1992c), this pretence of neutrality is an added oppression to women in many families. Structural and strategic family therapists are similarly condemned for

> modelling authoritarian behaviour associated with being male and white, and manipulative strategies and values that some see as consonant with the ideology of a male-dominated market economy.
>
> (Grunebaum, 1987: 647)

Thus, the models of the 'normal family' operated by family therapists are seen as, at best, androcentric, at worst, misogynistic.

Psychoanalysis – reductionist and phallocentric?

Freudian psychoanalysis has perhaps received the most vociferous criticism from feminists,[40] for being based on 'the strict determinism that characterized the scientific thinking of the Victorian era' (Friedan, 1965: 94), which is seen as both misogynistic and phallocentric. Freud is seen to have had 'no objective proof . . . in support of his notion of penis envy or of a female castration complex' and thus 'one is struck by how thoroughly the subjectivity in which all these events are cast tends to be Freud's own, or that of a strong masculine bias, even of a gross male supremacist bias' (Millett, 1970: 182). Psychoanalysis is seen as reducing women to biologically determined, perpetually envious, second-rate citizens; prescribing womanhood as a punishment to be borne; and seeing suffering or madness as an almost inevitable consequence. Again, the patriarchal environment which creates women's distress is seen to be ignored, whilst the woman herself is controlled through the therapy. As one critique puts it:

> Freud's basic view was that every woman was a square peg trying to fit into a round hole. It did not occur to him that it might be less destructive to change the shape of the holes rather than to knock all the corners off. The 'cured' patient is actually brainwashed, a walking automaton, as good as dead. The corners have been knocked off and the woman accepts her own castration, acknowledges herself inferior, ceases to envy the penis and accepts the passive role of femininity.
>
> (Figes, 1970: 147–8)

Rejecting therapy

I could produce an almost infinite list of feminist criticisms of the various therapies currently practised, all leading to the same conclusion. Whatever therapy is being considered, the woman herself is seen as a victim of the experts who look for trade in the market place of the mad. Women are indoctrinated into believing themselves mad and thus in need of help from those who can both interpret the anger or distress within their own theoretical frameworks, and offer a 'cure' under a mystifying and controlling shroud. Thus, as Mary Daly argues:

> . . . therapists create a market for their 'healing'. A woman seduced into treatment is 'inspired' with dis-ease she had never before even suspected. As she becomes more fixated upon her surfacing 'problems' she becomes more in need of Help. The multiplicity of therapies feeds into this dis-ease, for they constitute an arsenal for the manufacture of the many forms of *semantic bullets* used to bombard the minds of women struggling to survive

in the therapeutically polluted environment.

(Daly, 1979: 276; my emphasis)

What are the consequences of the feminist debate, of these vociferous criticisms? Not surprisingly, given an almost wholehearted condemnation of experts, many feminist critics have advocated the abolition of professional care, partly on the grounds that 'women confiding in therapists stops them from confiding in each other' (Daly, 1979: 256). It was as a result of exposure to these arguments that I stopped practising as a clinical psychologist. I could not reconcile myself to the notion that I was merely bombarding women with *semantic bullets*. The transfer of care into the community of women has been suggested as an alternative to professional therapy. Ehrenreich and English propose that:

> [We need] a society in which healing is not a commodity distributed according to the dictates of profit, but integral to the network of community life . . . in which wisdom about daily life is not hoarded by 'experts' or doled out as a commodity but is drawn from the experience of all people and freely shared among them. This is the most radical vision, but there are no human alternatives.
>
> (Ehrenreich and English, 1978: 324)

This is not, however, the only solution offered. For whilst feminist critics may be united in their disavowal of the patriarchs and their professional practices, there are many other theoretical frameworks within which alternative means of reconstructing women's madness have been explored, resulting in a number of alternative solutions, some therapeutic, some social – all reframing women's madness through the feminist prism.

Woman's different voice

It is as difficult to provide a synopsis of the 'feminist position' on women's madness as it is to unite the myriad of feminist scholars under one umbrella. There are virtually as many different theories and arguments in the feminist debate as there are feminists. Perhaps this is a sign of health, for only a stagnating ossifying discipline is complacent and without debate or controversy.[41] But for the novice, previously not exposed to feminist critiques, or for the woman attempting to constitute a feminist position which can be used in a reconstruction of women's experience of madness, these different arguments might present an almost impenetrable barrier. For it would be easy to be confused by the different shades of grey within the feminist debate, and lose sight of the primary need to challenge the dominant discourse which positions us as Other, in such a way as to provide some impetus for change. It would be easy to become embroiled in the controversy surrounding the different arguments, never moving forward as the minutiae of disagreement would always exert a stultifying influence. In addressing disagreements one can lose sight of the overall battle.

It is thus naïve to say 'the feminist position is . . .', for the theories of what have become known as radical (or cultural), liberal or egalitarian and socialist (or classical Marxist) feminists may be at odds with each other, both theoretically, and in terms of the prescriptions for change. Yet, as Janet Sayers argues, the position may not be as complicated as it first appears, for whilst there are disagreements between the different feminist camps, 'certain theories – such as those of biological essentialism and social constructionism – are shared by some within each of the different tendencies' (Sayers, 1982: 173). I will therefore attempt to summarize the main tenets of different feminist positions[42] to decide whether Freeman is correct in asserting that contemporary feminists are not at odds with each other at all (Freeman, 1975). This brief analysis of different forms of feminism illustrates that the various feminist alternatives to professional intervention are dependent on the particular stance taken by individual critics – whether they be working from an egalitarian or a woman-centred perspective. Whilst the present analysis is cursory it is a necessary overview of many of the different perspectives, which can be explored in depth elsewhere.

Liberal feminism: Working from within

> Simone de Beauvoir may be called the chief exemplar of metaphysical feminism, which holds that the male view of the world is the human view and that women should subscribe to it as much as possible.
>
> (Baruch and Serrano, 1988: 9)

The development of liberal or egalitarian feminism has been seen to have its roots in the bourgeois development of the free market economy, wherein sex discrimination was deemed a hindrance to the operation of the market, and thus should be overthrown (Sayers, 1982: 174). The doctrine of the liberal feminists – typified by writers such as de Beauvoir (1979), Friedan (1965) and Sherman (1977) – is that women and men are equal, and given opportunity and access to power, women will thrive and succeed. Biology is not seen as an insuperable obstacle to women's emancipation. In fact, it is argued that any biological limitations imposed on women by patriarchal society will be eradicated by fundamental changes in social structures so that women will no longer be systematically subjugated and excluded.

In the liberal feminist tradition, inequalities evident within society are largely engendered by the iniquitous socialization of males and females, in which girls are socialized into passivity and conformity, denied an autonomous existence, and prepared for subservience to men. Factors such as education (Sherman, 1977) the media (Coward, 1984) and relationships within the family (Chodorow, 1978) are believed both to create, and maintain, gender roles, preparing women for their existence as the 'second sex'. Thus it is argued that, if appropriate changes in both childhood socialization and institutional structures can only take place, then a liberal utopia, in which people achieve on the basis of individual ability rather than gender, will ensue. The free market economy will out. In disciplines such as psychology, liberal feminists such as Unger (1979) have concentrated on making 'egalitarian corrections to psychological theories' (Squire, 1989: 76), attempting to redress the balance and demonstrate the fallacy in much of the psychological theorizing about women.

In this view, women's madness is seen to be related to our position within the structures and institutions in society, and thus institutional change is one of the major keys to enlightenment and freedom, and to the alleviation of misery and madness. It has been claimed that 'the easiest target in removing sexual inequality involves legal statute change or judicial interpretation of rights in the public sector' (Rossi, 1969: 81), a claim based on the assumption that if women are allowed space to be equal, they will achieve their potential, throwing off the bonds of oppression, the bonds of madness. In the meantime, structural supports such as childcare, equal opportunity laws in the workplace, and both free abortion and contraception are seen as some of the means by which women will achieve this freedom.

Socialist feminism

A second brand of feminist thinking which also adheres to the notion of the social construction of female oppression, but which looks to the capitalist structure of society as the root of all evil, is socialist feminism. Its analysis has taken much of the rhetoric of Marxism: ownership of the means of production is deemed to be at the root of abuse of power and oppression; but it also focuses on the oppression of women by men, inherent within patriarchal societies. Marxist accounts alone are deemed to provide inadequate explanations for the continuation of sexism (Rubin, 1975), particularly of sexism in the proletariat where there is no access to property; for it is believed to be naïve to assume that absence of property would lead to equality between the sexes (cf. Engels, 1884: 135), as is demonstrated by the continuation of sexism and oppression of women in working-class (non-property-owning) communities, and in non-capitalist societies such as the USSR. Yet socialist feminists still see the explanation for women's oppression as located within social structures – determined by women's specific position of powerlessness within the family and our lack of access to the means of production within patriarchy (Mitchell, 1974). Biology itself is not central to these divisions between men and women, but the social construction of biology *is* central, in that it 'both reflects and contributes to the reproduction of patriarchy and existing divisions in society' (Sayers, 1982: 195).

Thus the socialist feminist account sees the route to change as being within the system, within social practices. For example, in a powerful account of socialist feminism, which is deeply critical of the other feminist standpoints, Lynne Segal has argued that:

> A feminist politics which can reach out to all women, as distinct from the privileged few, must concern itself with material inequalities – with questions of income, resources and the control of resources. This means struggles in and around the state and work around trade unions, however wearing and slow these may be.
>
> (Segal, 1987: 244)

Contrary to radical feminists such as Daly (discussed below), who espouse a separation from men and all that the phallus represents, socialist feminists such as Segal argue that, 'feminists . . . need to accept that part of their struggle must involve an alliance with men to transform the social inequalities, and the dangerous and destructive technologies, of existing capitalist economies' (Segal, 1987: 245). A very different journey indeed from the 'psychic voyage' of Mary Daly, during which women throw off the chains of men, escaping on their own self-determined flight from oppression. For whilst these two perspectives above focus on structures and divisions in society, seeing women as equal to men, and capable of all that is presently denied them, radical and cultural feminists take a different viewpoint in their analysis, arguing for women's inherent difference – in fact, for our superiority.

Radical feminists: Misogyny and essentialism

> Female self-actualization becomes the means to feminist revolution.
>
> (Squire, 1989: 79)

The radical, or women-centred or cultural feminists, as they are often known, are represented in force in the earlier parts of this book, particularly in the analysis of misogyny. They have rejected the egalitarian feminist assumptions that social factors determine women's oppression, asserting that women are very different from men and that biological differences are at the root of both misogyny and the subjugation of women. Critics such as Mary Daly, Adrienne Rich, Jean Baker-Miller, Susan Griffin and Andrea Dworkin have provided the background for the reconstruction of women's biology as a positive empowering force, and have inspired generations of newly emerging feminists in the process. The poetic language adopted, the rhythmic rhetoric and the clear denunciation of men is, for many, both seductive and exhilarating. My own adolescent awakening to structured explanations for woman's oppression was inspired by a diet of such authors, as was my rejection of clinical psychology at a later stage. What radical feminists espouse is the recognition of woman's essential difference – women's biological superiority and 'special nature', as well as the recognition that it is man's envy and fear of women's reproductive power, and women's essential self, that underlies oppression. In this view, men are very clearly the enemy – it is men who make women mad.

Daly, one of the most vociferous (and most anti-male) feminists, has argued that language is central to women's oppression. She argues that women must reject the male definitions of reality imposed upon us, reject the polluted patriarchal culture and the language which supports and maintains it, embarking instead on an individual 'psychic voyage'. Daly (1974: 4) focuses on language, on the 'radiant power of words', and this has led to the claim that the reframing of women's experience cannot take place within our present phallocentric language: we cannot rewrite the textbooks on madness in the language of the oppressors – we must use our 'different voice'. Through reclaiming words normally used to oppress women ('witch', 'hag', 'spinster'), and using them as positive words to empower women, Daly claims that we can discover new meanings for bad/old labels within the polluted male culture. Dale Spender has sanctioned this view, positing that 'to reclaim our minds' we must embrace feminism, and as such, the 'alternative meanings put forward by feminists' (Spender, 1982: 8). In this view, everything is reduced to language: it creates reality, and denotes power.

One of the other strong threads of argument within radical feminism has been the attention paid to heterosexual sex and the power of the phallus, to the objectification and control of women through sex. The historical roots of this discourse have been discussed in Chapters 2 and 3: sexuality has for centuries been seen to be a centre of power, and in particular power over women. Sexuality is thus a central component of the misogynistic discourse and of the feminist backlash.[43] Sexuality, used to control women, to objectify and pathologize us, is seen as being at the core of the misogynistic denigration of the female. The act of heterosexual sex, intercourse, is seen to enforce and reinforce men's power over women (Jeffreys, 1990: 31). Some feminists, such as Sheila Jeffreys and Andrea Dworkin, have laid the blame for women's oppression and their subsequent distress firmly at the bedroom door, arguing that:

> Intercourse occurs in the context of a power relationship that is pervasive and incontrovertible. The context in which the act takes place, whatever the meaning of the act in and of itself, is one in which men have social, economic, political and physical control over women.
>
> (Dworkin, 1987: 125)

Thus heterosexuality itself is damned, by many radical feminists, the heterosexual woman merely a dupe, signing her own certificate for madness if she does not throw off the bonds of men, and look for her sexual pleasure to women. These writers did not advocate sexuality for women, as did many of their nineteenth-century counterparts; rather, the expression of sexuality outside of the realms of men.

Other radical feminists have looked to the root of the hatred of women and found it in mothering. Thus Adrienne Rich has claimed that men's dominance over women and the subsequent positioning of women as mad is fundamentally based on men's envy of women's power to reproduce – the power to bear and rear children, an envy which is really jealousy of 'female creative energy in all of its forms' (Rich, 1977). This location of misogyny in a fear of woman's reproductive power is adopted not only by women-centred theorists. It is also taken up by those who would justify and maintain women's subordination. For example, the literary critic Holbrook berates feminists for attempting to become 'a rather nasty type of man' because they 'dress like men or bathe naked from the waist down' (Holbrook, 1989: 54). He also claims:

> Woman is . . . the creature we are terribly afraid of because she once had the power of life and death over us. She was once the creative mirror in whose face and response we saw our being emerge. But because she had this power and because we could have only seen a blankness in her face, we are afraid of her, because she could be a witch. Because we are afraid of her, we are often hostile to women.
>
> (Holbrook, 1989: 7–8)

Norman Mailer, who celebrates female denigration in his writing, is more explicit:

> It was men's sense of awe before woman, his dread of her position one step closer to eternity (for in that step were her powers) which made men detest women, revile them, humiliate them, defecate symbolically upon them, do everything to reduce them so one might dare to enter them and take pleasure of them . . . Men look to destroy every quality in a woman which would give her the power of a male, for she is in their eyes already armed with the power that she brought them forth.
>
> (Mailer, 1971: 116)

Certain radical feminists, such as Firestone, have reacted to the foregrounding of women's mothering as a source of oppression by advocating artificial reproduction (Sayers, 1982: 188), a dissociation of women and motherhood. A dangerous suggestion, perhaps, for it mechanizes the woman's body, and 'whereas formerly they were reified as sex objects, women are now utilized for their reproductive parts, which are the commodities, the products for largely male technicians' (Baruch and Serrano, 1988: 20). Others have taken the opposite stance, arguing that motherhood is woman's source of power, and should be *celebrated* as the means to freedom and emancipation. This 'cosmic essence of womanhood' is seen to be the root to power – if only women would realize and utilize it. Thus Adrienne Rich, in celebrating woman's essential difference, declares:

> I have come to believe . . . that female biology – the diffuse intense sensuality radiating out from the clitoris, breasts, uterus, vagina; the lunar cycles of menstruation; the gestation and friction of life which can take place in the female body – has far more radical implications than we have yet come to appreciate.
>
> (Rich, 1977: 39)

In the same way that Carol Gilligan espoused a theory of women's *moral* superiority, in her now classic text *A different voice* (1982), Rich is espousing a *biological* superiority. Thus whilst Gilligan presents women as inherently more empathic, compassionate and caring, showing more concern for the individual than for any cause or principle, Rich presents women as closer to nature, and argues that if only we carried out a 'repossession . . . of our bodies' we would be free (Rich, 1977: 290). The classic 'bleed-ins' of the 1970s, where women celebrated their menstruation together, and the use of the vagina as art form, epitomized by Judy Chicago's *Dinner party*, are examples of how this repossession has begun to take place.[44]

Thus, in the radical feminist view, women's difference is both at the root of oppression and the road to emancipation. A celebration of femininity is deemed not only one of the main keys to women's future, but to the future of society, where 'new ways of relating . . . [will] restore the world to its emotions, and literally to its senses' (Firestone, 1971: 38).

Psychoanalytic feminism

> . . . a rejection of psychoanalysis and of Freud's works is fatal for feminism. However it may have been used, psychoanalysis is not a recommendation *for* a patriarchal society, but an analysis *of* one. If we are interested in understanding and challenging the oppression of women, we cannot afford to neglect it.
>
> (Mitchell, 1974: xv)

Both the theories and the therapy of psychoanalysis were rejected by many early feminists in the 1960s and 1970s, as being misogynistic, as we have seen. Yet, in more recent years, the dissatisfaction with the inability of egalitarian or liberal theories to explain women's continued inequality despite increased opportunities, and the realization that patriarchal discourse is internalized by women, 'that the subjective experience of gender is not an entirely logical or consistent affair' (Squire, 1989: 95), marked the turn towards psychoanalysis as a means of understanding women's response to patriarchy.[45] Equally, as the role of sexuality, power and ideology (or discursive practices) in the subordination of women, and our subsequent madness, began to be acknowledged, psychoanalysis was seen to provide a framework for its investigation, offering 'an understanding of how subordination can be internalized deep in our personalities' (Cameron, 1985: 117). Whilst the radical and cultural feminists might look to the deconstruction of isolated mothering and the celebration of womanhood as a road to women's freedom, and explain misogyny through fear of the mother, psychoanalytic feminists have looked more closely at the role of language, of sexuality and the ambivalence felt towards the mother; and they have brought the whole array of psychoanalytic theorizing to bear upon explanations for the 'woman question'.[46] This places the relationship of the individual woman with society at the centre of the debate, as the unconscious is deemed to be 'the site of interaction between the body, history, and psychic representations' (Coward, 1974: 8).

As outlined in Chapter 5, psychoanalytic theory can be traced back to Freud, to the basic premise that both conscious and unconscious forces are working together, and that sexuality begins from the moment of birth, rather than at adolescence or adulthood. Our sexuality is seen to be the product of our history – both our own individual history and history in a wider sense, an acknowledgement of the role of wider social factors in the formation of identity.

Freud posited that the father plays a major role in the formation of women's sexuality through the feelings of desire and guilt which occur at the Oedipal stage of development. When the female child realizes her lack of penis she interprets it as a punishment of her sexuality, and, according to Freud, blames the mother for her penisless state. Female heterosexuality is seen as being formed by penis envy, and lesbianism as being the effect of the denial of penis envy, or as a retaliation for the father's rejection. This phallocentric view of women's psychology and sexuality has been challenged by many women psychoanalysts and feminist psychoanalytic theorists, who view the relationship with the mother as much more important in women's development and sexuality.[47] This focus on the mother, and the emphasis on the role of language in creating and maintaining the symbolic order, has most clearly marked the contribution of late-twentieth-century psychoanalytic thinking.

The psychoanalytic feminists have developed their theories from the work of Freud, Klein, Winnicott or Lacan. These marked divisions in perspective are often made along lines of nationality, with Freudian theory being dominant in the USA, Kleinian and object-relations theory dominant in Britain, and Lacanian theory in Europe, and particularly in France.[48] Yet, despite their different theoretical origins, one of the most influential theorists in feminist psychoanalytic terms, in his influence on post-structuralist artistic, literary and psychological critiques, has been Jacques Lacan. Drawing on theories of linguistics and semiotics, Lacan argued that, prior to the Oedipal crisis, the child belongs to the realm of the Imaginary, where it believes that it is part of the mother and can perceive no separation between itself and the world. On the acquisition of language, the child enters the 'symbolic order' where it takes up 'The Law of the Father', signified by the phallus, the symbol of patriarchal power and order. The male child possesses the penis, which is the signifier for the phallus, whilst the female child experiences only the absence of the penis and thus of access to power. Women thus are confronted with lack, with Otherness. For:

> . . . in its grandeur, the penis is like the phallus, the transitional object that helps the penis become the landlord of the world . . . we all, female as well as male, want the phallus, for in the symbolic patriarchal order, it is the representation of desire.
>
> (Baruch and Serrano, 1988: 19)

The term 'symbolic' refers to 'a set of meanings that define culture and are embedded in language, that lie outside the being of the individual child but represent an order of humanity in which each one of us has to take up a position, or risk psychosis' (Frosh, 1987: 193). The positing that the symbolic order is created by linguistic representations suggests that identity and subjectivity are ultimately linguistic constructs – that they cannot, in fact, exist outside of the language. Thus:

> There is then no identity outside of the language; subjectivity is only possible in an alienated identification of oneself as 'I', a pre-existing linguistic position in which each subject is positioned as either masculine or feminine.
>
> (Malson, 1992: 10)

This is a phallocentric language that defines the 'I', the One, as masculine, and thus the feminine as the 'not – I'. Women are thus 'the Other'. The phallus (which is not synonymous with the actual penis but rather is a representation of male pre-eminence and power), is central within the formation of both identity and sexuality; and, since women are defined as the Other in relation to the phallus, their identity and sexuality can never be positive. The woman does not have an identity of her own, but is defined as a not-male, denoting a negative identity. Women's relationship to the symbolic order will always be negative; they will always be represented as incomplete, as lacking (Lacan, 1977; Mitchell and Rose, 1982). The consequences of this are that femininity itself becomes an impossible conundrum because women are always defined as 'other' within the symbolic order.[49] Hence for many women madness is an almost inevitable outcome, inasmuch as women's gender is defined in terms of negative social relations and is contradictory. Within this framework the possibility of change may seem unlikely, for, as Irigaray comments,

> When he [Nietzsche] says that God is dead, it seems that the collapse of this keystone of a transcendental system leads to the carriers of the phallus becoming gods themselves. Why is phallic culture so important after the fall of the gods? Because the carriers of the phallus want to be gods themselves. It is terrifying.
>
> (Irigaray, 1988: 161)

Psychoanalytic feminists argue that the explanation for the need for the 'carrier of the phallus' to act God goes back to the mother, for men desire power over women so that 'they can create the earliest relationship with the omnipotent mother, this time with the positions reversed' (Baruch and Serrano, 1988: 18). When men realize the fragility and vulnerability of their position – the fact that the signifier, the penis, is in reality 'a pitiful instrument; little, weak, fragile, ineffectual, unpredictable, unreliable, passive, impotent [with] all the traits that men have stereotypically attributed to women' (Baruch and Serrano, 1988: 19) – their envy of the womb, their fear of the woman fuels their desire to maintain woman as the Other. In this position she is no threat, and the phallus can continue to reign supreme – the man, possessor of the sexualized signifier, the woman as Other: as mad. But perhaps not for long.

Dethroning the phallus

> In deconstructing the old psychoanalysis, the new one often reverses its terms. For example, we would say that the baby is less a substitute for a phallus than the phallus is a substitute for a baby.
>
> (Baruch and Serrano, 1988: 13)

What may initially appear to be a reductionist and pessimistic analysis of women's experience within a phallocentric symbolic order is reframed and reconstructed by numbers of feminist psychoanalytic theorists, each proposing a different arena for change, focusing either on the language, or on the body, in the post-structuralist Lacanian view, or on the position of the mother, in the object relations view; each offering hope for a world where the phallus is no longer 'the landlord of the world' (Baruch and Serrano, 1988: 19).

In the feminist revision of the Lacanian view adopted and developed by the French feminists, because the symbolic order is constructed through linguistic representation, it is in the sphere of language that change must take place in order to move towards a position where femininity is not deemed to be a negation, and where woman is not the Other. Thus the French analyst, Luce Irigaray, argues:

> The so-called universal discourse, whether it be philosophic, scientific, or literary is sexualised and mainly in a masculine way. It is necessary to unveil it, to interpret it, and at the same time to begin to speak a language which corresponds better to, and in continuity with, our own pleasure, our own sensuality, our own creativity.
>
> (Irigaray, 1988: 161)

Irigaray proposed a dismantling of the phallic discourse, advocating a gynocentric perspective, in which women's sexuality is celebrated through the creation of a new semiotic language for women. One of the ways in which this has been achieved is through the creation by the French feminists of *l'écriture feminine* which attempts to reach the pre-Oedipal language which preceded the pre-eminence of phallus, and instead to emphasize the body, blood and milk; women's pleasure; women's cycles.[50] Thus there is advocated a new form of women's writing which allows women to 'feel the political fecundity of mucus, milk, sperm, secretions which gush out to liberate energies and give them back to the world' (Chawaf, 1988: 178). This is how the phallus is dethroned – through language, and in particular through writing. As Hélène Cixous claims:

> It is by writing, from and toward women, and by taking up the challenge of speech which has been governed by the phallus, that women will confirm women in a place other than that which is reserved in and by the symbolic, that is, in a place other than silence.
>
> (Cixous, 1988: 251)

Luce Irigaray pursues this argument, emphasizing the woman's body and sexuality through declaring that women's femininity and identity are located in biology; a biology which is distinctive because of women's sexual organs. It is the self-contained nature of women's sexuality that is of the essence, for 'a woman "touches herself" constantly without anyone being able to forbid her to do so, for her sex is composed of two lips which embrace continually' (Irigaray, 1988: 100). Men alienate women from their essential selves, and from their sexuality, coercing them into passivity in the face of male desire, and causing women to be trapped in the voyeuristic gaze of men – 'captive when a man holds me in his gaze . . . abducted from myself . . . trapped in a single function – mothering' (Irigaray, 1981: 66). Like Rich, Irigaray commands women to take control of their destiny through their bodies and their sexuality, declaring, 'touch yourself, touch me, you'll see' (Irigaray, 1980: 78). One must write through the body, she urges, reclaiming and emphasizing sexuality, emphasizing pleasure, for 'woman has sex organs just about everywhere. She experiences pleasure almost everywhere' (Irigaray, 1986: 153). According to Irigaray, we need to affirm our womanhood, celebrate our difference:

> It is necessary that women discover their own autoeroticism, that they reveal themselves to each other and leave their rivalries, the hatreds that have been imposed on them as competitive merchandise in the marketplace.
>
> (Irigaray, 1986: 162)

This view, epitomized by Irigaray and Cixous, emphasizes women's essential *difference* from men, as do many of the radical feminists discussed above. By contrast, Julia Kristeva believes that women are repressed by their social position and confinement to a rhythmic, non-arbitrary, semiotic order. She emphasizes *similarity*, arguing that 'The woman' or femininity is not tied to gender – it can be possessed by both men and women, through a subversion of the symbolic order within semiotic language, a process most clearly seen in art. Thus women need not reject the phallic attributes of language, for they are not inevitably male. Women can subvert the language and reclaim it as their own. Both the phallus and the semiotic language are thus open to both men and to women:

> If women have a role to play . . . it is only in assuming a *negative* function: reject everything finite, definite, structured, loaded with meaning, in the existing state of society . . . By 'woman' I mean that which cannot be represented, what is not said, what remains above and beyond nomenclatures and ideologies. There are certain 'men' who are familiar with this phenomenon.
>
> (Kristeva, 1986: 137–8, 161)

The women of the *l'écriture feminine*, typified by Irigaray, Kristeva and Cixous, oppose the positioning of women's bodily experiences as negative within phallocentric discourse; and sexuality, the body, and the new female discourse and writing that comes from the body, all provide the means for women to discover what we really are, and thus escape from the phallocentric discourse that makes women mad.

However, the psychoanalytic feminists such as Dorothy Dinnerstein and Nancy Chodorow, who look to object relations theories for their inspiration and who argue for an emphasis on the *similarity* between men and women, see the problem differently. Their contention is that an understanding of oppression of women, and thus of madness, can be reached by examining childbearing patterns, for 'So long as the first parent is a woman, then, woman will be inevitably pressed into the dual role of indispensable quasi-human supporter and deadly quasi-human enemy of the self' (Dinnerstein, 1976: 111–12). Dinnerstein takes her lead from Melanie Klein, who described children as harbouring an idealized image of the mother as a being who can satisfy every desire, thus leading the child to both love and hate the mother as a result of being both gratified and frustrated by her (Klein, 1952). The child loves and desires the mother, yet is both angry and full of hatred for her as the all-powerful creature – part-monster, part-madonna – who can not fulfil all needs. The child is terrified of the mother, fearing that she may retaliate for this hatred. To cope with this conflict of feelings and desires, the love and hatred, the child splits off the bad feelings, resulting in an idealized image of the mother (and subsequently all women) as being good and bountiful. The joining together of the two split images of the mother, the loved and hated parts, can lead to what Klein termed the 'depressive position' – to madness. It is the creation of this split, idealized image of woman, and the fear of domination by her, which is seen as being the root of men's domination within society – we escape our fear of women by accepting domination by men, and positioning women as powerless victims, both denigrated and desired. In Dinnerstein's words:

> The early mother's apparent omnipotence, . . . her ambivalent role as ultimate source of good and evil, is a central source of human malaise . . . Women . . . are both the most acceptable and the most accepting victims of the human need for a quasi-source of richness and target of greedy rage. If this were not the case, if there did not exist a special category of human being who seems on an infant level of thought naturally fit to fulfil this infantile need, our species might be forced to outgrow it.
>
> (Dinnerstein, 1976: 100–2)

Here Dinnerstein is in agreement with the object relations theorist, Donald Winnicott, who argued that 'the woman figure of primitive unconscious fantasy has no limits to her existence or power' and that 'the tendency of groups of people to accept or even seek actual domination is derived from a fear of domination by fantasy woman' (Dinnerstein, 1976: 165). The fear of fantasy woman is found in images of women throughout history, in the juxtaposition of the ubiquitous madonna/whore. Both men and women are imbued with fears and fantasies about the mother, men wanting to dominate, women not being able to accept independence and separation.

Nancy Chodorow has explicitly examined some of the implications of mothering on the identity and psychological make-up of women, arguing that 'because of their mothering by women, girls come to experience themselves as less separate than boys, as having more permeable ego boundaries' and that 'girls come to define themselves in relation to others' (Chodorow, 1978: 93). Men are not immune to the effects of mothering either, as Chodorow says:

> Psychologists have demonstrated unequivocally that the very fact of being mothered by a woman generates in men conflicts over masculinity, a psychology of male dominance, and a need to be superior to women.
>
> (Chodorow, 1978: 185)

The difficulty women have in separating from the mother, and the way in which many mothers fulfil their own needs through their children, and particularly their daughters, is of central importance in any deconstruction of women's madness (Miller, 1982; Orbach, 1986). It is certainly not a healthy state of affairs for women as it is the centrality of women as mothers that ensures 'men's location in the public sphere' which 'defines society itself as masculine' and 'gives men power to create and enforce institutions of social and political control' (Chodorow, 1978: 9).

In this view, the willingness of women to be dominated by men, and the positioning of women as 'quasi-human enemy of the self ', is very much located within the family. One solution offered is that inequality and oppression could be overcome by a rearrangement of childcare patterns, with men taking a more equal role, so that the woman as mother is no longer feared and envied. This would apparently signal an end to misogyny, to pornography,[51] to male domination of society and to madness. For if 'women's mothering is a central and defining feature of the social organization of gender and is implicated in the construction and organization of male dominance itself ' (Chodorow, 1978: 9), a rearrangement of mothering roles will have far-reaching implications for every aspect of women's experience, madness included. It is a simple route from misery to emancipation and freedom. The consequences of 'collective childrearing' would be that:

> The unhappiness of many women would be eliminated if their men provided them with the same nurturance they offer them, if their children had loving fathers, and if they were able to use their other talents in the world.
>
> (French, 1978: 534)

The other solution to the dethroning of the phallus and the affirmation of women's sanity is therapy. For, whilst criticism of the traditional therapies is accepted by most protagonists in these debates, there are many who would consider the wholesale disregard of therapy a case of throwing out the baby with the bathwater. Although some theorists, such as the continuously critical Mary Daly, claim that 'the concept of "feminist" therapy is inherently a contradiction' (Daly, 1979: 282), many *have* advocated feminist therapy, which appears in many different incarnations, including the psychoanalytic, but in general it does not distinguish between the subjective and objective, and does not pathologize the woman. It allows us to recognize women's anger, women's despair, and offers more than a theoretical analysis of woman's situation.

Feminist therapy

> Now women are replacing this competitive way of relating to one another with collective co-operative systems; instead of fighting one another we lend each other support and are thereby building a base of strength, which, when translated into power politics, is effecting important social changes.
>
> (Mander, 1977: 285)

> Psychoanalytic psychotherapy *is* capable of offering insights and experiences which are congruent with, and can contribute to, progressive political changes.
>
> (Frosh, 1987: 211)

As I have outlined above, therapy has been placed under the feminist microscope and emerged not looking particularly healthy. Traditional therapy is seen as enforcing gender stereotypes, maintaining women's powerlessness and pathologizing women's anger. It diverts attention away from the *real* root of the problem – the social oppression of women – and, if it does anything positive, it provides merely a short-term panacea for distress, sticking plaster which may cause more harm in the long run, by stemming other protests or actions, and concentrating on the individual woman and her supposed madness. Yet women *are distressed*, and many feminists have acknowledged this reality by arguing that a new form of women-centred non-sexist or feminist therapy can evolve, where women are helped, but not blamed or made to feel at fault. Women could be working together, rather than experiencing pain in isolation.

Feminist therapy is generally acknowledged to be a perspective, rather than a technique. Those who practise under the umbrella of feminist therapy may use different techniques or theoretical paradigms, paradigms which draw on the theoretical positions of the different feminist groups, above, or which draw on the frameworks evolved by the theorists discussed in Chapter 4, such as psychoanalytic, behavioural, cognitive and humanistic. Through the use of therapy as a 'rich and inclusive political practice' (Ernst and Goodison, 1981: 303) feminists have attempted to reconcile the problems in traditional expert interventions and the structural and political problems in society with the needs of women to receive help. They acknowledge that the women are distressed, but that this is not because of an inherent weakness or illness within the woman. As there are few supports for women in their natural environments and many reasons for distress, feminist therapy is seen as beneficial through providing some support, and empowering women to seek solutions.

Power is of central concern within feminist analyses, and the critiques of the abuse of power in therapy are high on the agenda. The madness for which women are treated is seen as a response to powerlessness, whether it be manifested in eating disorders, depression, self-harm or anxiety. Feminist therapy attempts to allow women to speak in ways other than through their bodies, or through pain, or thwarted protest; to enable them to find a voice which is clear and strong, 'making explicit the social processes that delimit women's use of, and access to power . . . enabling the lessening of shame or blame women may feel about the power they use' (Watson and Williams, 1991: 10). Thus the therapeutic situation is not removed from the real world, for many would argue that:

> The inferior status of women is due to their having less political and economic power than men. Feminist therapists focus on social rather than hormonal or anatomical factors . . . feminists all agree that the basic problem is the power differential between males and females.
>
> (Rawlings and Carter, 1977: 54)

As there is a recognition that women are disempowered in their worlds, so there is a commitment to avoid reconstructing this power imbalance in the therapy setting. Thus there is emphasis on an egalitarian relationship between client and therapist, as Penfold and Walker illustrate:

> Hallmarks of feminist therapy are its commitment to feminist principles, the application of a feminist analysis to women's current situation, and its grounding in current research about women. The approach is egalitarian, with a careful avoidance of the one-down position and a recognition of the importance of the therapist as a role model.
>
> (Penfold and Walker, 1984: 233)

Others have averred that feminist therapy encourages women to recognize their self-worth and their need both to nurture and be nurtured, and that it encourages co-operation and solidarity between women (Ernst and Goodison, 1981: 318). It has been claimed that 'feminist therapy recognizes the interconnectedness of the "inner" psychological and "outer" social and material worlds' (Chaplin, 1988: 40) and that the effects of the oppression within a patriarchal society on women's inner feelings and experiences are high on the agenda. The woman herself is certainly not pathologized for her unhappiness. Instead, she is encouraged to have 'raised consciousness' about the role which patriarchal oppression plays in her madness:

> The assumption which is shared by all feminists involved in therapy . . . is that as women we are brought up to be second-class citizens in a male-defined world, and that this deeply affects our emotional lives. It follows that the role of a feminist therapist, or a feminist self-help therapy group, is not to adjust us to being second-class citizens but to help us to explore how this experience has affected us, what a struggle it is to have your ways of seeing the world validated, and how we can make ourselves stronger.
>
> (Ernst and Goodison, 1981)

Not only are women encouraged to consider their oppression in feminist therapy, they are frequently encouraged to be angry, to own their true feelings, and to shout out against the oppressors (Hunter and Kelso, 1985: 202). Women have thus transformed the consciousness training group into therapy. There is in this an assumption that therapy takes place as much *outside* the consulting room as within, with the personal and the political being inseparable. Thus, women therapists become involved in legal and social action alongside their clients, as in the White City project in London (Holland, 1992) or in rape crisis or incest survivor groups (Watson and Williams, 1991). The therapy is thus aimed at creating social change, as much as it is at creating personal change, for it is recognized that only through change in the patriarchal power structures will women ever be free. In feminist therapy:

> The commitment was to change, not adjustment, and to client not therapist defined change. It was widely assumed that women who engaged in this process of change were likely to become politically aware and involved in social action.
>
> (Watson and Williams, 1991: 4)

It has also been argued that all therapists themselves *should* become involved in social and political action (Rawlings and Carter, 1977: 63)

Many of the assumptions about women, and about madness and normality, are challenged in feminist therapies. For example, women's anger, which may be constructed as pathological, is deemed to be normal and healthy, and thus 'using a sex-role analysis a feminist therapist could assist the patient in articulating the basis of her anger and channel it in constructive ways' (Rawlings and Carter, 1977: 83).

The actual work which goes on within the therapy, and the way in which problems are addressed will depend on the orientation of the therapists. There can therefore be no 'shopping list' of ingredients for feminist therapy, no list of steps to follow to produce the right solution, no recipe which, successfully followed, will produce the perfect feminist therapist. Attempts have been made to summarize some of the essential ingredients in the therapy, which include demystifying both the therapy process and the therapist, strengthening the client's rights in therapy, encouraging the client's active participation and seeing the client as expert.[52] Others contend that any written information should be made available to the client, the use of diagnostic labels should be avoided and the therapist should make clear her own values and beliefs as a vital part of the therapeutic agenda (Rawlings and Carter, 1977: 53). The power imbalances inherent within traditional therapy would thus be eroded.

Using many of these premises as part of the therapeutic contract, a whole gamut of different therapeutic approaches has been brought into feminist therapy, on either an individual, a group or a family basis. For example, the principles of humanistic therapy, where the client is valued and treated in a caring and equal manner, have been incorporated by feminists, as it has been claimed that:

> What feminist therapy does, in part, is to explicitly extend the humanistic view of human nature to include women as well as men . . . feminist therapy has developed a feminist humanism.
>
> (Sturdivant, 1980: 88)

Others have advanced the idea that feminist behaviour therapy can be developed using the principles of modelling, assertiveness training and social skills training (Hunter and Kelso, 1985). More recently, however, this emphasis on skills teaching has been criticized as it emphasizes the *deficit* in women, rather than attending to the social change that is needed (Fodor, 1985). It also encourages women to behave in ways valued within competitive patriarchal society, rather than challenging the very values of this society, the patriarchal discourse itself.

Group therapy which emphasizes the importance of sharing feelings of oppression and pain, has also been a major aspect of feminist alternatives to patriarchal therapies, as has feminist family therapy. It has been argued that feminist theories can reformulate gender divisions within the family, enabling them to 'lend family therapists a coherent theory of how gender is constructed within families' (Leupnitz, 1988), and thus to reconstruct family theories within an historical perspective which acknowledges the oppression of women. Family interventions that *don't* blame the mother are seen as being able to reconstruct a positive psychology of women for more than one generation (Vetere, 1992; Malson, 1991).

Yet the area of theory and therapy which has produced the most prolific writers and critics in the last decades has been the one perhaps most vigorously criticized by the early feminists – psychoanalysis. Object relations theory has been incorporated into the work of women such as Orbach and Eichenbaum, who set up the Women's Therapy Centres in London and New York, and who believe that 'the work that the therapist and the client do is a work of creation' (Orbach, 1986: 165). Equally, Freudian, Kleinian and Lacanian theories have all been incorporated into a feminist psychoanalysis[53] as ideas have changed:

> Formerly, the little girl, the adolescent girl, and the woman all had to turn to the father or his representatives in order to be separate from the mother. Father, instructor, seducer, were one in their internal fantasy. It is now the analyst (often the woman analyst) who has become the mother/mentor, who allows the daughter to separate and individuate . . . the father has been largely replaced . . . women want to enter and define culture directly, not through the intermediary of a male surrogate . . . the new psychoanalysis . . . will further that quest (Baruch and Serrano, 1988: 24)

Psychoanalysis thus allows feminists to work directly in the area where the effects of the phallocentric discourse are felt – the unconscious – enabling 'patients to become fully conscious of the gap that exists between illusory and actual fulfilment of their needs' (Sayers, 1986: 180). It thus works towards changing their reality.

Para-therapeutic proposals

In addition to acknowledging the problems inherent in 'therapy' whilst making a response to women's need for help that recognizes the reality of women's madness, women have put forward proposals that I would term 'para-professional'. These might include consciousness raising, crisis intervention (such as rape crisis), or social and practical support such as that found in women's refuges or in community interventions.[54] Feminist responses to the reality and direct consequences of women's madness are thus not solely therapeutic.

Conclusion

In the main, the criticisms made by feminists are not dissimilar from those of the male dissenters. They acknowledge the sociopolitical roots of madness, they refute the concept of madness as illness, and they condemn the experts, be they physicians, psychologists or psychiatrists. The feminists move away from pathological explanations for women's madness, presenting a different analysis, a 'different voice'. The phenomenon treated by the medical profession as illness is seen by feminists as the result of women's position in society, their subjective experiences of their gendered identity, not the result of a biological vulnerability. And, if the body has a role in this madness, it is because of the phallocentric discourse which positions the woman as Other, not because of an inherent weakness or lack of ability. Thus there is a deconstruction of existing frameworks, and some suggestions for alternatives in the form of a feminine language, changes in childrearing and feminist therapy. It is, perhaps, more constructive than the male dissenters who seemed content to deconstruct and be damned.

But this is not the end of the story. This is not the solution to the analysis of women's madness. It is not enough to deconstruct the existing order and its power structures in an effort to explain women's inequality and madness. Merely to propose political change, change in childrearing practices, a new form of women's writing, to reclaim the body, or offer a feminist therapy are insufficient. We cannot simply accept the criticisms and sweep away the existing concepts and controls. For if we do, we may be left with nothing more than empty rhetoric and polemical arguments; arguments which offer very little of substance to the object of the critical gaze – the woman deemed mad – as her experience is reduced to the status of a theoretical construct. Many of the theories and solutions proposed by the antipsychiatrists, the sociologists and the feminist critics are insubstantial and unsubstantiated. They are as full of holes as a sieve, and ultimately fail to answer the questions: What is women's madness? and What can we do for the woman herself? Thus the challenge to the dissenters themselves is on. We need to turn our critical gaze on the critics themselves.

Notes

1. See Brown and Harris 1978.
2. See Russo 1990; Eaton and Kessler 1985; Gove and Tudor 1973.
3. European Mental Health statistics.
4. See Gove 1979 for a review of these different studies. See also *Social trends* (HMSO) for more recent information on gender differences in hospitalization in Britain.
5. The motivation behind such research is to overcome the bias and unrepresentative nature of studies of psychiatric referrals or hospital admissions.
6. See Gove and Tudor 1979; Weissman and Klerman 1976; Goldman and Ravid 1980; Mowbray and Benedek 1988.
7. From Mental Illness Tables A2.2 and A2.3 (*mental health statistics for England, 1986*, Booklet 1).
8. All of the epidemiological surveys point to the conclusion that 'personality disorders' are also more common in men: summarized by Gove 1979, Briscoe 1982.

9. See *mental health statistics for England, 1988*; Russo and Sobel 1981; Dohrenwend and Dohrenwend 1966, for evidence that men are diagnosed more frequently as having alcohol problems.
10. Working-class men, those who are unemployed and ethnic minorities are also at higher risk of diagnosis of madness. See, for example, Jenkins 1986; Hollingshead and Redlich 1958.
11. Reliability of psychiatric diagnosis is poor, varying between 20 per cent and 63 per cent consistency between experts making the diagnosis in different studies (Busfield 1986: 66). There are also suggestions that the 'symptoms' used as indices of schizophrenia in men are different from those used in the diagnosis of schizophrenic women (Al-Assa 1980), which may mean that different criteria may be used in making official diagnoses of men and women.
12. See Jones and Cochrane 1981; Philips 1985; Thorne 1984; Swenson and Ragucci 1984, for more recent research replicating the Broverman findings.
13. This was suggested by Bassoff and Glass 1982 in a meta-analysis of twenty-six studies on gender and mental health, carried out between 1961 and 1980.
14. Abromowitz *et al.* 1976 showed that women who challenge accepted values were more likely to be given a psychiatric diagnosis; Feinblatt and Gold 1976 reported that aggressive girls were deemed more disturbed than aggressive boys.
15. Freud 1895 (7): 28. Briefly, Dora was a sixteen-year-old woman whom Freud treated in 1900, on the instigation of her father. Dora had been 'approached' sexually by Herr K, a friend of her father, and husband of the woman with whom her father was having a sexual liaison. This approach was the second such incident, Herr K having previously attempted a forced seduction when Dora was fourteen. Dora responded to the attempted sexual assault, perhaps not surprisingly, by running away. This is deemed unnatural by Freud, who declared: 'Instead of the genital response which would certainly have been felt by a healthy girl in such circumstances . . . Dora was overcome by the unpleasurable feeling . . . that is disgust'. Dora's rejection of her pursuer was interpreted as pathological and in Mary Daly's eyes 'announces that any woman who does not enjoy rape is hysterical' (Daly, 1979: 267).
16. See Allen 1987: 113 for a further discussion of this process.
17. Section 3 of the British Mental Health Act forcibly contains those deemed to be a danger to themselves or others for periods of six months at a time. Section 37, a hospital order, detains those undergoing criminal proceedings for which the mitigating circumstance are deemed to be psychiatric illness (Burns 1992a).
18. There are some instances of secure psychiatric treatment wherein men do not clearly predominate. For example, the statistics on regional secure units for 1986 in Britain showed that 2,592 men as opposed to 2,021 women were detained. These women are those who would have been most likely to have been treated as criminals and sentenced to prison, had they been men: women whose deviant behaviour was not merely mad, but also bad.
19. As Valerie Hey (1985: 76) suggests: 'Are women's "non-feminine" actions more likely to be interpreted by a medical model because we cannot accept that women commit such actions for the very same reasons as men? Or is it that women have reasons apart from biology to account for violent criminal and destructive urges?' To position women's deviant behaviour as mad is to dismiss it, to remove any onus on the society to reflect upon *why* this act was

carried out, and to remove any element of reason from the woman herself. She is pathologized as she is dismissed. For men their crimes, their violence, are seen almost as a normal part of masculinity. For as Jan Burns argues, 'It seems to be the expectation that men inherently have strong, violent emotions which they constantly have to keep under control, but which under "unreasonable" provocation, especially sexual jealousy, can break out of control and have violent and irreversible consequences. The blame for such consequences may lie at the man's feet for losing control, but the provocation he was under is usually used and accepted as powerful mitigating circumstances' (Burns 1991: 9).

20. Plath, 'Poem for a Birthday', 1959, in Plath 1981.
21. Quoted by Showalter 1987: 207.
22. Elaine Showalter reviews much of the women's literature on this subject in a concise and lucid manner (Showalter 1987: 210–19).
23. Quoted by Showalter 1987: 211.
24. See Burman 1990 for a discussion of women who have left psychology.
25. Although Freud was adamant that sex between therapist and patient could only be harmful, Jung engaged in sexual relationships with at least one of his female clients, as Masson 1989: 218 outlines.
26. Taylor and Wagner 1976 review this early research.
27. Davidson 1984: 364 discusses the suppression of such a report by Dahlberg, and speculates on how many others have met a similar fate.
28. Schoener *et al.* 1984 report that out of 250 known cases only four were of female therapist/male client.
29. *Report of the senate task force on psychotherapists' and patients' sexual relations*, March 1987. Quoted in Masson 1988: 224.
30. *Ibid.*
31. Chesler 1972, Masson 1984 and Dahlberg 1970 cite such examples.
32. Schoener *et al* 1984 cite the most common effects of sex with a therapist as being guilt and shame, grief, anger, depression and loss of self-esteem, ambivalence and confusion, fear and massive distrust.
33. Stone 1984 and Davidson 1984 discuss these explanations for the absence of action in these cases.
34. See Holmes and Lindley 1989 for further discussion of this issue.
35. As Lynne Segal argues, in her discussion of the eroticization of power in pornography, 'Feminists need to admit, rather than to deny, that at present many standard images of pornography do arouse women as well as men. Given the link between sex and the intensities of feeling about dependence and power which transport us back to those of childhood, perhaps we will always, at least in fantasy, tend to eroticize relations of power and hostility' (Segal 1990: 231–2).
36. Chesler 1972 provides graphic evidence of this in the quotations from abused women.
37. Estimates are that over 45 per cent of women who are receiving therapy or psychiatric care have been sexually abused.
38. Citing Dahlberg 1970 and Boas 1966 as evidence.
39. Also see Leupnitz 1988 for a general critique of family therapy, with suggestions for feminist alternatives. See Malson 1992 for an analysis of family therapy in relation to anorexia and Vetere 1992 in relation to clinical psychology.
40. Juliet Mitchell 1974 provides an analysis of some of these feminist critiques

in her book which reclaims Freud as positive for feminism.

41. There are also many women who actually reject the term 'feminism', seeing it as something which has been co-opted by the dominant order, as yet another -ism. Yet many of these women are still critical, are still challenging the discourses associated with women and thus have much in common with those such as myself who still espouse the feminist label.
42. Those well versed in feminist theory may find this a superficial and simplistic analysis: however, it is not intended to provide a complete dissection of the many strands of feminist theory, for which the reader is referred to more specialist texts.
43. See Segal 1987: 70–116 for a lucid and critical account of the role of sexuality in feminist theorizing.
44. See Chadwick 1990: 344 for a discussion of this in relation to art history.
45. See Sayers 1986 and Mitchell 1974 for excellent and readable accounts of psychoanalysis and feminism. To examine the role of psychoanalysis in feminist literary theory see Rose 1986. Interested readers should also examine the source materials of Klein, Winnicott, Freud and Lacan, as these form the foundations of the feminist critiques.
46. Although Rich 1979 draws on psychoanalytic theories in her understanding of the mother–daughter relationship.
47. See Sayers 1991 for a discussion of women analysts and their revaluing of the mother.
48. See Baruch and Serrano 1988 for a discussion of the different analytic theorists and their views of feminism and women, in their interviews with British, American and French women analysts.
49. 'The women' does not mean real women, for when Lacan says 'the woman does not exist' he is referring to the feminine/not-I position rather than actual women (Mitchell and Rose 1982).
50. Marks and de Courtivron 1986 provide an anthology of these writings which are an excellent introduction to the subject.
51. Susan Griffin 1981 has argued that the pleasure gained from pornography can be understood in terms of the defences children adopt in order to cope with the pain of the mother's separate nature.
52. These are the main themes discussed by Watson and Williams 1992.
53. See Baruch and Serrano 1988, Mitchell 1974 for descriptions of feminist psychoanalysis.
54. See Watson and Williams for a discussion of the various feminist practices. Also see Holland 1992 for a discussion of a community-based intervention. Eichenbaum and Orbach 1983 discuss many of the general issues.

PART Four

Moving forwards; facts, fictions, realities

8

The challenge to the critics

myopia...
Theoretical myopia, associated with a striking degree of know nothingness, left the radical psychiatrists unable to pay attention to the real subjective phenomena of emotional disturbance.

(Kovel, 1982: 100)

failure...
Their challenge to the role of traditional psychology and psychiatry as tools of social control was limited by their failure to create a fundamentally new form of psychology that not only considered the racial or gender background of the practitioner ... or broke down authoritarian therapist/patient relationships, but which sought to challenge the traditional bottom line commitment to adaptation and sought to replace it with a commitment to empowerment.

(Fulini, 1987: xvi)

action...
The revisionists ... can expose the hypocrisies and annotate the tragedies of official psychiatry, but the concepts which they have developed enable them to engage in no public action grander than that of wringing their hands.

(Sedgewick, 1982: 41)

mothering...
In its fascination with the mother–child relationship [mothering theory] cannot offer a full account of patriarchy as a social structure which operates over and above the interactions between individuals and which, indeed, structures those interactions. The fact of female mothering cannot hold all the explanatory weight

> placed upon it, because without a theory of the positioning of this fact it has no power at all.
>
> (Frosh, 1987: 92)

> *sexuality. . .*
> Is women's sexuality so monolithic that a notion of a shared, typical femininity does justice to it? What about variations in class, in race and in culture among women? What about changes over time in *one* woman's sexuality (with men, with women, by herself)? How can one libidinal voice – or two vulva lips so strikingly presented by Irigaray – speak for all women?
>
> (Jones, 1985: 93)

Is it the case that the radical critiques which attempted to overturn our models of madness are inevitably faded and jaded, that 'today's radicalism ossifies into tomorrow's dogma' (Bynum *et al.*, 1988: 4). The dissension epitomized by the antipsychiatry movement reopened and placed in the public arena the debate about the meaning of madness, the role of the experts and the relationship between biological and social phenomena. The feminist theories placed the 'woman question' at the centre of the discussion. They all challenged and questioned, providing impetus for change which can still be seen today. Yet their radicalism has been short-lived. Much of the early work, particularly that carried out in the ever-hopeful sixties and seventies, did not fulfil its promise. It has perhaps proved naïve in many of its assumptions, often doing a disservice to those it claimed to defend, when it resulted in the removal of basic services, criticized as oppressive, but not replaced with any different framework or support. The dissenters rightly condemned the old order, the exploitations of power, the inadequacies in the theorizing; but they fell into the old trap of criticizing without effectively revising, deconstructing without reconstructing, since no real working alternative to the oppressive treatment or models of madness was ever mooted. The deconstruction of madness alone does not remove a woman's unhappiness, nor does it remove her 'symptoms'. Thus a purely deconstructionist academic or a seductive polemical approach is short-sighted, and ultimately can be as oppressive as the models and methods it sets out to condemn. The solutions offered by the critics are invariably unidirectional, idealistic and utopian – or no different from the vigorously criticized models, in spite of all the relabelling and renaming.

Recent critics, while exposing the failures in the supposedly radical arguments, have turned their sceptical gaze on the antipsychiatrists, on the feminists, on the dissenters themselves, arguing that many of their theories were naïve rather than revolutionary, and that they too have failed as clearly as the experts they condemn.[1] Women's madness is still misunderstood.

Illness and madness – worlds apart?

> All diseases are hypothetical, all are labels. There is no such thing as diabetes, there are only individuals who have certain experiences and physical symptoms which are said to have some relation to the hypothetical disease.
>
> (Siegler and Osmond, 1966)

One of the major objectives of many of the antipsychiatrists was to emphasize the subjective, value-laden and political nature of psychiatric diagnosis, and consequently the inapplicability of positivistic methodologies in the field of madness. They dismissed psychiatry whilst simultaneously supporting the notion that physical medicine is apolitical, value-free and objective – a notion which does not bear any careful scrutiny. Madness may well be a social construction, but it could also be argued that *all* illness is socially constructed. For as Dingwall has argued, the debate centring on the applicability of illness concepts to psychiatry has 'almost invariably presupposed a split between mind and body, between physical and psychiatric illness' (Dingwall, 1976: 49) – a split which may be erroneous. This Cartesian dualism has haunted the debates on health and illness since Hippocrates. The radicals have fallen into the same trap, and, as a result, may prevent our reaching a greater understanding of women's mental and physical health.

So one of the main tenets of the antipsychiatrists' case, that diagnosis of madness is subjective and political in contrast to the more objective diagnosis of physical illness, may be erroneous. As Clare illustrates, in his analysis of dyspepsia, physical medicine involves a 'complicated evaluative process' which is certainly not as cut and dried as is claimed by some (Clare, 1976). The dissenters' arguments have thus been termed 'semantic gymnastics' (Clare, 1976: 3), serving only to obscure reality.[2]

But, as Sedgewick argues, rather than attempting to strip psychiatric diagnosis of its politics, should we not recognize that there is an element of politics, of subjectivity, of value judgements, in *all* illness? Should we not, recognizing that our definitions of physical illness are also largely socially constructed, be examining the very concept of illness itself?

Sedgewick claims that 'the attribution of illness always proceeds from a gap between the behaviour (or feeling) and some social norm' (Sedgewick, 1982: 34). Thus the man who complains to the doctor that he cannot climb the stairs without resting every few seconds might be deemed ill, until we have the information that he is ninety-eight years old and lives on the sixth floor of a tower block. We then see his need to rest as normal behaviour. The woman complaining of aches and pains on waking every morning escapes a diagnosis of illness when we discover that she is a traveller who sleeps in a tent on uneven ground. How many people, having experienced the 'morning after' sensation of a hangover after consuming alcohol, have tolerated symptoms which in any other circumstances would result in an immediate visit to the doctor? Thus the person's perception of themselves as ill is an important variable and is not a consistent objective factor. Diagnosis of any 'illness', physical or mental, will depend on an evaluation by the patient and the observer. It is not as cut and dried as the dissenters would have us believe.

It has also been shown that tolerance or acceptance of symptoms, or conversely, the attribution of illness to one's self varies between people, between cultures,[3] and between social classes.[4] As Clare notes:

> No objective norms of physical well-being exist and what one man defines as personal malaise or ill health another tolerates as one of the slings and arrows that flesh is heir to.
>
> (Clare, 1976: 10)

It has, in fact, been suggested that every person experiences some symptom which, if presented to the relevant clinician, could be seen as a symptom of illness (Briscoe, 1982). So are we all 'ill' in reality?

It has also been demonstrated that what is clearly 'disease' in one culture is 'health' in another. For example, in one South American Indian tribe the disease of dyschronic spirochetosis, which is marked by the appearance of coloured spots on the skin, was so 'normal' that those who did not have them were regarded as pathological and excluded from marriage (Sedgewick, 1982: 32). Drug use (conceived always as addiction) is now deemed an 'illness' in Britain, but a normal part of life in other cultures, particularly where the so-called 'soft' drugs are concerned. Hyperactivity in children, premenstrual syndrome, post-natal depression and the menopausal syndrome are among other supposed 'illnesses' which have been challenged as legitimate entities, and which are not found cross-culturally.[5]

One of the difficulties in the organic versus social debate in relation to madness is that the social constructionist analysis beloved by the dissenters really precludes the presence of any physical symptomatology or physical aetiology. Thus they exclude from their analysis any type of madness which might have some organic basis or organic correlates, such as types of dementia, or some psychosis. Where no organic basis can be established, the dissenters (including Laing and Szasz, as well as, ironically, Eysenck and Freud')[6] agree that a social or psychological analysis is appropriate, disputing medical control over these types of madness. The supposedly organic cases can stay in the hands of the medical professionals. Thus, if the cause is physical, it is illness, and thus medical; if it is social, it is madness, and not 'real', but constructed.

But this is far too simple an analysis. It assumes a dichotomy between physical and psychological symptoms, physical and psychological aetiology. This distinction cannot be drawn very easily. Many psychological problems have physical concomitants or symptoms: anxiety, with a clear 'social' aetiology such as worry about an examination, can produce physical symptoms of panic such as hyperventilation, sweating and high blood pressure. Conversely, physical or organic illness can be associated very closely with psychological difficulties: the high incidence of psychological problems experienced by people with AIDS (PWA's) is testimony to that (Ussher, 1990b).[7] Many 'psychological illnesses' such as depression, and psychosis, are undoubtedly *associated* with biochemical changes, or 'brain changes' (Claridge, 1990) but this is not to say that depression or psychosis is *caused by* these physical factors. These might be merely physical concomitants – parts of the whole jigsaw. It is the simple reductionist theory which sees physical (or even social) factors as the single cause of disease that is flawed. These factors may be contributory, or provide reasons for symptomatology, but to imply causation is to apply a reductionist analysis which both strips the individual of control and implies the absence of reason (Ingleby, 1982).

Equally, to imply that madness has *no* physical component is to place it on a different plane from all other human behaviour, as Claridge has argued:

> Some commentators would even wish to deny an inheritable component in *any* human psychological differences, whether these refer to healthy variations or to pathology . . . [this is] to make an absurd assumption: that the nervous system – which is after all the biological vehicle for psychological processes – constitutes the only system in the body immune to genetic influences.
>
> (Claridge, 1990: 175)

This dualism is not only damaging to the development of a useful understanding of psychological and social phenomena, it also encourages a partisan attitude on the part of professionals who restrict themselves to factors deemed to be within their own particular jurisdiction, be they medical or social. It ultimately acts to isolate the individual, in this case the 'mad' woman, from her own experience. And whilst the 'medical model' has been attacked by an array of dissenters, from sociologists to feminists, these critics are in danger of adopting a naïve oppositional position. For, as Sedgewick argues, 'the blanket use of the term "medical model" renders impossible the intelligent discrimination of medicine by its consumer' (Sedgewick, 1982: 146).

One of the further consequences of the rejection of the medical model, and with it all things positivistic, is a rejection of science *per se*. This is not really a step forwards. For whilst there are undoubtedly problems in the positivistic paradigm, which indicate the need for careful interpretation of research results, and scepticism in applying the positivistic methodology to research on human behaviour, there are also contexts where scientific findings are useful. They may not be able to illuminate the complete picture, but the unaminous rejection of positivism is as limited as the approach which uncritically *accepts* scientific findings. The rejection of rigid positivistic analyses should not imply a rejection of rigour or systematic inquiry, although this often appears to be the case.[8]

The tendency for the dissenters to adopt a dichotomous approach to physical/mental illness also reinforces the legitimacy of the role of experts such as psychiatrists, in types of madness deemed to involve a physical aetiology, as would be argued with certain types of schizophrenia. Other non-medical professionals, such as those in clinical psychology in Britain, have reinforced this tendency by stating that their role is with the neurotic population, and that the psychotics should remain under medical control (Eysenck, 1957). As Pilgrim has said, this results in a diversion of attention away from other factors which could alleviate difficulties experienced by those manifesting *all* forms of madness, factors such as:

> A widespread educational policy concerning the tolerance of deviance; a massive increase in the housing stock . . . a democratization of the mental health services to break down medical dominance and to make decisions about patients a matter of negotiation with them not about them; a greater availability of non-coercive, non-invasive methods of helping patients . . . a massive reduction in unemployment . . . and the availability of settings tailored to a variety of needs.
>
> (Pilgrim, 1990: 224)

Thus if the dissenters in any way support the notion that certain types of madness such as those with a physical component should remain in medical hands, they are obviating any other form of societal intervention.

What's in a name? The problems with labelling theory

> Arguably, the use of the term 'mental illness' is in itself not necessarily offensive (what after all is in a name?) and Szasz's

> preoccupation with this issue can be described as moralistic, rather than moral.
>
> (Pilgrim, 1990: 215)

One of the foremost aims of the antipsychiatry movement, both academic and populist, was to remove the 'stigma' of the labels of madness. As in the feminist critiques, the deconstruction of medicalized madness fundamentally challenges the notion of expert intervention, or the existence of madness itself, for it assumes that madness, like beauty, is in the eye of the (prejudiced) beholder. But is this a justifiable endeavour which will result in the de-institutionalization of those formerly labelled as deviants – or is it principally an academic exercise, which actually results in the removal of services which may be beneficial? Is it actually *preventing* a revolution in mental health care?[9]

The other question is this: does it change the experience? As I have argued elsewhere, it is a common practice to change the label of a phenomenon or object which has received bad press (Ussher, 1989). The nuclear power station Windscale had its name changed to Sellafield; PMT changed to PMS. With madness there has been a considerable casting off of derogatory labels in the 1980s, with supposedly radical professionals espousing the 'new' labels in a way which purports to empower, rather than disempower, their 'clients' (no longer 'patients', as this denotes 'illness'). Thus the label 'mental handicap' has been replaced by 'learning difficulties', 'mentally ill' by 'mental health difficulties', 'behavioural disturbance' by 'challenging behaviour' . . . the list is endless. But in a very short space of time, these new labels come to be associated with the same stigma, the same denigration of the individual. They may even be more damaging, partly because they disguise the process of derogatory labelling through the apparently 'positive' new label, and also because they allow the experts to look no further for reform than changing the label they use to refer to their clients. Labels *are* important, and they are certainly powerful, but removing or changing the label may do more to salve the conscience of the professional or the liberal-minded political activist, than it does to serve the needs of the person who is labelled. We need to do more than rename the madness in order to change things. The change to 'mental health problems' rather than 'mental illness' might reduce the stigmatization of those in distress (although this is doubtful, given the research on negative attitudes to madness, whatever its nomenclature). But what it certainly does achieve is a considerable widening of the net of 'expert care', for many different professional groupings can claim jurisdiction over 'mental health'. It is certainly not the sole property of the medical professionals. Renaming may demystify interventions for madness. It may dethrone the reductionist monopolistic medical men. But it empowers a *new* breed of experts to enter the market place of the mad, to pronounce and pontificate, to profit from despair, profiting from madness through peddling the latest cure: the latest therapy. This is not empowering. It further disempowers and objectifies the 'mad'.

There are also many limitations in the socio-statistical model which sees madness as primarily a disturbance in functioning; an inability of an individual to fulfil role functions or carry out their customary role performance (cf. Schwab and Schwab, 1978). The schizophrenic, the agoraphobic and the frigid wife have all been conceptualized in these terms. Yet this cannot account for all types of madness, or provide a complete explanation for *any* madness, and particularly more serious or seriously debilitating forms; and it is thus limited. Madness is much more than deviation from a social role. This view is also limited by its emphasis on relativity, and its tendency, because of its mechanistic emphasis on norms and frequencies, to deny the existence of the distress experienced by those labelled as mad.

The critics seem to be working in a theoretical myopia, using abstract analogies to emphasize their point or, as Scull has argued (1979), using extremes to support their rhetoric. The danger in this is that they may have little to say to those in real distress. The natural culmination of many of the theories of madness is the removal of the labels, but this does not remove the basic problems: the pain, the misery, the distress. The new label, too, soon takes on the old associations.

The negation of reality

> The great value of Foucault's work lies in his insight that madness was a speculum in which normal people saw their own image reversed and distorted. Its major weaknesses are that abstractions confront abstractions in his book and his descriptions of how real men and women thought and acted are often vague and fanciful.
>
> (MacDonald, 1981: xi)

This criticism levelled at Foucault can also be addressed to the other dissenters. In fact, one could argue that much of the discussion and criticism seems to be an intellectual exercise – what Sedgewick termed 'the intelligentsia toying with madness at the end of a pen' (Sedgewick, 1982). Szasz's image of the forcibly incarcerated victim was never a reality for those deemed mad in recent years. Today it is more likely that people are desperately hanging on with the hope of some salvation, whilst the waiting list of the psychiatrist or psychologist on which they have placed themselves recedes slowly in front of them. And whilst the definitions of madness may have been widened to include 'problems with living', it is untenable that we either deny the reality of these problems, or continue to take the extreme cases of psychiatric abuse as the norm. We are left with cobwebs when we attempt to integrate the critical theory into any form of practical intervention or attempt to introduce changes in practices. What Sedgewick said of Foucault, we could also say of the other dissenters:

> Foucault never presents an intelligible account of any psychological syndrome. We are invited to reflect on a number of distressing and unsatisfactory cultural stereotypes of insanity, and then to enter into a human relationship with those unfortunate figments of past or present diagnosis. It is true that the demolition of inaccurate stereotypes may be a preliminary to real dialogue, but we are left without much of a clue how to proceed after Pinel, Tuke and Freud have done their worst.
>
> (Sedgewick, 1982: 146)

Thus there are dangers inherent in the application of rhetorical critiques to the real world because of the neglect of constructive advice as to how to reframe madness other than that of shifting the blame to other institutions such as the family, or to psychiatry itself.

The dissenters profit from the rhetoric, from the critiques, but they do not want to dirty their hands with the *real* questions: What to do about madness? What to say to those who demand help? Their pronouncements may be spellbinding on the conference platform but they can have a hollow ring in the hospital ward or in the doctor's surgery; in the lonely, desperate isolation of the world of many who feel mad, and who want this to be recognized so that the fear can abate. They need someone to understand, not merely to have their pain deconstructed through clever linguistic manipulation. By denying the reality of madness in its myriad forms, with its myriad causes, and using the most extreme examples of abuse as the norm, the dissenters not only make a mockery of themselves, but they insult the people whom supposedly they support – the mad. Their defence may be that the rhetoric and hyperbole are essential in order to highlight the abuses inherent in expert power and 'care'. But they can become captivated by their own mesmerizing arguments, moved or thrilled by the shocking horror of the extremes they portray, forgetting the essential reality and unglamorous actuality of madness as it is for the majority.

The extreme example

The original radical dissenters invariably took very limited views of madness. Thus the work of Laing, Esterman, Cooper and Berke was confined to these diagnosed as schizophrenics, yet it was used, at least by those who emulate the original dissenters, to extrapolate about *general* theories of madness. The manifestations of madness specifically labelled as neuroses, such as anxiety, depression or phobia, were given short shrift by the dissenters. This results in blanket judgements, blanket statements about the aetiology and treatment of extremely complicated human behaviours. We would never lump together physical illnesses such as influenza, heart disease and asthma, assuming a common path of causation and explanation. Yet this is what the dissenters appear to do: madness is a social construction, oppression exemplified. Even if oppression *is* part of madness, and if labelling *is* tyranny in practice, we cannot claim that all the different experiences of those positioned mad are a result of a common chain of events, or that they can be ameliorated in an homogeneous way. As schizophrenia, the archetypal case of madness in the dissenters' eyes, is by far the least common 'presenting problem', the case has even less validity.

In the critiques, hyperbole abounds. It has been argued that Szasz 'takes the worse cases of compulsory detention and treatment of mental patients, and represents them as typical' (Holmes and Lindley, 1989: 102). Jeffrey Masson has done the same. Mental health treatment is represented as abusive, oppressive, demoralizing, coercive and degrading. Treatment may have elements of these damaging constituents inherent within it, and it is undoubtedly true that some mental health professionals behave in a way that adds to the problems of their patients, however inadvertently. But to argue that *all* intervention is analogous to torture, to slavedriving, to the Nazi persecution, to witch trials, as do Szasz and Masson, is surely to take such an extreme case that it is bound to be rejected, and thus will have little impact on the services it sets out to condemn. One explanation for this use of hyperbole is that if the example presented is less extreme, it is more difficult to expose the horrors of therapy and psychiatry: the rhetoric could not unfold seductively, nor could the dissenter present himself (*sic*) as hero.

A further explanation is that the extreme case or simplistic analysis provides an 'intuitively appealing bandwagon construct' (Mednick, 1989: 1120). In the face of political inertia, or appalling obstacles to reform which would involve careful negotiation and complicated application of theory, it is tempting to advocate a simple analysis, a dichotomous approach, which attracts support without actually necessitating the proposal of constructive solutions. As Mednick argues in criticism of the women-centred feminists:

> The 'different voice/women's special nature' views came along at a time when feminists were losing at the political level and had not yet developed

> strategies for dealing with such losses . . . it was apparently easier to turn from social action and to think about women's nature, even a better, glorified nature, than to continue to change society in the face of loss and resistance.
>
> (Mednick, 1989: 1122)

Perhaps the love of rhetoric and hyperbole is a necessary part of being a successful reformer, for as Scull argues, 'the man [*sic*] who seeks to alter certain aspects of this socially constructed reality, must characteristically carry such cognitive significations to an extreme' (Scull, 1979). Yet at what cost? The dissenters simplify a complex process in their arguments, thus leaving themselves open to assault, whilst simultaneously providing a short-sighted and blinkered understanding of the experience of those they claim to support, the mad. The one-sided thinking of the reformers is often no more helpful than that of the traditionalists whom they vilify. These criticisms are not directed solely at the male dissenters: the feminist critics are not immune to such weaknesses. The feminists may succeed in placing the position of women at the top of the agenda, but they fall into many of the same traps as their male colleagues.

The monstrosity of men

The radical feminist critiques of women's madness have a seductive appeal. They allow the difficulties of women to be attributed to the ultimate scapegoat – men. If society is indicated in the search for the source of women's misery, it is in its role of maintaining and being maintained by misogynistic discourse. Yet the situation is not this simple. We cannot subsume all men under the same umbrella of oppressive masculinity any more than we can claim that all women have the same experience, or are similarly affected by their positioning within a patriarchal discourse. For whilst women may share a common oppression, it is not enough to look solely to sex (or heterosexuality), the body, the mother–child relationship or to institutionalized oppression for the root of madness. As there are a multitude of mad women, so there are a multitude of causes for madness.

One of the major flaws in many of the feminist arguments is that they assume all men are equally dominant, and all women oppressed, that women are an homogeneous group. Yet it is rarely *all* men who hold the reins of power in society and who maintain the discursive practices which regulate us. Men from the dominant social groups – those who are white, middle-class, heterosexual and able-bodied – undoubtedly have more power. To analyse women's experience, of madness or of any other oppression, *solely* from the perspective of gender is naïve. There are many other societal oppressions which may be equally important in the analysis, if not more so. Social class, ethnicity and sexuality are the most obvious examples, examples which often seem to be removed from the feminist agenda. And if they are present, they often appear to be of secondary importance, or are mentioned only in passing, without real analysis. Again, the theorists take a one-sided, simple analysis: good for rhetoric and polemic; bad for the individual woman attempting to understand her own experience.

Feminist élitism?

Much of the radical feminist theorizing is potentially very anti-women in its implications and very divisive, setting up criteria for how 'good' women, 'good' feminists should behave, and dismissing those who do not comply. For example, only the chosen few, the élite, are able to join Mary Daly on her psychic journey, as Segal says:

> Not only all men, but most women, are excluded from any possible creative being or salvation. The 'painted birds' (the stereotypically feminine), the 'token feminists' (those seeking or offering reforms for women), the 'fembots' (female robots or professional women), and a host of other 'parasites' are too 'blinded' and 'damaged' by patriarchy to free themselves.
>
> (Segal, 1987: 20)

Women who do not manage to throw off the bonds of patriarchy and women who live with men are deemed inadequate or incomplete. They are seen as dupes or fools, not deserving the attention of 'real' feminists. Non-radical or insufficiently political feminists are seen as frauds, as when Celia Kitzinger confidently proclaims, 'I have never yet met a psychologist colleague at a feminist campaign meeting or a picket line', and asks 'Are feminist psychologists reading feminist political journals with the same attention they devote to professional psychological journals – and if not, why not?' (Kitzinger, 1990: 131–2). This reminds me of the 'reds under the bed' panics of the McCarthy era in the 1950s in the USA – except that now the search is for the closet reactionaries, those who are not *real* feminists. By positioning women not living up to this particular feminist ideal as *not* of the 'Race of Women', Daly and many radical feminists reinforce the very élitist practices which feminism is surely meant to preclude. This theorizing, produced by self-acclaimed radicals in an arrogant self-congratulatory manner, divides women, and induces feelings of inadequacy in those not fulfilling the exact criteria of 'successful feminism' as defined by the self-appointed experts.

It also establishes a cosy élite which can be entered only by the chosen few. Yet the few women who manage to survive the perils of patriarchy to reach the feminist utopia are likely to share many of the characteristics of the castigated male oppressors. These women are invariably white, able-bodied, middle-class, without dependants, well educated and articulate. The majority of women who fight for survival on a daily basis, whose worries centre around feeding their families, arranging childcare, and maintaining some semblance of sanity in the face of adversity, will be completely alienated by this brand of feminist rhetoric. Who can take a psychic journey when the reality of unpaid bills, screaming children and an unsupportive partner are glaring her in the eye? Such women may, from the radical feminist view, be duped by patriarchy; but can they enter a state of higher spirituality when the demands of reality are so overwhelming?

As well as excluding women burdened with the chains of children and unsupportive (but still desired) male partners, many feminists exclude women who do not see men as their primary enemies. Women can be enemies of each other – we can (and do) oppress (or dismiss) each other. This is ignored. The Black feminist, bell hooks, has argued that there are stronger bonds between women and men of the same cultural or socio-economic group, than there are between women of different cultural groups (hooks, 1985: 4). Likewise, the white middle-class feminist who commands her audience with poetic rhetoric may have little to say to the majority of working-class women. She will be perceived as representative of the dominant élite, who act to marginalize and alienate working-class women in innumerable ways. Not all women are affected equally by patriarchy, by misogyny. Many women hold a privileged position in society, and may oppress women less powerful than they.

In recent years there has been an increasing awareness of the importance of issues other than gender for the feminist agenda. Oppression of race, class, age, sexuality and disability are frequently referred to and acknowledged.[10] Yet these avowals by feminists who do not want to appear to be biased or bigoted may be merely paying lipservice to the now fashionable rhetoric of 'equality of opportunity'. Feminists may be guilty of the same crime as those who would change the label of madness to 'mental health problems' yet still continue the oppression of the mad through the traditional practices of expert care. It is easy to jump on the bandwagon, and claim to be adding awareness of class, race and sexuality to the litany of oppressions women experience – but is this awareness really happening, or are many feminists claiming such wide understanding and interest in women's many oppressions simply in order to increase their own credibility? How many of these supposedly radical feminists, profiting from the written discourse on women's oppression, are prepared to move out of their ivory towers or their publishing-house-funded islands of security to address issues of class, race and sexual orientation in anything other than a theoretical context?

It is a dangerous tendency – successful feminists espousing equality, revelling in rhetoric, and yet in reality aiming only (or mainly) at personal prestige and power. This is a brand of feminist élitism that sneers at women who have fallen from grace – women who *dare* call themselves feminists when they are deemed not to have fulfilled the criteria set by the self-appointed arbiters of 'good' feminist standards, whether by engaging in relationships with men,[11] or for example, if they are psychologists, not attending 'feminist conferences, workshops and summer schools' as frequently as they attend professional gatherings such as 'psychology conferences and meetings' (Kitzinger, 1990: 132). This arrogant dictating of appropriate 'feminist' behaviour is no different from the élitism and oppression practised by the patriarches for centuries. Such feminists may have rejected the phallocentric discourse, but they have in its stead created new discursive practices which are as oppressive and misogynistic as those of the men. Perhaps this is why some women, actively engaged with oppressions other than gender, would reject feminism itself, seeing it as racist,[12] classist[13] and limited.

It is also generally denied in the feminist discourse that many men may be oppressed. The 'male is bad/female is good' equation is much too simplistic. Feminists such as Susan Griffin and Dorothy Dinnerstein look to negative and bifurcated images of women in our culture as evidence of misogyny, attributing these images to defences adopted in childhood against recognizing the mother's power and separateness.[14] But they cannot explain the presence of powerfully negative images of *men*. Nor can their analysis account for the denigration of certain groups of men, prevalent throughout history and across cultural groups, denigration such as that of Blacks or Jews or Arabs. Abuse of power and oppression is not restricted to women. Misogyny and mother-hatred cannot be the only explanation.

The celebration of the body – emancipation or essentialism?

This positioning of women as essentially good, as different, as somehow better, is one of the weakest points in the women-centred theories advocated by many feminists, both radical and psychoanalytic alike. For these theories reek too heavily of the biological essentialism advocated by the nineteenth-century patriarchs, of discourses used in a previous era to maintain women's subordinate position. Is it not the same argument in a different guise that Darwin, a strong antifeminist, and Daly, a committed radical feminsit, are making? Darwin stated that 'with women the powers of intuition, of rapid perception, and perhaps of imitation, are more strongly marked than in men' (Darwin, 1871: 563). Daly's claim is that 'we are rooted, as are animals and trees, winds and seas, in the earth's substance. Our origins are in the elements' (Daly, 1984: 4). Both are similar to the psychoanalytic theorists such as Dinnerstein, Rich, Chodorow and Irigaray who celebrate woman's essential difference. The message is clear – women are closer to nature. One would hope, however, that the feminists would not agree with the second half of Darwin's statement: 'These faculties are characteristic of the lower races, and therefore of a past and lower state of civilisation.' The feminists are in danger of banging the same drum as the reductionists who would bar women from any autonomy or responsibility on the basis that women are not fit to think, unfit to be independent, because of their essential biological selves. Can we have it both ways?

The implication of the women-centred theories is that nothing can be changed since women's biology is seen as a fixed entity, even if it is socially constructed as negative only within a patriarchal society. To locate oppression, and thus madness, solely within biology presents us with a depressingly static perspective. As Schwarzer contends:

> This so-called new femininity – with an enhanced status for traditional feminine values, such as woman and her rapport with nature, woman and her physical being . . . [is] an attempt to pin women to their traditional role . . . to try to keep women quiet . . . Once again women are being defined in terms of 'the other', once again they are being made 'the second sex'.
>
> (Schwarzer, 1984, 103)

The ideas regarding women's essential sexuality (the biological specificity which distinguishes women from men), advocated by the French feminists Kristeva, Irigaray and Cixous, may be equally damaging, even if their theories appear emancipatory for women. Irigaray's writing that 'woman has sex organs just about everywhere. She experiences pleasure almost everywhere. . .' may initially appear to be a celebration of female sexuality and sensuality, but how representative is it of women's experiences of their sexuality? And is it not reductionist in the extreme? Cixous' argument that 'it is [their] psychosexual specificity that will empower women to overthrow masculinist ideologies and to create new female discourses' (Jones, 1985: 89) seems essentialist and idealistic. Our 'psychosexual specificity' has long been used to *dis*-empower us, and cannot easily, at least outside feminist theorizing, be used in a revolutionary context. The view of sexuality proposed in these theories seems to strip it of any social context, locating it solely in women's biology, an untenable position in the light of our knowledge that sexuality is not an innate construct, but results from the complex interaction of a number of social and symbolic systems.[15] It is hard to conceive of a uniform ubiquitous 'feminine sexuality', which is not affected by class, race or culture; a single libidinal voice that all women share.[16]

The location of women's strength and women's voice[17] within the body places too much emphasis on the physical, at the expense of the social, political and economic forces that both motivate and confine women. It also dichotomizes women's and men's voices – their writing, their protests – in a way which is too simplistic and biologistic.

The essentialist theories of the 'New French Feminists' are initially seductive and appealing. The concept of powerful and positively sexual women creating their own discourse, their own semiotic writing, is compelling. But it is only women who are freed on an economic, a social and a political level who can exercise the luxury of the play with words, the parody of phallocentric discourse in the '*écriture feminine*' in which Irigaray and Kristeva engage. Cixous declares that, 'By writing her self, woman will return to the body which has been more than confiscated for her', and that, 'To write. An act which will not only "realize" the decensored relation of woman to her sexuality [but] . . . will give her back her goods, her pleasures, her immense bodily territories that have been kept under seal' (Cixous, 1986: 250). Is this not élitist? Is this not the response to oppression of an intellectual? And is the replacement of a phallocentric discourse with a women-centred discourse the real answer to our misery? Of course we need to deconstruct the linguistic and material representations of phallocentrism. But erecting a new, potentially damaging (because of being reductionist) 'woman's language' may please only those who are paid to play with words. To pervert and parody on a solely intellectual and apolitical/ahistorical level is not enough.

Equally to place the emphasis solely on language and on discursive practices is not enough. It is too abstract; it does not engage fully with material reality, reality which does make many women 'mad'. For as Frosh argues,

> The description of the construction of the subject in language needs to be contextualised by an account of those power relations which construct the system itself, which give rise to the order of language that centres on the phallus and that creates the human subject in accordance with a patriarchal law.
>
> (Frosh, 1987: 207)

The biological chains used as a justification for tying us to men, and to the home cannot be the same chains we celebrate and which are used to emancipate us in the way that the radical feminists suggest. The majority of women do not have the luxury of a psychic voyage, and emphasizing our biology will inevitably lead to further oppression. We can acknowledge our difference, our sexuality, our reproductive ability, but to place it at the centre of all debate as the core of women's identity will be an act of emancipation only for the (few) women already emancipated from physical and economic ties to men, who can therefore afford to revel in a female-centred world.

A particular example of this is Vita Sackville-West, English poet, novelist and gardener, who clearly enjoyed and celebrated her womanhood and sexuality through her verse and her succession of lesbian relationships. She may have represented the epitome of emancipation – exploring avenues of pleasure and achievement without having to concede to the demands of patriarchy. But she was also a member of the English aristocracy, and could afford to be economically free (and to support her husband financially) allowing herself to be spiritually free. Few women can achieve this, even today. It is cruel to try to make us believe that we can and that we only need to find a different voice, when the odds are stacked so heavily against most women.

Mothering – the root to equality?

The ideal of Dinnerstein and Chodorow – that women should no longer be pre-eminent in mothering, and that men should take an equal role within the home, as a means of eradicating sexual inequality and misogyny – may also be naïvely limited. First, it implies a very narrow view of the source of our oppression as women, locating the problem as solely within the family rather than within larger social structures. It is actually in line with the misogynistic discourse in which the mother is blamed for everything – madness and war. But it is a too narrow account.

The very notion of mothering as the root of madness, and shared child-rearing as the solution, is unsubstantiated and insubstantial. Even if we were to advocate such solutions as an improvement on the existing patriarchal nature of family life, the proposals might well fall on deaf ears. For these theories imply that women have a choice: that they have a man to share with (this 'new family' is heterosexual). Is this not another rerun of the fantasy of the stereotypical family, this time with mummy and daddy sharing the tasks equally, rather than mummy doing everything in the home? How many families today have a mummy and daddy? As single parents (almost invariably mothers) now form on average one-third of the families in the Western world, this particular feminist vision of the egalitarian family is still far from reality, and impossible for many women. It also implies that women *want* to give up their power within the home. For many, it is the only power base they have. And whilst this power may have a shallow basis, and be in reality a figment of the (powerless) imagination, it is at least *something*. Shared parenting, ideal on paper, is impractical for many in the light of the harsh reality of economic necessity wherein men cannot obtain paternity leave, and where at least one full-time income is a necessity for the family. The middle-class bourgeoisie or the yuppie couple with their baby as designer accessory may be able to experiment with egalitarian family patterns. It is not so easy for those on the lower rungs of capitalism, who have little flexibility in their working practices, and who would be laughed out of the workplace at the merest suggestion of paternity leave. Masculinity, as it is presently constructed, leaves little room for such experimentation. Perhaps most importantly in the shared parenting debates, many men do not wish to mother. This is perhaps not surprising given the low status attached to parenting in most societies, and the power and prestige pertaining to unencumbered full employment. For as Lynne Segal comments:

> Men's resistance to change, however, not only reflects real economic and social pressures, and both sexes' attempts to shore up a man's sense of self-esteem around a traditional masculinity; it also enables men to remain cushioned and privileged in relation to women. It is simply not in men's interests to change too much, unless women force them.
>
> (Segal, 1990: 41)

Men with dependent children work, on average fifty, and sometimes seventy, hours a week, much longer than their childless peers, and invariably longer hours than their female partners (Segal, 1990: 37–8). Childcare and housework are low on the agenda when they return home.

Reification of the phallus

One of the other criticisms to be levelled at the radical feminist analysis is the pre-eminence given to heterosexual sex, to the phallus, as the root of women's oppression. In both the psychoanalytic and radical feminist accounts the phallus is castigated – and yet it is simultaneously reified through the attention given to it. According to Daly, to Dworkin, to Jeffreys, and by implication many other radical feminists, women who are engaged in heterosexual relationships are brainwashed dupes. They are violated, degraded, subordinated and objectified by penetration with the all-powerful penis, the literal representation of the phallus. Women are reminded of their subjugated status as they are fucked, and fooled into thinking it pleasurable. But is it not ridiculous to claim that 'the basic elements of rape are involved in all heterosexual relationships' (Griffin, 1971)? Many women desire men, and many women have not been sexually abused or assaulted by men. Those women who have are dismissed by this analysis of all heterosexual sex as rape for, as Segal argues (1987: 37), 'It diminishes rather than clarifies rape's hideous reality and prevalence.'

Equally it is naïve to claim that, by freeing ourselves from the sexual oppression of men by embarking on sexual relationships with women, we will be free. For there is no lesbian utopia where women live together in peace and harmony without conflict or oppression. If it exists, it is only in the pages of feminist fiction.[18] The continuation of this particular brand of rhetoric and its use as an explanation for women's madness is both naïve and short-sighted. We cannot replace one restrictive discourse (that of compulsory heterosexuality) with another (that of compulsory lesbianism). Sexuality *is* part of our oppression as women – but the radical feminist answer does not suit all women.

It is naïve to place a pre-eminent emphasis on heterosexual sex and the phallus as being at the root of women's difficulties, for it ignores and denies all other factors which are central to the oppression of women. It also, paradoxically, glorifies the phallus, celebrating it as the powerful symbol in a discourse analogous to that used by the misogynistic males so comprehensively castigated. As Lynne Segal argues:

> Are there not sturdier weapons than the penis? . . . we are forced to leave behind the complex historical formation of men's social power – and how this social power confers a symbolic power to the penis as the defining characteristic of the male – to return to a naked sexual capacity which can be, and therefore is, used to control women. In the description of the relentless power of the steely prick, the biological, so forcefully ejected from the front door, swaggers in, cocksure, through the back.
>
> (Segal, 1987: 101)

This preoccupation with male sexuality and with heterosexual sex solely as the act of vaginal penetration – an act presented in the same graphic form in much radical feminist polemic as it is in pornography – is also short-sighted. As women's sexuality cannot be reduced to penetration – to pleasure from fucking (as it was in the myth of the vaginal orgasm) – neither can men's. To reduce men's pleasure (and power) to this one act is to ignore the many complex factors which form the discourses of male sexuality.[19] As much as we need to explore women's sexuality, creating new ways of exploring our desire, so we need to understand and not simplify men's sexuality, if women are to remain in sexual relationships with men, as many women wish to do. For men's sexuality can be no more reduced to a single experience (fucking powerfully and oppressively) than can women's (passively receiving without pleasure). Male sexuality is clearly 'the site of any number of emotions of weakness and strength, pleasure and pain, anxiety, conflict, tension and struggle, none of them mapped out in such a way as to make the obliteration of the agency of women in heterosexual engagements inevitable' (Segal, 1990: 215). To deny this, by positing that sexual or marital therapy merely coerces women into heterosexuality, or that heterosexual sex is always oppressive for women, is a nonsense, and denies the existence of pleasure in heterosexual sex. In the same way that it is insulting to women who are distressed, women who are mad, to imply that *all* women are mad within a patriarchal culture, it is insulting to imply that *all* heterosexual women are oppressed.

Liberal feminism – reifying society?

Inasmuch as the psychoanalytic or radical feminists place too much (or sole) emphasis on the essential quality of 'woman', looking towards the body and sexuality, whilst ignoring the material realities, liberal or egalitarian feminists are in danger of denying the biological, the sexual, and the role of the unconscious in women's madness. Guilty of denying difference, they pathologize the woman who does not reach out and claim her rightful prize of equality in the market place. It is her fault. She fails if she does not succeed. As Valerie Walkerdine argues:

> Equal opportunities and much work on sex-role stereotyping deny difference in a most punitive and harmful way. Operating in these practices is a partial and shaky denial of castration. The 'clever girl' is positioned as though she could and can possess the phallus, while she has to negotiate other practices in which her femininity is what is validated . . . a denial of the reality of difference means that the girl must bear the burden of her anxiety herself.
>
> (Walkerdine, 1990: 46)

To claim that women have only to reach out to claim the phallus and all the power it possesses is a cruel trick to play on us. If we believe that we have only to try harder, work longer, seek further and we will succeed, but yet we fail, whom will we blame? Invariably our own failings; our own stupidity and weakness. If we are second-rate, it is because we make ourselves so. This is the message of the rhetoric of the liberal feminists (and of the reactionary reductionists). But it is not enough to say that we are mad because we are oppressed by structural or institutional forces and that we fail because we have not claimed the phallus for our own. These egalitarian, social constructionist accounts cannot explain madness (or misogyny) completely. They cannot explain the continuation of women's subservient status and distress despite (admittedly small) changes in opportunity. The oppression and subjugation goes much deeper, operating on levels other than the structural. Free childcare, equality of opportunity and freedom in the market place will not release women from the chains of madness or misogyny. It is utopian to think so, and it exonerates the oppressors and reinforces the subjugation of women. The finger of blame is still pointing in the same direction – at women.

Feminist therapy: old goods in a new wrapping?

The other alternative within the feminist framework, feminist therapy, is offered by many as the panacea for all ills, seemingly, not only addressing the personal, but also taking on the political. The feminist chant of the sixties and seventies has moved into the consulting room, therapists now claiming to be able to 'facilitate women's assuming equality in society' (Rawlings and Carter, 1977: 49) and simultaneously to 'lend each other support and . . . thereby build a base of strength which, when translated into power politics, is effecting important social changes' (Mander, 1977: 287). But how different is feminist therapy from the more traditional or supposedly sexist therapies that it sets out to replace? As it is clear that feminist therapy is an approach, rather than a specific practice, is it really anything new, anything different? Cannot the feminist therapist be guilty of dressing up old goods under a new label and selling them as radical?

One of the problems with feminist therapy, as with any of the solutions offered by the dissenters, is that it is a unidimensional approach, looking to the psychological, the therapeutic, as *the* solution to women's problems. For whilst it might be claimed that feminist therapists should be as active outside the consulting room as inside, rallying for the cause of their women clients in the courts, the housing offices or the streets, how realistic is this? Who would pay for it? Unless these idealistic feminist therapists have other sources of income, which present health system, whether state- or privately funded, would maintain their income? For we do not, and cannot become therapists merely for love – it is a job. To dictate that 'engaging in social action is an essential professional responsibility of therapists' (Rawlings and Carter, 1977: 63) suggests a complete absence of awareness of the pragmatics of being a therapist, where a day spent lobbying or 'taking social action' means that eight women who might have received some support have been left waiting. It also implies the feminist therapist knows what to do to achieve her 'socially active' end – how could we all be experts on the legal and social service systems? Is it not difficult enough to be a therapist? Is there not an argument for specialization, for a division of skills and liaison between workers who are actively supporting women's interests? We should certainly be aware of the practical and social needs of women clients, but to suggest that one person can take on the whole gamut of problems is naïve. Interdisciplinary working, information giving and liaison with outside agencies may be appropriate. Marching to the town hall on a regular basis is not.

Given that feminist therapists are at work within the psychological domain, how different is their practice? As all types of interventions, from the psychoanalytic to the behavioural, can be offered under the feminist label are not the problems inherent within these interventions still present in the feminist version of the therapy? And, whilst the feminist retort might be that gender is at the centre of their therapeutic agenda, that politics are present in the interaction, is not the focus on the category 'women' in danger of ignoring the almost infinite sources of a woman's pain and despair? Again, may it not ignore class, race and age in its assumption that gender is the main focus of intervention; that sexism and misogyny are at the root of madness; that all women are the same; and that a feminist therapeutic, or political solution is best for one and all? The perennial problem of the conflict between the needs of women as a group and the needs of individual women is perhaps most clearly evident in this arena. Women as a group would undoubtedly benefit from social and political change and from an end to patriarchal oppression. Individual women have more personal (and pressing) needs which can rarely be fulfilled within a solely political analysis, at least in the short term.

Women seek help expecting some results, some solutions – not an abstract theoretical explanation.[20] What does the woman do when she realizes her father/husband/boss is a prime mover in her misery? Leave him? Change him? Most women have *in reality* little power in their lives, and cannot simply leave the luxury of the consulting room and change their worlds. There are many powerful structures mediating against them. The educated, affluent middle-class woman may be empowered by the feminist message to move outwards and change her world, unlike the majority of women. A feminist therapy which allows women to see an alternative to their current desperate lives, yet does not fully facilitate change might be accused of being some form of subtle torture. To allow women to see the possibility of change, to have hope which we cannot realize, to envisage a feminist utopia we cannot achieve, may only make matters worse.

The notion of feminist therapy can also be used as a rhetorical device, serving the interests of its proponents more than those of women who are mad. It is in danger of being as élitist as its predecessors, offered chiefly to middle-class women who are amenable to the analysis it entails. The working-class woman who might benefit from an egalitarian non-pathologizing therapy, whose pain is still genuine and tied up with the real strains and stresses of her life, may well be completely alienated by the language and by the assumption of the possibility of equality in a world where oppression operates on levels other than (or additional to) gender. The misogynistic stereotype of feminist women also has powerful consequences. 'Feminism' as a concept still provokes images of strident, marching, powerful women, causing alienation from the very term 'feminist' for many women in our society. 'I'm not a feminist but. . .' is a common expression. Many women would not countenance even the thought of feminist therapy, leaving it for those whose 'consciousness had been raised' and who are aware that feminists do not really march around burning their bras. In the meantime, the remainder of women are invariably offered other 'care', usually consisting of drugs.[21] Can it claim to be feminist therapy if it is available or offered or acceptable only to women who are the chosen (middle-class) few?

The notion of an 'equal' relationship in feminist therapy is also problematic, for how egalitarian and equal can any therapy be? One person is paid, is secure, has knowledge and training. The other is distressed, often frightened, and needing help. This can never be an equal relationship, and to pretend that it is may actually be dangerous and disempowering as it pays lipservice to egalitarian practice without fundamentally changing anything. And women may want to seek help and advice from an 'expert', from someone who they feel has the ability to know what to do. As one woman said of her psychiatrist:

> The psychiatrist is the specialist in the field. If he cannot help nobody can. You've got to believe that he will help you, just got to believe it, other wise you lose all hope.
>
> (Miles, 1988: 124–5)

The feminist therapist who deskills herself through her need to demystify her power may be well-intentioned, but she may be adding to her patient's anxiety.

If feminist therapists decry all notions of theoretical descriptions of problems, are they offering nothing other than friendship? But it is an empty hollow friendship, because one woman has come to it in pain, wanting help, the other has not. The therapist is supposed (and paid) to have the answer, to know why, to know how this madness can be healed. To pretend that this is equality makes a farce of friendship as well as of therapy.

Feminist therapists have had training, and thus have certain privileges many women do not have. They have an occupation and an autonomous existence. They are involved in professional structures which militate against change; and, whilst women may form their own structures, such as those of the Women's Therapy Centres in London and New York, are these really any different? They may be more supportive, and the extreme elements of psychiatric and psychological abuse may be absent, but they are still offering an expert service within a system, and the woman is still the patient. Feminist therapists are offering a particular theoretical explanation for women's distress based on the feminist expert model of madness. Even if it is a social or political model, it is still an expert theory, offered as explanation, and used as a basis for intervention. Is it really any different from the other theories and therapies? The rhetoric of equality may be there but is the practice not the same?

The gap between theory and practice in feminist therapy is wide and potentially hazardous. The theoretical explanation for women's distress, women's inequality, may be complex and many-faceted, but translating this into a mandate for therapy is neither simple nor always convincing. Gender equality through therapy seems an untenable concept. It places the burden of change on the woman herself, implying that if only she expressed her anger, realized the root of her oppression, demanded equality and refused to be pathologized, she would be free – or at least happy. This is a grandiose, short-sighted and limited view. It blames the woman for her situation as effectively as the more traditional interventions that feminist therapy sets out to replace. Therapy, of any type, is not going to resolve the question of women's madness. It will not prevent misery. Feminist therapists are right to want to empower their clients, but feminist theory does not yet offer adequate tools for this empowerment: the woman is pushed to 'free' herself without being given the means to do it. Feminist therapy is thus laudable in its aims and intentions, but on its own it is not enough, and must not be accepted without question.

Thus, in taking the extreme example, appearing to be addicted to rhetoric, and suggesting only utopian or one-dimensional solutions, the feminist critics and the male dissenters effect few real changes for women.

Radical rhetoric – restricting reform

> Cynics are, quite simply, people who have no hope, and therefore have no capacity to express any demands for the future. The sociological critics of the 'mental illness' concept are, as ideologists, deeply cynical . . . And the cynic cannot really be a critic; the radical who is only a radical nihilist, or a radical tragedian, is for practical purposes the most adamant of conservatives.
>
> (Sedgewick, 1982: 42)

The male dissenters and feminist critics have presented sophisticated analyses of madness, challenging the orthodox medical models with an arsenal of ammunition. But are they guilty of 'an extreme form of theoretical abstraction which in practice has left little space for political engagement' (Segal, 1987: 131)? Their theories do not suggest any reconstruction, any real alternatives to the expert authorities they abhor. If the dissenters' argument, that mental illness is a myth and forcible incarceration is perpetuated by the 'madness mongering' of psychiatrists, is taken to its full conclusion, all forms of traditional mental health care will be removed, as psychiatrists, psychologists and therapists will be recognized as agents of the state, merely legitimating the scapegoating of those deemed mad. In fact, following the de-institutionalization and unpopularity of psychiatry in the wake of the criticism of the dissenters, services have been removed in wholesale fashion. It is interesting that this is one area where the political right and left agree in their aims,[22] the dissolution of institutional power over the mad. The right might want this because of a belief in the liberty of the individual and the dangers of the welfare state; the left because of the oppressive power of institutions. The consequences are the same – a removal of services, and a vacuum in care. Institutions have been closed down, and the 'community care' which has taken their place, whilst it has been excellent in instances, has largely meant care in the family, unresourced and unnoticed.

That desolation in the back ward of the psychiatric hospital has been largely replaced with desolation on the streets or in lonely bedsits seems to go unnoticed. As Sedgewick baldly states:

> There is no primal Arcady into which mental patients can slip, away from the modern institution of care and intervention. If they slip anywhere at all, it will be into the gutter or the graveyard.
>
> (Sedgewick, 1982: 146)

For, as we cannot remove the label of madness and hope that all will be well, so we cannot dissolve therapy, psychiatry and psychology and expect this to remove oppression and distress. For the distress, the madness, is not generally caused by the professional care; and the distress is real – there is no doubt about that. Madness is not merely a process of definition, a label for arbitrary behaviour. Many of those deemed mad are desperate, angry, unhappy people, with real worries and crises. The role society plays in creating this distress cannot be denied, but a deconstruction of the label serves only to deny the existence of the pain. Thus those who would deny the existence of despair, who would re-label madness, run the risk of 'marginalising and excluding the ill from their own world' (Gilman, 1988: 9). We may want to criticize the traditional positivistic psychiatric treatment of madness, to question the very concept of madness as illness, and acknowledge the ethical and moral aspect of diagnosis and treatment, but we cannot leave it at that.

Recent critics have argued that instead of providing institutionalized care, we should be 'taking care' of each other – that friendship, or lay healing is the answer to human misery.[23] Thus, Masson notes:

> Many times I sat behind a patient in analysis and became acutely aware of my inability to help . . . Any advice I might have had to offer would be no better than that of a well-informed friend (and considerably more expensive).
>
> (Masson, 1989: 299)

So years of psychoanalytic training are deemed to be no more helpful than the attention of a friend. In the same vein, David Smail, a clinical psychologist, acknowledges that pain exists, but disputes the unequal power structure inherent in therapy, and the location of the problems with the individual, advocating instead an 'environmental psychology' (Smail, 1991). But this places the burden of 'care' firmly on the shoulders of others – others in a non-professional role.

Is it not a utopian vision of the world that Smail and Masson present? Is it really likely that we will suddenly open our eyes to the damage we do to each other, and start 'taking care'? Or is it more likely that a small group of non-paid and unacknowledged *female* carers will carry out the role presently done by professionals? The same army of unpaid and low-status carers who look after the elderly and the handicapped in our present society? The wives and the mothers – the door-mats of the welfare state. The implications for women of the removal of professional care are not positive. Women predominate in those presently seeking help, as well as in those providing it unofficially – and unpaid. Even the feminist critics seem to ignore this reality.

The psychiatric backlash

> In trying to remove and reduce the concept of mental illness, the revisionist theorists have made it that bit harder for a powerful campaign of reform in the mental health services to get off the ground.
>
> (Sedgewick, 1982: 41)

The idealism, cynicism, and what Sedgewick saw as inherent conservatism of the dissenters has provoked a psychiatric backlash, providing impetus to those who would frame all mental health services within an organic biological framework. It provided a rallying call for the reductionists, and consequently prevented the introduction of progressive reform because the complete dismissal of existing theories and therapies allowed those who advocated psychiatry and psychology to reject the dissension outright, and maintain the status quo. As Pilgrim argued, there have been two major waves of response from the psychiatrists in reaction to the sixties critics (Pilgrim, 1990: 218), ranging from 'outraged condemnation of any critique'[24] to calmer but equally reactionary replies.[25] The latter acknowledge some validity in the sociological arguments, but dismiss the most radical of the critiques whilst bolstering the existing system by paying lipservice to liberal reforms. Those outraged by the very notion of reform don't even pay lipservice.

For example, one of the defenders of psychiatric control of madness, Roth, describes the dissenters as guilty of 'dogmatic oratory, diffuse and inconsistent . . . utterances' (Roth, 1973: 373)[26] and uses this dismissal to defend his case that scientific psychiatry should maintain its position of pre-eminence. Thus, the dissension may have served to strengthen the position of the experts. As Claridge (1990: 157) has outlined:

> The subsequent backlash in orthodox psychiatry was such that it has now entered an even more vigorous phase of organic explanation, revitalized by fresh discoveries in biochemistry (Haracz 1982), psychiatric genetics (Gottesman and Shields 1982), and neuropathology, including the newly developed science of brain imaging.
>
> (Weinberger *et al.*, 1983)

Thus, because the dissenters positioned themselves outside the current mental health services, 'above the battle' (Sedgewick, 1982: 41), their theories have actually had little effect other than to provide a seductive theorizing for academics and a rhetoric for service user groups, all of which was ignored by those holding the reins of power.

Madness as artistry

One of the tenets of the dissenters' case most strongly rejected by those professionals involved in the reactionary backlash was the idea of madness as thwarted creativity. It has been used to ridicule the critics, as the mad in the back wards are clearly revealed not to be tortured artists. Yet, were not the dissenters' claims too simplistic? Was it not disingenuous to imagine that the thousands of people receiving psychiatric intervention could have been saved if only they had been allowed to express their pain in another form? Or to claim that they are all protesting, and if heeded, will cease their protest? There may be an element of protest in madness – but it is not that simple.

The view of madness as protest may similarly detract from the campaign to provide effective political action for those in distress. It presents too naïve and romantic a view of the reality of madness. For every famous painter and every tortured poet, there are a thousand 'ordinary' people who would be ignored by those glorifying and reifying the mad. And how helpful is this celebration of madness in the long run? Does it not serve the rhetoric of the dissenters more than it serves the individuals deemed mad? It is no help to the woman in distress to be placed on a pedestal and told that she is a victim of societal oppression, a hero of the people, a political dissident. I am again inclined to agree with Sedgewick when he suggests that the dissenters have some investment in maintaining the grievances and misery of the mad, for the very existence of madness provides fuel for the fire to burn down the establishment:

> It is as though people believe that there is only a finite pool of grievances and maladjustments available in this society for radicals to work with. The fear is that psychiatry, with its tranquillisers, hospitals and whatnot, may succeed in mopping up this limitless supply of miseries, discharging patients into the hell of the factory and the purgatory of the home as 'cured' and adjusted robots . . . if capitalism could really 'adjust' people, through psychiatry or any other technology, who would want to quarrel with it?
>
> (Sedgewick, 1982: 42)

The adjusted world smacks of that outlined in Aldous Huxley's *Brave new world*, where, to maintain the social order, the automated workers take their daily drugs, their 'soma', in a fantasy of orgasmic happiness. The dissenters may be accused of maintaining the misery in order to avoid this, for to address it is to address the question of the need for intervention on a level other than that of the social, the revolutionary, or the rhetorical. Is not one of the issues whether it is better to be cognizant and in pain, or senseless and serene? For all their faults, the psychiatrists can offer a panacea, a therapy to dull the pain – even if it also dulls all else. The dissenters would rather the mad face up to the pain, and society face up to its role in the creation and maintenance of madness. But they are not the ones suffering: they are merely pronouncing on the sidelines. If the two perspectives are in opposition, no constructive change will take place. Medication and therapy may be thrown out of the window. Nothing is provided in its stead.

The liberal, radical and psychoanalytic feminist bandwagons have their ardent followers, as had the antipsychiatry bandwagons before them, but how progressive are they? How much do they achieve? The risk is that any really innovative or positive solutions or theories are lost in the morass of sycophantic rhetoric. The blind lead the blind. The lemmings follow the rest. No one attempts to address issues outside the current party line of thinking. This may guarantee research publications, and thus help the careers of the critics themselves – but it stifles real scholarship.[27] It stifles innovation; it stifles change.

Conclusion

Where, then, does this leave us? There is certainly a great deal of value in many of the critiques offered by the dissenters. Labels are important. Reality is mystified. Culture is implicated in the definitions and diagnosis of madness. Madness is an effective means of social control, and symptoms may be protest by the powerless. Therapy may be coercive and oppressive, whether it be the widely condemned physical interventions, or the 'talking cure' of psychotherapy: the expert is certainly powerful in either context. But, whilst we may want to acknowledge the critiques of the dissenters, and the feminists, surely each analysis on its own is really too simplistic, too one-dimensional, as are the expert theories and therapies they condemn. Each line of argument can be defended and justified within its own narrow world view – but it can also be refuted. And, as there are few (if any) attempts to produce any integration of the theories and criticisms, one is left with a sense of frustration and impotence, which is based on a realization that, whilst in the abstract the criticisms are seductive, in practice they are often idealistic and unworkable. As an explanation for my mother's 'madness' or as a tool in my clinical practice, none of the dissenters' theories fulfilled my expectations. They offered very little other than (often poorly worked out) theoretical explanations, and vilifications of professional care.

Yet, whatever the experts or the critics may say, madness is a spectre in many women's lives. There are many reasons why women are mad – many roads to despair which the individual woman will travel. Madness is more than a label, far more than a theoretical construct. The feminists have demonstrated that women dominate in the psychiatric statistics, and have attempted to understand the subjugation of women within a number of different frameworks, liberal, radical and psychoanalytic. But the reality of the difficulties inherent within many women's lives in the late twentieth century is not always evident within these individual frameworks, or within the critiques, with their concentration on extremes, or on single dimensions of experience. Before reconstructing women's madness, the many roads there require a more careful examination and women should speak for themselves.

Notes

1. One of the most notable, as well as most readable, is Peter Sedgewick, who exposed the flaws and 'inherent conservatism' in much of the supposedly radical dissension, in his book *Psychopolitics* 1982: 42.

2. In order to cleanse the diagnosis of madness of its subjectivity, the dissenters have suggested that the ideal should be the expulsion of all cultural, normative or subjective references, which would then place psychiatry on a par with the supposed 'objective medicine': 'Long indeed is the road to be travelled before we can hope to reach a definition of mental-cum-physical health which is objective, scientific and wholly free of value judgements, and before we shall be able, consistently and without qualification, to treat mental and physical disorders on exactly the same footing' (Wooton 1959: 225).
3. Zborowski 1952 carried out an analysis of reaction to physical pain in a New York hospital, and found that whereas Jewish and Italian patients showed an emotional response to pain, 'Old Americans' displayed an 'objective' stoical attitude, and Irish patients exhibited complete denial. This was interpreted in terms of personal and cultural differences in coping with and experiencing physical distress: differences which undoubtedly have a significant effect on the experience of pain or illness itself.
4. Koos 1954 has argued that the upper classes were more likely to view themselves as ill when they experience particular symptoms. This is supported by work (see Rosenblatt and Suchman 1965) which demonstrated that blue-collar workers are more likely to ignore symptoms which would be reported to the doctor by their white-collar counterparts – sometimes to their own detriment.
5. In order to contend with these difficulties in definition, it has been suggested that we should take 'health' as our starting point, and see deviation from that as illness. But if we take the World Health Organization definition of health as: 'a state of *complete* physical, mental and social well-being and not merely the absence of disease and infirmity [my emphasis]', can any of us be defined as healthy, as enjoying a *complete* sense of well-being? If this definition is the norm, there are very few of us not ill. In a system of medicine based on fiscal resources, the only person to be satisfied with this definition of health would be the doctors.
6. For example, Eysenck argues that a distinction can be made between neurotic illness which can be treated by a psychologist, and organic illness which can be treated by a medical professional (Busfield 1986: 105).
7. This is not to suggest that the physical presence of AIDS will inevitably cause psychological difficulties, but that psychological factors are an important part of the PWA's experience.
8. See Ussher 1992c for a discussion of science and clinical psychology.
9. This is discussed in more detail in Chapter 6.
10. For example, a new journal, *Feminism and psychology*, has claimed in its editorial to be influenced by 'developments in the feminist movement which have sought to challenge academic feminisms's predominant focus on white, Western culture . . . in order to address difference and diversity, including the multiple oppressions of race, class, sexuality, and disability (amongst others)', *Feminism and psychology*, vol. 1, 1, 1991: 6.
11. Daly 1979, Jeffreys 1990 and Dworkin 1987 are amongst those who have castigated such women.
12. Anurdha Sayal-Bennet, who describes both feminism and psychology as sharing a 'Eurocentric élitism which continues to oppress and invalidate the black women', sees the *real* interests of many feminists as being themselves: 'Job rejections are to be expected if one is black . . . Never once was I

offered a job in inner-city areas, where black people may form a majority of the population. In several instances these posts were taken up by less-qualified feminist women, who talked about equal opportunity but who in my view will never give up their power and will continue to climb the ladder at the expense of their black colleagues' (Sayal-Bennet 1991: 76).

13. Laguiller 1986: 23 argued that, 'Feminism, except on very limited issues (abortion) cannot bring together all women in a common struggle. Class oppression is stronger. Men are as hassled as women, within the couple and in their militant action.'
14. Sayers 1986: 60 discusses Griffin 1981 and Dinnerstein 1976.
15. Both Freud and Lacan, as well as Foucault and more modern theorists such as Weeks and Jeffreys, make this point, if from a different perspective.
16. See Jones 1985 for a further analysis of this.
17. The French feminists have argued that women must 'write from the body . . . let the body flow' (Gagnon 1986: 179).
18. See Burns 1992b for a discussion of some of the issues concerning lesbian health. Lesbian women may free themselves from many of the chains and oppressions of relationships with men, but they still have problems in relationships (Ussher 1991d) and are still open to the many other factors which make women mad (See Chapter 9).
19. See Hollway 1989 for a discussion of these discourses.
20. Many feminist therapists undoubtedly avoid abstract theoretical explanations, but the literature on feminist therapy does not represent this.
21. Miles 1988 has shown how women going to their GP with any psychological problem are initially offered psychotropic drugs. See Chapter 9 for a discussion of this.
22. They also agree on the abolition of pornography.
23. 'We suffer pain because we do damage to each other, and we shall continue to suffer pain as long as we continue to do the damage. The way to alleviate and mitigate distress is for us to *take care of* the world and the other people in it, not to *treat* them' (Smail 1987: 1).
24. For example Hamilton 1973; Roth 1973.
25. For example Clare 1976; Wing 1978.
26. Quoted by Pilgrim 1990.
27. In the academic world the quantity of publications counts largely towards continuation in a job, or towards promotion.

9

The routes to madness

madness. . .
There is something every woman wears around her neck on a thin chain of fear – an amulet of madness. For each of us, there exists somewhere a moment of insult so intense that she will reach up and rip the amulet off, even if the chain tears at the flesh of her neck.

(Morgan)[1]

woman. . .
Where is she?
Activity/passivity,
Sun/Moon,
Culture/Nature,
Day/Night,

Father/Mother,
Head/Heart,
Intelligible/sensitive,
Lagos/Pathos.

Form, convex, step, advance, seed, progress.
Matter, concave, ground – which supports the step, receptacle.

Man

Woman

(Cixous, 1988: 90)

pain. . .
It happens. Will it go on? –
My mind a rock,
No fingers to grip, no tongue,

My god the iron lung

That loves me, pumps
My two
Dust bags in and out,
Will not

Let me relapse
While the day outside glides by like ticker tape.
The night brings violets,
Tapestries of eye,

Lights,
The soft anonymous
Talkers: 'You all right?'
The starched, inaccessible breast.

Dead egg, I lie
Whole
On a whole world I cannot touch
At the white, tight

Drum of my sleeping couch. . .

(Plath, 1963)[2]

despair. . .
This wandering, this despair, this cry for help, this powerlessness to express oneself that I know and understand well. Something poignant. The alienation of the neurotic is tragic, because it is an alienation which doesn't tip the whole world into madness. There is only you, on the inside, who have tipped into the useless, into disorder. On the outside, everything is normal, you seem to be fit for society, while on the inside you don't understand anything about it. The more you plunge into neurosis, the less you can insert yourself into society, and not for political reasons or any other kind. For reasons you don't understand, don't know, you are surrendered to an unknown which wishes you harm and hunts you ceaselessly. It is hell.

(Cardinal, 1977: 30)[3]

fear. . .
Sandra, 31, two children 5 and 12: I am terribly afraid that I am going to die . . . I know I am hypochondriac and it worries me terribly . . . I shout at the children, I feel so irritable with them, I know it's wrong . . . I am worried about my heart, I feel breathless and my heart is bumping, but the tests show it's all right . . . I am so poorly on some says, I feel I can't cope.

anger. . .
Susan, 21, no children: I feel depressed and worried . . . some days

> I feel I can't go on and I shut myself away . . . I have dreadful rows with my husband; after one row I cut my wrists, just in anger you know, it wasn't serious . . . I cry a lot and feel terrible . . . I think I have agoraphobia a bit, I don't want to go out . . . I can't cope very well, I feel irritable.[4]

> *the experts. . .*
> All the data on mental illness . . . indicates that in modern Western industrial societies more women than men are mentally ill. It is especially important to note that this finding is not dependent on who is doing the selection. For example, if we look at admissions to mental hospitals, where societal response would appear to be of prime importance, women have higher rates; if we look at treatment by general physicians, where self-selection would appear to be of prime importance, women have higher rates; and if we look at community surveys, where the attempt is to eliminate the selection process, women have higher rates.
> (Gove and Tudor, 1973: 54)

The reality of madness

Throughout this whole debate, in common with all academic discourse on madness, the voice which is seldom heard, if not silenced, is that of the woman herself, the woman who is positioned as mad. This madness may take many forms, have many roots, be manifested through a myriad of symptoms, be given different names: hysteria, mania, neurasthenia, schizophrenia, neurosis, depression, post-traumatic stress; they all share a common history, common effects, even if they differ in manifestation of 'symptoms'.[5] In different cultures, at different points in history, at different times in the individual woman's life cycle, the madness may be distinct. The 'symptoms' may be seclusion in the home, obsessive cleanliness, refusal to wear the Muslim veil, promiscuity, starvation, self-injury, or hallucinations of God, the devil or a favourite singer.[6] But there are common threads, common experiences, common consequences. It is painful and frightening, as it envelops and encumbers the woman. The woman herself is invariably stigmatized, feared, positioned as doubly dangerous, for she is Woman and she is Mad. She is the eternal outsider, her gender marking her as different and deficient; her madness sealing her fate, her experience, her pain. Her despair is undoubtedly real, but her experience of it, the meaning attached to it and the solutions offered to (or withheld from) her are framed by the current discourse of madness. In any deconstruction of madness it is easy to forget the individual woman in distress – but we must not. I have started this chapter with women's own voices as a reminder. But to listen, to sympathize, to offer empathic understanding is not enough. We want to know why we are mad or why we are framed as mad. We want to be more than 'the opaque screen', the eternal Other.

The feminist theorists have demonstrated that women are positioned as Other and labelled as mad, when they step out of line. Women are pathologized and thus dismissed. Psychologists, psychiatrists, therapists all act as agents of a patriarchal discourse exacting control through their expert interventions, convincing women of the existence of disease they did not know they had.

This is not the only analysis of women's madness to have any credence, for there are those who would vehemently maintain that women are mad, that for many the distress, the misery, the despair is real. I would certainly agree with this position. Anyone who has stepped outside the ivory tower of academia, or stepped off the political platform, where radical rhetoric is all too seductive, to walk into the streets, the doctor's waiting room, the council estates, the psychiatric hospital, will recognize that this phenomenon we call madness is certainly a reality for many women. My own rude awakening to the flimsiness of the facade of radicalism within the antipsychiatry and labelling theories came very quickly when I first worked with women who were distressed and desperate and realized that the rhetoric would not have ameliorated my mother's madness. The madness was there, whether I named it as such or not. The desperation was certainly real.

Women's vulnerability – biological or social?

To acknowledge the power of labels, and the power of the androcentric or phallocentric discourse of psychiatry and psychology, as well as to admit the existence of madness does not have to be a problematic position to take. Sedgewick has criticized feminists for adopting both stances, claiming that, 'the stance of psychiatric radicalism has been of having one's cake in the form of stress-theory as well as eating it in the substance of labelling or antipsychiatry theory' (Sedgewick, 1982: 237). I'm afraid I want to have my cake *and* eat it. We need to acknowledge the importance of labels, the gender differences in diagnosis and treatment; the association between femininity and pathology. But we also need to look at why women are mad – look critically at those experts variously asserting that women are victims of our biology (as madness is in the brain), or are victims of an oppressive society (as madness is socially constructed). For, perhaps unsurprisingly, there is little consensus about what actually causes this distress; where the roots of madness actually are.

To move towards an understanding of madness which is useful for women, that does not objectify or vilify us and which incorporates the feminist critiques, we need to examine the different explanations which are freely offered, but also to look wider than the official discourse on madness to the many aspects of woman's role in our society which may make us mad. This is where the analysis is as much about women as it is about madness – but the two are intertwined; their histories go hand in hand.

The biological burden of woman

The discourse which positioned women as biologically inferior, and thus prey to all manner of disorders, both physical and psychological, became well established in the Victorian era, as we have already seen (Chapter 4). Women are still seen by many authorities today as biologically labile, and madness as caused by biology. Women's predominance in mental health statistics is not seen as peculiar, and it is assumed that we simply need to correct a woman's biological deficiencies, modify her raging hormones, and she will be put back on the right track. If only it were so simple. If I could take a pill which would make me eternally happy, without dulling my mind and my emotions or impeding my work, I might take a less cynical view of the drug companies who promulgate the biological theories. But the perfect pill is still a pipe dream, a reality only in the imaginations of the advertisers who reap profits from the trade in chemical interventions. Along with the multinational drug companies, they are interested in their own profits, not in providing an alleviation of misery.[7] Capitalism and care do not easily go hand in hand. Cynicism apart, biological explanations for madness are still rife, allowing a plethora of experts to proclaim with confidence that the root of madness (specifically labelled depression) is in the brain and that it is genetically transmitted. And women are positioned as particularly vulnerable, as biologically more susceptible.

Thus, Slater and Cowie claimed that the gene for depression was located in the X chromosome; and thus women, who have two X chromosomes, would be more liable to become the victims of this (unquestioned) genetically transmitted illness (Slater and Cowie, 1971). The other favourite of the medical misogynists is women's wandering womb, which makes a transition from the Victorian disease, hysteria, to the late-twentieth-century syndromes, premenstrual syndrome (PMS), post-natal depression (PND) and the menopausal syndrome. The dictat 'biology as destiny' has in the twentieth century taken on the status of scientifically supported fact, reifying the connection between the womb and the brain by elevating the problem to that of objectively defined syndrome. The message is still the same – women's bodies send them mad.

The return of the raging hormones

> Abnormal hormone patterns may be a biological risk factor which predisposes [women] patients to anorexia nervosa.
>
> (Kaplan and Woodside, 1987: 648)

> Since by definition premenstrual syndrome occurs cyclically, it is tempting to consider that the symptoms are related to some hormone or other compound which varies cyclically. . . . The problem is more likely to be related to an underlying effect in such substance as a natural opiate which affects mood and behaviour and which in turn is responsible for the minor hormonal abnormalities.
>
> (Butt, Watts and Holder, 1983: 23)

PMS, PND and the menopausal syndrome neatly cover the major part of a woman's life cycle, allowing any madness to be attributed to the effects of those supposedly dangerous raging hormones. They exemplify the discourse of woman as biologically labile, and have far-reaching consequences in terms of the way in which women are treated.[8] The inability of clinicians to 'cure' women of our (supposed) hormonally induced madness is put down, again, to the present inability of research to identify the 'exact' hormone, not to the fact that physical aetiology might not be what we should be looking for. But the researchers live in hope. One day their prince – in the form of the hormonal key to the mystery of reproductive madness – will come. As the middle-class woman in the nineteenth century was incarcerated in the prison of femininity, so are her twentieth-century descendants. Women are categorized as labile, unstable, at the mercy of a biology which, whilst it prepares us for woman's greatest fulfilment, motherhood, leaves us open to all manner of ailments and adversities.[9]

Yet one can easily expose these modern reproductive syndromes for the counterfeit concoctions that they really are. PMS was a syndrome first described in 1931 by a medical man, Frank, in its earlier incarnation of PMT (premenstrual tension). It was used as a label to categorize the (supposedly) monthly fluctuations in mood and behaviour experienced by women, the disparate physical symptoms, anxiety, tiredness, hostility and irritability. The menstrual cycle, or more precisely, the hormonal fluctuations taking place during the cycle, were assumed to be at the root of all these problems. Over the yars, the symptoms of PMT were continuously updated and revised, so that today the renamed PMS includes over 150 different symptoms, ranging from the 'classics', above, to others such as elation, palpitations, increased/decreased sexual desire, constipation, diarrhoea, emotionality . . . I could go on. In fact, name a symptom, and it is likely to be part of PMS.[10] Different studies maintain that between 5 and 95 per cent of women suffer from this monthly ailment, the estimates of prevalence being dependent on the definition used and the population studied (Harrison *et al.*, 1985). Yet there are major problems in arriving at an agreed definition of PMS as there is little agreement on 'core' symptoms.[11]

The supposed effects of these raging hormones, now elevated to the status of psychiatric syndrome, are legion. As well as the monthly fluctuations in mood, which purportedly render women so unstable, PMS is said to be at the root of performance debilitation[12] (thus rendering women unreliable at work, in sports activities and in childcare – Tuch, 1975), and innumerable other more 'deviant' activities, such as suicide (Mandell and Mandell, 1967), psychiatric admissions (Luggin *et al.*, 1984), accidents (Lees, 1965; Dalton, 1964), violence (Morton *et al.*, 1953) and even murder (see Hey, 1985). These raging hormones certainly seem dangerous: the picture painted of the premenstrual woman is certainly of one who is 'mad'.[13] Yet there is no consistent empirical evidence for any of these supposed deleterious effects. Performance is not significantly affected by menstruation (Sommer, 1991; Ussher, 1992d), neither is there consistent evidence of mood variability (Ussher, 1991a), increased psychiatric admissions, accidents, suicide (Ussher, 1989), or cyclical violence (Nicolson, 1991). Thus the notion of menstrual lability is a fiction linked to fantasy, seen as fact, with no basis in reality.

Before unpeeling the layer of pseudo-scientific rhetoric which validates the existence of this syndrome, I would like to turn to the big sister of PMS, post-natal depression, a syndrome which further reinforces the mad/bad body discourse. PND is the label given to the depression, sadness, anger, or any other negative symptom, experienced by women following the birth of a child. Perhaps not surprisingly, given the reality of motherhood for many women, some degree of unhappiness is often experienced following childbirth, by both men and women. This may take the form of mild mood change, or be manifested in severe depression or anxiety. The woman may be tired. She may be experiencing a major reconsideration of her identity, particularly after the first child. She may feel overwhelmed by the myriad different responsibilities facing her – as may her partner. Whilst the reductionists would turn to the raging hormones for their explanation of this phenomenon, I would be more inclined to agree with theorists such as Paula Nicolson, who argues for a more social explanation, seeing PND as the grieving for the lost self after childbirth, a natural experience given the nature of childbirth as a life event; and suggesting that we should face 'up to the possibility of depression as a healthy and normal grief reaction, which, given conducive support, will enable a successful transition to motherhood' (Nicolson, 1990: 694). For whilst many women experience the 'blues' following childbirth (Nicolson, 1990; Elliot, 1984), the majority recover after a matter of days.[14] Hardly a debilitating illness; a 'syndrome'. Yet PND has become established in the psychiatric textbooks as an illness which 'infects' women after childbirth, and has come to be seen as an entity which *causes* the symptoms in the first place.

As I have argued elsewhere, there are many similarities between PMS and PND, which bodes ill for women (Ussher, 1989: 87). PND is now the blanket term used to describe and categorize all aspects of female discontent which occur following the birth of a child. It has a firm place in both medical and popular discourse, again said to affect between 5 and 95 per cent of women, depending on definition. As with PMS, there are major disagreements between researchers and clinicians as to exactly what PND is, and exactly when it can occur. Is it necessary for it to follow immediately on from childbirth, or can a woman who has a two-year-old child be suffering from post-natal depression? Given this, is not PND merely a convenient label for women's distress?

With both PMS and PND there is no clear evidence for a hormonal aetiology – the raging hormones just cannot be pinned down. Despite the wide range of different aetiological roots suggested, no one biochemical cause can be isolated.[15] In fact psychotropic interventions in the, rarely executed, double blind trials have been shown to be no more effective than a placebo. In the case of PMS, it has been claimed that over 80 per cent of women who are 'treated' with *any* form of intervention are 'cured' (Parlee, 1989). Given the negative side effects of many of the chemical PMS treatments, one might argue that biochemical interventions are unnecessary, as they will not achieve anything not achievable by less invasive means. There is also no evidence to suggest that the vast majority of women who complain of PMS have any hormonal abnormality. This has lead proponents of the reductionist hypotheses, such as Katrina Dalton, to declare that only a tiny percentage of women have 'true PMS' (Parlee, 1989). Yet considerable numbers of women flock to these researchers and like-minded clinicians, as they are seen as providing a 'cure' for an indeterminate number of symptoms and ailments which modern medicine has decreed are cyclical phenomena.

Protagonists of the raging hormones theory, such as Katrina Dalton (1964) are acclaimed as saviours of women from their uncontrollable biological selves; and the drug companies reinforce the message, through providing research funding, promotional material for both the 'curse' and their own particular 'cure', and continuous copy for the sensation-seeking newspapers.[16]

The menopausal syndrome is no different. Despite the popular belief (as prevalent in the nineteenth century as the twentieth) that the cessation of menstruation at the menopause brings with it a cornucopia of ailments, both physical and mental, there is little evidence for this. But, within the discourse of woman as biological creature, women are deemed ruled by our wombs. Hence, the end of the reproductive life (and, it is assumed, of active sexuality) is expected to signal a morass of misery and an end to any sense of usefulness. Only hormones, in the form of the miracle drugs in HRT (hormone replacement therapy) can offer the key to happiness. Again, the problem is seen to be within, raging through the woman's veins. But the reality is far from this. What limited research there is suggests (Hunter, 1990; Greene, 1984) that whilst women may experience some physical discomfort as a result of dryness of the vagina, dizzy spells or hot flushes during the menopause, there is no evidence for the 'menopausal madness' of popular myth (Ussher, 1989); a madness once described as the 'horror of this living decay' (Wilson, 1966). In fact, many women report that they find a new lease of life when their childbearing years are over, a challenge to the ageist and sexist construction of the menopausal woman as 'spent'.

However, despite the evidence to the contrary, PMS, PND and the menopausal syndrome are used as justifications for biological theories of women's madness, for describing women as biologically labile, once again attributing madness to the female body, source of all temptation and vulnerability. Modern madness has thus been attached to the female body in the same way that femininity and madness became synonymous in the nineteenth century. This functions to make man immune to such afflictions, as he cannot be affected by the dreaded hormones. It is also a way of tying women to our beleaguered bodies and offering no way out of madness other than that of the medical expert. For if our bodies are at the root of the problem, only physical treatments will provide the cure. Inevitably, the patriarchs are in control of this cure: women certainly cannot help themselves.

Reclaiming the body

In recent years there has been a new wave of feminist writing reconsidering the discourse associated with the female body, and reclaiming this particular territory as women's own (outlined in Chapter 7).[17] There has been a deconstruction of the myths and taboos associated with menstruation, pregnancy and the menopause, and of the ways in which the discourse associated with the woman's body is used to control women's lives. This view, which I myself advocate, says that it is not biology *per se* which is at the root of madness or distress; but because woman's reproductive cycle and sexuality are socially constructed as unnatural, polluted, and somehow indecent, and are represented within patriarchal or phallocentric discourse as a liability rather than a strength, women learn to experience our biology as negative. We are taught that our bodies are weak; that our bodies make us mad. Is it any wonder, then, that we turn to our bodies and to reproduction as a source of attribution when we *feel* mad?

However, whilst we may gaze with a critical eye at the medical discourse associated with the reproductive syndromes, we must also acknowledge that women's reproductive biology is a reality. We cannot explain it away with a new form of words. We cannot say to the woman who feels irritable or tense premenstrually or the woman who is tired and anxious after childbirth, 'It is all a social construction.' We cannot deny the existence of reproductive reality. For some women, the interaction of biological or hormonal factors with other social factors may lead to anxiety or depression.[18] For others, biology may have no effect. But biology is an undeniable reality. The other important factor is that women's *perceptions* of our biology may be of central importance. For if a woman believes herself to be affected detrimentally by her body, by menstruation, this may result in poor use of coping skills, or internal attributions for any difficulties she is experiencing.[19]

Thus there are limitations to a purely social constructionist approach to menstruation, to the stance taken by those whom I have previously described as the radical-feminist outsiders (Ussher, 1992b).[20] These theorists would argue that PMS is merely an ascription of pathology placed upon women's out-of-role behaviour, analogous to the general labelling arguments discussed above. But this analysis has problems. To deny completely the effects of biology itself, and argue that its only effects are those created by negative social constructions is not helpful to all women. One of the contradictions facing feminists is that between the social or cultural construction of syndromes such as PMS which pathologize and dismiss women, and which can be seen to have little basis in reality, and the increasing number of women who seek treatment for PMS, claiming that it is seriously disrupting their lives. As Parlee notes:

> What is strategically difficult for feminists is that many women now derive genuine benefits in their personal lives from an ideology that functions to explain and obscure social contradictions in their lives and those of other women.
>
> (Parlee, 1989: 20)

In fact, the most vehement proponents of PMS as a concept are frequently women who claim to suffer from it. It is a disservice to women to deny completely the effect of biology, as some feminists have done; menstruation, pregnancy and the menopause are a reality for the majority of women – not necessarily a negative reality, but there none the less, and part of the path to madness.

The woman – the mirror

> Women have served all these centuries as looking-glasses possessing the magic and delicious power of reflecting the figure of man at twice its natural size. Without that power probably the world would still be swamp and jungle. The glories of all our wars would be unknown . . . Whatever their use in civilised societies, mirrors are essential to all violent and heroic action. That is why Napoleon and Mussolini both insist so emphatically upon the inferiority of women.
>
> (Woolf, 1929: 36)

Virginia Woolf eloquently describes what she sees as woman's eternal role – the mirror for man's glory. She is always second best, always the second sex. If this is so, it is no wonder that women are mad. The relationship between madness and society, particularly that of patriarchal society, has been discussed earlier in this book, but it is important to renew acquaintance with the debate, for it is one of the most consistent themes in the sociological debates on women's mental health.

As was disclosed above, it is not all women who fall into the contaminating diagnostic categories; only those in particular social roles. Thus, it is not something inherent in femininity or womanhood that makes us mad. Rather, it is a result of the construction of femininity in our society and the way in which women are treated; a result of the roles were are compelled to play.

The economic root of madness

The raw facts on women's social role, which to a certain extent speak for themselves, make for a depressing picture. Women are significantly poorer than men. It is an oft-repeated statistic that whilst women do

Table 9.1 Occupation group earnings, 1988, for the UK (Equal Opportunities Commission, 1990, UK)

		Females £ (weekly earnings)	Males £ (weekly earnings)
I	Professional and related supporting management and administration	270.4	365.4
II	Professional and related in education, welfare and health	206.9	290.8
III	Literary, artistic and sports	228.7	310.0
IV	Professional and related in science, engineering, technology and similar fields	197.7	291.8
V	Managerial (excluding general management)	198.9	289.7
VI	Clerical and related	150.5	194.1
VII	Selling	128.5	221.5
VIII	Security and protective servicing	232.1	255.4
IX	Catering, cleaning, hairdressing and other personal service	116.7	158.7
X	Farming, fishing and related	—	151.2
XI	Materials processing (excl. metals)	125.6	201.2
XII	Making, repairing (excl. metal and electrical)	120.3	207.2
XIII	Processing, making, repairing and related (metal and electrical)	140.2	223.4
XIV	Painting, repetitive assembling, products inspection, packaging and related	130.4	194.0
XV	Construction and mining	—	200.7
XVI	Transport operating, materials moving and storing and related	132.8	196.4
XVII	Miscellaneous	—	181.5

90 per cent of the work in the world they own 1 per cent of the wealth (World Health Organization). In Britain, for example, whilst 70 per cent of women are, in statisticians' jargon, 'economically active' with 36 per cent working full-time and 28 per cent part-time, women earn significantly less than men, on average achieving only three-quarters of men's earnings.[21] This is not explained by the fact that men are taking up the better-paid positions: at all levels of employment, women earn less – even in the same-level job as a man. The rhetoric of equal opportunities is, unfortunately, merely rhetoric, as the figures in the table above demonstrate.

These figures do not reflect educational achievement, for although fewer women are enrolled as full-time undergraduates at university (in 1988 in Britain, 98.6 women to 130 men, per thousand), a higher percentage of women than men embark on full-time further education, other than the traditional degree (92.3 women to 62.8 men, per thousand). In fact, the gender difference in education is not reflected in the numbers of women achieving qualifications, but in the type of qualifications they receive: girls are over-represented in the arts subjects, and boys in the science subjects (EOC, 1990).[22] Statistics from North America reflect a similar picture: women are as well educated as men (with an average of 12.5 years' schooling), yet they earn 40 per cent less than men, are more likely to be employed in part-time or low-status positions, and earn less when occupying the same positions as men.[23]

Poverty and madness have a close relationship. As one recent authority claimed, 'The correlation between poverty and psychiatric disorder is one of the most well-established research findings in psychiatric epidemiology' (Russo, 1990: 370). Those in low-income groups are more likely to be subjected to uncontrollable and threatening life events, to experience crime and violence, and to be subjected to the stress of poor housing and financial uncertainties (Brown and Harris, 1978; Makosky, 1982). Poverty is often associated with poorer social support,[24] and thus with an absence of any buffer from stress. Across the board those in the economically poorer groups in society (the elderly, women and ethnic minorities) are more likely to receive a psychiatric diagnosis, and to be subjected to the (often unwanted) attention of a variety of official agencies.[25] This can increase an individual's sense of powerlessness, placing her further along the road to madness.

Patriarchy and power

The other clear fact illustrated by the statistics on women's occupations is that women are represented in far greater numbers in the low-status positions – positions which also have low access to power. So women's feelings of powerlessness are certainly not irrational. The patriarchs are still at the helm, despite the myth of the post-feminist age. To take the very top of the tree of power, government: in Britain, women make up only 6.3 per cent of the elected Members of Parliament (Social Trends, 1990) – a position not dissimilar to that in other European countries (Table 9.2).

In the judiciary the position is similar: in Britain in 1988 there were three female and seventy-six male High Court judges, thirteen female and 378 male circuit judges. In medicine in 1991 only 15 per cent of medical consultants were female (Department of Social Services, 1991). I could go on – the picture is effectively the same in every profession. Even in professions which are predominantly female – clinical psychology or nursing[26] – those in control are male. The ubiquitous pyramid of power seems always to have men firmly placed at the pinnacle.

Table 9.2 Women elected to Parliament at the most recent election: in Western European countries[27]

	Total no. of members	Total no. of women members	Date of General Election	% Women
United Kingdom	650	41	June 1987	6.3
Austria	183	21	Nov. 1986	11.5
Belgium	212	18	Dec. 1987	8.5
Denmark	179	52	June 1988	29.1
Finland	200	63	Mar. 1987	31.5
France	577	23	June 1988	4.0
Germany (Fed. Rep.)	519	80	Jan. 1987	15.4
Greece	300	13	June 1989	4.3
Iceland	63	13	Aug. 1988	20.6
Irish Rep.	166	13	June 1989	7.8
Italy	630	81	June 1987	12.9
Luxembourg	60	9	June 1989	15.0
Netherlands	150	32	May 1986	21.3
Norway	165	60	Sep. 1989	36.4
Portugal	250	17	July 1987	6.8
Spain	343	23	June 1986	6.7
Sweden	349	133	Sep. 1988	38.1
Switzerland	246	33	Oct. 1987	13.4

The burden of care

Not only are women disadvantaged in the workplace and powerless in public life – they are placed in the position of greatest responsibility in the home. Despite the fact that 70 per cent of women are in paid employment, 95 per cent still carry out *all* the household tasks (Social Trends, 1990). The shopping, cooking and cleaning are largely done by women even when both partners are in full-time work. Women are effectively carrying out two full-time jobs; and, as Oakley has argued, housework is a depressing, alienating occupation, thankless and unrewarding (Oakley, 1976). The long working hours (on average seventy-seven a week), the isolation, confinement and heavy responsibility make many 'housewives' mad (Sharpe, 1984). Woman's work is silent and forgotten; never ending, never relenting – always demanding.

Women also carry out the major part of childcare. In Britain, only 14 per cent of women use a creche, or nursery, the rest relying on partner (44 per cent), grandmother (40 per cent), or child minder (23 per cent) to care for the children when they are at work. The situation in the

USA is similar. Yet, as 12 per cent of families in Britain (EOC, 1988) and 14 per cent of families in the USA (US Department of Labor, 1980) are headed solely by a woman, it is clear that, for a significant number of women, childcare is a singularly isolated task. Even when they have a partner, women carry the major part of the burden. The 'new man', who cooks, cleans and cares, seems to be a figment of the advertisers' imaginations.

The madness in motherhood

Children themselves may also contribute to women's madness – however inadvertently. The idealized image of the glowing madonna gaining pleasure and fulfilment from her angelic offspring is far removed from the reality of many women's experience. High rates of depression are reported by women with children – and this is not the result of raging hormones unbalancing the woman's mind, as some would have us believe.

Women experience more change and greater impact on identity development than men in the transition to parenthood (McBride, 1990) and they feel more responsibility for the health and well being of the child. Women who work outside the home must cope with the often conflicting demands of their dual roles, whilst those who stay at home often experience isolation and identity conflict (Ussher, 1989; McBride, 1990). And for women whose children have continuing behavioural or health problems, the transition to parenthood is particularly difficult. For it has been found that rates of depression in women are highly correlated with 'behavioural disturbance' or health problems in their children (McBride, 1988; Richman, 1978). A woman who is depressed is more likely to have a child with sleep problems, temper tantrums, continuous crying, or any other of the difficulties found in children. Whether the problems experienced by the child cause the woman to be depressed, or vice versa, is uncertain: the relationship may work either way (Pound *et al.*, 1985; Hunt, 1986). For women who find they have a difficult child often report feeling they have somehow failed, and perceive the problems as a reflection of their own inadequacy. (As women are invariably blamed, it is not surprising that we easily blame ourselves.) Equally, a mother who is withdrawn and unhappy may communicate her feelings, however unintentionally, to her child, causing tension and disturbance. What *is* certain is that a vicious spiral may ensue, with depressed mother and difficult child moving together in a helpless and hopeless dance of misery.

Having children can be a rewarding and fulfilling experience for women. It can also be soul-destroying, tiring and frustrating, leaving a woman with little sense of identity other than that of 'mother'. Men who mirror the traditional mothering role (and they are few) experience much of the same isolation and depression (Hunt, 1986; Jenkins, 1986); and it surely cannot be their 'raging hormones'. Is it any wonder that the hard work and drudge of childcare is usually carried out by women, women who are told that this activity is the culmination of their creative powers, whilst men get on with the 'real' work, reaping the joys and benefits of children as they grow, without the same soul-destroying sacrifice? So the very fact of being the mother – the major role in many women's lives – can drive women mad.

It is not only children who place women in the seemingly endless role of carer and nurturer, for in our increasingly elderly society, when 'care in the community' is the catchphrase on every politician's lips, women increasingly take on the burden of caring for the sick and the elderly. Women make up the vast majority of unpaid and often unnoticed carers (Eichler and Parron, 1987; Horowitz, 1985). The stresses of such a role are often interminable: financial hardship, deteriorating personal relationships, physical and emotional collapse – a recipe for madness (Brody, 1983; Cantor, 1983).

Women are also over-represented in the elderly population itself – a population which is both one of the poorest groups in society (Eichler and Parron, 1987), and one prone to physical and psychological problems. Madness is not an inevitable consequence of ageing, but may be due to the treatment of the elderly in our society: the general lack of care, respect and status given to those perceived to be 'past their prime'. The consequences of Alzheimer's disease, which affects 25 per cent of people over eighty-five years of age (Cohen, 1988), in addition to other physical health problems, the dependency and the absence of support for the elderly (Mowbray and Beneder, 1988) cannot be ignored. And most of those affected are women (Cohen, 1988; Horowitz, 1985).

To return to the mirror metaphor – women as a group have less access to power, less access to resources in society, and yet are expected to care, to mother, to provide that particularly female gift, nurturance and security. At the same time, women are subjected to abuse, verbal, physical and sexual – abuse which erodes a sense of positive identity. The all-caring, coping woman is both marginalized and derided. And who cares for women? Perhaps that is part of the problem. Even when they are in supposedly supportive relationships, such as marriage, women seem to suffer – or, at least, escape from the general assumption that relationships are a protective factor for mental health,[28] for marriage is not good for our health – despite the myth of 'happy ever after' we are reared on.

Marriage and madness

> Marriage is a step so grave and decisive that it attracts light-headed, variable men by its very awfulness . . . Marriage is like life in this – that it is a field of battle, and not a bed of roses.
>
> (Robert Louis Stevenson)[29]

That marriage is bad for men is a popular illusion. For a man to receive condolences at the news that he has finally been 'hooked' is a not uncommon experience – it is the stuff of much jolly joke-making in our society. Men might convince themselves that they are reluctant to wed, but the reality is that, whilst in general marriage is not a bed of roses for women, it is men who bloom. In fact, it is not married men, but single men who are more likely to be deemed mad, to be diagnosed and treated as such. Empirical research, examining both the community surveys and the officially recognized 'cases', shows that married status is one of the major factors correlated with women's diagnosis as depressed. Married women are at higher risk of receiving a psychiatric diagnosis, of reporting distress and of relapsing after diagnosis than married men or single women.[30] Thus, according to these studies, married women and single men are the groups who appear to be at highest risk of psychiatric diagnosis, with marriage acting to protect men, and place women at risk.

It is not marriage *per se* which sends women mad, for not all married women receive a psychiatric diagnosis![31] But the particular role which women adopt in traditional marraige, a passive, subservient role – the classic mirror of man – is that which is detrimental to women's health. As we well know, 'Married women occupy a subservient position relative to married men and carry out numerous social and physical support services for their husbands' (Mulvey and Dohrenwend, 1983): the position of unpaid housekeeper, or servant. It is particularly those women who are married, not in paid employment, with children living at home, who are most at risk of being positioned as mad and slipping into madness. In fact, it has been claimed quite categorically that:

> The data indicate that married men who work are in the best mental health, that married women who are unemployed are in the worst mental health, and that the mental health of employed housewives falls in between. Having children in the household generally contributes to poor mental health.
>
> (Gove and Geerken, 1977: 68)

The sociological work carried out by Brown and Harris in the 1970s was one of the milestones in this area. It showed that working-class women at home with three children under fourteen years of age were five times as likely to suffer from depression. The absence of a supportive relationship with a partner was deemed to be a major risk factor here (Brown and Harris, 1978). In fact, interestingly, more recent work has shown that single mothers with children were *less* likely to report depression than those who were married, as the single women had good supportive networks in the community (Brown *et al.*, 1986). So the presence of a partner is not enough to buffer the effects of a stressful environment, as many partners are ineffective in reality.

The statistics presented above show that women's position in society can have a sepulchral effect; burial under the burden of boredom and isolation. It may be the absence of a meaningful role outside the home which marks women as mad. It may be the effect of being tied to the frustrating, boring, low-status, unpaid role of housewife. Or the fact that women's work is deemed second-rate, supplementary to that of her man. We educate women to expect equality in many cases, and then we expect them to be happy with the crumbs from the table. It is no wonder we feel mad.

A woman's role is diffuse, unclear, and her work never-ending. As a 'housewife'[32] she has little structure to her day, and no clear delineation of tasks. She has few rewards. She is often a door-mat for her family, with little or no control. Women who are in work, in egalitarian relationships, women who are economically independent, women who have support with childcare, will be at less risk of going mad. Analogies can be made between the role of the classically depressed housewife and the unemployed man, who is also at high risk of depression, a similarity permitting the conclusion that:

> Many fewer women than men are in employment, and it is towards unemployment, rather than marital status, that we should be looking as a major determinant of sex differences in psychopathology.
>
> (Cochrane and Stopes-Roe, 1981: 380)

A simple and sensible analysis one might think, leading to the conclusion that we should merely change women's roles, and their madness will disappear. These theories have had a fundamental effect on the way in which madness in women has been framed within the dominant discourses of patriarchy, allowing for social theories of depression to be supported, and for more socially supportive interventions to be advocated. It has also shifted the focus of search from a biological aetiology to that of a more social one: the madness resulting from living in a high-rise block with three children and little social support is not seen as hormonally induced, but as a direct consequence of the environment. All well and good. But these theories have a serious underside, a more malevolent function.

One of the dangers in these liberal social theories is that they mask the reality of the power differential in marriage. They imply that all we need to do is make relationships more egalitarian, give women more support, open up the employment market for women, and change will take place. In fact some authors seem to think this has already taken place. For example, speaking in 1981, Cochrane and Stopes-Roe dismissed the argument that marriage was a health hazard for women, claiming:

> Although Gove cites evidence from community surveys in the US supporting the existence of a real marital status difference in psychopathology these studies pre-date the changes in sex role definitions, the trends towards a less rigid division of labour in marriage and the fuller participation of married women in the labour force that have undoubtedly occurred in the last decade.
>
> (Cochrane and Stopes-Roe, 1981: 380)

Here we are again – the myth of the post-feminist era with its misleading argument that, since equality is here, feminists should put down their banners, and turn their attentions to other sorts of injustice. This is patently not the case, as the statistics cited above testify. Just take marriage as an example. Whilst marriage may be more egalitarian today (and this is debatable if you look at the divisions of labour, the violence, the oppression), in terms of women's increasingly keeping their own name or having independent tax rights, it is still an institution which has negative effects on many women's mental health. The changes have been merely on the surface – superficial niceties, not fundamental changes in power.

The tyranny of marriage

> Marriage is an institution which robs a woman of her individuality and reduces her to the level of a prostitute.
>
> (Dennison, 1914)

> Marriage laws sanctified rape by reiterating the right of the rapist to ownership of the raped. Marriage laws protected the property rights of the first rapist by designating the second rapist as an adulterer, that is, a thief. Marriage laws also protected the father's ownership of the daughter. Marriage laws guaranteed the father's right to sell a daughter into marriage, to sell her to another man.
>
> (Dworkin, 1974: 27)

Traditionally in marriage, the woman has been passed from the father to the husband, an exchange 'of her person for the means of subsistence' (Hamilton, 1909: 36). This 'traffic in women' maintains social cohesion, social order, and sustains the continuation of the status quo, the existing patriarchal power structures. At the most fundamental level, it is based on the transfer of property, the ownership of women, and the maintenance of a woman's sexuality within a contractual agreement. Whilst their main function within post-industrial capitalist society is the maintenance of an economic relationship in which 'each household operates as an economic entity much like a corporation' (Millett, 1971: 59), marriages are represented as romantic or religious rites, when in reality, to some, they represent an institution 'worse than prostitution. To call them sacred or moral has been seen as a desecration' (Aveling and Aveling, 1886). Marriage is represented in popular discourse as a loving, trusting sincere relationship, the pinnacle of a woman's achievement (she has caught her man) and the fulfilment of all desires. In reality, it is often a 'crisis, trial, struggle, trauma, problem [a] perilous journey over a rocky road' (Quinn, 1984). The juxtaposition of the fantasy perpetuated by women's magazines and the media with reality is cruel.

Over the last hundred years, from the era of the Victorian mad woman to the present-day 'neurotic', the institution of marriage has been fundamentally connected to women's experience of distress. It is no coincidence that the women who attempted to escape from their husbands through the 1870 Divorce Act were deemed mad (Showalter, 1987). It is no coincidence that women who are today diagnosed as suffering from syndromes such as 'agoraphobia' or 'depression' (the modern-day maladies) are often found on closer inspection to be experiencing 'marital difficulties'. It is not a surprise for a well-meaning clinical psychologist to 'cure' a woman of agoraphobia, only to find that she is deeply unhappy in her relationship with her husband (as in the case discussed in Chapter 1). The answer for many is to involve the husband in the 'treatment'; or to acknowledge that the woman is experiencing 'symptom substitution' – manifesting her distress in symptoms of agoraphobia or depression rather than admitting to the 'real' issue; to say that the 'symptom bearer [is the] marital distance regulator' (Byng-Hall, 1980). But is this not just skirting the issue, a refusal to acknowledge that marriage as an institution is often one which strips a woman of her identity and her power? Perhaps Bruley was right when she commented:

> Someone coming from another planet and looking at a marriage contract and the semi-slavery it entails for that woman would think it insane that she should enter into it voluntarily.
>
> (Bruley, 1976: 44)

From a feminist perspective, it is these aspects of marriage which link with madness – not the seemingly innocuous 'role' which is stripped of its real connection with oppression and power. It is no coincidence that many married women are mad. Anyone embarking upon what is seen as 'slavery' within the institution which is the 'bastion of male power' (Rivers, 1977: 40) would be mad.

Within marriage a woman has traditionally given up her right to autonomous sexuality, to say 'no' to her husband if he desires sexual intercourse.[33] It is still the case that, 'It is within marriage that a woman is most likely to be slapped and shoved about, severely assaulted, killed or raped' (Dobash and Dobash, 1979). In fact, the majority of women who are sexually assaulted are not the victims of a stranger, the monstrous man who jumps out of the dark in popular myth. Over 80 per cent of women who are sexually assaulted know the man who attacks them (Koss, 1990: 102). And sadly, the physical and sexual abuse of women within marriage is endemic (Barshis, 1983). It may no longer be the case that a man can legitimately beat his wife if he uses a stick 'no wider than his thumb', as he could in the nineteenth century (a law only abolished in the 1930s in the USA – Martin, 1976), but marital violence is still seen as a private affair. If we hear women scream, we feel we shouldn't interfere. We should scream softly, for the neighbours may hear. And if the estimates are accurate that one in seven women are raped and one-third of women experience violence in marriage, a lot of women are screaming.[34]

If the neighbours do hear, they will not interfere: 'Family violence, in contrast with violence outside the family, is more often perceived as normal, legitimate, and instrumental' (Hilberman, 1984: 214). Some facts bear testimony to this. A high percentage of murders occur within the family, with estimates ranging between 20 and 50 per cent, depending on the country in question and the time studied (Hilberman, 1984). About 40 per cent of women who are murdered are killed by their spouse, compared to 10 per cent of men, so it is clear which party is more at risk (Dobash and Dobash, 1978). Cases of murder are only the tip of the iceberg: the number of women brutalized and battered by their partners is incalculable. We cannot know the reality of it for many women remain silent.

Whilst there is increasing concern about 'wife battering',[35] as the reality of women's persecution is realized, those who might intervene are often loath to do so. The police see it as a 'family affair'. And while, in Britain anyway, the public discourse of the police is now one of sympathy towards battered wives, the reality is often very different. The women are often not taken seriously since it is believed that they will not prosecute; that in the final analysis they will retract their claims.[36] When the consequence of prosecuting their husbands, via the unwieldy machinery of the law, is invariably poverty, fear and isolation (for the woman must fight every step of the way without the man who has financially supported her) it is not surprising that many women are forced to scream in silence. They see no other way out. And many who scream will be deemed to deserve it, will be blamed anyway, for, as Klein comments:

> Pervasive abuse of wives is reflected in media images of sexually vulnerable females and in everyday social life, with its repertoire of jokes about nagging wives inviting their just deserts.
>
> (Klein, 1982: 85)

This may seem a wholly depressing picture, but marriage does not inevitably make women mad. It is not an inevitably oppressive relationship. Undoubtedly many men and women do manage to create relationships which are egalitarian, caring and loving. Family relationships are not all abusive, either physically or sexually. But not all families are loving and caring and supportive. The 'return to Victorian values' advocated by the Thatcher and Reagan governments in Britain and the USA in the 1980s does not mean a return to love and care. It can mean a return to isolation, oppression, control, and to powerlessness. In many families it is already there. And its effects are clear – even if we choose not to recognize them.

Sexual violence

One other aspect of a woman's experience worthy of consideration is the issue of sexual harassment and violence, in both the public and private arenas. This is another area of silence, of taboo, only recently (in terms of women's history) exposed, encouraged by the type of feminist analysis of sexual violence discussed in Chapter 2. Sexual abuse of women and girls is endemic in our society. We can only guess at the reality of its prevalence, and balk at the astounding figures produced from different epidemiological studies. The evidence we do have tells a chilling picture. It is estimated that 70 per cent of women experience sexual harassment at work (Stockdale, 1991), ranging from continuous salacious comments, to outright attack, or rape. On a daily basis many women feel that their very person is under attack, that they must continuously watch for their safety, that their sexuality is under constant surveillance.

And this experience of surveillance is not based on paranoia. For as Koss comments, when reporting the results of epidemiological studies:

> Sexual abuse and assault has been experienced by 30% to 67% of adult women recalling the period before the age of 18, 12% of adolescent girls, 15% of college women, and approximately 20% of adult women.
>
> (Koss, 1990: 375)

Others estimate that one in four women has been raped (Baker-Miller, 1986). But these are all estimates: whilst we can look to statistics and social trends to demonstrate women's absence from positions of power in society, there are few statistics on sexual assaults, for the women largely remain silent. As Koss argues, only '5% to 8% of adult sexual assault cases were reported to the police . . . by comparison, 61.5% of the robberies and 82.5% of the burglaries were reported' (Koss, 1990: 375). If women are silent, our experiences can be ignored; and the abuse continues, unnoted and unchecked. Another vicious spiral.

Adult women are not the only victims. It is estimated that between one in ten and one in three children is sexually abused (Herman and Hirschman, 1984; Whitewell, 1990). In the late twentieth century Western society has woken up to the reality of sexual abuse.[37] And while over 90 per cent of rape and sexual abuse victims are female (suggesting that a considerable number of boys and men are sexually assaulted), 99 per cent of those charged with rape are men (Koss, 1990: 374).

Sexual abuse exerts a deleterious effect on women's mental and physical health, as Herman and Hirschman argue:

> The testimony of these victims,[38] and the observations of their therapists, is convincing evidence that the incest experience was harmful to them and left long-lasting scars. Many victims had severely impaired object relations with both men and women. The overvaluation of men led them into conflictual and often intensely masochistic relationships with men. The victims' devaluation of themselves and their mothers impaired development of supportive relationships with women. Many of the victims also had a well-formed negative identity as witch, bitch, or whore. In adult life they continued to make repeated ineffectual attempts to expiate their intense feelings of guilt and shame.
>
> (Herman and Hirschman, 1984: 253–4)

Recent evidence from research studies, clinical reports and the reports of women themselves, provides compelling support for the belief that sexual abuse is one of the major factors which lead to women's madness.

It has been argued that women who are victims of violence are more likely to be diagnosed as 'mad', being likely to be diagnosed specifically as having depression, alcohol/drug abuse, generalized anxiety, obsessive compulsive disorders, post-traumatic stress disorders, eating disorders, multiple personality or borderline syndrome (Burnam *et al.*, 1988; Kilpatrick *et al.*, 1985; Koss, 1990; Parrot and Bechhofer, 1991). In one recent study of 140 women psychiatric outpatients, 64 per cent had a history of physical or sexual abuse, and the abused women reported more symptoms than the non-abused women (Surrey *et al.*, 1990).

Women who have been abused are also more likely to engage in self-injurious behaviour or attempts to commit suicide (Koss, 1990). They often experience a distorted sense of reality as the victimization creates a negative sense of the world, where little seems meaningful (Taylor, 1983) and where the woman herself feels weak, needy, frightened and out of control (Horowitz *et al.*, 1980). The woman's image of the world, and of herself, can become imbued with negative overtones. Yet the whole issue of sexual abuse was ignored by many researchers and practitioners in the past (Jacobson and Richardson, 1987; Koss, 1988); and, as women were not routinely asked about abusive experiences, they did not report them. Given the recently emerging evidence (Jehu, 1988), this was a serious omission.

Women often remain silent about sexual abuse, possibly because of the 'forced secrecy that is almost uniformly demanded by perpetrators of abuse' (Koss, 1990: 375), or because once again women are positioned as responsible (Burt, 1980), which means that support and help are not forthcoming. Even when women do disclose, many find the response they receive is less than helpful, as few professionals are able to provide the ameliorative support so desperately sought (Wheeler and Berliner, 1988). Is it surprising then that many women attempt to forget or deny the abuse, developing survival strategies that often 'form the basis of the damaged self ' (Koss, 1990: 376). It seems that violation of the self – both physically and psychologically – may continue to be a part of many women's lives until we can face up to it, and no longer allow it to go unspoken.

The discourse which positions women as mad spreads its influence much wider than the family and is often more covert than in the practice of sexual violence and abuse. For it is the misogynistic discourse which positions woman as the mirror, as powerless, as the Other, which underlies the images of women pervasive in Western society – the images which confront us on a daily basis, reminding us of our place as the second sex.

The guilty secret: The defined sex

> There is then, for women, an ambivalence between fascination and damage in looking at themselves and images of other women. The adult woman near totally abandons the love which the little girl had for her own image, in the period of narcissistic glory. But this culture damages the glory and turns it into a guilty secret. The girl-child discovers herself to be scrutinised, discovers herself to be the defined sex, the sex on which society seeks to write its sexual and moral ideals.
>
> (Coward, 1984: 81)

Women are caught in the voyeuristic gaze, caught as fragmented objects of desire. Castrated and castigated, we are cut off from our own experiences, from any positive representations, and forced to live through images provided for us, images as pervasive as they are powerful. We may be seduced by the images, but they are also powerful instruments of destruction. They destroy a woman's identity, her autonomy, and her freedom. Strong words, but justified.

Images of women are everywhere – glaring down at us from every advertising hoarding, looking up from the newspaper page, gazing into our lives from the television and cinema screens. The visual image may be the most archetypal and most limiting to real women, but the image of women in written or spoken discourse is not fundamentally different. The role of language in maintaining the position of woman as 'other' has been one of the most prolific areas of discussion in the seventies and eighties, as discussed above. Novels, academic discourse, newspapers and magazines present and perpetuate particular images of women, images which define the boundaries of our experience by creating the models against which we compare ourselves, thus shaping our existence. They create a potentially deleterious context within which a woman's identity is formed. For women internalize the images, internalize the underlying messages, internalize the inherent constraints and entreaties to compliance. What we see is what we are. The images define us. The images contain us. And perhaps the images drive us mad.

What the images achieve is the verbal or pictorial representation of the archetypal woman – the woman I have traced through history as represented in art, literature, science and the spoken discourse. The Victorian 'angel in the house', the madonna or the whore, the castrating sexual monster, the sex object, the submissive wife, the pedestalled princess, all are present in today's prolific images. And just as these images dictated the representation and treatment of the Victorian woman or the witch, so they shape our experiences and understanding of women today. The medium may be more sophisticated, but the message is the same. Women are dangerous. Women are weak. Women are imbued with sexuality and as such must be controlled and contained. The pedestal, represented today in the image of the 'perfect woman', to which the majority of us cannot aspire, serves well.

During the last twenty years feminist scholarship has been actively exploring and exposing the images of women which fill our gaze.[39] Examining this material can be uncomfortable. It can provoke anger, shame and despair. Anger and despair at the negativity of the images, shame at the way we are drawn to them, and emulate them. It can also provoke humour at the ridiculous posture in which women are positioned. We laugh at the almost prehistoric images of the consumer woman or the 'little woman' represented in the advertisements of the 1950s: the wife waiting for her man; ecstatic about her new vacuum cleaner;

orgasmic in her clean kitchen; driven to cries of delight by the power of the cleaning product foisted on her. How ridiculous we exclaim. How things have changed! But have they?

The soft sell: Advertising

> In ads women are frequently represented in a fragmented way . . . signified by their lips, legs, hair, eyes or hands, which stand metonymically . . . for the sexual woman.
>
> (Winship, 1987: 25)

> The consumer is not a moron, she is your wife!
>
> (David Ogilvy, advertising director)[40]

The late twentieth century has become the era of the advertiser. From every street corner, from every newspaper or magazine, from the very walls of the trains on which we travel and the packets of food we eat startling images leap out, entreating us to buy, to live a particular lifestyle, to be a particular person. We may claim to be immune to such pressures, resistant to the advertisers' pleas, but we internalize the messages, and we do buy. We do believe. The advertisers tell it how it is, and we soak it up.

Advertisers are selling more than their products: they are selling a lifestyle. And they are selling a particular image of woman. She who is caring. She who is nurturant. She who is always available to man, for his sexual pleasure, or as his domestic slave. The two roles are complementary, for the woman in the advertisements is caught in the gaze of man for his pleasure, always ready to serve, in the bedroom or in the kitchen. As women look at these images, we cannot avoid taking in the message that we are there for *Him*.

In the dawn of the advertising era in the 1950s the characteristic image of woman was in the role of wife, mother or seductress. Woman as consumer was perhaps the most popular theme, the woman encouraged to believe that she needed the goods on offer in order to be fulfilled. Without them, she was incomplete: she is persuaded that she 'cannot live another day without acquiring whatever it is you are offering' (Faulder, 1977: 37). In this role, woman is compliant. She washes the clothes, scrubs the floor, cooks the food – and she loves it! How many women gain pleasure from the dull monotony of housework as does the advertiser's woman who manages to be attractive and happy as she bends to her task? She enjoys feeding her family, serving her man. As we see these women, comparing our feelings of drudgery, observing our dishevelled image and experiencing boredom and frustration, we know that we are failures. It is not only the image of the woman as eager consumer that seduces us. It is also the image of her home, the home that cocoons and satisfies her. We too want to be satisfied, satiated by material possessions. When we look at the 'ideal homes' occupied by the media women, we strive to emulate: to be perfect, to be happy. For as Coward argues:

> Home-writing encourages a narcissistic identification between women and their 'style'. The language of home-improvement in fact encourages an identification with women's bodies and their homes; houses like women are, after all, called stylish, elegant and beautiful.
>
> (Coward, 1984: 63)

The image of the woman and her home almost merge into one. The message is clear. Fulfilment achieved is through striving for perfection; having the perfect home; being the perfect woman.

In the final decade of the twentieth century advertisers have begun to wake up to the fact that women are no longer chained to the kitchen sink, that we occupy roles outside those prescribed by patriarchy, and that the housewife at home is a media myth. Despite this, she is still the dominant image presented, as shown by a recent survey of European TV advertising where 43 per cent of images overall were of women in the home, 18 per cent of women at work. In some countries the differential was more notable; for example, in Britain 50 per cent and in Luxembourg 57 per cent of images were of the woman as home-maker (Thoveron, 1987: 56). The woman as independent careerist, as independent consumer is, however, beginning to infiltrate our TV screens and occupy our advertising hoardings. In Britain in 1990 one of the most successful TV campaigns has featured a 'yuppie' career woman who travels on Concorde, as an advertisement for 'Gold Blend' coffee. Sales have soared since the on-screen romance with her eligible (male) neighbour has been serialized. Similarly, 'power dressed' women sell car phones, sell mineral water, seemingly sell an emancipated lifestyle. But have things really changed? These glossy, beautiful women are as unrepresentative of real women's lives as is the image of the mother who is fulfilled by her family's washing. And in whose interests have these changes occurred? Have the changes taken place as a result of commercial interests, a recognition of the fact that women are no longer willing to buy the image of the passive home-maker?

Even the career woman is portrayed in a seductive and appealing light. Her sexuality is of more interest and importance than her veneer of professionalization. Her seriousness and efficiency are skin-deep: underneath she is like all women, ready for her man. As Coward comments on the now infamous 1970s bra advert, 'underneath they're all lovable':

> The woman is shown dressed in glamorous but business-like clothes. It's

> night time and she is scowling into the camera, as if stopped for a moment as she goes about her business. In the right-hand corner, the same woman is shown in a posture directly taken from pornography. She's opening up her blouse to reveal her bra . . . the suggestion is that however tough and resistant women appear they are still sexual, sensual, soft and lovable.
> (Coward, 1984: 60)

The aforementioned coffee advert is the same. The emancipated woman falls for the man. Underneath the tough exterior, women all want the same thing: to be desired, to be seduced, to be consumed by the all-embracing male presence. We return to the power of the phallus, the instrument of female pleasure and male power. And how the media woman loves it! As she consumes she is consummated. She might feign resistance, but this serves only to increase her pleasure, and that of her man. In the patriarchal discourse resistance is an attractive part of femininity. Here it is portrayed as false, like the beauty which conceals the danger within. It is part of the veil concealing the 'seething passion', the dangerous sexuality. The man is encouraged to overcome the resistance, possess the woman, and thus neutralize her danger. He believes the woman wants it.

The look of 'aggressive resistance' is now common parlance of the seductive beautiful women who fill the advertising hoardings. The 1950s saw the cheesecake grin, the bright and beaming young bride. The 1970s, 1980s and 1990s seem to be characterized by the pout, the woman feigning independence. But this image is not resistant, it is not inspired by strength or autonomy. It denotes availability and arousal. For as Coward argues, 'the woman's seriousness denotes readiness for sex. If the expression appears to say, "Fuck you", it actually reads, "Fuck me" ' (Coward, 1984: 59). Whether as temptress, as powerful bitch, or as scantily clad innocent virgin, the woman is presenting herself as available. Her beauty and her sexuality enhance the product she sells. She sells herself as she sells the goods. And as goods can be discarded once their 'shelf life' is over, the woman also can be discarded. She too is to be taken and used as conveniently and thoughtlessly as the products she proffers in the advertisements. The images are a part of the same misogynistic process examined in the discussion of pornography, for, as Wallsgrove claimed, 'pornography can be seen as merely an extension of images of women in adverts as shiny decorative objects' (Wallsgrove, 1987: 172).

The body beautiful

One of the features of advertisements which reinforces the objectification of women, and the belief that we can be consumed and discarded, is the portrayal of women in fragmented images of dislocated and disconnected parts of the body.[41] The hand which holds the desired object is clearly female; the elegant fingers, the painted nails, mark it as such. The shapely legs which advertise slinky stockings convey the same message, representing a woman disconnected from herself, useful only in parts, cut up into pieces. We thus see ourselves as dislocated, and examine ourselves as separate parts, some good, some bad. And thus:

> . . . because of the fragmentation of the body into separate areas, most women value certain aspects of their bodies: eyes, hair, teeth, smile. This positive self-image has to be maintained against the grain for the dice are loaded against women liking themselves in this society.
>
> (Coward, 1984: 45–6)

This denial of wholeness, this scrutiny of ourselves as a collection of fragmented 'bits', contains, controls and depresses. The female body is displayed and revealed as a desirable commodity to be admired, revered – and emulated by mere mortal women. Whether in fashion pieces (Myers, 1987), in advertisements for 'healthy products' (Coward, 1984: 22) or in exhortations to women to 'stay slim', to loose that extra weight,[42] the ideal and beautiful female body is exposed for our delight. But the body that we see, perfect in its flawlessness, is unreal. It taunts us as it tempts us. We compare, and we despair. We are encouraged to believe that there is hope, that we too can look delectable in the latest fashions or on the beach if we only follow the correct regime, take the correct exercise, buy the right products. What a con! Women often feel guilty, anxious, depressed about their own appearance, filled with the '*disgust* of fat and flesh' (Coward, 1984: 43). But the image of beauty is a mirage; and if we attempt to emulate it, rather than accepting the reality of our bodies as beautiful, as female, we will indeed despair. As this woman who can never compete comments:

> To attract and keep the Father-God men, I have to be feminine, which means being short, slim, blonde, blue-eyed, domesticated but stylish, and either stupid or deceitful so that they will always feel they have the upper hand. I'm neither physically nor temperamentally suited to the part. I'm five feet eight inches tall, weigh 180 pounds and am black haired, wild eyed, ferociously intelligent, kinda wild and determined to run as much of my life and world as I can get under my control. Conflict.
>
> (Simmons, 1987: 70)

The effect, however, of these images is more serious than merely positioning each woman as second-rate or incomplete because of her failure to achieve perfection. For the images control women through concentrating concern on the external, on transitory beauty, thus ensuring that we do not question or revolt. They make certain that we expend our energies on ourselves, on our own (supposed) inadequacies; and by ensuring that we worry about our appearances, they prevent us from thinking, from creating, from writing. Is it any wonder that women have been silenced? As Tillie Olsen argued:

> . . . invisible worms are finding out the bed of crimson joy. Self-doubt; seriousness, also questioned by the hours agonizing over appearance; concentration shredded into attracting, being attractive; the absorbing real need and love for working with words felt as hypocritical self-delusion ('I'm not truly dedicated'), for what seems (and is) esteemed is being attractive to men.
>
> (Olsen, 1978: 30)

The images also position us as simultaneously sexual and powerless, subject to the whims and wills of man:

> The sexually immature body of the current ideal . . . presents a body which is sexual – it 'exudes' sexuality in its vigorous and vibrant and firm good health – but it is not the body of a woman who has an adult and powerful control over that sexuality. The image is of a highly sexualised female whose sexuality is still one of response *to* the active sexuality of a man.
>
> (Coward, 1984: 43)

The advertisers' dream woman who fills the pages of newspapers and magazines and populates the TV adverts is certainly seething with sexuality, even if it is thinly disguised. The woman is the 'bait used to sell products' (Gallagher, 1979), as well as to tantalize the man. That sexuality pervades the images of women paraded before us for our delectation and delight is never more clear than in other media outlets – newspapers and magazines, purveyors of the almost pornographic image of woman, exemplified in the 'page three girl' of the British tabloid press.

News, views and nudity

> One has only to pick up any newspaper to realise that one is living in a patriarchy.
>
> (Woolf, 1928)

> The *Sun*[43] has located is pleasure around sexuality – heterosexual sexuality. Its features and its presentations of 'news' are organised around forms of arousal ranging from shock and disgust to thrills and celebration, but sexual stimulus is a constant underlying theme, with the page three 'girls' – that particular stylised presentation of the female body as spectacle – those 'luscious ladies you drool over at breakfast' (September 20 1982) as a central image.
>
> (Holland, 1987: 105)

The British tabloid press presents examples of the crudest images of women as objects, as creatures always available for man's pleasure. The 'page three girl' stands bare-breasted gazing up at the devouring eyes of the male viewer. She is the reason for buying the newspaper. She is the stuff of board-room jokes, of factory-floor fantasies. She reaches out to all men, declaring her willingness to please, her actual unavailability (for it is only her image which the man can possess) enhancing her attractiveness. She is desired as she is reviled: she is the woman men would love to bed, but not to wed. Great for a 'mistress', but not for a wife. She is the modern representation of the madonna/whore dichotomy – and no prizes for guessing on which side of the fence she falls. And 'fall' is certainly the operative word. She is Eve incarnate, the temptress who must be controlled. Bring out the mighty penis to disempower her!

But the page three girl is not very different from the image projected in the advertisements and the fashion shots. She is merely more blatant in her message. Each represents the discourse of woman as object, each is the product of the culture which positions women as the 'not-I', the Other.[44] Women are not consumers, they are the consumed: the commodity. The newspaper do not present women as active, as intelligent, as thoughtful – even as *human*. When women are clever, they are expected to be asexual and unattractive. If not, there must be something wrong:

> What the press does, in fact, is to reinforce the traditional stereotypes of what women are in relation to what men are. It is therefore rather uncomfortable to admit, for example, that women can be both beautiful and clever.
>
> (Barr, 1977: 70)

Although there has been an increase in the numbers of women in positions of authority in the male-dominated newspaper empires over the last ten years, women are still in a minority. Women journalists are more likely to be found on magazines, or on women's pages than on the serious news pages, and any mention of women, particularly since the demise of Margaret Thatcher as British Prime Minister, is likely to be similarly restricted. The message is clear. Women are absent from the centre stage of world affairs, and are available only to titillate or trivialize. Their interests should be separate, not intruding on the 'real' world: the world of men.

Magazines and educational materials: A pervasive message continues

The representations in women's or in teenage magazines are no different.[45] As Faulder has claimed, 'Women's magazines are like those toy kaleidoscopes which you twist so that the same coloured shapes fall into different patterns' (Faulder, 1977: 176). In this case the different pieces portray the same glossy (and unreal) image: of unobtainable beauty, of sexualized consumption, of powerlessness. The fiction in the magazines mirrors the romantic fiction which sells by the ton every year, with its fictionalized rape scene, the strong dark hero who sweeps the woman away, the fantasies of power and passion, the escape and the final orgasmic union. Such images, which are an insidious force, pervade magazines, romantic novels and even comics read by adolescents. Thus, the message starts at an early age, exerting a damaging influence, as Braman has argued:

> Isn't the influence which these comics exert pernicious, in that they encourage girls to dream rather than to act, to follow rather than to lead? Many girls may admit that the stories are escapist nonsense and yet still have their expectations moulded and limited by them; to jobs, not careers; to glamour, not to reality; to finding a boyfriend and then to marrying; at which point fiction ends. What comes after is literally a closed book.
> (Braman, 1977: 92)

It is not only pulp fiction which sells these images. Surveys of educational material aimed at children show it too to be seriously sexist (Lobban, 1975; Spender and Sarah, 1980; Whyld, 1983). The message of the passive woman, reified in romance, infiltrates academic discourse as effectively as it does the newsagent's stand.

In romances the heroines have no existence of their own. The modern romance may have a veneer of emancipation, the heroine may have a career, may espouse independent values, but ultimately she wants what every woman supposedly wants: a man. Only then is she fulfilled. This is the pervasive image, a damaging, as well as a limiting one for women. Possibly, however, we should expect it: 'We are conditioned by society to view women as one-dimensional beings, so it isn't surprising that women emerge from the pages of most mass-market fiction as paper dolls' (Kavet, 1977: 103).

The representation of the independent woman who succumbs, or of the adolescent, orphaned, suffering and perpetual victim (pervasive in schoolgirls' comics – Walkerdine, 1990) provides powerful images, ensuring that women realize they are wasting their efforts looking for satisfaction in a career or through any life of their own, for fulfilment lies elsewhere, as Valerie Walkerdine indicates:

> The heroines suffer in silence; they display virtues of patience and forbearance and are rewarded for silence, for selflessness, for helpfulness. Any thought for the self, any wanting, longing, desire or anger is in this way reduced within the texts as bad. This provides for the readers a

> value-system in which certain kinds of emotion are not acceptable, and a set of practices in which their suppression is rewarded by the provision of the longed-for happy family, the perfect bourgeois setting.
>
> (Walkerdine, 1990: 95)

Is it surprising that we are disappointed, if not depressed, when reality hits us; when the promised happy ending turns out to be as fictional as the hunky hero and as chimerical as the bourgeois family fantasy peddled so furiously and falsely?

It is not only pulp fiction and magazines which present women frozen within the archetypal image. As we have already seen, throughout the nineteenth century literature portrayed the woman behind the veil, the monstrous castrating bitch, the angel or the whore. It still continues. For, with the notable exception of feminist literature, the archetypal and negative images of women still populate the pages of novels, high- and low-brow alike. Fiction deemed worthy of adulation by critics, academics and the reading public, such as the works of Kingsley Amis, D. M. Thomas and Anthony Burgess, contain negative stereotyped images of women which promote misogyny (Smith, 1989). We cannot escape at all.[46]

Moving images – still lives

> During the day, male presenters and disc-jockeys retain exclusive rights to the airwaves. They address their listeners as 'girls' or 'ladies'. The talk between the records is light, trivial, though friendly enough in the ingratiating manner of the smooth good-with-the-ladies salesman. In a way, the DJ is sound broadcasting's equivalent of the pin-up model girl in the 'glamour' pictures in the tabloid newspapers.
>
> (Ross, 1977: 14)

> A news announcer needs to have authority, consistency and reliability. Women may have one or two of these qualities, but not all three.
>
> (Jim Black, presentation editor, Radio 4)[47]

The moving images of women on TV, on film, and the voices on the radio are part of the same subjugating process. They give the same message, and though more technically sophisticated, they too purvey the discourse of the passive available woman.

The radio is an interesting example of a feminine medium, in that it is estimated that women form the bulk of daytime listeners (Ross, 1977). The image of the lonely housewife kept company by the male DJ is still prevalent, and the airwaves are kept clean and 'suitable' for such an audience. Entertaining without being challenging, radio addresses the lonely woman who passes her days with her smooth-voiced entertainer. It is a sorry image with sorry consequences, as Ross suggests:

> Every disc-jockey reports that his daily post bag is filled with sad letters from women telling of boredom, loneliness, empty lives. The possibility that there could be a link between the diet of verbal trivia that pours over the air to these women and their boredom is never given a passing thought. (Ross, 1977: 14)

The popular music that fills the programmes perpetuates the image of woman as subject to men, available for man's sexual pleasure or as his menial server. Estelle Philips, analysing images of women in popular music from the 1950s to the 1980s, concluded that demeaning and stereotyped images of women have been the stuff of the lyricists for decades (Philips, 1990). Women (and men) will internalize the messages continuously played to them through songs, not even noticing them, rarely questioning them, but all the time being reminded of woman's role, woman's function. The recent influx of female lyricists is changing this picture, but they are still only a drop in the ocean.

The DJ and his music provide company and solace for many women, as do the daytime 'soaps', the chat shows, and the women's programmes, all designed to provide an illusion of community, an illusion of association with others, to fill the chasm of loneliness faced by millions of women. For many women the soaps have become more real than real life. Life is arranged around them. Programmes in the USA such as the 'Oprah Winfrey Show' come to dominate the lives of these women, with arrangements made 'before Oprah' or 'after Oprah' as if the chat show has more reality than life itself (Squire, 1990). In Britain in 1990, the same can be said of the Australian soap 'Neighbours' or of 'Coronation Street'. The lives of the characters in these TV programmes seem more real to us than those of friends, and for many they are the only friends.

Whilst women can be subdued by the messages of the small screen (Koerber, 1977), seduced by the smooth-voiced radio DJ, or dulled by the 'soaps', they are startlingly absent from serious TV. The first woman newsreader in Britain, as recently as 1973, became an immediate media celebrity, as notable for her shapely legs as for her newsreading. Her arrival was not greeted with glee – for how could women seriously read the news? As one female journalist commented:

> Recently the BBC broke through the sex barrier with the first woman newsreader, Angela Rippon. Ms. Rippon is a joy to Women's Lib, but a pain in the ear to honest women, like me, who have to admit – even though it hurts – that a woman reader is too lightweight to sustain

Chrysler's crash or even Franco's coffin.

(Jean Rook, *Daily Express*, 28 November 1975)

Outdated comments reflecting a different era, we may declare. Women now regularly present the news, and even the weather! But have things changed? A recent EC report on women in the media provides a depressing picture: it seems as if the surface of sexism has merely been scratched. For example, women make up only 14 per cent of news broadcasters in the EC, with the best statistics from France (25 per cent), Great Britain (12.6 per cent) and French-speaking Belgium (18.8 per cent): not numbers to be proud of. The voices off-screen who provide a commentary on the news were also generally male: 83.3 per cent overall. This is a similar finding to that found in advertisements, where 76.6 per cent of the voices off were male. Thus, when serious business (or serious selling) is on the agenda, men are definitely in the driving seat. The other findings are that only 1.4 per cent of news items concerned issues related specifically to women, and that whilst men occupy the central role in 81.8 per cent of newsreel material, women do so in only 13.2 per cent. So the news which is considered worthy of attention and dissemination is collected and collated from an androcentric position. Women's news is not news; it is mere padding, the cosy item at the end of the broadcast, the happy family item used to convince viewers that everything is all right, really.

All of these images have similar effects. They represent women as objects, the not-I, the Other. They represent women as subject to men. And these images maintain women's silence. To neutralize their effect we need to expose the images for what they are, and allow women's voices to be heard.

Silencing women

> How much it takes to become a writer. Bent (far more common than we assume), circumstances, time, development of craft – but beyond that: how much conviction as to the importance of what one has to say, one's right to say it. And the will, the measureless store of belief in oneself to be able to come to, cleave to, find the form for one's own life comprehensions. Difficult for any male not born into a class that breeds such confidence. Almost impossible for a girl, a woman.
>
> (Olsen, 1978: 256)

The images of woman as object, not as active agent or creative autonomous subject, ensure that women remain on the outside, that women's voices are not heard. As history describes the doings of men, as fine art is the art created by men, as literature is writing produced by men, and as classical music is that composed by men, so the science, the news, the art, the literature, the music of today is that produced by men. The patriarchs are adamant that this should be so. The conductor, Sir Thomas Beecham, pronounced, 'There are no women composers, never have been, and never will be.'[48] John Ruskin confidently declared 'No woman can paint.'[49] And Swinburne claimed that, 'When it comes to science we find women are simply nowhere. The feminine mind is quite unscientific.'[50] Virginia Woolf's ponderings on the (im)possibility of 'Shakespeare's sister' who might have wanted to write, characterize the position of women in the creative sphere. As Tillie Olsen illustrates, in her now classic text, *Silences*, woman's voice has been absent from the world's creative arena for centuries. Unfortunately, it seems as if it still is.

But why are women so silent in the scientific, professional or creative spheres of life? The traditional reductionist argument, rehearsed earlier, is that women are somehow unable to think, to paint, or to write because of affinity with nature and lack of intellect. Or is it rather that we are not allowed to, through the systematic exclusion of women's work in the public sphere, or through the maintenance of women's work in the home – the maintaining of women as servers, as the 'angel in the house', rather than as active creators of artistic discourse? Is it that women are producing creative material, but it is being systematically ignored? For there are many who profit from the reification of the male creator and the simultaneous reduction of women's creativity to the sphere of childbirth, as this extract from a misogynistic male critic illustrates:

> A few years back I read a neo-feminist's approving review of another neo-feminist's book. The reviewer said that she agreed with the author that for a woman, a career is more creative than being a mother. That puzzled me: *without having given much thought to it*, I had assumed that about the closest the human race can get to creation is when a woman bears a child, nurtures him, and cares for him [*sic*].
>
> (Himmelfarb, 1967: 59; my emphasis)

If women can believe that childbirth is unsurpassable as a creative act, perhaps they will put down their pens and their paints, cease thinking and continue breeding. Is it a coincidence that the male pronoun is used to refer to the product of female creativity? Is it as creative to produce a female child? Or is this yet another comment produced *without having given much thought to it*?

The reason for women's absence on the world stage of creativity is not biological inferiority, nor an absence of desire to create beyond the realms of the family. The real reasons for the silence are not very difficult to discern; nor are the effects. Take the case of art, as many feminist scholars recently have, rewriting the history of art through a feminist prism:[51] our Old Masters and masterpieces – the art which fetches astronomical prices, elevating the artist to an almost godlike status, his creativity seen to be drawn from some higher power – are all the work of men. The history of art is peopled with men, not women. The male artist is the hero; the female artist is invisible. The woman is present only as the object of the artist's gaze, to be consumed, to be frozen and framed, to be possessed. Feminist analysis has identified the way in which women's voices and women as active agents have been suppressed; the way in which women are destined 'to be spoken' (in Lacanian terms) rather than to speak. It is the same process that silences women in any sphere. The silence not because of lack of creativity or talent, as recent texts on the 'forgotten' women artists,[52] scientists,[53] or authors[54] has shown. It is produced by a systematic suppression – a systematic oppression – achieved by promoting and validating the work of men whilst ignoring, or denying the existence of, the work of women.

Whilst women writers from Aphra Behn[55] to Mary Wollstonecraft[56] have been rediscovered by feminist literary scholars and feminist publishers,[57] many others have not. Many women never had the time or opportunity to publish – and their voices will never be heard. Many women remain silent, following in the painful footsteps of our foremothers who never have the time or legitimacy for reflection and creation. It is moving to consider how many brilliant voices have not been heard, how many brilliant careers have been thwarted. As Olive Schreiner reflected:

> What has humanity not lost by suppression and subjection? We have a Shakespeare; but what of the possible Shakespeares we might have had who passed their life from youth upward brewing currant wine and making pastries for fat country squires to eat, with no glimpse of freedom of the life and action necessary even to poach on deer in the green forests; stifled out without one line written, simply because of being the weaker sex, life gave no room for action and grasp on life?[58]

In addition to marginalizing women, and ensuring that we cannot find a voice with which to declare our anger, our desperation, or our fears, the images can be seen to have a more invidious function in that they objectify women. They ensure that we have few role models to turn to for inspiration. We expect to be confined and constricted. We expect to serve men. Is it any wonder that we despair, that we cry out, that we are mad? And if the woman herself was not treated as mad for daring to be creative, she may have been driven so by the restrictions upon her. It is an insidious double bind: women who do attempt to create may be vilified for their talent, and for their temerity in daring to speak out. Whether a woman's creativity is an expression of inner conflict and turmoil, or merely a desire for self-expression, it is in danger of becoming the tool which condemns, a centuries-old process, as Virginia Woolf eloquently shows:

> . . . any woman born with a great gift in the sixteenth century would certainly have gone crazed, shot herself, or ended her days in some lonely cottage outside the village, half witch, half wizard, feared and mocked at. For it needs little skill in psychology to be sure that a highly gifted girl who had tried to use her gift for poetry would have been so thwarted and hindered by other people, so tortured and pulled asunder by her own contrary instincts, that she must have lost her health and sanity to a certainty.
>
> (Woolf, 1928: 48)

The feminist martyrs, diagnosed as mad, 'treated' by patriarchal experts, and (often) destroyed by their own hands, have fuelled arguments that madness is protest, an expression of thwarted creativity. And within a culture which refuses to recognize women's creativity (except in the area of motherhood) it is argued that its frustration leads to madness. Phyllis Chesler opens her book, *Women and madness*, with a testimonial to four such women, Elizabeth Packard, Ellen West, Zelda Fitzgerald and Sylvia Plath. In her description of their madness as 'an expression of female powerlessness and an unsuccessful attempt to reject and overcome this state', Chesler argues that the experiences of these women symbolize the oppression of women's power, women's creativity – an oppression with fatal consequences (Chesler, 1972: 16). Her argument – that the inability of these women to express themselves, their silencing by men, has led to their madness and their suicide – has obviously struck a chord in the hearts and minds of many women. Their icons and heroines are women like Sylvia Plath, women seen as victims of the individual men who thwarted their intellect, as well as victims of a society which sees women, not as active subjects, but as objects. When we read Plath's words, 'Dying/Is an art, like everything else./I do it exceptionally well,'[59] a chill hand clutches the heart: although many would like to emulate her creativity, they fear the fate that befell her. We must, however, be careful not to glorify these women, raising them to the status of martyrs, for, as Tillie Olsen demonstrates, suicide is rare among creative women.[60] What is undoubtedly more common is the slow creeping frustration, the inability to think, to breathe, to work at anything other than the daily grind. For women's creativity is not frustrated only by the structural barriers provided by the male-dominated academies and universities, and the male publishing houses, but also by the lack of time. For if male writers such as Hardy, Gerard Manley Hopkins and Joseph Conrad can share this experience described by Conrad, how must it be for the woman whose main task is the care of her children, her husband, her home?

> I sit down religiously each morning, I sit down for eight hours, and the sitting down is all. In the course of that working day of eight hours I write three sentences which I erase before leaving the table in despair.[61]

It is no coincidence that 'in our century as in the last, until very recently, all distinguished achievement has come from childless women' (Olsen, 1978: 31). How many women can find time to await the visit of the muse in moments snatched between children and housework? It is a wonder that Jane Austen managed to write – hiding her papers under a blotter in her parsonage drawing room – by snatching a few lines, a few thoughts, when the scarce moments of solitude were upon her. How many others must have given up, despairing, angry and defeated?

Even those women who manage to ward off the angel in the house, and can find a room of their own, may be remembered chiefly for aspects of their personal lives, their work forgotten, and their creativity reduced to voyeuristic intrusions on their sexuality. As French says:

> Whether a woman had a sex life, what sort of sex life it was, whether she married, whether she was a good wife or a good mother, are questions that often dominate critical assessment of female artists, writers and thinkers.
> (French, 1985: 97)

The critics who pore over men's work with an academic glee, hardly noticing their personal lives, seem unnaturally interested in the woman creator's personal habits and especially in her sexuality. This allows the creative woman to be presented as unbalanced, unnatural, and certainly not representative of women. Thus, 'Harriet Martineau is portrayed as a crank, Christabel Pankhurst as a prude, Aphra Behn as a whore, Mary Wollstonecraft as promiscuous' (Spender, 1982: 31). Sylvia Plath, one of the foremost creative women of the late twentieth century, has been similarly treated. Biographers, commentators and critics seem more interested in her adolescent sexuality, her relationships with men during her college years, and her marriage, than with her work.[62]

That a woman who produced brilliant poetry could also be sexual is seen to be a peculiarity. That she killed herself allows her to be seen as mad, and thus as not a normal woman. This over-concern with her sexuality and sanity detracts from her work, and is an insult to this gifted poet, and to others who might follow her. The message to women is clear – dabble with the muse, attempt to enter the male world of learning, of thinking, of creativity, and you may pay the highest price.

The mirror – the muse – the madwoman

This somewhat depressing analysis makes it clear why many women are distressed. Many women are angry; many women are mad; and many others are labelled as such. When we look at the discursive practices which regulate women's lives, at the reality of the misery of many women's existence, at the absence of alternatives to madness as a form of expression, this is not surprising. These women may appear as statistics, but they are more than that. Their pain and despair drives them to desperate measures: to withdrawal, to throwing themselves into the arms of anyone offering succour, to suicide. And as we have seen, there are many who offer explanations and ameliorations, ranging from the biological to the social; many who offer a complicated theoretical analysis or a quick remedy. But none can really offer the solution women seek. They all fail, for each is blinkered, each is blinded in its one-dimensional approach. So where does that leave us? And most of all, where does that leave the woman herself, the woman at the centre of the debate, the woman who is 'mad'? Where does it leave woman, for whom madness is a sepulchral signifier? Together the explanations, the theories, the remedies, the critiques, make up a complex jigsaw. Each piece on its own is not enough; but when we put them together the picture becomes more clear.

Notes

1. Morgan, R. 'Goodbye to all that', in *Going too far*, quoted by Dworkin 1981: 101.
2. Plath, 'Paralytic' (1963), in Plath 1981.
3. Translated and quoted by Valerie Walkerdine 1990: 112.
4. Two cases cited by Miles 1988: 23.
5. As we have seen above, there is much disagreement as to the actual symptoms associated with each of these syndromes, with a great deal of dissension between diagnostic agents. Their common history is the genealogy of madness as a signifier.
6. In a paper where she argued that the symptoms of her 'schizophrenia' were culture-specific, as they were tied to the sixties pop culture, Plumb 1990 argued that madness cannot be seen in isolation from the context in which it is experienced and that part of her own 'symptoms' involved hallucinations about a sixties pop singer.
7. As Rowe 1990 has argued, the multinational drug companies have budgets which exceed those of many governments, with one major company in the USA grossing 100 million dollars in one year. In Britain, drug companies spend £5,000 on every general practitioner per year, promoting drugs, with enough tranquillizers prescribed in 1981 to allow thirty for every man, woman and child.
8. See Ussher 1989: 49 for an analysis of the different treatments for PMS.
9. See Ussher 1989 for a more detailed analysis of the reproductive syndromes and their history.
10. See Laws 1985: 38, for a cynical and amusing discussion of the symptoms of PMS.

11. See Ussher 1989 for a more complete discussion of these issues.
12. Sommer 1991 outlines the evidence against the theories of performance debilitation during the menstrual cycle. Parlee 1974 has examined the ideological implications of such theories.
13. Nicolson 1991 discusses the representations of PMS in the media and the image of the premenstrual woman as murderess.
14. A minority of women experience psychosis; but these women are exceptions, and have often experienced previous episodes of psychosis, which in this case may have been precipitated by the childbirth (Elliot 1984).
15. See Ussher 1989: 48 for a review of the different biochemical theories. Richardson 1991 discusses these further. See Steiner and Carroll 1977 for a discussion of hormonal theories of PND, and Nicolson 1986 for a critical review.
16. Nicolson 1991b discusses this in detail. See Ussher 1991c for a discussion of the role of the menstrual cycle researchers in all of this.
17. Ussher 1989; Martin 1989; Laws, Hey and Eagan 1985.
18. See Ussher 1992b for an analysis of this relationship.
19. Koeske 1983 outlined the importance of attributions and the menstrual cycle, showing that women were liable to attribute positive moods to life events, and negative moods to the menstrual cycle.
20. For an example, see Laws 1990.
21. Equal Opportunities Commission (EOC) statistical unit, 1990. Figures are based on 1988.
22. See Walkerdine 1990 for a discussion of this in relation to girls and maths.
23. US Department of Labor in *Twenty facts about women workers* (Office of the secretary, Women's Bureau, Washington DC, 1980).
24. Particularly for women who are married who receive little support from husbands (Brown and Harris 1978).
25. See Belle 1990 and Russo 1990 for analyses of poverty and women's mental health.
26. See Nicolson 1991 for a discussion of this.
27. Social Trends 1990: 20, Table 11.14.
28. Generally, research suggests that social support protects against or buffers stress (Ganster and Victor 1988).
29. Robert Louis Stevenson, 'Virginibus puerisque' in *The Oxford book of quotations*: 521.
30. Gove 1972; Gove 1979; Russo and Sobel 1981; Weissman and Klerman 1977.
31. Fox 1980 reported that women were more likley to be diagnosed as mentally ill in all marital categories; Warheit *et al.* 1976 and Cochrane and Stopes-Roe 1981 found no relationship between marital status and symptomatology.
32. Many feminists use the term 'home worker' instead of housewife. I prefer the latter in this context, as it refers to the married relationship which acts to make women subservient and mad.
33. In many US states a man cannot legally be prosecuted for raping his wife. It was only in 1991 that the first case of this kind was allowed in England, setting a legal precedent. See Parrot and Bechhofer 1991.
34. See Hall 1986; Hanneke *et al.* 1986.
35. For a discussion of 'wife battering' see Straus 1976, 1977; Hilberman 1980; Dobash and Dobash 1979; Klein, D. 1982; Finn 1985; Janoff-Bulman and Freize 1983.

36. In Britain, the Crown cannot prosecute an abusive husband without the wife's support. If women retract their accusation, the case is dropped.
37. Finkelhor 1984 argued that there are stages to acknowledgement of abuse, where a society can accept its existence. We now believe that sexual assault exists, but society is not yet ready to accept the existence of organized abuse such as child sex rings. Acceptance will come at a further stage of development. See also Glaser and Frosh 1988 for a discussion of the politics of sexual abuse.
38. Many of those subjected to sexual abuse prefer to call themselves 'survivors' in recognition of their ability to overcome the pain.
39. Two of the most readable and persuasive texts, which are recommended, are Betterton 1987 and Coward 1984.
40. Quoted by Faulder 1977: 37.
41. Winship 1987 discusses the meanings of the dislocated images in advertising.
42. See Orbach 1979 for a discussion of *Fat is a feminist issue*.
43. The British tabloid newspaper which first exposed the breasts of women on 'page three' and continues to do so in the 1990s.
44. As Myers 1987: 59 argues, 'The fashion image and the pornographic image are in the first instance produced within quite distinct sets of social and economic circumstances. Those differences affect the way in which the image is constructed as a *commodity*, as well as in the pleasures it makes available [my emphasis]'.
45. Braman 1977 carried out an analysis of sexism in comics, and discovered the following pervasive messages: 'females tidy up after males'; 'women are acceptable as sex-symbols, slaves or goddesses'; 'powerful women are dangerous'; 'girls who want to be strong are a figure of fun'; 'girls will do anything for boys who are nice to them'; 'the most important thing in life for a girl is a boy'.
46. See Ferguson (1981) for a number of contemporary stories representing the different images of women.
47. Quoted by Ross 1977: 23.
48. Quoted by Morgan 1989: 163.
49. Quoted by Morgan 1989: 165.
50. Quoted by Walton 1986: 12.
51. See Chadwick 1990; Parker and Pollock 1987; Tickner 1988.
52. See Chadwick 1990 for a good illustrated collection of women artists. See Williams 1986 for a discussion of women photographers from 1900.
53. See Alic 1986.
54. See Spender 1982.
55. Aphra Behn (1640–80) produced sixteen plays and numerous novels in an era before the 'first' novel (the first male novel).
56. Mary Wollstonecraft (1759–97) has often been acknowledged as the first feminist writer with her book *A vindication of the rights of woman*.
57. See Spender 1982, and the Virago publishing house.
58. Olive Schreiner, *From man to man*, 1883, quoted by Olsen 1978: 151.
59. 'Lady Lazarus', 1962.
60. Olsen 1978: 225 has documented the few cases of suicide in women writers, juxtaposing them with the many women who lived relatively healthily until their natural deaths.
61. Conrad, *Letters*, quoted in Olsen 1978: 157. Olsen documents details of the despair of various male authors at the absence of the muse.
62. For example, Wagner-Martin's 1987 biography of Plath contains a

litany of boyfriends and lovers, detailed in prose and photographs, presenting the image of artist as sexual object. Plath is presented as engaging in sex but not enjoying it; a double crime.

10

Reconstructing women's madness

blinded horses . . .
With their heads and their bodies finally liberated, with their eyes wide open, women will no longer be like those blinded horses who turn in circles around the well to which they are attached; they will no longer turn blindly, lovingly around you, Sir. You will no longer be the opaque screen between the woman and the world . . . They will no longer bury themselves in you . . . They will admit that even for a free body happiness is the exception . . .

There will be a revolt of feminine minds against a world made by men for men where so much horror, blood, weeping and torture inflicted on what is alive proclaims that domination is a vice.

(Parturier, 1986: 235)

imprisonment . . .
The cure for female despair must be spiritual as well as physical, aesthetic as well as social . . . when a supposedly 'mad' woman has been sentenced to imprisonment in the 'infected' house of her own body, she may discover that, as Sylvia Plath . . . put it . . . she has 'a self to recover, a queen'.

(Gilbert and Gubar, 1979: 92)

speech . . .
We are beginning to speak our histories, and as we do it will be to reveal the burden of pain and desire that formed us and, in so doing, expose the terrible fraudulence of our subjugation.

(Walkerdine, 1990: 170)

time-bomb . . .
No more, I will acept no more
be sorry no more

be quiet no more
They will have to hear my story
and they will not dare to say it
made me mad
Of course it made me mad
After all they pathologised
my history
No more, no more
my shouts today will be
so loud
My tears drops of pure fire
you will no longer take away
my past
for today I take my life
into these two hands

I am a time-bomb
and I have started ticking

(Walkerdine, 1990: 160)

Deconstructing madness

Madness – an emotive term, laden with meaning, with memories, with mythology. Madness is a secret, a fiction linked to fantasy, seen as fact; a fact of life we might prefer to turn away from, to forget. For to attempt to understand women's madness is to face up to the pain, the subjugation, the misogynistic discourse which regulates our lives. As women, madness affects us all; not just women who cry out in pain, or women who are caught in the psychiatric gaze, but all women. For within the patriarchal discourse femininity and madness are closely aligned. Madness both signifies what it means to be woman, regulating us through the discourse of madness, and serves as a description of the distress of many individual women. Any analysis of madness needs to acknowledge the reality of the pain of individual women, the needs of women as a group, and the construction of 'woman' as a signifier,[1] where madness plays a central role.

Through deconstructing the discourse of madness I have shown that what we call 'madness' is the product of systematic and regulated discursive practices, whose genealogy can be historically traced to show their connections with other discourses, such as that of 'witch' or 'hysteric'. We can prise apart the meanings and assumptions fused together in the ways we understand women's madness in order to see our present practices as historically determined phenomena rather than as timeless and incontrovertible facts. Such an analysis of the construction of the modern form of women's madness is a prerequisite for understanding and bringing about change.

This deconstruction demonstrates that madness cannot be understood either in the isolation of the consulting room, the research laboratory, the deconstructed literary texts or through the subjective reports of an individual woman. Madness is more than a hormonal imbalance, a set of negative cognitions, a reaction to a difficult social situation, or the reflection of underlying unconscious conflict. Madness is more than a label. It is more than a protest. It is more than a representation of women's secondary status within a phallocentric discourse, a reaction to misogyny and patriarchal oppression. To understand madness we must look further and wider than the individual – to the whole discourse which regulates 'woman'. Yet we must also look beyond the category of 'woman' to the reality of the pain and desperation which is a part of this experience for the individual in distress. It is not an easy task, and thus far it has not been accomplished at all, by either the mental health experts or the radical dissenters.

The experts, the critics: Dictating and deficient

On the question of 'women and madness', the experts expound, the 'radical' theorists claim insight and knowledge; from whatever quarter, the rhetoric flows freely. Publishers and authors rake in royalties and credit, expanding on their latest 'complete understanding' of women's distress, belittling their predecessors and rivals in the battle for academic supremacy. Professionals and critics attempt to demonstrate the efficacy of their own approach over all others. Popular books and magazines cry out to the supposed victims that the answer can be found within, thus perpetuating the discourse of helplessness and illness.

To untangle the web of theory and advice is no mean task. As I have shown, the myriad theories are comprehensive, convincing and confusing. Psychiatrists might suggest that dopamine is deficient, that neural pathways are malfunctioning. Psychologists might argue that women in distress are troubled by negative cognitions, making dysfunctional attributions which result in depression, or exhibiting learned helplessness. A sociologist (or socially orientated psychologist) might argue that lack of social support and poor living conditions were of aetiological significance, and that the answer lies in social and political change. The dissenters might argue that women, alongside men, are victims of a stigmatizing labelling process, which functions as a means of social control, pathologizing behaviour which is deemed unacceptable; that society is disposing of such people through the label of 'mental illness' and incarceration in the metaphorical strait-jacket of psychiatric categorization or professionally mediated treatment. A feminist might argue that women are victims of patriarchal oppression, of misogyny, and that madness is an understandable and natural reaction to the demeaning role enforced upon women, the protest of the powerless, or that labels of madness are merely tools of patriarchy and that our position as other within phallocentric discourse, makes us mad.

In this tangled web, where is the woman in distress, to whom can she turn for a complete understanding of her experience? Are the disparate theories and theses compatible, or do they all individually provide an incomplete picture of a woman's madness?

The psychiatric or psychological perspective is rarely critical, offering individualized solutions to complex problems, buttressed by the institutional frameworks within which these professions operate. Science is still the God, and gender is rarely acknowledged. As health care is organized as a commodity within the capitalist culture, each profession outbidding the other for monopoly, how much investment in madness do these professionals actually have? The existence of this 'illness' is their livelihood; the controversy over its exact roots provides their academic credibility through the protracted debates which serve to extend their academic publications, the CVs upon which their professional livelihoods depend. Psychiatric, psychological or therapeutic solutions may have their place, but they cannot be elevated to the status upon which their proponents have so long insisted. Each theory, each therapy has its weaknesses and shortcomings, and the whole concept of expert intervention cannot go unquestioned. For, whatever the context, expert interventions are not the only answer. They can provide only a partial and perhaps short-term solution. Women's experiences are marginalized and subsumed under general diagnostic categories and classifications; explanations which lead to simple solutions. Waiting for the latest wonder drug, the new development in therapy, the theory that will completely explain and cure madness is a fruitless exercise; like waiting for Godot.

Yet the critics fare no better in this deconstructed world of the mad. For although the perspectives offered by the dissenters are (rightly) critical, they are all unidimensional in their critical theory and, if any are offered, in their solutions; all somewhat naïve, in most cases ignoring real distress. All except the feminists ignore gender issues. Yet a feminist thesis which advocates social restructuring and raised consciousness, or (doubtfully different) feminist therapy may be as guilty of leaving women out in the cold as the traditional psychiatrist who is only interested in neural pathways. Social and political restructuring may be the perfect solution, the answer to every woman's problems, but until the perhaps unlikely event of such social change, women are unhappy, depressed, or 'mad'. Where does this leave them? Criticism is vital for development and change: it is healthy, if not essential, for feminists and antipsychiatrists to challenge the existing order, to challenge our understanding of mental health problems, of madness. Yet is this merely rhetoric which ignores the reality of women's lives, the reality of many women's depression? Elevating madness to sainthood, to the status of protest of the powerless, is ultimately useful only as a rhetorical device, or a short-term panacea to shore up the ego of the distressed. As women we must be careful about the reification of witches, of the mad woman, for it may go against us; we must '*beware of those Thrones for "Woman" that turn her into an altar*' (Marks *et al.*, 1986: 221). We must turn away from the pedestal that separates us as the Other, either reified or denigrated, and reconstruct the discourse of madness in a way which works *for* women.

All of those speaking and writing on the subject of madness propose a single theory, a single solution. Whether it is ECT, drugs or lobotomy, therapy, a feminine writing, changes in childrearing or a 'psychic voyage', political change or social supports – each is offered in isolation as *the one* solution (or one of a few in some perspectives). Here again is the parallel with witchcraft theorists; witches were martyrs, or mad, or feminist heroines, or evil harridans. Each theorist could find examples to support her or his supposition; no one theory could explain the complete phenomenon of witchcraft. Each authority invariably ignores all others in the battle to convince.

So what are we left with?

I have deconstructed on many levels, exposing the weaknesses in both the dominant models of madness and the treatments meted out by the experts, together with the weaknesses in the critiques which have arisen in their wake, and the dissenters' inability, in the main, to formulate any workable alternatives to the treatments they condemn. The critiques of the antipsychiatrists and feminists have their place. They challenge directly our taken-for-granted assumptions about the world, about women, and about madness. But this is not enough, for they negate the importance of the individual woman trapped within the system which pronounces upon her condition in paternalistic and patronizing ways. They deny women who need an answer, who have no voice; women who find little comfort in the deconstructions and find that the tranquillizers dull the pain. Whilst we spin our webs of discontent and deconstruction, those with the power, the medical professionals and the therapists, are handing out their answers and their remedies to all women who come to them. And they are not being questioned; they are believed.

I must not, therefore, be guilty of the crime for which I vilify the critics – of merely exposing the weaknesses in the different arguments, of entering an academic debate where criticism or annihilation of another's theories are the sole object of the exercise. It is easy to criticize, to deconstruct. It is what I have been trained to do: to look for weakness in arguments, chinks in the armour of others. But whilst we are looking for chinks in the armour, we may be missing the view of the whole, attending to the minutiae of academic debate rather than thinking for ourselves, and attempting to *reconstruct* rather than merely *deconstruct*. For as one critic says of experimental methods in psychology, we can say of the whole range of theorizing on madness:

> Too much emphasis has been placed on having experimental procedure without any perceptible flaws or ambiguities; and all too often this emphasis takes place at the expense of considering what is an interesting or important problem . . . once an interesting demonstration has been introduced into the psychological literature, dozens of other experimenters devote their attention – and their methodological zeal – toward finding the vulnerabilities in the experiment. And ultimately, nearly all of these experiments get shown up (and ultimately abandoned) for their limitations. These trends combine to produce a science that has progressed rather less than it should have, and that still consists more of a set of impressive but isolated findings than of a truly cumulative discipline.
>
> (Gardner, 1985: 135)

The critiques, the expert theories, the interventions for madness form a series of sometimes impressive but ultimately isolated findings, pitched in a battle against each other, their promulgators determined to achieve the position of pre-eminence. Their determination to stay blinkered, continuously critical, and unidimensional, prevents the development both of a 'truly cumulative discipline' and of any real understanding of women's madness. It cannot go on.

There cannot be one simple answer to the question, 'Why are women mad?' for many routes take us to madness. There cannot be one solution to the problem of women's madness, no simple recipe which will alleviate pain, elevate women to a position of equality, and eliminate oppression. We would all like the simple answer. It is what I sought when I began this quest, burning with the need to solve my own problem of why my mother was mad. I thought I would find the answer in psychology. When I did not, I turned to feminism, to deconstructionism, to the critiques. But no one can offer the single solution I needed. There is no magic wand. There is no simple 'cure'. There is no simple explanation. This may be difficult to face, and many would prefer to believe in the one cure, the magic wand. Such a belief will ensure that the various experts and critics will maintain their followings. We are deluding ourselves if we share that belief but the situation is not hopeless. There is much we can do to understand women's madness and reconstruct means of alleviating women's pain which do not act to position woman as the Other. We need to operate on the level of the political and of the individual: at the level of discursive practices, and individual solutions for misery. The two must go hand in hand if we are to move forward.

We must reconstruct our discourse of madness so that it does not deify the woman in a way that prevents her from speaking honestly of her unhappiness. We need solutions which look at the individual woman, yet also acknowledge the needs (and oppression) of women as a group, solutions which acknowledge the position of woman in patriarchal society, recognizing the function of Woman's position as 'the Other'. We need solutions that reject utopian ideals which serve only to display empty rhetoric and polemic; solutions which do not blame or pathologize the woman, which do not see only her surface symptoms, and control her through dulling her pain momentarily. Such short-term solutions, used in isolation, may cause more harm than good in the final analysis. As the boy whose finger plugged the first hole in the flooding dyke seemed to stop the flow of water for a time, yet ultimately failed because of his short-sightedness and the ineffectiveness of his remedy, so do we fail in many of our treatments for women's madness. And as the boy allowed the flood water to build whilst he concentrated on the one small hole, many of the solutions for madness, such as the most widely used panacea, chemotherapy, may function not only to silence the woman, but also to cause her more pain.[2] Each solution on its own is not enough.

Post-feminism – a mirage

Radical feminist rhetoric may sometimes seem to be short-sighted or élitist or utopian, but we cannot ignore the relationship between misogyny and madness. We cannot ignore the control of women through misogynistic devices, be they sexual slavery, clitoridectomy or psychiatric diagnosis. To reject the feminist perspective through adherence to the belief that we are in a 'post-feminist era' is dangerous and short-sighted. The concept of 'post-feminism' in a world where inequality is still pervasive, where women are more likely to be treated as commodities if not elevated to a pedestal (a pedestal ringed with barbed wire) is a nonsense. The existence of this very concept acts as a device to placate us, to control us, to reassure us that we need no longer fear or protest. It persuades us that our battles have been won, the vote gained, contraception available, beating or marital rape now illegal. This is merely window dressing, for it is clear that women are not yet free. If we believe we are, if our daughters forget how to protest, if we are lulled into a false sense of freedom, we will lose all. Is this why each generation of feminists has to rediscover the arguments, to rekindle the fight, to reinvent the wheel? Is this why the work of women throughout history, women who campaigned and fought for our rights and freedom, is forgotten? Women may well be silenced, as I have argued above, but we must beware of silencing ourselves by believing in post-feminism, and thus giving up the fight.

Feminist theorists or activists may not have all the answers, but they are asking the right questions and exposing the oppression of women. The feminist solutions are at least on the right tracks, even if they are not enough on their own. But we should not dismiss them for not providing all of the answers. This would be to have double standards, for who does have the answer?

We need to build on this work, examine it critically, and enter into the debates not taking anything for granted. We should not allow ourselves to be lulled into a false sense of security by surface gains such as the formation of women's therapy centres, or by the visibility of a few women who have succeeded and seemingly escaped from the position of the second sex. Feminist theories and arguments will be opposed, they will be dismissed; they are a threat to the dominant order, to patriarchy. Who would give up power easily? Who would hand over control merely because the inequity is identified, the injustice exposed? The 'law of the father' will not be overturned or replaced merely by our identifying its inherent misogyny, its damaging effects on women. This is only the first step. We must not become complacent or be caught up in our own rhetoric, seduced by the belief that we have won. We have not. Post-feminism is a utopian concept: women will not become free easily. Our freedom would threaten those who benefit from the phallocentric discourse. Woman as the Other serves a powerful function in maintaining patriarchy. If women challenge the One, and no longer 'readily volunteer to become the object, the inessential' (de Beauvoir, 1986: 45), we are challenging the very foundations of the Law of the Father. We must expect resistance. But we can stop being the object. Woman does not have to be the Other.

Misogyny and élitism

We must be clear, then, about the misogyny inherent in madness; the misogyny underlying much of the discourse about 'woman', the misogyny which frames us, which undermines us and which defines us as the Other. We must continue to deconstruct, and to make connections with the treatment and control of women in other cultures and at other points in history. The feminist analysis has clearly done this. Yet it is, as yet, a theoretical analysis, based on academic discourse and training, open only to the privileged few who succeed by threatening the law of the phallus, the law of the father. On its own it is élitist, and may say little to women.

The critiques must be accessible. They must go further in their impact than the narrow academic world or the closed and self-satisfied (because already free) world of the feminist activist. Rhetorical critics and complex academic theorizing are important; they are the first step, providing inspiration and enlightenment. But they are only the first step, not the final end or the solution. Too much of feminism or academic deconstruction speaks to the converted, and through its creation of new rules for living and behaving which a majority of women cannot achieve, it creates a new impossible élite, a new way for women to fail. Is this feminist? Feminist theorizing is often unintelligible to those not steeped in its traditions, those who do not have the privilege of education, of learning, or time to unravel the complex theorizing and time to understand the new and often difficult language. Is it surprising that feminism frightens many women; and that the academic élitism, exemplified by some of the French feminist literary theorists, or by the new language adopted by radical feminists such as Daly and her followers, is alienating to those not conversant with the rules of the game? If feminism is for women it must be accessible to women. This does not mean 'pop' psychology, or 'pop' feminist theories translated into monosyllables or into simple analyses of a one-dimensional world. Since the questions are difficult, the theories must reflect the complexity of the issues we are addressing. But feminism must be available to women in general, not merely to the chosen few. We must climb down from our feminist pedestals: they look too much like the towers which perpetuate the power of the phallus.

It is tempting for women theorists to adopt the language of the phallus, the language of power, in order to have a voice; in order to compete: tempting to set up a feminist Arcady to supplant that Arcady of the father in which the phallus has reigned for so long. But in this world only a few women can wear the crown, can find 'a self to recover, a queen'. The rest are still outside, are still the second sex, and do not even have a voice, for they are not able to speak in the language of the élite, which will always be the language of the phallus. We must beware of adopting the mantle of our oppressors in order to be free. We may free ourselves, but reinforce the oppression of other women. Our critiques, read only by those already converted to the arguments, may avoid real analysis, prevent real change.

Interdisciplinary discussion

Equally, affiliation and allegiance to single disciplinary approaches is short-sighted and ultimately limited. Deconstruction and subsequent reconstruction needs to take place across traditional disciplinary boundaries, rather than safely within our own cosy yet blinkered worlds. Thus it is not enough to take a solely medical, sociological, anthropological, historical, psychoanalytic or psychological approach. We must look across these traditional distinctions for the commonalities present in all. For too long theorists and critics have looked inwards, have kept blinkers on, refusing to recognize the importance of the vast wealth of knowledge available in disciplines other than our own. The debate on women and madness is no more the prerogative of the medical theoreticians than it is of the literary theorists, the sociologists, the psychologists, or the psychoanalysts. The historical perspective by itself no more gives a complete picture than does the anthropological. All are important.

This is a fundamental attack on the insularity of academic disciplines and political theorizing; an attack on the expert critics who look for their answers within a limited field, spinning webs of intricate and complex theories. Their insularity makes them blind and deaf, prevents them from asking the right questions and thus from receiving the right answers (or any answers other than those they want to hear). We can no more understand madness in this way than we could understand witchcraft.

The implications of this are enormous. First, it would involve co-operation rather than competition, listening rather than pronouncing. We must learn from each other rather than turn our eyes and ears away from anything that does not fit in with our own perspective, that is not within our field of expertise. This means that no one person, no one body of 'experts' can claim monopoly on madness. No single person can hope to understand everything, to have access to all information or to all aspects of knowledge. The era of the egotistical expert will be over – and this cannot come too soon. For the insistence on expertise and on power, on the validity of our own pet theories and solutions, which characterizes the insular and arrogant theorizing of the current experts and critics, seeks only to serve the interests of the élite at the expense of those deemed mad: women.

We might not want to give up our claims to expertise and our hopes of monopoly over madness. It is difficult for me to recognize that my nine years of psychology training has not really equipped me to provide solutions for women's despair. I would like to believe I could provide such solutions; many professionals do. How many of the medically trained, having endured long and arduous training, having experienced the acquisition of skills and expertise, having recognized the respect and pre-eminence their professional training accrues, will give it up? How many sociologists, having studied structures, social groups, organized oppression and the role it plays in madness, will admit that theirs is not the only answer? How many therapists, analysts or counsellors, having sacrificed much to achieve their professional training, will acknowledge that it is not enough? Many will privately arrive at such an understanding whilst presenting their professional solidarity (their blinkers) to the world. The continuation of the professions and the academic disciplines which support them depends on this. To admit to the need for interdisciplinary explanations and solutions would challenge the power of these élites, undermining the chances of achieving power for those who presently clamour after it. Just as those who perpetuate the 'law of the father' will not easily reject the phallocentric discourse, so those steeped in the rhetoric of their chosen profession or academic discipline will not easily let go of their insularity. But they must. Or they will ensure the ossification of progress, prevent the development of any positive solutions for those women who are in distress, and stand in the way of the reconstruction of a discourse of madness which does not mark woman as other.

The woman – the pain – the answer

Whilst we must look to the academic deconstruction, to the discursive, to address the misogyny inherent in madness, we must also look to the political, to the structural. That is, the world of the real, to the individual women positioned as mad, women labelled, diagnosed and treated, women who are more than representations of discursive practice: women who bleed when they are pricked; women who scream.

I am not going to offer a recipe for happiness, a formula for alleviating distress, for treating madness, because there is no one formula. Each woman is different. Each woman's pain has its own history, its own roots – and its own solution. Any woman in distress may have unconscious conflicts, negative cognitions, low self-esteem, poor social support, or have learnt to be anxious through previous experience. Her hormones may fluctuate. She may be beaten by her husband. She may care for many young children alone. She may have internalized the sense of powerlessness and otherness with which patriarchy brands women. Her sexuality may be experienced as a bind, a lack. Her relationship with her mother may have been ambivalent. Her lack of power and autonomy may be real. She may be poor. Shall I go on? No one woman (hopefully) would fit into all of these categories – but any group of women in distress might. To adhere to just one approach for all is obviously nonsensical.

We must stop treating women as a homogeneous group, expecting one solution for all, one analysis for all. As there are many things which divide us as women, such as class, sexuality, race, culture and age, the 'sisterhood of women' is a utopian ideal. Our shared sexuality, our gender, may draw us together, but many other factors keep us apart. We do not need either to celebrate or deny difference, whether between women, or between women and men. We share a lot as women, but as individuals we cannot be subsumed under some category, some all-encompassing label which predicts that our experiences will all be the same. Each woman's experience is still unique to her. I know this is an argument which is anathema to many, such as those within the sociological arena, but the acknowledgement of both the individual and the social is the only way in which we can heed the individual woman in need, and stop madness from being a mantle for all women.

As there are many manifestations and routes to madness, so there are many solutions. In reality, we need them all. Each individual woman may benefit from a different group of solutions. She may want physical treatments, she may benefit from therapy (be it psychoanalytic, cognitive, behavioural or feminist), she may want to work with other women in a supportive group setting, or become involved in political action. Or none of these tried, tested – and vilified – solutions may help. We cannot paint a simple picture of women's madness without acknowledging the myriad roots to distress, the complex genealogy of the discourse of madness. Nor can we paint a rosy picture of the one perfect solution. It is time to acknowledge the complexity of the issue of madness, to stop attempting to find 'the cure'. We have to look to the individual woman's needs, her personal path to misery, and offer help accordingly. But we also need to attack the underlying structures and institutions which perpetuate women's oppression. Both lines of attack need to happen simultaneously, not necessarily activated by the same individuals, for we cannot take on all the world's ills at a personal level. We do not want to set ourselves up as the hero-innovators who fail. We need to work together to effect change.

Structural change: Were the liberal feminists right?

On a structural level, many of the arguments of the liberal feminists and sociologists ring true. Oppression of the other is built in to the fabric of our society, and women are disadvantaged on many levels. We need to effect change at the level of work, the family, in the media, and in education. Women are powerless within patriarchy, and powerlessness is one of the routes to madness. To empower women is an enormous task, which must take place both on an individual level (as recognized by the feminist therapists) and on a wider societal level, through changes in social structures.

For example, we need more than a rhetoric of equality of opportunity at work. Women are gravely disadvantaged and literally oppressed by the present organization of work. Whether we talk of glass ceilings which prevent us from rising through organizations, lack of availability of childcare so that women can work, levels of pay, educational opportunities, old boy networks, sexual harassment in the workplace, or beliefs about women's labile performance, we are talking of a situation where women are doomed to fail. Only the few escape through the net. Real change is needed so that women can have equal rights and equal opportunities, not merely the opportunity to look longingly (or resentfully) at the few women who do succeed, whilst feeling more of a failure ourselves.

We need to educate women to succeed, not to take second place, not to be second best. We need to go back to the infant school and the primary school, changing the way teachers reward children. Girls and boys should be rewarded equally – not girls for acquiescence and obedience, boys for assertiveness and achievement. If we do this, our boys will be healthier too. We need women in the academic subjects where they are presently under-represented, such as the sciences or mathematics. A world of science where women are absent is an impoverished one.

The family has for too long been the seat of women's oppression and depression. The role of archetypal housewife and mother, isolated and economically dependent (repository of mythology and maintained by misogyny) has for too long been the site of women's madness. We know that mothering, dependency, powerlessness, make many women mad. We know that motherhood is not always the joyous fulfilling task we are led to believe. We may also suspect that mothering fuels misogyny – that the fear of the mother, the dread of her power, provokes hatred of the woman; the madonna/whore dichotomy affects us all, women and men. Equally many men now want to mother: where parenthood is concerned, they no longer want to be left in the cold. Whilst we should be wary about giving only the good parts of parenting over to men (the cosy bedtime stories and 'quality time'), and whilst we must acknowledge that many women do not have a relationship with a man (from choice or necessity), parenting as a sole task for one person is often both soul-destroying and destructive of the self. It is not enough for individual women (or men) to fight to share the parenting: fundamental changes to our social structures need to take place in order to make it happen. The neuroticism of the nuclear family as a site of madness, abuse and aggravation will have to come to an end.

Images of women position us as the Other, as objects for the gaze of man. In media representations, in advertising, in pornography, we are framed outside the domain of the One. We are reminded of our position as the second sex. These images burn into us. We are so inured to their effect that we may no longer even notice them. As we turn away from madness, we turn away from these images of woman – but we must not. A society which reminds itself of the status of woman through our position as commodity, as object of (male) desire, as dislocated and disconnected from any sense of autonomous existence, cannot expect women to be anything but mad. By themselves the images do not make us mad. But they remind us, they mark us out, and they perpetuate the Law of the Father, the phallocentric discourse.

The Law of the Father – the law of the phallus

The deconstruction of the phallocentric discourse is present in the radical feminist, the post-structuralist and the psychoanalytic critiques. On its own as a solution to madness it may seem esoteric and abstract in the extreme, reinforcing the power of the phallus through concentrating solely on the discursive practices. But it is an essential aspect of a reconstruction of women's madness. We must recognize the phallocentric nature of language. We cannot deny the way in which women are framed within patriarchal discourse. A reclamation of woman's voice through writing, art, science and academic discourse is essential to our emancipation from the chains that bind us. The French feminists argue this most eloquently. Irigaray, Kristeva and Cixous spin a seductive web in which women can create their own language, a woman's voice. This may be only the start, and the feminist polemic inaccessible to many women, but it gives us hope. It demonstrates that the Law of the Father does not have to reign supreme. Women have been silenced too long. It is time to speak out. And to speak out loudly, for we need to be heard.

Sexuality is at the centre of women's oppression. It is at the centre of the misogynistic discourse, of the discourse of madness. Women need to reclaim their own sexuality, to challenge the negative construction of our sexuality imposed upon us by the patriarchs, to move away from definitions of our sexuality as a lack, as 'a flaw'[3] serving only to satisfy men, and to develop an autonomous sexuality which allows a woman pleasure. This does not necessarily mean always emphasizing sexuality as a central part of what it means to be woman, for we must be wary about constructing a new cage in which to confine ourselves. A positive sexuality for women is possible without always reducing ourselves to the level of the body, a reduction used to bind us for so long. Many women may want to 'speak through the body', to write through the body and thus reject the phallocentric discourse. This can only be of benefit if women can develop a positive sexual identity on a fundamental level, not at the level of the abstract, but at the level of the real.

We should not need to prescribe what this sexuality will be – autonomous, with women, or with men. (The separatist feminist Arcady is a trap to avoid.) But women should be able to express and experience their sexuality in a way which does not mark it as a terror, a danger, a wound or a lack. The misogynistic discourse of woman's sexuality has had free rein for too long. We cannot ignore it any longer. We must leave the myth of the sexually dangerous woman behind and move forwards into a sexuality which allows a woman to experience herself, to give and receive pleasure; and to integrate her sexuality as part of herself, not be compelled to split it off as forbidden or denied.

Acknowledging pain – feminism or therapy?

All the resolutions discussed so far operate at the level of woman as a group, and, whilst they will have some impact on the individual woman in distress, they will not offer any resolution to her pain. So something is needed for women who are in despair. This alleviation of pain cannot be carried out in isolation, or it will act only as a first-aid measure, covering a gaping wound with a flimsy bandage. But if it is part of a widespread process of challenging the conflation of woman and madness, looking beyond the individual woman, whilst being able to acknowledge her despair, it can work for women.

I have reviewed many of the treatments presently offered to women within the professional world of psychiatric or psychological care. Each can be deconstructed, and seen to act to pathologize the woman, treating her as the person who is sick, whilst ignoring the route she has travelled to arrive at the position of madness. Any solution which treats the symptoms without looking to the cause of the problem is short-sighted, be it a physical, therapeutic or sociopolitical change. Many interventions reconstruct the woman's life in order that she fit into the current theoretical framework – her past is reconstructed to show childhood deprivation, or negative cognitions or faulty learning; her current state of anxiety and tension is interpreted as being the result of her faulty neural pathways, or social deprivation. With our clever professional and scientific rhetoric we can construct a convincing picture of anything.

But the alternative to these solutions is invariably nothing. Self-help is not enough. Caring in the community of women is still a utopian ideal, and assumes a commonality between women which is fantasy, not fact. There is also the danger of unscrupulous unregulated therapists taking advantage of any deconstruction of professional care and wielding power over women, as the experts have done for centuries. We cannot rely on trust, on honesty, on altruism. Women can wound each other, can turn against each other and can exploit, however unpalatable a thought that is.

Equally, by tarring all professional interventions with the same brush, dismissing them all, as many of the dissenters and feminists have done, we are denying women the right to any form of panacea, any form of alleviation of their misery. No one can do this. It is arrogant and divisive, and lacks any awareness of the reality of many women's suffering. The misery may be the result of misogyny, of patriarchal oppression, or of unconscious conflicts, but it is real to the woman herself. She will wait a long time for the effects of the political and structural changes prescribed by the critics. But we cannot look to one intervention and say it is less oppressive, less punishing, for that is to evaluate from our own perspective, denying individual women the right to choose. So I would avoid endorsing one method or one solution, and look to the woman herself. Let her choose.

Re-educating the experts

This does not remove from the professionals the onus to change. One of the first steps towards any form of positive mental health care for women is in the education of the experts so that they acknowledge the myriad routes to a woman's madness. They should acknowledge the complexity of the phenomena, and not dismiss the woman by merely categorizing her and mentally castrating her with uni-dimensional treatment. Just as the academic deconstruction needs to be interdisciplinary, so must the professional intervention. A woman may need economic support, child-care, psychotropic medication or therapy. She may need different forms of intervention at different times in her life, or at different points in the course of her crises. It is naïve to dismiss one avenue of help, looking at it in isolation, but it is equally naïve to depend solely on one.

We could insist that therapists acknowledge politics and gender in their work, through individual practice, service development, research and liaison with other professionals. That they no longer marginalize feminist issues, allowing them instead to pervade all avenues of therapy, as well as service development and delivery. Everyone cannot practise feminist therapy – it would be naïve to suggest that they do. But we can all be informed by feminist arguments. Thus there is a clear need for a continuing debate and reflexivity both in theory and in practice.

Re-educating women

We must also educate women. We no longer need take the opinions of the patriarchal prelates as revealed truth. Women can have a voice in the market place of the mad. We can speak out against our oppressors, rejecting their solutions if they seem to disempower us. We can choose to take the answers of the experts, but it has to be within our power to say no. For this we need to be informed; to know about the alternative solutions for alleviating despair; to have access to these services, and the power to use them as we wish; and to know that the one answer presented to us may be only one view, often merely opinion, or a judgement based on professional loyalty, not a judgement from some higher power, incontrovertible and conclusive. We need to make it public that professionals have not been educated in all avenues of intervention, afterwards making a rational choice to work with the most effective. Professionals are invariably informed about only one approach – their own. We need a demystification of the rhetoric of madness; a stripping of the polemic which surrounds the mental health professions; a movement out of the élitist ivory tower, the parochial consulting room. We need movement in the direction of a health care system that works with women, and for women, away from a system which is imposed upon us. Women often know why they are mad, why they are miserable. Given the opportunity, women will be able to know what interventions they will choose. Women should be listened to, our opinions validated, and the experts dethroned.

Dethroning the experts

The history of expert intervention in the market place of madness is long and complex. Our present practices have clear links with the ascent of the nineteenth-century psychiatrists, and the misogynistic practices of other cultures, and other points in history. The deconstruction of women's madness exposes that clearly. To reconstruct a positive system of comfort for women we must acknowledge this history, and dethrone the patriarchs who have imposed their will upon us. This will be the most difficult step – the most obviously threatening to the power of the phallus, the Law of the Father. For we are attempting to undermine systems with centuries of investment, power structures that serve the One, whilst they maintain us as the Other. As women working inside these systems we are part of the oppression of women, and we cannot use our gender to obtain exemption from the criticism.

In dethroning the patriarchs we do not have to throw all of their theories away, to dismiss their arguments completely, or deny all validity in their methods of intervention. To fail to offer positive solutions merely because those solutions have evolved within a phallocentric discourse would be self-defeating. We can be cleverer than that. We can dethrone the patriarchs, but distil from their methods aspects of care that suit us as women. The feminist therapists have attempted this. They are moving in the right direction by acknowledging the person and the political, working to empower women, and avoiding the prescription of dictates from above.

Other forms of women-centred practices are developing: community projects where women work with professionals in their own locality, where issues of age, race and class are high on the agenda,[4] and where 'therapy' is part of a wider project of social intervention, childcare, local political action and supportive working practices. Practical and physical interventions, such as women's refuges for survivors of domestic violence and abuse, are a positive step. We should not have to live in a society where violence is endemic, but, since it exists, we must acknowledge the women's pain. The development of rape crisis lines and women therapy centres is also a positive step which shows that it is possible to work within existing frameworks and services, and not blame the woman for her unhappiness. Community health centres and Well Women's clinics can act to take the stigma away from mental health care. For too long women have suffered in silence because to be mad is to be outside, marked as fallen from sanity, fallen from reason. We must prevent this misery from becoming a secret, a woman's silent pain, her silent scream. There are many understandable reasons why we are mad. To move towards change we have to allow women to speak without stigmatizing them as the Other. Madness must not be a secret.

Another positive step is the development of women's networks, but we also need professional help from women acting to legitimate the rights to the services and to have recognized the worth of women's caring. Whilst we can work with and care for each other, we must not expect women to do for nothing what the patriarchs have for centuries been rewarded for. Caring is often hard work – we must recognize that. Therapy may be a part of women-centred services, but so may the traditional (and often vilified) asylum: space away from family, from society. For many women it is a welcome relief, and the move to the community in psychiatric care often denies this. To acknowledge the need for asylum does not mean that we should lock women in 'mad houses' for expressing their pain, that we should allow women to become institutionalized. We need safety without coercion. Equally, chemical interventions may be helpful, particularly in alleviating the depths of depression – but they should not be seen as the sole 'cure'. They are an aid for treatment, not the answer. Addictive drugs may be a thing of the past, but the woman who is offered only chemical intervention will not be helped in the long run. Her pain will merely be dulled.

The problem of men

What of men? Are they to be involved in this reconstructed world of madness, where women are to be freed to speak, to challenge, to be empowered? I started this book by arguing that we do not need to look at men, that it is legitimate to focus on women, leaving the analysis of men's madness to the men. But now we need to let the men back in. A positive future for women cannot ignore men, or continue to denounce men as oppressive holders of the phallus. We cannot ignore men and hope that they will be made impotent: they are part of the framework of many women's lives. Many women do not wish to give up men; and we cannot hope to make a world which is more hopeful for women without changing men. A world of women is a mirage, a reality for the very few. Yet we must be wary of turning our focus again on to men, the default option for so many. Our history, our psychology (Squire, 1989), has been developed for men, by men, but masculinity itself is rarely examined.[5] An analysis of masculinity will work for women as well as for men.

Looking at the misogynistic discourse (the discourse of madness) one could be excused for arguing that women are not the problem, men are. Men whose power is based on the myth of the all-powerful penis, envy women. They revere or denigrate us, projecting their envy and their fear on to us; and, as the baby splits off the good and bad mother, women are split in men's eyes. If as women we are confident and, not having to be always angry, we can work together, on both the individual and the structural level, using the knowledge from our deconstructions of woman and madness, then we can reconstruct. We can move away from the man-made definitions of our lives which cause our pain. We do not have to hold hands with men to do this: we can walk on our own. (Too many times men, holding the hands of women as friends and allies, steal the power for themselves.) But I would caution against a feminist state where women oppress men, or deny men access to their desires as men have done to women for centuries. We must build a world for women which is not based on oppression or subjugation. We do not want to turn men into the victims, however tempting it may be to turn the tables on our oppressors.

Men will have less fear if they are not on the outside, if they cannot construct elaborate and misogynistic fantasies about gatherings of women. Witches, midwives, working women – we are all reviled for grouping together and apparently excluding men. If we are secure we can work with men on our terms, not being coerced.

Conclusion: Listen to women

There can be no simple answer to the question of whether women's madness is a misogynistic construct, or a mental illness. It is both. It is neither. It cannot be encapsulated within one explanation, one interpretation. As women, we are regulated through the discourse of madness. But the woman herself is real, as is her pain – we must not deny that. So we must listen to women.

I do not pretend to have all the answers, but I would emphasize the need for critical debate and examination of discourses surrounding women's madness in a way which acknowledges both individual women and the oppression of women as a group. Neither current therapeutic practices, nor feminist analyses are doing this. We have spent decades criticizing. Now it is time for attention to be given to constructive and workable alternatives.

My own quest for a single solution to women's madness I now realize was naïve. I was looking for the impossible, the magic wand. No one solution would have solved my mother's misery; the medical treatment she did receive was most damaging in that it was offered as the panacea that did not work. Had other types of help been offered at the same time, the outcome may have been different. So my adolescent anger at the ECT has been misplaced. It should have been directed at the single- (and narrow-) minded approach of the professionals.

Equally, my rejection of my own clinical psychology training as hypocritical and oppressive was also naïve. It is short-sighted to reject all therapy. Many women are saved by these professional interventions. But to practise, as I will again, I must widen my agenda, and look beyond the professional rhetoric, the constraints of my chosen profession, and listen to the women I shall work with. I have skills that I can offer, but I must be able to accept rejection of those skills, and to acknowledge that for many women I do not have the answers, but that I might help them to find answers elsewhere. Professional egos must be challenged. If I accept that, I can accept a role in working with women in an attempt to alleviate their misery. This is less seductive a conclusion than the extreme rhetoric beloved by the feminist critics and the antipsychiatrists, by the experts who hold out their professional solution as *the* one. But the multi-dimensional approach, the individual approach combined with critical analysis, is the only answer for women. Each professional, each critic can offer something, but women must make the decisions themselves. Since women are the best judges of their own needs, we must listen.

I shall end with a quotation from a nineteenth-century feminist, herself diagnosed as mentally ill and treated with therapy, for in all of our analysis the voice least often heard is that of the women at the centre of the debate, those who are actually distressed.[6] If we spend more time listening to women, and less time expounding our own pet theories, perhaps we will move forward. Here is Charlotte Perkins Gilman's voice:

> Mental illness . . . for women [is] often a form of logical resistance to a 'kind and benevolent enemy' they are not permitted to openly fight. In a sick society, women who have difficulty fitting in are not ill but demonstrating a healthy positive response.
>
> (Charlotte Perkins Gilman, 1892)

I would hope that both feminists and professionals can move towards a more complete understanding of this response, an understanding which can only have benefits for those at the heart of the debate, the women positioned as mad.

Notes

1. See Chapter 1 for a discussion of this.
2. In terms of side effects, addiction, inability to function and reluctance to seek other solutions.
3. See Irigaray 1986: 100 for a discussion of woman's sexuality as a flaw in patriarchal discourse.
4. See Holland 1990 for a discussion of how this is translated into action.
5. Segal 1990 examines masculinity in an interesting and insightful way.
6. See Chamberlain 1988 and Fraser 1989 for more recent accounts from women who have received psychiatric treatment.

Bibliography

Abrahams, R. 1990: 'Deathmaking: The evidence and trends in Britain and Europe', *Changes*, 8, 4, 294–303.

Abramowitz, S., Roback, H., Schwartz, F., Yasuna, A., Abramowitz, C. and Gomes, B. 1976: 'Sex bias in psychotherapy: A failure to confirm', *American journal of psychiatry*, 133, 706–9.

Abramson, L. Y., Seligman, M. E. P. and Teasdale, J. D. 1978: 'Learned helplessness in humans: Critique and reformulation', *Journal of abnormal psychology*, 87, 49–74.

Aden, G. 1976: 'Lithium carbonate versus ECT in the treatment of manic state of identical twins with bipolar affective disease', *Diseases of the nervous system*, 37, 7, 393–7.

Al-Assa, I. 1980: *The psychopathology of women*, Prentice Hall, New Jersey.

Alexander, F. G. and Selesnick, S. T. 1966: *The history of psychiatry*, Allen and Unwin, London.

Alic, M. 1986: *Hypatia's heritage: A history of women in science from antiquity to the late nineteenth century*, Women's Press, London.

Allen, H. 1987: *Justice unbalanced: Gender, psychiatry and judicial decisions*, Open University Press, Milton Keynes.

Allen, M. G. 1976: 'Twin studies of affective illness', *Archives of general psychiatry*, 33, 1476–8.

Antaki, C. and Brewin, C. R. (eds) 1982: *Attributions and psychological change: Applications of attributional theories to clinical and educational practice*, Academic Press, London.

Aristotle (trans.) Peck, A. L. 1965: *History of animals: Historia animalium*, Heinemann, London.

Arlow, J. 1989: 'Psychoanalysis', in R. Corsini and D. Wedding (eds) *Current psychotherapies*, 4th edn, FE Peacock Pub., Illinois, 19–64.

Armstrong, S. 1991: 'Female circumcision: fighting a cruel tradition', *New scientist*, 2 February, 42–7.

Aveling, E. and Aveling, E. 1886: 'The woman question: From a socialist point of view', *Westminster review*, 207–22.

Avery, D. and Winoker, G. 1976: 'Mortality in depressed patients treated with electroconvulsive therapy and antidepressants', *Archives of general psychiatry*, 33, 9 1029–37.

Bachman, J. A. 1972: 'Self-injurious behaviour: A behavioural analysis', *Journal of abnormal psychology*, 80, 3, 211–24.

Baker Brown, I. 1866: *On the curability of certain forms of insanity, epilepsy, catalepsy and hysteria in females*, Robert Hardwicke, London.

Baker-Miller, J. 1986: *Towards a new psychology of women*, 2nd edn, Beacon, New York.

Bancroft, J. 1974: *Deviant sexual behaviour*, Clarendon Press, Oxford.

Bandura, A. 1977: 'Self efficacy: Toward a unifying theory of behavioural change', *Psychological review*, 84, 191–215.

Barker-Benfield, G. J. 1976: *The horrors of the half-known life: Male attitudes towards women and sexuality in nineteenth century America*, Harper and Row, New York.

Barnes, M. and Berke, J. 1971: *Mary Barnes: Two accounts of a journey through madness*, MacGibbon and Kee, London.

Baroja, J. 1973: *The world of witches*, University of Chicago Press, Chicago.

Barr, J. 1912: 'What are we? What are we doing? Whence do we come? and Whither do we go?', *British medical journal*, 2, 157–63.

Barry, K. 1979: *Female sexual slavery*, New York University Press, New York.

Barshis, V. G. 1983: 'The question of marital rape', *Women's studies international forum*, 6(4), 383–93.

Baruch, E. H. and Serrano, L. 1988: *Women analyse women: In France, England and the United States*, Harvester Wheatsheaf, Hemel Hempstead.

Baruch, G. and Treacher, A. 1978: *Psychiatry observed*, Routledge and Kegan Paul, London.

Bassoff, E. and Glass, G. 1982: 'The relationship between sex roles and mental health: A meta-analysis of twenty-six studies', *Counselling psychologist*, 10, 4, 105–12.

Beck, A. 1976: *Cognitive therapy and emotional disorders*, International Universities Press, New York.

Beck, A. and Weishaar, M. 1989: 'Cognitive therapy', in Corsini, R. & Wedding, D. (eds), *Current psychotherapies*, 4th edn, FE Peacock Pub., Illinois, 285–322.

Becker, H. 1963: *Outsiders: Studies in the sociology of deviance*, Free Press, New York.

Becker, M. H. and Maiman, L. A. 1975: 'Sociobehavioural determinants of compliance with health and medical care recommendations', *Medical care*, 13, 10–24.

Bell, R. M. 1985: *Holy anorexia*, University of Chicago Press, Chicago.

Belle, D. 1990: 'Poverty and women's mental health', *American psychologist*, 45, 3, 385–9.

Benedict, R. 1935: *Patterns of culture*, Routledge and Kegan Paul, London.

Bentall, R. P. 1990: 'The syndromes and symptoms of psychosis', in Bentall, R. P. (ed.), *Reconstructing schizophrenia*, Routledge, London, 23–59.

Bentall, R. P., Jackson, H. F. and Pilgrim, D. 1988: 'Abandoning the concept of "schizophrenia": Some implications of validity arguments for psychological research into psychotic phenomena', *British journal of clinical psychology*, 27, 303–24.

Berke, J. 1979: *I haven't had to go mad here*, Penguin, Harmondsworth.

Berkwitz, N. 1974: 'An up-to-date review of shock therapies: Are convulsive shock therapies "moral treatments?" ', *Diseases of the nervous system*, 35, 11, 523–7.

Betterton, R. (ed.) 1987: *Looking on: Images of femininity in the visual arts and media*, Pandora, London.

Biron, M., Risch, N., Hamburger, R., Mandel, B., Kushner, S., Newman, N., Drummer, D. and Belmaker, R. H. 1987: 'Genetic linkage between X-chromosome markers and affective illness', *Nature*, 326, 289–92.

Blier, R. (ed.) 1988: *Feminist approaches to science*, Pergamon Press, New York.

Boas, C. 1966: 'The doctor–patient relationship', *Journal of sex research*, 2, 215–18.

Bouhoutsos, J., Holroyd, J., Lerman, H., Forer, B. and Greenberg, M. 1983: 'Sexual intimacy between psychotherapists and patients', *Professional psychology: Research and practice*, 14, 2, 185–96.

Bowers, J. 1990: 'All hail the great abstraction: Star Wars and the politics of cognitive psychology', in Parker, I. and Shotter, J. (eds), *Deconstructing social psychology*, Routledge, London.

Braman, O. 1977: 'Comics' in King, J. and Scott, M. (eds) *Is this your life? Images of women in the media*, Virago, London.

Breggin, P. 1979: *Electroshock: Its brain-disabling effects*, Springer, New York.

Breuer, J. and Freud, Z. 1957: *Studies on hysteria*, Hogarth Press: London.

Brewin, C. R. 1990: *Cognitive foundations of clinical psychology*, Lawrence Erlbaum, London (2nd edn).

Briscoe, M. 1982: 'Sex differences in psychological wellbeing', *Psychological medicine*, Monographs, Supplement 1.

Brody, E. M. and Schoonover, C. B. 1986: 'Patterns of parent care when adult daughters work and when they don't', *The gerontologist*, 26, 372–82.

Brooks, K. 1973: 'Freudianism is not a basis for Marxist psychology', in Brown, P. (ed.), *Radical psychology*, Tavistock, London, 315–74.

Broverman, K., Broverman, D., Clarkson, F., Rosenkrantz, P., and Vogel, S. 1970: 'Sex role stereotypes and clinical judgements of mental health', *Journal of consulting and clinical psychology*, 34, 1, 1–7.

Brown, G. and Harris, T. 1978: *Social origins of depression*, Tavistock, London.

Brown, G. W., Andrews, B., Harris, T., Adler, Z. and Bridge, L. 1986: 'Social support, self-esteem and depression', *Psychological medicine*, 16, 813–31.

Brown, P. (ed.) 1973: *Radical psychology*, Harper and Row, London.

Browne, S. 1923: 'Studies in feminine inversion', *Journal of sexology and psychoanalysis*, 101.

Browne, W. A. F. 1837: 'What asylums were, are and ought to be', 1976 reprint, Arno Press, New York.

Brownfain, J. 1971: 'The American psychological association professional liability insurance program', *American psychologist*, 6, 648–52.

Brownmiller, S. 1975: *Against our will: Men, women and rape*, Secker and Warburg, London.

Bruely, S. 1976: 'Women awake, the experience of consciousness raising', in Feminist anthology collective (ed.), *No turning back: Writings from the women's liberation movement 1975–80*, Women's Press, London.

Brumberg, J. 1988: *Fasting girls: The emergence of anorexia nervosa as a modern disease*, Harvard University Press, Cambridge, MA.

Burman, E. (ed.) 1990: *Feminists and psychological practice*, Sage, London.

Burnam, M. A., Stein, J. A., Golding, J. M., Sorenson, S. B., Forsyth, A. B. and

Telles, C. A. 1988: 'Sexual assault and mental disorders in a community population', *Journal of consulting and clinical psychology*, 56, 843–50.

Burns, J. 1992: 'Mad or just plain bad: Gender and the work of forensic clinical psychologists', in Ussher, J. M. and Nicolson, P. (eds), *Gender issues in clinical psychology*, Routledge, London.

Burrows, G. 1828: *Commentaries on insanity*, Underwood, London.

Burt, M. R. 1980: 'Cultural myths and supports for rape', *Journal of personality and social psychology*, 38, 843–50.

Burton, R. 1620: quoted in F. Morgan 1989: *A mysogynist's source book*, Jonathan Cape, London, 148–52.

Busfield, J. 1986: *Managing madness: Changing ideas and practice*, Hutchinson, London.

Butler, S. 1872: *Erewhon*, 1954 reprint, Penguin, London.

Butt, W., Watts, J. and Holder, G. 1983: 'The biochemical background to the premenstrual syndrome' in Taylor, R. (ed.), *Premenstrual syndrome*, Medical news tribune, 16–24.

Byng-Hall, J. 1980: 'Symptom bearer as marital distance regulator: Clinical implications', *Family processes*, 19, 355–62.

Bynum, W. F., Porter, R., and Shepherd, M. (eds) 1988: *The anatomy of madness: Essays in the history of psychiatry*, Tavistock, London.

Byrd, M. 1962: *Visits to Bedlam: Madness and literature in the eighteenth century*, University of South California Press, Columbia, South California.

Cabinis, P. J. C. 1958: *Ouvres philosophiques*, 2 vols, Paris.

Cadoret, R. J. 1978: 'Psychopathology in adopted-away offspring of biologic parents with antisocial behaviour', *Archives of general psychiatry*, 35, 176–84.

Cameron, D. 1985: *Feminism and linguistic theory*, Macmillan, London.

Cameron, D. and Frazer, E. 1987: *The lust to kill: A feminist investigation of sexual murder*, Polity Press, London.

Camp, J. 1974: *Holloway Prison*, David and Charles, London.

Cantor, M. H. 1983: 'Strain among caregivers: A study of experience in the United States', *The gerontologist*, 23, 597–604.

Cardinal, M. 1977: *Autrement dit*, Grasset, Paris.

Carmen, E., Russo, N. and Baker-Miller, J. 1984: 'Inequality and women's mental health: An overview', in Rieker, P. P. and Carmen, E. (eds), *The gender gap in psychotherapy*, Plenum Press, New York, 369–74.

Carney, M. and Sheffield, B. 1974: 'The effects of pulse ECT in neurotic and endogenous depression', *British journal of psychiatry*, 125, 91–4.

Caroll, B. J. 1982: 'The dexamethasone suppression test for melancholia', *British journal of psychiatry*, 140, 292–304.

Carter, A. 1979: *The Sadeian woman*, Virago, London.

Casement, P. 1985: *Learning from the patient*, Tavistock, London.

Chadwick, W. 1990: *Women, art and society*, Thames and Hudson, New York.

Chagnon, N. A. 1977: *Yanomamo: The fierce people*, 3rd edn, Holt, New York.

Chamberlain, J. 1988: *On our own*, Mind publications, London.

Chawaf, C. 1986: 'Linguistic flesh', in Marks, E. and de Courtivron, I. (eds), *New French feminisms: An anthology*, Harvester, Sussex, 177–8.

Chesler, P. 1972: *Women and madness*, Doubleday, New York.

Chodorow, N. 1978: *The reproduction of mothering: Psychoanalysis and the sociology of gender*, California University Press, California.

Choiton, A., Stitzer, W. O., Roberts, S. R. and Delmore, T. 1976: 'The patterns of medical drug use', *Canadian medical association journal*, 114, 33.

Cixous, H. 1986: 'Sorties', in Marks, E. and Courtivron, I. (eds), *New French feminisms*, Harvester, Sussex, 90–9.
Cixous, H. 1986: 'The laugh of the medusa', in Marks, E. and Courtivron, I. (eds), *New French feminisms*, Harvester, Sussex, 245–64.
Clare, A. 1976: *Psychiatry in dissent: Controversial issues in thought and practice*, Tavistock, London.
Claridge, G. 1990: 'Can a disease model of schizophrenia survive?', in Bentall, R. P. (ed.), *Reconstructing schizophrenia*, Routledge, London, 157–83.
Cloninger, C. R., Bohman, M. and Sigvardson, S. 1981: 'Inheritance of alcohol abuse: Cross fostering analysis of adopted men', *Archives of general psychiatry*, 38, 861–8.
Cochrane, R. and Stopes-Roe, M. 1981: 'Women, marriage, employment and mental health', *British journal of psychiatry*, 139, 373–81.
Cohen, D. 1988: *Women's mental health research agenda: Older women's issues*, Women's mental health occasional paper series, National institute of mental health, Rockville MD.
Conrad, P. 1982: 'On the medicalization of deviance and social control', in Ingelby, D. (ed.), *Critical psychology*, Penguin, Harmondsworth, 102–19.
Cooper, D. 1973: 'Being born in a family', in Brown, P. (ed.), 1973, *Radical psychology*, Harper and Row, London.
Cooper, D. 1974: *The grammar of living: An examination of political acts*, Penguin, Harmondsworth.
Cooper, G. F. 1988: 'The psychological methods of sex therapy', in: Cole, M. and Dryden, W. (eds) *Sex Therapy in Britain*, Open University Press, Milton Keynes, Chapter 7.
Cooperstock, R. 1976: 'Women and psychotropic drugs', in MacLennan, A. (ed.), *Women: Their use of alcohol and other legal drugs*, Addiction research foundation, Toronto.
Cooperstock, R. 1978: 'Sex difference in psychotropic drug use', *Social science and medicine*, 12, 3B, 179–86.
Costrich, N., Feinstein, J., Kidder, L., Marecek, J., and Pascale, L. 1975: 'When stereotypes hurt: Three studies of penalties for sex-role reversals', *Journal of experimental social psychology*, 11, 520–30.
Coward, R. 1984: *Female desire: Women's sexuality today*, Paladin, London.
Cowie, C. and Lees, S. 1987: 'Slags or drags', in *Feminist review* (eds), *Sexuality: A reader*, Virago, London.
Cowie, E. 1978: 'Woman as sign', *m/f* 1, 49–64.
Dahlberg, C. 1970: 'Sexual contact between patient and therapist', *Contemporary psychoanalysis*, 6, 107–24.
Dalton, K. 1964: *The premenstrual syndrome*, Carles Thomas, Springfield, Illinois.
Daly, M. 1979: *Gyn/Ecology: The metaethics of radical feminism*, Women's Press, London.
Daly, M. 1984: *Pure lust*, Women's Press, London.
Darwin, C. 1871: *The descent of man*, 1889 reprint, Princeton University Press, Princeton, NJ.
Davidson, V. 1984: 'Psychiatry's problem with no name: Therapist–patient sex', in Reiker, P. and Carmen, E. (eds) – *The gender gap in psychotherapy*, Plenum Press, New York, 361–8.
Davison, G. and Neale, J. 1990: *Abnormal psychology*, 5th edn, Wiley, New York.

Dawkins, R. 1976: *The selfish gene*, Open University, Milton Keynes.
de Beauvoir, S. 1953: *The second sex*, Jonathan Cape, London.
de Beauvoir, S. 1979: Interview by Alice Jardine, *Signs*, 5, 228.
de Fonseca A. F. 1989: 'Psychiatry in the 1990's,' in Hindmarsh, I. and Stoner, P. D. (eds), *Human psychopharmacy: Measures and methods*, vol. 2, Wiley, New York.
de Sade and Bataille, G., 1950: *Justine, ou, les malteurs de la vertu*, Preface de George Bataille, Soleil Noir, Paris.
Deutch, A. 1937: *The mentally ill in America*, Doubleday, New York.
DHSS 1991: *Women doctors and their careers: Report of the joint working party*, DHSS, London.
Dingwall, R. 1976: *Aspects of illness*, Sedge, London.
Dinnerstein, D. 1976: *The mermaid and the minotaur: Sexual arrangements and the human malaise*, Harper, New York.
Dobash, R. and Dobash, R. 1978: 'Wives: the "appropriate" victims of marital violence', *Victimatology: An international journal*, 2, 3/4, 426–42.
Dobash, R. and Dobash, R. 1979: *Violence against wives: A case against patriarchy*, Free Press, New York.
Dohrenwend, B. P., and Dohrenwend, B. S. 1969: *Social status and psychological disorders: A casual inquiry*, Wiley, London.
Dohrenwend, B. S. and Dohrenwend, B. P. (eds) 1981: *Stressful life events and their context*, Proudist, New York.
Duquesne, T. and Reeves, J. 1982: *A handbook of psychoactive medicines*, Quartet Books, London.
Durkheim, E. 1897: *Suicide: A study in sociology*, Felix Allan, 1951 reprint Free Press, London.
Durkheim, E. 1938: *The rules of sociological method*, Collier Macmillan, London.
Dworkin, A. 1974: *Woman hating*, Dutton, New York.
Dworkin, A. 1981: *Pornography: Men possessing women*, Women's Press, London.
Dworkin, A. 1987: *Intercourse*, Secker, London.
Easlea, B. 1980: *Witchhunting, magic and the new philosophy: An introduction to the debates of the scientific revolution 1450–1750*, Harvester Press, Brighton, University Books.
Eaton, W. and Kessler, L. G. 1985: *Epidemiological field methods in psychiatry: The NiMH epidemiological catchment area program*, Academic Press, Orlando.
Edwards, S. 1986: 'Neither mad nor bad: The female violent offender re-assessed', FL. *Women's studies international forum*, 19, 1, 79–87.
Ehrenreich, B., and English, D. 1974: *Witches, midwifery and nurses: A history of women healers*, Glass Mountain pamphlets, 1, Compendium, London.
Ehrenreich, B., and English, D. 1978: *For her own good: 150 years of the experts' advice to women*, Anchor Doubleday, New York.
Eichenbaum, L. and Orbach, S. 1983: *What do women want?* Fontana, London.
Eichhler, A. and Parron, D. 1987: *Women's mental health: Agenda for research*, National institute for mental health, Rockville, MD.
Elliot, S. 1984: 'Pregnancy and after', in S. Rachman (ed.), *Contributions to medical psychology*, 3, Pergamon Press, Oxford, 93–116.
Ellis, A. and Bernard, M. (eds) 1985: *Clinical applications of rational emotive therapy*, Plenum Press, New York.
Ellis, H. 1897: *Sexual inversions: Studies in the psychology of sex*, vol. 2, reprinted 1927, F.A. Davis, Philadelphia.

Engels, F. 1884: 'The origin of the family, private property and the state', in Marx, K. and Engels, F. *Selected Works*, Lawrence and Wishart, London.
Erikson, K. T. 1962: 'Notes on the sociology of deviance', *Social problems*, 9, 307–14.
Ernst, S. and Goodison, L. 1981: *In our own hands: A book of self help therapy*, Women's Press, London.
Esquirol, J. E. 1845: *Mental maladies: A treatise on insanity* (1965 facsimile of English edition of 1845), Library of the New York Academy of Medicine, Hafner Publishing Co., New York.
Eysenck, H. J. 1952: 'The effects of psychotherapy: an evaluation', *Journal of consulting psychology*, 16, 319–24.
Eysenck, M. W. 1984: *An introduction to cognitive psychology*, Lawrence Erlbaum, London.
Faulder, C. 1977: 'Women's magazines', in King, J. and Scott, M. (eds), *Is this your life? Images of women in the media*, Virago, London, 173–94.
Fee, E. 1988: 'Critique of modern science: The relationship of feminism to other radical epistemologies', in Blier, R. (ed.), *Feminist approaches to science*, Pergamon Press, New York, 42–56.
Feinblatt, J. A. and Gold, A. R. 1976: 'Sex roles and the psychiatric referral process', *Sex roles*, 2, 109–22.
Ferguson, M. A. H., 1981: *Images of women in literature*, Houghton Miflin, London.
Ferguson, M. 1983: *Forever feminine: Women's magazines and the cult of femininity*, Heinemann, London.
Fernando, S. 1988: *Race and culture in psychiatry*, Croom Helm, London.
Figes, E. 1970: *Patriarchal attitudes*, Faber and Faber, London.
Finklehor, D. 1984: *Child sexual abuse: new theory and research*, Free Press, New York.
Finkelhor, D. *et al.* 1986: *A sourcebook on child sexual abuse*, Sage, Beverly Hills, CA.
Finn, J. 1985: 'The stresses and coping of battered women', *Social casework*, 66(6), 341–9.
Firestone, S. 1971: *The dialectic of sex: The case for feminist revolution*, Cape, London.
Fitch, J. G. 1890: *Notes on American Schools and training colleges*, Macmillan and Co., London.
Fodor, I. G. 1985: 'Assertiveness training in the eighties: moving beyond the personal', in Rosewater, L. B. and Walker, L. (eds), *Handbook of feminist therapy, women's issues in psychotherapy*, Springer, New York.
Foucault, M. 1967: *Madness and civilization: A history of insanity in the age of reason*, Tavistock, London.
Foucault, M. 1970: *The order of things*, Tavistock, London.
Foucault, M. 1979: *The history of sexuality: vol. I, An introduction*, Allen Lane, London.
Fox, J. W. 1980: 'Gove's specific sex-role theory of mental illness: A research note', *Journal of health and social behaviour*, 21, 260–7.
Frame, J. 1961: *Faces in the water*, 1980 reprint, Women's Press, London.
Frame, J. 1984: *An angel at my table*, Women's Press, London.
Frank, J. 1985: 'Therapeutic components shared by all psychotherapies'; in Mahoney, M. J. and Freeman, A. (eds), *Cognition and psychotherapy*, Plenum,

London.

Frank, R. T. 1931: 'The normal causes of premenstrual tension', *Archives of neurology and psychiatry*, 26, 1053–7.

Fraser, S. 1989: *My father's house: A memoir of incest and of healing*, Virago, London.

Frazer, J. G. 1938: *The golden bough: A study in magic and religion*, Macmillan, London.

Freeman, J. 1975: 'The woman's liberation movement: its origins, structures, impact and ideas', in: Freeman, J. (ed.), *Women: A feminist perspective*, Mayfield Publishing Co., Palo Alto, California.

French, M. 1985: *Beyond power: Men, women and morals*, Cape, London.

Freud, S. 1895: *The standard edition of the complete works of Sigmund Freud*, v1 Pre-psychoanalytic publications and unpublished drafts. Hogarth Press, London, 1966 reprint.

Freud, S. 1933: 'New introductory lectures on psychoanalysis', *Pelican Freud Library*, Penguin, Harmondsworth.

Friedan, B. 1965: *The feminine mystique*, Gollancz, London.

Friedberg, J. 1976: *Shock treatment is not good for your brain*, Glide, London.

Frith, C. D., 1979: 'Consciousness, information processing and schizophrenia', *British journal of psychiatry*, 134, 225–35.

Frosh, S. 1987: *The politics of psychoanalysis*, Macmillan, London.

Fulani, L. 1987: 'All power to the people! But how?', in Fulani, L. (ed.), *The psychopathology of everyday racism and sexism*, Harrington Park Press, New York, 65–74.

Gage, M. J. 1972: *Women, church and state*, Arno Press, New York.

Gagnon, M. 1986: 'Body I', in Marks, E. and de Courtivron, I. (eds), *New French feminisms: An anthology*, Harvester, Sussex, 179–80.

Gallagher, M. 1979: *The portrayal and participation of women in the media*, UNESCO report, Paris.

Ganesan, V. 1986: 'Electroconvulsive therapy under fire', *Indian journal of clinical psychology*, 13, 2, 145–7.

Ganster, D. and Victor, B. 1988: 'The impact of social support on mental and physical health', *British journal of medical psychology*, 61, 17–36.

Gardener, A. 1872: cited in Barker-Benfield 1976, *The horrors of the half-known life: Male attitudes towards women and sexuality in nineteenth century America*, Harper and Row, New York.

Gardner, H. 1985: *The new mind's science: A history of the cognitive revolution*, Basic Books, New York.

Garfunkel, P. E., Garner, D. M., Rose, J., Darby, P. L., Brandes, J. S., O'Hanlon, J., Walsh, N. 1983: 'A comparison of characteristics in the families of patients with anorexia nervosa and normal controls', *Psychological medicine*, 13, 821–8.

Gauthier, X. 1986: 'Why witches?', in Marks, E. and de Courtivron, I. (eds), *New French feminisms: An anthology*. Harvester, Sussex, 199–203.

Gilbert, S. and Gubar, S. 1979: *The madwoman in the attic: The woman writer and the nineteenth century*, Yale University Press, New Haven.

Gilligan, C. 1982: *In a different voice: Psychological theory and women's development*, Harvard University Press, Cambridge MA.

Gilman, C. P. 1892: *The yellow wallpaper*, 1988 reprint, Virago, London.

Gilman, S. L. 1988: *Disease and representation: Images of illness from madness to AIDS*, Cornell University Press, Ithaca.

Glaser, D. and Frosh, S. 1988: 'Child sex abuse', *Practical social work series*, Macmillan, Basingstoke.
Goffman, E. 1961: *Asylums: Essays on the social insituation of mental patients and other inmates*, Doubleday, New York.
Gold, N. 1986: *The good news about depression*, Bantam Books, New York.
Goldman, N. and Ravid, R. 1980: 'Community surveys of sex differences in mental illness', in Guttentag, M., Salasin, S. and Belle, D. (eds), *Mental health of women*, Academic Press, New York.
Goodwin, D. W., Schulsinger, F., Hermansen, L., Guze, S. B. and Winoker, G. A. 1973: 'Alcohol problems in adoptees raised apart from alcoholic biological parents', *Archives of general psychiatry*, 128, 239–43.
Gottesman, I. and Shields, J. 1972: *Schizophrenia and genetics: A twin study vantage point*, Academic Press, New York.
Gottesman, I. I., McGuffin, P. and Farmer, A. 1987: 'Clinical genetics as clues to the "real" genetics of schizophrenia', *Schizophrenia bulletin*, 13, 23–47.
Gould, A. and Shotter, J. 1977: *Human action and its psychological investigation*, Routledge, London.
Gove, W. 1972: 'The relationship between sex roles, marital status, and mental illness', *Social forces*, 51, 34–44.
Gove, W. 1979: 'Sex differences in the epidemiology of mental illness: Evidence and explanations', in Gomberg, E. and Franks, V. (eds), *Gender and disordered behaviour*, Brunner/Mazel, New York.
Gove, W. and Geerken, M. 1977: 'Response bias in community surveys: An empirical investigation', *American journal of sociology*, 82, 1289–317.
Gove, W. and Tudor, J. 1973: 'Adult sex roles and mental health', *American journal of sociology*, 78, 812–35.
Greene, J. G. 1984: *The social and psychological origins of the climacteric syndrome*, Gower, Aldershot.
Griffin, S. 1981: *Pornography and silence*, Women's Press, London.
Groult, B. 1986: 'Night Porters,' in Marks, E. and de Courtivron, I. (eds) *New French feminisms: An anthology*, Harvester, Sussex, 68–75.
Grover, S. 1981: *Towards a psychology of the scientist: Implications of psychological research for contemporary philosophy of science*, University Press of America, Washington.
Grunebaum, J. 1987: 'Multidirected partiality and the "parental imperative" ', *Psychotherapy*, 24, 35, 646–56.
Gull, W. W. 1874: *Anorexia nervosa*, Transactions of the clinical society of London; 7.
Haldane, C. 1927: *Motherhood and its enemies*, Chatto and Windus, London.
Hall, K. 1985: 'The two spinster ladies', in Bradshaw, J. and Hemmingway, M. (eds), *Girls next door: Lesbian feminist stories*, Women's Press, London.
Hall, R. E. 1986: *Ask any woman: A London inquiry into rape and sexual assault*, Falling Wall Press, London.
Halliday, A. 1828: *A general view of the present state of lunatics and lunatic asylums in Great Britain and Ireland*, Underwood, London.
Hallisey, M. 1987: *Venomous women: Fear of the female in literature*, Greenwood Press, New York.
Hamilton, C. 1909: *Marriage as a trade*, 1981 reprint, Women's Press, London.
Hamilton, M. 1973: 'Psychology in society: End or ends?', *Bulletin of the British psychological society*, 26, 185–9.

Hanneke, C. R., Shields, N. M. and McCall, G. J. 1986: 'Assessing the prevalence of marital rape', *Journal of interpersonal violence*, 1, 350–62.
Harding, J. 1986: *Perspectives on gender and science*, Falmer Press, Sussex.
Harding, S. J. 1986: *The science question in feminism*, Cornell University Press, Ithaca.
Harcz, J. C. 1982: The dopamine hypothesis: An overview of studies in schizophrenic patients', *Schizophrenia bulletin*, 8, 438–69.
Harre, R., and Secord, P. 1972: *The explanation of social behaviour*, Blackwell, Oxford.
Harrison, W., Shapre, L. and Endicott, J. 1985: 'Treatment of premenstrual symptoms', *General hospital psychiatry*, 17, 1, 54–65.
Haslam, J. 1817: *Considerations on the moral management of the insane*, R. Hunter, London.
Hawthorne, N. 1852: *The Blithedale romance*, 1958 reprint, Norton, New York.
Hays, H. R. 1972: *The dangerous sex: The myth of feminine evil*, Pocket Books, New York.
Healy, D. 1990: *The suspended revolution*, Faber and Faber, London.
Heninger, G. R., Charney, D. S. and Menkes, D. B. 1983: 'Receptor sensitivity and the mechanism of action of antidepressant treatment', in Clayton, P. J. and Barrett, J. E. (eds), *Treatment of depression: Old controversies and new approaches*, Raven Press, New York.
Henriques, J., Hollway, W., Urwin, C., Venn, C. and Walkerdine, V. 1984: *Changing the subject: Psychology, social regulation and subjectivity*, Methuen, London.
Herman, J. and Hirschman, L. 1984: 'Father–daughter incest', in Reiker, P. and Hilberman, E. (eds), *The gender gap in psychotherapy: Social realities and psychological processes*, Plenum Press, New York.
Heston, L. L. 1966: 'Psychiatric disorders in foster home reared children of schizophrenic mothers', *British journal of psychiatry*, 112, 819–25.
Hey, V. 1985: 'Getting away with murder: PMT and the press', in Laws, S., Hey, V. and Eagan, A. (eds) *Seeing red: The politics of premenstrual tension*, Hutchinson, London.
Hilberman, E. 1980: 'Overview: The "wife beater's wife" reconsidered', *American journal of psychiatry*, 137, 1336–47.
Hilberman, E. 1984: 'The "wife beaters wife" reconsidered', in Reiker, P. and Hilberman, E. (eds), *The gender gap in psychotherapy: Social realities and psychological processes*, Plenum Press, New York.
Himmelfarb, M. 1967: 'Varieties of Jewish experience', *Commentary*, July, 59.
Hite, S. 1977: *The Hite report: A nationwide study on female sexuality*, Dell, New York.
Holbrook, M. 1989: *Images of women in literature*, New York University Press, New York.
Holland, P. 1987: 'The Page Three girl speaks to women, 2', in: Betterton, R. (ed.) *Looking on: Images of femininity in the visual arts and media*, Pandora, London.
Holland, S. 1989: 'Women and community mental health: Twenty years on', *Clinical psychology forum*, 22, 35–7.
Holland, S. 1990: 'Psychotherapy, oppression and social action: Gender, race and class in black women's depression', in Perelberg, R. J. and Miller, A. C. (eds), *Gender and power in families*, Routledge, London.
Holland, S. 1992: 'From social abuse to social action: A neighbourhood

psychotherapy and social action programme for women', in Ussher, J. M. and Nicolson, P. (eds), *Gender issues in clinical psychology*, Routledge, London.

Hollingshead, A. B. and Redlich, F. 1958: *Social class and mental illness*, Wiley, New York.

Hollway, W. 1989: *Subjectivity and method in psychology: Gender, meaning and science*, Sage, London.

Holmes, J. and Lindley, R. 1989: *The values in psychotherapy*, Oxford University Press, Oxford.

Holroyd, J. and Brodsky, A. 1977: 'Psychologist attitudes and practices regarding erotic and non-erotic physical contact with patients', *American psychologist*, 32, 843–9.

hooks, b. 1989: *Talking back: Thinking feminist – thinking black*, Sheba, London.

Horney, K.: *Feminine psychology*, 1973 reprint, Norton, New York.

Horowitz, A. 1985: 'Sons and daughters as caregivers to older parents: Differences in role performances', *The gerontologist*, 25, 612.

Hoskins, E. 1979: 'The Hoskin report: Genital and sexual mutilation of females', *Women's internationalnetwork*, Lexicon, USA.

Houck, J. 1972: 'The intractable female patient', *American journal of psychiatry*, 129, 27–31.

Hughes, P. 1952: 'Psychology: Science and/or profession', *American psychologist*, 7, 441–3.

Hughes, P. 1965: *Witchcraft*, Penguin, London.

Hunt, H. 1986: 'Women's private distress: a public health issue', *Medicine in society*, 12, 2.

Hunter, M. 1990: *The menopause*, Pandora, London.

Hunter, P. and Kelso, E. 1985: 'Feminist behaviour therapy', *Behaviour therapist*. 8, 10, 201–4.

Ingelby, D. (ed.) 1982: *Critical psychiatry: The politics of mental health*, Penguin, Harmondsworth.

Irigaray, L. 1980: 'When our lips speak together', *Signs*, 6, 1, 66–79.

Irigaray, L. 1981: 'And the one doesn't stir without the other', *Signs*, 7, 1, 60–7.

Irigaray, L. 1986: 'The sex which is not one', in Marks, E. and de Courtivron, I. (eds), *New French feminisms: An anthology*, Harvester, Sussex, 99–106.

Irigaray, L. 1988: Interview in Baruch, E. H. and Serrano, L., *Women analyse women: In France, England and the United States*. Harvester Wheatsheaf, Hemel Hempstead 149–66.

Jackson, M. 1984: 'Sex research and the construction of sexuality: A tool of male supremacy?' *Women studies international forum*, 7, 43–51.

Jacobson, A. and Richardson, B. 1987: 'Assault experiences of 100 psychiatric inpatients: Evidence of the need for routine inquiry', *American journal of psychiatry*, 144, 900–13.

Janoff-Bulman, R. and Freize, I. 1983: 'A theoretical perspective for understanding reactions to victimization', *Journal of social issues*, 39, 1–17.

Jeffreys, S. 1985: *The Spinster and her enemies: Feminism and sexuality 1880–1930*, Pandora, London.

Jeffreys, S. 1987: *The sexuality debate*, Routledge, London.

Jeffreys, S. 1990: *Anticlimax: A feminist perspective on the sexual revolution*, Women's Press, London.

Jehu, D. 1990: *Sexual abuse and beyond*, Wiley: Chichester.

Jenkins, R. 1986: '*Sex differences in minor psychiatric morbidity*,' *Psychological*

medicine, Monographs, Supplement 7.
Jenner, F. A. 1989: 'Democracy and ECT', *Asylum*, 3, 4.
Jones, A. R. 1985: 'Writing the body: Towards an understanding of *l'écriture feminine*', in Newton, J. and Rosenfelt, D. (eds), *Feminist criticism and social change: Sex, class and race in literature and culture*, Methuen, New York, 86–101.
Jones, L. and Cochrane, R. 1981: 'Stereotypes of mental illness: A test of the labelling hypothesis', *International journal of social psychiatry*, 27, 2, 99–107.
Jordanova, L. J. 1989: *Sexual visions: Images of gender in science and medicine between the eighteenth and twentieth century*, Harvester Wheatsheaf, Hemel Hempstead.
Kaplan, A. and Woodside, D. B. 1987: 'Biological aspects of anorexia and bulimia nervosa', *Journal of consulting and clinical psychology*, 55, 5, 645–51.
Kardener, S., Fuller, M. and Mensh, I. 1973: 'A survey of physicians' attitudes and practices regarding erotic and non-erotic contact with patients', *American journal of psychiatry*, 130, 1077–81.
Karet, T. 1977: 'Popular fiction', in: King, J. and Scott, M. (eds) *Is this your life? Images of women in the media*, Virago, London.
Kayton, R. and Biller, H. 1972: 'Sex role psychopathology in adult males', *Journal of consulting and clinical psychology*, 38, 208–10.
Keller, E. F. 1985: *Reflections on gender and science*, Yale University Press, New Haven, Conn.
Kendler, K. S. 1983: 'Overview: A current perspective on twin studies of schizophrenia', *American journal of psychiatry*, 140, 1413–25.
Kesey, K. 1962: *One flew over the cuckoo's nest*, Picador, London.
Kety, S. S., Rosenthal, D., Wender, P. H., and Schulsinger, F. 1968: 'The types and prevalence of mental illness in the biological and adoptive families of adopted schizophrenics', in Rosenthal, D. and Kety, S. S. (eds), *The transmission of schizophrenia*, Pergamon Press, New York.
Kety, S. S., Rosenthal, D., Wender, P. H., Schulsinger, F. and Jacobson, B. 1975: 'Mental illness in the biological and adoptive families of individuals who have become schizophrenic: A preliminary report based on psychiatric interviews', in Fieve, R. R., Rosenthal, D. and Brill, H. (eds), *Genetic research in psychiatry*, Johns Hopkins University Press, Baltimore.
Kilpatrick, D. G., Best, C. L., Veronen, L. J., Amick, A. E., Villeponteaux, L. A. and Ruff, G. A. 1985: 'Mental health correlates of criminal victimization: A random community survey', *Journal of consulting and clinical psychology*, 53, 866–73.
King, H. 1990: 'Hippocratic hysteria', paper presented at the Wellcome symposium on the history of medicine: History of hysteria, 6 April 1990, London.
Kitzinger, C. 1987: *The social constructions of lesbianism*, Sage, London.
Kitzinger, C. 1990: 'Resisting the discipline', in Burman, E. (ed.), *Feminists and psychological practice*, Sage, London.
Klein, D. 1982: 'The dark side of marriage: Battered wives and the domination of women', in Rafter, N. and Stanko, E. (eds), *Judge, lawyer, victim, thief: Women, gender roles and criminal justice*, Northeastern University Press, Boston.
Klein, M. 1952: *Some theoretical conclusions regarding the emotional life of the infant*, Hogarth, London.

Kline, P. 1977: *Fact and fantasy in Freudian theory*, Methuen, London.

Koerber, C. 1977: 'Television', in King, J. and Scott, M. (eds), *Is this your life? Images of women in the media*, Virago, London, 123–42.

Koeske, R. 1983: 'Sociocultural factors in the premenstrual syndrome: Review, critiques and future directions', paper presented at the Premenstrual syndrome workshop, National institute of mental health, Rockville, MD, 14–15 April 1983.

Koos, E. 1954: *The health of Regionville: What the people thought and did about it*, Columbia, New York.

Koss, M. 1990: 'The women's mental health research agenda: Violence against women', *American psychologist*, 45, 3, 374–80.

Kovel, J. 1982: 'The American mental health industry', in Ingelby, D. (ed.), *Critical psychology: The politics of mental health*, Penguin, Harmondsworth.

Kovelman, J. and Schiebel, A. 1986: 'Biological substrates of schizophrenia', *Acta neurologica Scandanavia*, 73, 1, 1–32.

Kreitman, N. 1962: 'Psychiatric orientation among psychiatrists', *British journal of medical psychology*, 46, 75–81.

Kristeva, J. 1986: 'Woman can never be defined', in: Marks, E. and de Courtivron, I. (eds) *New French Feminisms*, Harvester Press, Brighton.

Kuhn, T. S. 1962: *The structure of scientific revolutions*, 2nd edn, University of Chicago Press, Chicago.

Lacan, J. 1958: 'The signification of the phallus', in Mitchell, J. and Rose, J. (eds), *Feminine sexuality: Jacques Lacan and the Ecole Freudienne*, Macmillan, London.

Lacan, J. 1977: *Ecrits: A selection*, Tavistock, London.

Laguiller, A. 1986: From an interview in Marks, E. and de Courtivron, I. (eds) *New French feminisms: An anthology*, Harvester, Sussex, 121–4.

Laing, R. D. 1960: *The dividend self: A study of sanity and madness*, Tavistock, London.

Laing, R. D. 1967: *The politics of experience*, Penguin, Harmondsworth.

Laing, R. D. 1972: 'Interview', *London Times*, 4 October.

Lambert, M., Shapiro, D. and Bergin, A. 1986: 'The effectiveness of psychotherapy', in Garfield, S. and Bergin, A. (eds), *Handbook of psychotherapy and behaviour change*, Wiley, London, 157–212.

Laws, S. 1985: 'Who needs PMT? A feminist approach to the politics of premenstrual tension', in Laws, S., Hey, V. and Eagen, A., *Seeing red: The politics of premenstrual tension*, Hutchinson, London.

Laws, S. 1990: *Issues of blood*, Macmillan, London.

Laws, S., Hey, V. and Eagen, A. 1985: *Seeing red: The politics of premenstrual tension*, Hutchinson, London.

Lea, H. 1906: *History of the inquisition in Spain*, vol. IV, Macmillan, New York.

Lees, P. 1965: 'The vulnerability to trauma of women in relation to periodic stress', abstract, The medical commission on accident prevention, second annual report.

Leflowitz, M. 1981: *Heroines and hysterics*, Duckworth, London.

Lemaire, A. 1977: *Jaques Lacan*, translated by Macey, D., Routledge, London.

Leupnitz, D. 1988: *The family interpreted: Feminist theory in clinical practice*, Basic Books, New York.

Levy, H. S. 1966: *Chinese footbinding: The history of a curious erotic custom*, Walton Rawls, New York.

Lewinsohn, P. M., Steinmetz, J. L., Larsen, D. W. and Franklin, J. 1981: 'Depression-related cognitions: Antecedent or consequences?' *Journal of abnormal psychology*, 90, 213–19.

Littlewood, R. and Lipsedge, M. 1982: *Aliens and alienists: Ethnic minorities and psychiatry*, Penguin, Harmondsworth.

Lobban, G. 1975: 'Sex-roles in reading schemes', *Educational review*, 27, 3.

Lorber, J. 1986: 'Dismantling Noah's ark', *Sex roles*, 14, 11–12, 567–80.

Luborsky, L., Singer, B. and Luborsky, L. 1975: 'Comparative studies of psychotherapy', *Archives of general psychiatry*, 32, 995–1008.

Luggin, R., Bensted, L., Petersson, B. and Jacobsen, A. 1984: 'Acute psychiatric admission related to the menstrual cycle', *Acta psychiatrica Scandanavia*, 69, 6, 461–5.

Macdonald, M. 1981: *Mystical bedlam*, Cambridge University Press, Cambridge.

Maddock, A. 1854: 'The education of women', in *On mental and nervous disorders*, Simpkin Marshall, London.

Mailer, N. 1971: *The prisoner of sex*, Weidenfeld, New York.

Makosky, V. 1982: 'Sources of stress: events or conditions', in Belle, D. (ed.), *Lives in stress: Women and depression*, Sage, Beverly Hills, CA, 35–53.

Malcolm, J. 1984: *In the Freud archives*, Flamingo, London.

Malen, D. H. 1979: *Individual psychotherapy and the science of psychodynamics*, Tavistock, Boston.

Malla, A. 1988: 'Characteristics of patients who receive electroconvulsive therapy', *Canadian journal of psychiatry*, 38, 8, 696–701.

Malson, H. 1992: 'Anorexia nervosa – feminist, psychoanalytic and family theories', in Nicolson, P. and Ussher, J. M., *The psychology of women's health and health care*, Macmillan, London.

Mandell, A. and Mandell, J. 1967: 'Suicide and the menstrual cycle', *Journal of the American medical association*, 200, 792–3.

Mander, A. 1977: 'Feminism as therapy', in Rawlings, E. and Carter, D. (eds), *Psychotherapy for women*, Charles and Thomas, Springfield, Ill.

Mappen, M. (ed.) 1980: *Witches and historians: Interpretations of Salem*, Kreiger, New York.

Marcuse, H. 1966: *Eros and civilization*, Beacon Press, Boston.

Marks, E. and de Courtivron, I. 1986: 'Variations on common themes'. Marks, E. and de Courtivron, I. (eds), in *New French feminisms: An anthology*, Harvester, Sussex, 212–32.

Marshall, R. 1990: 'The genetics of schizophrenia', in Bentall, R. P. (ed.), *Reconstructing schizophrenia*, Routledge, London.

Martin, D. 1976: *Battered wives*, Glide, San Francisco.

Martin, E. 1989: *The woman in the body: A cultural analysis of reproduction*, Open University, Milton Keynes.

Martin, P. 1987: *Mad women in romantic writing*, Harvester, Sussex.

Masson, J. M. 1989: *Against therapy*, Collins, London.

Masters, W. and Johnson, V. 1981: *Human sexual inadequacy*, Bantam Books, Boston, MA.

Maudsley, H. 1873: *Body and Mind*, Macmillan, London.

May, P. R. A., Tuma, A. H., Yale, C., Potepan, P. and Dixon, W. J. 1976: 'Schizophrenia: A follow-up study of treatment: II. Hospital stay over two to five years', *Archives of general psychiatry*, 33, 4, 481–6.

Mayo, K. 1927: *Mother India*, Blue Ribbon Books, New York.

McBride, A. 1988: *Women's mental health research agenda: Multiple roles*, Women's mental health occasional paper series, National institute of mental health, Rockville, MD.

McBride, A. 1990: 'Mental health effects of women's multiple roles', *American psychologist*, 45, 3, 381–4.

McGuffin, P., and Katz, R. 1989: 'The genetics of depression and manic depressive disorders', *British journal of psychiatry*, 155, 294–304.

McLaughlin, E. C. 1974: 'Equality of souls, inequality of sexes: Women in medieval theology', in Radlord Buetler, R. (ed.), *Religious and sexism*, Simon and Schuster, New York.

McNeal, E. T. and Cimbolic, P. 1986: 'Anti-depressants and biological theories of depression', *Psychological bulletin*, 99, 361–94.

Mechanic, D. 1969: *Mental health and social policy*, Prentice Hall, Englewood Cliffs, NJ.

Mednick, M. 1989: 'On the politics of psychological constructs: Stop the bandwagon, I want to get off', *American psychologist*, 44, 8, 1118–23.

Medvedev, Z. A. and Medvedev, R. A. 1971: *A question of madness*, Macmillan, London.

Meltzer, H. 1987: 'Biological studies in schizophrenia', *Schizophrenia bulletin*, 13, 1, 77–111.

Melville, H. 1962: 'Hawthorne and his mosses', in Miller, P. (ed.), *Major American writers*, New York.

Micale, M. 1990a: 'Hysteria male/hysteria female: Reflections on comparative gender construction in nineteenth-century medicine', paper presented at the Wellcome symposium on the history of medicine: History of hysteria, 6 April 1990, London.

Micale, M. 1990b: 'Hysteria and its histography: The future perspective', *History of psychiatry*, 1, 1, 33–124.

Michelet, J. 1862: *Satanism and witchcraft: A study in medieval superstition*, translated by Allinson, A. R., 1965, Citadel, New York.

Midelfort, H. C. 1972: *Witchhunting in south western Germany 1562–1684: The social and intellectual foundations*, Stanford, University Press, California.

Miles, A. 1988: *Women and mental illness*, Harvester Wheatsheaf, Hemel Hempstead.

Miller, A. 1982: *The drama of being a child and the search for the true self*, Virago, London.

Miller, H. 1938: *Black spring*, Grove Press, New York.

Miller, N. 1973: 'Letter to her therapist', in Brown, P. (ed.), *Radical psychology*, 484–9, Tavistock, London.

Millett, K. 1971: *Sexual politics*, Hart-Davis, London.

Milner, M. 1960: *The hands of the living God: An account of a psychoanalytic treatment*, Hogarth Press, London.

Minuchin, S. 1974: *Families and family therapy*, Harvard University Press, Cambridge MA.

Mitchell, J. 1974: *Psychoanalysis and feminism*, Allen Lane, London.

Mitchell, J., and Rose, J. 1982: *Feminine sexuality: Jacques Lacan and the école Freudienne*, Macmillan, London.

Mitchell, S. W. 1877: *Fat and blood: And how to make them*, J. B. Lippincott, Philadelphia.

Mollica, R. F. and Mills, M. 1986: 'Social class and psychiatric practice: A revision of the Hollingshead and Redlich model', *American journal of*

psychriatry, 143, 1, 12–17.
Morgan, F. 1989: *A misogynist's source book*, Jonathan Cape, London.
Morton, J., Additon, H., Addison, R., Hunt, L. and Sullivan, J. J. 1953: 'A clinical study of premenstrual tension', *American journal of obstetrics and gynaecology*, 65, 1182–91.
Mowbray, C. and Benedek, E. 1988: *Women's mental health research agenda: Services and treatment of mental disorders in women*, Women's mental health occasional paper series, National institute of mental health, Rockville, MD.
Mulvey, A. and Dohrenwend, B. 1983: 'Issues in mental health nursing', 59(1–4); 219–37.
Murray, M. 1921: *The god of witches*, Sampson Low, London.
Myers, K. 1987: 'Fashion 'n' passion', in Betterton, R. (ed.), *Looking on images of femininity in the visual arts and the media*, Pandora, London.
Nairne, C. and Smith, G. 1984: *Dealing with depression*, Women's Press, London.
Nathenson, C. A. 1975: 'Illness and the feminine role: A theoretical review', *Social science and medicine*, 9, 57–62.
Nicolson, P. 1986: 'Developing a feminist approach to depression following childbirth' in Wilkinson, S. (ed.), *Feminist social psychology*, Open University, Milton Keynes.
Nicolson, P. 1990: 'Understanding post-natal depression: a mother-centred approach', *Journal of advanced nursing*, 15, 689–95.
Nicolson, P. 1991: 'Menstrual cycle research and the construction of female psychology', in Richardson, J. (ed.), *Cognition and the menstrual cycle*, Lawrence Erlbaum, London.
Nicolson, P. 1992: 'Gender issues in the organisation of clinical psychology', in Ussher, J. M. and Nicolson, P. (eds) *Gender issues in clinical psychology*, Routledge, London.
Noddings, N. 1984: *Caring: A feminine approach to ethics and moral education*, University of California Press, Berkeley.
Noddings, N. 1989: *Women and evil*, University of California Press, Berkeley.
Notestein, W. 1911: *A history of witchcraft in England from 1558–1718*, Russell and Russell, New York.
Oakley, A. 1976: *Housewife*, Penguin, Harmondsworth.
Olsen, T. 1978: *Silences*, Delta, New York.
Orbach, S. 1979: *Fat is a feminist issue*, Hamlyn, London.
Orbach, S. 1986: *Hunger strike*, Fontana, London.
Orwell, G. 1949: *Nineteen eighty-four*, Harcourt, London.
Parker, R. and Pollock, G. (eds) 1987: *Framing feminism: Art and the women's movement 1970–85*, Pandora, London.
Parlee, M. 1974: 'Stereotypic beliefs about menstruation: A methodological note on the Moos menstrual distress questionnaire and some new data', *Psychosomatic medicine*, 36, 229–40.
Parlee, M. 1989: 'The science and politics of PMS research', paper presented at the Association for women in psychology annual research conference, Newport, Rhode Island, 10–12 March, 1989.
Parloff, M. B. *et al.* 1978: 'Research in therapist variables in relation to process and outcome', in Garfield, S. and Bergin, A. (eds), *Handbook for psychotherapy and behaviour change*, Wiley, London.
Parrot, A. and Bechhofer, L. 1991: *Aquaintance rape*, Wiley, New York.
Parturier, F. 1986: 'An open letter to men', in Marks, E. and de Courtivron, I.

(eds), *New French feminisms: An anthology*, Harvester, Sussex.

Pattenson, L. and Burns, J. 1990: *Women, assertiveness and health: A rationale for the use of assertiveness training in promoting women's health*, Health education authority, London.

Paulham, J. 1970: *A slave's revolt: An essay on the story of O*, addendum to Reage, P. translated by Estree, S., *The story of O* (translation of *L'histoire d'O*), Corgi, London.

Pauls, D. L., Butcher, K. D., Crowe, R. R. and Noyes, Jr, R. 1980: 'A genetic study of panic disorder pedigrees', *American journal of human genetics*, 32, 639–44.

Penfold, S. and Walker, G. 1984: *Women and the psychiatric paradox*, Open University, Milton Keynes.

Peterson, C. and Seligman, M. E. P. 1984: 'Causal explanations as a risk factor for depression: Theory and evidence', *Psychological review*, 91, 347–74.

Philips, D. and Segal, B. 1969: 'Sexual status and psychiatric symptoms', *American sociological review*, 34, 58–72.

Philips, E. 1990: 'From the 50's to the 80's: The changing face of women as represented in thirty years of popular songs', paper presented the British psychological society annual conference, Swansea, April 1990.

Philips, R. 1985: 'The adjustment of men and women: Mental health professionals' views today', *Academic psychology bulletin*, 7, 2, 253–60.

Pilgrim, D. 1990: 'Competing histories of madness', in Bentall, R. (ed.), *Reconstructing schizophrenia*, Routledge, London.

Pinel, P. 1806: *A treatise on insanity*, translated by Davis, D. D., Cadell and Davies, London.

Plath, S. 1963: *The bell jar*, Faber and Faber, London.

Plath, S. 1981: *Collected poems*, Faber and Faber, London.

Plumb, A. 1990: *The challenge of self-advocacy*, paper presented at the Women in psychology conference, 14 July, 1990, Birmingham.

Poggi, D. 1986: 'A defence of the master slave relationship', in Marks, E. and de Courtivron, I. (eds), *New French feminisms: An anthology*, Harvester, Sussex.

Porter, R. 1987: *Mind-forg'd manacles*, Athlone, London.

Porter, R. 1990: 'Men's hysterica in corpore hysterico?', paper presented at the Wellcome symposium on the history of medicine: History of hysteria, 6 April 1990, London.

Pound, A., Cox, A., Puckering, C. and Mills, M. 1985: 'The impact of maternal depression on young children', in Stevenson, J. E. (ed.), *Recent research in developmental apthology*, Pergamon Press, Oxford.

Quinn, N. 1984: 'American marriage and the folk psychology of need fulfillment', unpublished manuscript, Duke University and Institute for advanced study.

Rainer, J. D. 1982: 'Genetics of schizophrenia', in Wing, J. and Wing, L. (eds), *Handbook of psychiatry*, vol. 3, Cambridge University Press, Cambridge.

Rand, A. 1943: *The fountainhead*, 1963 reprint, Bobbs-Merrill, Indianapolis.

Rawlings, E. and Carter, D. (eds) 1977: *Psychotherapy for women*, Charles and Thomas, Springfield, Ill.

Reage, P. 1970: translated by Estree, S. *The story of O* (translation of *Histoire d'O*), Corgi, London.

Reiker, P. and Carmen, E. (eds) 1984: *The gender gap in psychotherapy*, Plenum Press, New York.

Reil, J. 1803: *Rhapsodien uber die andwendung der psychischen curmethode auf*

geisteszerruittungen, Curt, Halle.
Rich, A. 1977: *Of woman born*, Virago, London.
Richardson, J. 1991: 'Paramenstrual symptomatology', in Richardson, J. (ed.), *Cognition and the menstrual cycle*, Lawrence Erlbaum, London.
Richman, N. 1978: 'Depression in mothers of young children', *British medical journal*, 288.
Rickels, N. K. 1971: 'The angry woman syndrome', *Archives of general psychiatry*, 24, 91–4.
Rivers, C. 1977: 'Egalitarian marriage: No more ring around the collar', *Mother Jones*, November, 40–1.
Roberts, T. and Burns, J. 1987: 'Women and mental handicap: The oppression of the normal', paper presented at the Women in psychology conference, 11–12 July 1987, Brunel, London.
Rogers, C. 1961: *On becoming a person*, Houghton Miflin, New York.
Rose, J. 1986: *Sexuality in the field of vision*, Verso, London.
Rose, N. 1990: 'Individualizing psychology', in: Shotter, J. and Gergen, K. (eds) *Texts of identity*, Sage, London.
Rosen, B. 1969: *Witchcraft*, Edward Arnold, London.
Rosen, J. 1968: *Selected papers on direct psychoanalysis*, Grune and Statton, New York.
Rosenblatt, D. and Suchman, E. A. 1965: 'Blue collar attitudes and information towards health and illness', in Shostrack, A. B. and Comberg, W. (eds), *Blue collar world*, Prentice Hall, Englewood Cliffs, NJ.
Rosenhan, D. L. 1973: 'On being sane in insane places', *Science*, 179, 250–8.
Rosenthal, D. 1977: 'Searches for the mode of genetic transmission in schizophrenia: Reflections and loose ends', *Schizophrenia bulletin*, 3, 268–76.
Ross, M. 1977: 'Radio', in: King, J. and Scott, M. (eds) *Is this your life? Images of women in the media*, Virago, London.
Rossi, A. 1969: 'Sex equality: The beginnings of ideology', in Kaplan, A. G. and Bean, J. (eds) *Beyond sex role stereotypes: Readings towards a psychology of androgyny*, Little, Brown, Boston.
Roth, M. 1973: 'Psychiatry and its critics', *British journal of psychiatry*, 122, 374.
Rowen, J. and Dryden, W. 1988: *Innovative therapy in Britain*, Open University, Milton Keynes.
Rowe, D. 1990: 'A gene for depression? Who are we kidding?', *Changes*, 891, 15–29.
Rubin, G. 1975: 'The traffic in women: Notes on the "Political economy" of sex', in Reiter, R. (ed.), *Toward an anthropology of women*, Monthly review press, New York.
Rush, A. J., Beck, A. T., Kovacs, M. and Hollon, S. D. 1977: 'Comparative efficacy of cognitive therapy and pharmacotherapy in the treatment of depressed outpatients', *Cognitive therapy and research*, 1, 17–39.
Russo, N. and Sobel, S. 1981: 'Sex differences in the utilization of mental health facilities', *Professional psychology*, 12, 1, 7–19.
Russo, N. F. 1990: 'Forging priorities for women's mental health', *American psychologist*, 45, 3, 368–73.
Salkovskis, P. M. and Clark, D. M. 1986: 'Cognitive and physiological approaches in the maintenance and treatment of panic attacks', in Hand, I. and Wittchen, H. M. (eds) *Panic and phobias*, Springer-Verlag, Berlin.
Savage, W. 1988: *A Savage enquiry: Who controls childbirth?* Virago, London.
Sayal-Bennett, A. 1991: 'Equal opportunities: Empty rhetoric?, *Feminism and*

psychology, 1, 1, 74–7.

Sayers, J. 1982: *Biological politics: Feminist and anti-feminist perspectives*, Tavistock, London.

Sayers, J. 1986: *Sexual contradictions: Psychology, psychoanalysis and feminism*, Tavistock, London.

Sayers, J. 1991: *Mothering psychoanalysis*, Hamish Hamilton, London.

Scheff, T. J. 1966: *Being mentally ill*, Weidenfeld and Nicolson, London.

Schoener, G., Hofstee Milgrom, J. and Gonsiorek, J. 1984: 'Sexual exploitation of clients by therapists', *Women and mental health*, 3, 3–4, 63–9.

Schultz, J. H. 1952: *Psychotherapie: Liebanund Werk grosser Arzte*, Hippokrates-Verlag Marquardt, Stuttgart.

Schwab, J. J. and Schwab, M. E. 1978: *Sociocultural roots of mental illness: An epidemiological survey*, Plenum, New York.

Schwartz, H. 1986: *Never satisfied. A cultural history of diets, fantasies and fat*, Anchor Books, New York.

Schwarzer, A. 1984: *After the second sex: Conversations with Simone de Beauvoir*, Pantheon, New York.

Scot, R. 1584: *The discoverie of witchcraft*, Centaur Press, New York.

Scott, A. F. 1989: 'Which depressed patient will respond to electroconvulsive therapy?' *British journal of psychiatry*, 154, 8–17.

Scull, A. T. 1975: 'From madness to mental illness: Medical men as moral entrepreneurs', *Archives européennes de sociologie*, 16, 218–61.

Scull, A. T. 1979: *Museums of madness: The social organization of insanity in nineteenth century England*, Allen Lane, London.

Scull, A. T. 1981: *Mad houses, mad doctors and madmen: The social history of psychiatry in the Victorian era*, Athlone, London.

Sedgewick, P. 1982: *Psychopolitics: The politics of health*, Pluto, London.

Segal, L. 1987: *Is the future female? Troubled thoughts on contemporary feminism*, Virago, London.

Segal, L. 1990: *Slow motion: Changing masculinity, changing men*, Virago, London.

Seligman, M. E. P. 1975: *Helplessness: On depression, development and death*, Freeman, San Francisco.

Selvini Palazolli, M., Cecchin, G., Boscolo, L. and Prata, G. 1978: *Paradox and counterparadox*, Jason Aronson, New York.

Shapiro, D. A. and Firth, J. 1987: 'Prescriptive versus exploratory psychotherapies: Outcomes of the Sheffield psychotherapy project', *British journal of psychiatry*, 151, 790–9.

Sharpe, S. 1984: *Double identity*, Penguin, Harmondsworth.

Sherman, J. 1977: 'Effects of biological factors on sex-related differences in mathematics achievement', in Fox, L. H., Fennema, E. and Sherman, J., *Women and mathematics: Research perspectives for change*, National Institute for Education, Washington.

Showalter, E. 1987: *The female malady*, Virago, London.

Showalter, E. 1990: 'Double flowers: Hysteria, feminism and gender', paper presented at the Wellcome symposium on the history of medicine: History of hysteria, 6 April 1990, London.

Shreeve, C. 1984: *The premenstrual syndrome*, Thorsons, Wellingborough.

Shuttle, P. and Redgrove, P. 1978: *The wise wound: Menstruation and everywoman*, Gollancz, London.

Shyrock, R. 1966: *Medicine in America: Historical essays*, John Hopkins Press, Baltimore.
Siegler, M. and Osmond, H. 1966: 'Models of madness', *British journal of psychiatry*, 112, 1193–203.
Simmons, J. 1987: 'The necessary bitch', in Fulani, L. (ed.), *The psychopathology of everyday racism and sexism*, Harrington Park Press, New York.
Skodal, A. and Spitzer, R. 1983: 'ICD-9 and DSM III: A comparison', in Spitzer, R., Williams, J. and Skodal, A. (eds), *International perspectives on DSM III*, American Psychiatric Press Inc., Washington, DC.
Slater, E. and Cowie, V. 1971: *The genetics of mental disorders* (Oxford monographs in medical genetics), Oxford University Press, Oxford.
Smail, D. 1973: 'Clinical psychology and the medical model', Bulletin of the British Psychological Society, 26, 211–14.
Smail, D. 1987: *Taking care: An alternative to therapy*, Dent, London.
Smail, D. 1991: 'Towards a radical environmentalist psychology of help', *The psychologist*, 2, 61–5.
Smith, J. 1989: *Misogynies*, Faber and Faber, London.
Smith, M. L., Glass, G. V. and Miller, T. I. 1980: *The benefits of psychotherapy*, Johns Hopkins Press, Baltimore.
Sneddon, J. and Kerry, R. 1984: 'Puerperal psychosis: A suggested treatment model', *American journal of social psychiatry*, 4, 4, 30–4.
Social Trends, Great Britain Central Statistical Office, London.
Sommer, B. 1991: 'Cognitive performance and the menstrual cycle', in Richardson, J. (ed.), *Cognition and the menstrual cycle*, Lawrence Erlbaum, London.
Spender, D. 1982: *Women of ideas and what men have done to them: From Aphra Behn to Adrienne Rich*, Routledge, London.
Spender, D. and Sarah, E. (eds.) 1980: *Learning to lose: Sexism and education*, Women's Press, London.
Spense, J. T. 1985: 'Achievement American style', *American psychologist*, 40, 1285–95.
Spitzer, R., Williams, J. and Skodal, A. (eds) 1983: *International perspectives on DSM III*, American Psychiatric Press Inc., Washington, DC.
Sprenger, J. and Kraemer, H. *Malleus maleficarum*, Nuremberg, 1494 translated by Ashwin, E. A., introduction by Summers, M. Rev., London, 1928 reprint.
Squire, C. 1989: *Significant differences: Feminism in psychology*, Routledge, London.
Squire, C. 1990: 'Representations of "race", gender, psychology and politics in the Oprah Winfrey Show', paper presented at the Women in psychology conference, 15 July 1990, Birmingham.
Steiner, M. and Carroll, B. 1977: 'The psychobiology of premenstrual dysphoria: A review of theories and treatments', *Psychoneuroendocrinology*, 2, 4, 321–35.
Stekel, W. 1930: 'Frigidity in mothers', in Calverton, V. F. and Schmalhausen, S. D. (eds), *The new generation*, Allen and Unwin, London.
Stevenson, J. 1985: *Recent research in developmental psychopathology*, Pergamon Press, Oxford.
Stock, W. 1988: 'Propping up phallocracy: A feminist critique of sex therapy and research', *Women and therapy*, 2–3, 23–4.
Stone, A. 1984: 'Sexual misconduct by psychiatrists: The ethical and clinical

dilemma of confidentiality', in Rieker, P. P. and Carmen, E. (eds), *The gender gap in psychotherapy*, Plenum Press, New York.

Stone, L. 1980: 'A new interpretation of witchcraft', in Mappen, M. (ed.), *Witches and historians: Interpretations of Salem*, Kreiger, New York.

Straus, M. 1976: 'Sexual inequality, cultural norms, and wife-beating', *Victimatology*, 1, 54–76.

Straus, M. 1977: 'A sociological perspective on the prevention and treatment of wife-beating', in Roy, M. (ed.), *Battered Women*, Van Nostrand Reinhold Co., New York.

Strickler, G. 1977: 'Implications of research for psychotherapeutic treatment of women', *American psychologist*, 32, 14–22.

Strupp, H. H. and Hadley, S. W. 1978: 'Specific versus non-specific factors in psychotherapy: a controlled study of outcome', *Archives of general psychiatry*, 36, 1125–36.

Summers, M. 1929: *The history of witchcraft and demonology*, Routledge and Kegan Paul, London.

Surrey, J., Swett, C., Michaels, B. and Levin S. 1990: 'Reported history of physical and sexual abuse and severity of symptomatology in women psychiatric outpatients', *American orthopsychiatrist*, 60, 3, 412–17.

Sutherland, S. 1987: *Breakdown*, Weidenfeld and Nicolson, London.

Swenson, E. and Ragucci, R. 1984: 'Effects of sex role stereotypes and androgynous alternatives on mental health judgements of psychotherapists', *Psychological reports*, 54, 2, 475–81.

Szasz, T. 1961: *The myth of mental illness: Foundations of a theory of personal conduct*, Secker, London.

Szasz, T. 1971: *The manufacture of madness: A comparative study of the inquisition and the mental health movement*, Routledge, London.

Szasz, T. 1974: *The ethics of psychoanalysis: The theory and method of autonomous psychotherapy*, Routledge, London.

Szasz, T. 1979: *Schizophrenia: The sacred symbol of psychiatry*, Oxford University Press, Oxford.

Szasz, T. 1981: *Sex: Facts, frauds and follies*, Basil Blackwell, Oxford.

Taggart, M. 1985. 'The feminist critique in epistemological perspective: Questions of context in family therapy', *Journal of marital and family therapy*, 11, 113–26.

Taub, S. 1987: 'Electroconvulsive therapy, malpractice, and informed consent', *Journal of psychiatry and law*, 15, 1, 7–54.

Taussig, M. 1980: 'Reification and the consciousness of the patient', *Social Science and medicine*, 148, 3, 3–13.

Taylor, B. and Wagner, N. 1976: 'Sex between therapists and clients: A review and analysis', *Professional psychology*, 7, 593–601.

Taylor, S. E. 1983: 'Adjustment to threatening events: A theory of cognitive adaptation', *American psychologist*, 38, 1161–73.

Teasdale, J. D. 1983: 'Negative thinking in depression: Cause, effect or reciprocal relationship?', *Advances in behaviour research and therapy*, 5, 3–25.

Thorne, B. 1984: 'A social perspective on women's mental health problems', *Women and therapy*, 3, 3–4, 45–50.

Thoveron, G. 1987: 'How women are represented in television programmes in the EEC', *Part 1, Images of women in news, advertising, series and serials*, Office for official publications of the EC, Luxembourg.

Tickner, L. 1988: 'Feminism and art history', *Genders*, 3, 92–128.

Tissot, S. 1769: *Advice to the people in general with respect to their health*, W. Pine, Bristol.

Tizard, B. 1990: 'Research and policy: Is there a link?', *The psychologist*, 3 October 1990, 10, 435–40.

Treacher, A. and Baruch, G. 1982: 'Towards a critical history of the psychiatric profession', in Ingelby, D. (ed.), *Critical psychiatry*, Penguin, Harmondsworth.

Trevor-Roper, H. R. 1967: *The European witch-craze of the 16th and 17th centuries*, Harper, New York.

Tuch, R. 1975: 'The relationship between a mother's menstrual status and her response to illness in her child', *Psychosomatic medicine*, 37, 388–94.

Unger, R. 1979: *Female and male: Psychological perspectives*, Harper and Row: New York.

US Department of Labor 1980: *Twenty facts about women workers*, Office of the secretary, Women's bureau, Washington DC.

Ussher, J. M. 1989: *The psychology of the female body*, Routledge, London.

Ussher, J. M. 1990a: 'The future of sex and marital therapy in the face of widespread criticism: Caught between the devil and the deep blue sea', *Counselling psychology quarterly*, 3, 4, 317–24.

Ussher, J. M. 1992a: 'The demise of dissent and the rise of cognition in menstrual cycle research', in Richardson, J. (ed.), *Cognition and the menstrual cycle*, Lawrence Erlbaum, London.

Ussher, J. M. 1991b: 'Family and couples therapy with gay and lesbian clients: Acknowledging the forgotten minority', *Journal of family therapy*, 13, 2, 131–48.

Ussher, J. M. 1991c: *The role of clinical psychologists in HIV and AIDS*, British psychological society, Leicester.

Ussher, J. M. 1992a: 'Female sexuality: Constructions and contradictions', in Ussher, J. M. and Baker, C. (eds) *Psychological perspectives as sexual problems: New directions for theory and practice*, Routledge, London.

Ussher, J. M. 1992b: 'Reproductive rhetoric and the blaming of the body' in Nicolson, P. and Ussher, J. M. (eds), *The psychology of women's health and health care*, Macmillan, London.

Ussher, J. M. 1992c: 'Science sexing psychology', in Ussher, J. M. and Nicolson, P. (eds), *Gender issues in clinical psychology*, Routledge, London.

Ussher, J. M. 1992d: 'Sex differences in performance: Fact or fantasy?', in Jones, D. and Smith, A. (eds), *Factors in human performance*, Laurence Erlbaum, New York.

Van de Velde, T. 1931: *Sex hostility in marriage, its origins, prevention and treatment*. Heinemann, London.

Veith, I. 1965: *Hysteria: The history of a disease*, University of Chicago press, Chicago.

Vetere, A. 1992: 'Working with families', in Ussher, J. M. and Nicolson, P. (eds), *Gender issues in clinical psychology*, Routledge, London.

Wagner-Martin, L. 1987: *Sylvia Plath*, Cardinal, New York.

Waisberg, U. and Page, S. 1988: 'Gender role nonconformity and perception of mental illness', *Women and health*, 14, 1, 3–16.

Wakeman, T. 1890: cited in Ehrenreich, B., and English, D., *Witches, midwifery and nurses: A history of women healers*, 1978. Glass Mountain pamphlets, 1, Compendium, London.

Walker, B. 1968: *The Hindu world: An encyclopedic survey of hinduism*, 2, Praeger,

New York.
Walkerdine, V. 1990: *School girl fictions*, Virago, London.
Walkowitz, J. 1980: *Prostitution and Victorian society: Women, class and state*, Cambridge University Press, Cambridge.
Wallace, A. F. C. 1967: 'Anthropology and psychiatry', in Freedman, A. and Kaplan, H. (eds), *Comprehensive textbook of psychiatry*, Wilhause and Wilkins, Baltimore.
Wallsgrove, R. 1987: 'Between the devil and the deep blue Whitehouse', in Betterton, R. (ed.), *Looking on: Images of women in the visual arts and media*, Pandora, London.
Warheit, G. J., Holzer, G. E., Bell, R. A. and Arey, S. A. 1976: 'Sex, marital status and mental health', *Social forces*, 55, 459–70.
Watson, G. and Williams, J. 1991: 'Feminist practice in therapy', in Ussher, J. M. and Nicolson, P. (eds), *Gender issues in clinical psychology*, Routledge, London.
WAVAW (Women Against Violence Against Women): 'What is pornography? Two opposing feminist viewpoints', in Betterton, R. (ed.), *Looking on: Images of women in the visual arts and media*, Pandora, London.
Weeks, J. 1989: *Sex, politics and society: The regulation of sexuality since 1800*, Longmans, London.
Weideger, P. (ed.) 1985: *History's mistress: A new interpretation of a nineteenth century ethnographic classic*, Penguin, Harmondsworth.
Weinberger, D. R., Wagner, R. and Wyatt, R. J. 1983: 'Neuropathological studies of schizophrenia: A selective review', *Schizophrenia bulletin*, 9, 193–212.
Weiner, B. 1985: 'Spontaneous causal thinking', *Psychological bulletin*, 97, 74–84.
Weissman, M. and Klerman, G. 1977: 'Sex differences and the epidemiology of depression', *Archives of general psychiatry*, 34, 98–111.
Weisstein, N. 1973: 'Psychology constructs the female: Or the fantasy life of the male psychologists', in Brown, P. (ed.), *Radical psychology*, Tavistock, London.
Weith Knudsen, K. A. 1928: *The woman question from ancient time to the present day*, Constable, London.
Wheeler, J. and Berliner, L. 1988: 'Treating the effects of sexual abuse in children', in Wyatt, G. E. and Powell, G. J. (eds), *Lasting effects of child sexual abuse*, Sage, California.
Whitewell, D. 1990: 'The significance of childhood sexual abuse for adult psychiatry', *British journal of hospital medicine*, 43, 346–62.
Whyld, J. (ed.) 1983: *Sexism in the secondary curriculum*, Harper and Row, London.
Wilkinson, S. 1991: 'Equal opportunities: Empty rhetoric?', *Feminism and psychology* 1, 1.
Williams, J. and Watson, G. 1991: 'Open forum: Clinical psychology training: Training in oppression?', *Feminism and psychology*, 1, 1, 55–110.
Williams, V. 1986: *Women photographers from 1900 to the present*, Virago, London.
Willis, E. 1981: *Beginning to see the light*, Alfred A. Knopf, New York.
Wilson, G. 1988: 'The sociobiological basis of sexual dysfunction', in: Cole, M. and Dryden, W. (eds) *Sex Therapy in Britain*, Open University Press, Milton Keynes.
Wilson, R. A. 1966: *Feminine forever*, M. Evans, New York.
Wing, J. K. 1978: *Reasoning about madness*, Oxford University Press, Oxford.

Winokur, G. 1979: 'Unipolar depression', *Archives of general psychiatry*, 36, 47–52.

Winship, J. 1987: 'A girl needs to get streetwise', in Betterton, R. (ed.), *Looking on: Images of women in the visual arts and the media*, Pandora, London.

Wollstonecraft, M. 1792: *A vindication of the rights of woman with strictures on political and moral subjects*, Whitstan, Troy, NY, reprinted 1982.

Wolpe, J. 1973: *The practice of behaviour therapy* (2nd edn) Pergamon, New York.

Woolf, V. 1928: *A room of one's own*, 1977 reprint, Virago, London.

Wooton, B. 1959: *Social science and social pathology*, Allen and Unwin, London.

Yager, J. 1982: 'Family issues in the pathogenesis of anorexia nervosa', *Psychosomatic medicine*, 44, 1, 43–60.

Zborowski, M. 1952: 'Cultural components in responses to pain', *Journal of social issues*, 8, 16–30.

Zeman, A. 1977: *Presumptuous girls: Women and their world in the serious woman's novel*, Weidenfeld and Nicolson, London.

Zilboorg, G., and Henry, G. 1941: *A history of medical psychology*, Norton, New York.

Subject Index

Name Index